STUDY GUIDE

Principles of Macroeconomics
SECOND EDITION

Principles of Macroeconomics

SECOND EDITION

John B. Taylor

Prepared by

David H. Papell
University of Houston

John Solow
University of Iowa

Wm. Stewart Mounts, Jr.
Mercer University

Houghton Mifflin Company   Boston   New York

Editor-in-Chief: Bonnie Binkert
Basic Book Editor: Ann West
Project Editor: Margaret Kearney
Editorial Assistant: Patricia English
Senior Manufacturing Coordinator: Priscilla Abreu
Marketing Manager: Juli Bliss

Cover Design: Harold Burch, Harold Burch Design, NYC

Printed in the U.S.A.

ISBN: 0-395-87455-6

23456789-PO-01 00 99 98

Contents

Preface

The chapters of this study guide follow those of John B. Taylor's *Principles of Macroeconomics*. Why use this study guide? The best reason is to help you learn the course content more efficiently. For each chapter of the book, this study guide highlights the major concepts, defines the most important terms, shows you how to work problems, and provides you numerous opportunities to test your understanding of the material.

What You'll Find Here

Each chapter begins with a *Chapter Overview*, which introduces the major topics covered in the text. This is followed by a *Chapter Review*, which defines and explains the key terms and concepts. Next comes a section called *Zeroing In*, which provides a more in-depth look at several of the chapter's most important topics. In this section, figures are often used to illustrate concepts.

The focus of the study guide chapter changes with the next section, called *Active Review*, which consists of a total of 40 to 50 fill-in, true-false, and short-answer questions. You will find answers to all review questions, including explanations for the true-false and short-answer questions, at the back of each chapter.

An important part of studying economics is learning how to solve problems, and the study guide provides you with extensive assistance in this area. The section called *Working It Out* begins by explaining how to use the techniques covered in the chapter. These may be analytic, graphical, numerical, or algebraic. Next come several *Worked Problems*, for which complete answers are provided. These are followed by *Practice Problems*, for which the answers can be found at the end of each chapter.

Each chapter ends with a twenty-question multiple-choice *Chapter Test*. This test covers material from throughout the chapter and contains several graph-based and table-based questions. The answers to the chapter test can also be found at the end of the chapter.

This study guide also contains a thirty-question multiple-choice Sample Test at the end of each text part – covering material from all the chapters in that part. There are three of these Sample Tests (and answers) in this volume.

How to Make the Best Use of this Book!

Every student studies differently, and we do not presume to tell you how to study most effectively. Nevertheless, here are some suggestions. First, read the chapter in the text but don't worry too much about understanding everything. Second, read the *Chapter Overview, Chapter Review,* and *Zeroing In* sections in the study guide. When you find a concept that you do not understand, look it up in the text. Third, answer the *Active Review* questions. Write down your answers and provide explanations for the true-false questions. When you miss a question, refer back to the text or study guide. Fourth, learn how to solve the problems in the *Working It Out* section. Study the *Worked Problems*, and answer the *Practice Problems*. Fifth, carefully read the chapter in the text to make sure that you understand it completely. Sixth, take the *Chapter Test* as if you were taking an exam. If you miss any questions, don't just find the correct answer at the back of the chapter, but go back to the appropriate sections of the text and study guide to make sure that you learn the material. Finally, when you reach the end of a part, take the multiple-choice Sample Test, again under exam conditions. You will be well prepared for the midterm and final. Good luck!

PART 1

Introduction to Economics and Its Foundations

Scarcity exists because people's wants exceed their resources (or means). This forces them to make choices concerning the wants they will fill and the way they will use their resources. Economists investigate this behavior in order to explain facts and observations about the economy. Economists establish patterns by carefully organizing data and present this information in tables and graphs. They develop models of behavior and test them with data that have been collected. Chapters 1 through 4 address the fundamental questions of economics and the basics of "economic thinking."

Within a market economy, basic economic questions are answered by buyers (demand) and sellers (supply) interacting in markets, guided by prices. Changes in demand and supply (seen as shifts in the demand and supply curves) introduce surpluses or shortages into the market and thereby change the market price. In addition, the price elasticity of demand and supply quantifies the responsiveness of market participants to changes in prices. While governments can affect market processes by instituting price ceilings and price floors, free competition between buyers and sellers promotes economic efficiency, maximizes social welfare, and minimizes the deadweight loss.

CHAPTER 1

Observing and Explaining the Economy

CHAPTER OVERVIEW

What is economics? If you are tempted to answer "everything," you are at least partly correct. Economics is a way of thinking. It entails *describing* economic events, *explaining* why they occur, *predicting* whether they might occur in the future, and *recommending* appropriate courses of action to policymakers. When you listen to your professor in class, read the text, or work through the study guide, you should be learning to actively analyze economic events. This chapter introduces some of the tools of analysis. We consider the timely issue of health-care spending, and see what economists attempt to explain and how to interpret what they find. We look at economic models, and learn how economists abstract reality in order to make it manageable. We see how economics is used for public policy, and consider some of its limitations. Finally, we introduce some tools that economists use in their analysis. Using both graphs and algebra, we begin to learn how to document and quantify observations about the economy.

CHAPTER REVIEW

1. Economists divide people into broad categories. *Households* are either individuals or groups of individuals who share the same living quarters. *Organizations,* which include firms and governments, are producers of goods and services. *Firms* are private organizations that produce goods and services. *Governments* also produce goods and services, such as national defense and education.

2. A **market** is an arrangement through which exchanges of goods or services between people take place. Households supply their **labor** to the firms that employ them. The resources used by firms to produce goods and services are called **capital**. Labor and capital are called **inputs** or **factors of production**.

3. An **economic model** is an explanation of how the economy or a part of the economy works. Economic models, like models in other sciences, are always simplifications of reality. Economic models can be described with words, with numbers, with graphs, or with algebra, and you will use all four as you work through the text and study guide. The study of economic events of the past is called **economic history**.

4. An **economic variable** is any economic measure that can vary over a range of values. **Correlation** means that two variables move together, either in the same direction or in opposite directions. There is a positive correlation, and the two variables are **positively related**, if the two variables move in the same direction: One increases when the other increases. There is a negative correlation, and the two variables are **negatively related**, if the two variables move in opposite directions: One decreases when the other increases. **Causation** means that the movements in one variable bring about, or cause, the movements in another variable. Correlation does not imply causation. Just because two variables move together does not mean that the movements of one caused the movements of the other.

5. The assumption of *ceteris paribus*, which means "all other things equal," is often used by economists for prediction. The idea of *ceteris paribus* is easiest to explain through an example. Suppose that you wanted to predict the effect of cold weather on football attendance. In making your prediction, you would want to hold other things, such as the team's won-lost record, equal.

6. Keeping other things equal is not easy in economics. In many sciences, such as physics, researchers perform **controlled experiments** to determine whether one event causes another. In economics, as in astronomy, controlled experiments are rare. If you want to study the causes of the Great Depression of the 1930s, you cannot ask the government to go back and change policy. In **experimental economics**, a new and growing area of economics, researchers have begun to conduct economic experiments in laboratory settings.

7. The two main branches of economics are microeconomics and macroeconomics. **Microeconomics** studies the behavior of individual firms, households, and markets. Questions such as how much milk consumption would fall if the price of milk rises or how much a college education increases an individual's lifetime earnings are part of microeconomics. **Macroeconomics** focuses on the whole national, or even world, economy. Questions such as what were the effects of lowering inflation in the early 1980s in the United States or what are the prospects for economic reform in the former Soviet Union are part of macroeconomics.

8. There are two basic types of economic systems: **market economies**, where the vast majority of prices are free to vary, and **command economies**, where the vast majority of prices are determined by the government. Command economies are also called *centrally planned* economies. In modern market economies, the government plays a large role, and such economies are sometimes called **mixed economies**.

9. Economics is an important part of public policy making. **Positive economics** describes or explains what happens in the economy. **Normative economics** makes recommendations about what the government should do. For example, interest rates in the United States were increased in the spring and summer of 1994. Positive economics describes the effects of the higher interest rates and explains why interest rates were raised. Normative economics is concerned with recommending whether they should be raised further. The work of the **Council of Economic Advisers**, which gives policy advice to the president, is an example of normative economics.

ZEROING IN

1. Health-care reform has been a major domestic issue since the election of President Clinton in 1992. Although Congress adjourned in the fall of 1994 without passing a bill, health care provides a good introduction to thinking about economics.

    a. Two facts about health-care spending stand out. First, health-care spending has grown more rapidly than the rest of the U.S. economy during the last 25 years. Second, the price of health care has increased faster than most other prices. It is the task of economics to quantify, document, and explain these observations.

    b. Let's look at the first observation, that health-care spending has grown more rapidly than the rest of the U.S. economy. In order to evaluate this assertion, we need to measure both health-care spending and the economy as a whole. **Gross domestic product (GDP)** is the most comprehensive measure of the size of an economy. GDP for the United States is the total value of all goods and services made in the United States during a specified period of time, usually one year. In 1995, GDP for the United States was $7,246 billion, or about $7.2 trillion.

    c. We can measure health-care spending the same way we measure GDP, by adding up what we spend on all categories of health care. That number was $784 billion in 1995. If you doubt that health-care spending is important, you probably don't realize that $784 billion is three times as large as the entire automobile industry.

    d. Health-care spending as a *share* of GDP (in percentage terms) can be calculated by dividing health-care spending by GDP and multiplying by 100:

    $$\text{Health-care spending as a share of GDP} = \frac{\text{health-care spending}}{\text{GDP}} \times 100$$

    In 1995, health-care spending as a share of GDP was $784/7,246 \times 100 = 10.8$ percent. [If we did not multiply by 100, the share would have been .108 (out of 1) instead of 10.8 (out of 100). While we will usually represent shares in percentage terms, you should understand that the two numbers represent the same thing).

    e. Now let's turn to prices. The **overall price level** is a measure of the average price of all the goods and services in GDP. **Real GDP** equals GDP divided by the overall price level. **Inflation** is the general increase in prices over time, and the **inflation rate** is the percentage increase in the overall price level from one year to the next. The price of health care is a measure of the average price of all the items included in the measure of health-care spending. The **relative price** of health care can be calculated by dividing the price of health care by the overall price level:

    $$\text{Relative price of health care} = \frac{\text{health-care price}}{\text{overall price level}}$$

    f. Health-care spending and GDP for all years from 1977 to 1996 are reported in the text. Although both health-care spending and GDP have been rising, health-care spending has been increasing more quickly. The share of health-care spending as a percent of GDP has therefore been rising. The overall price level and the price of health care for the same years are also reported in the text. The relative price of health care has increased since 1977 because the price of health care has risen more rapidly than the overall price level.

2. Graphs and diagrams are used extensively in economics. They are useful both for uncovering correlations in economic variables and for understanding economic models.

   a. In a **Cartesian coordinate system**, pairs of observations on variables can be represented in a plane by designating one axis for one variable and the other axis for the other variable. Each point on the plane corresponds to a pair of observations. In economics, the axes are usually designated the vertical axis and the horizontal axis.

   b. A **time-series graph** plots a series—several values of the variable—over time. Figure 1.1 plots two variables, called x and y, over time. The value of the variable is depicted on the vertical axis, and time is on the horizontal axis. More than one variable can be plotted on the same graph. If the scales of measurement of the variables are very different, a **dual scale** can be used.

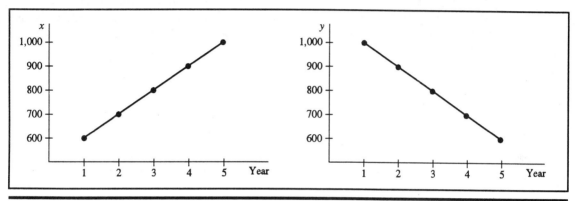

Figure 1.1

   c. Two variables can also be depicted with a **scatter plot**, where the vertical axis is used for one variable and the horizontal axis is used for the other variable. Figure 1.2 shows a scatter plot for the variables x and y, with x on the horizontal axis and y on the vertical axis. Connecting the dots in the scatter plot creates a curve. If the curve is a straight line, as in Figure 1.2, it is called *linear*. Economic relationships do not have to be linear.

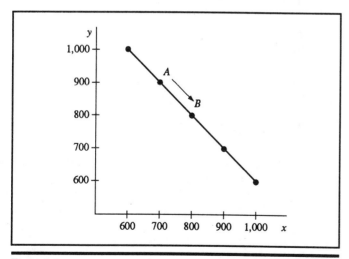

Figure 1.2

d. The **slope** of the curve is the change in the variable on the vertical axis divided by the change in the variable on the horizontal axis. If the curve slopes up from left to right, it has a **positive slope** and the two variables are positively related. If the curve slopes down from left to right, it has a **negative slope** and the two variables are negatively related. In Figure 1.2, the slope of the curve is negative because the curve slopes down from left to right and is constant along the curve because the curve is linear. Because y decreases by 100 for every increase of x by 100, the slope is -100/100 = -1.

e. When the value of one of the variables on the two axes changes, it causes a **movement along the curve**. For example, if x rises from 700 to 800 in Figure 1.2, y falls from 900 to 800. This is a movement along the curve, and is shown by a movement from point A to point B. But suppose that the relationship between the variables x and y is affected by the value of a third variable, z. In Figure 1.3, a change in the value of z causes a **shift of the curve**. We will consider movements along and shifts of curves many times in this course. It is important for you to understand that changes in the values of variables that are depicted on the axes cause movements along a curve, whereas changes in the values of other variables cause shifts of the curve.

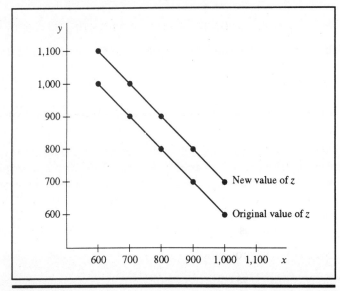

Figure 1.3

ACTIVE REVIEW

Fill-in Questions

1. _____ are individuals or groups of individuals who share the same living quarters.

2. Private organizations that produce goods and services are called _____.

3. A(n) _____ is an arrangement through which exchanges of goods or services between people take place.

4. Two factors of production are _____ and _____ .

5. A(n) _____ is an explanation of how the economy or a part of the economy works.

6. Two variables have a(n) _____ if they move in the same direction.

7. The assumption of _____ means "all other things equal."

8. The two main branches of economics are _____ and _____ .

9. _____ economics makes recommendations about what the government should do.

10. The most comprehensive measure of the size of an economy is _____ .

12. _____ is the general increase in prices over time.

13. In a(n) _____ , pairs of observations on variables can be represented in a plane by designating one axis for one variable and the other axis for the other variable.

14. A(n) _____ plots a series over time.

15. In a(n) _____ , the vertical axis is used for one variable and the horizontal axis is used for the other variable.

True-False Questions

T F   1. Governments produce goods and services.

T F   2. Money and capital are called factors of production.

T F   3. It is desirable to make economic models as realistic as possible.

T F   4. If two economic variables have a positive correlation, one must cause the other.

T F   5. The question of by how much a college education increases an individual's lifetime earnings is part of microeconomics.

T F   6. The question of what were the effects of lowering inflation in the early 1980s in the United States is part of macroeconomics.

T F   7. Gross domestic product (GDP) is measured for a specified time period.

T F   8. Health-care spending is over 10 percent of GDP in the United States.

T F   9. In the United States, we spend more for automobiles than for health care.

T F   10. Health-care spending as a share of GDP has been rising during the last 20 years.

T F   11. The relative price of health care has increased since 1970.

T F   12. In a time-series graph, the value of the variable is depicted on the horizontal axis, and time is on the vertical axis.

T F 13. If the curve depicting two variables in a scatter plot is linear, the two variables are positively related.

T F 14. When the value of one of the variables on the two axes changes, it causes a shift of the curve.

Short-Answer Questions

1. What is a market?

2. What is the difference between labor and capital?

3. What is the difference between correlation and causation?

4. Why is scarcity a central theme in economics?

5. What is the assumption of *ceteris paribus*?

6. What is experimental economics?

7. In the context of public policy making, what is the difference between positive and normative economics?

8. What are two important facts about health-care spending during the last 20 years?

9. How do economists calculate health-care spending as a share of GDP?

10. What is the overall price level?

11. What is the difference between inflation and the inflation rate?

12. How do economists calculate the relative price of health care?

13. When is a dual scale used?

14. What is the relation between the slope of the curve in a scatter plot and the correlation between the variables on the axes?

15. What types of changes cause movements along a curve, and what types cause shifts of the curve?

WORKING IT OUT

1. We have studied how to calculate health-care spending as a share of GDP and how to compute the relative price of health care. These techniques are applicable to any category of spending. Let's consider housing spending for a fictional economy, starting in the year 2000.

   a. Suppose you are given the following data on GDP and housing spending:

Year	GDP	Housing Spending
2000	1,000	50
2010	2,000	120
2020	4,000	280
2030	8,000	640

GDP and housing spending are in billions of dollars. You can calculate housing spending as a share of GDP (in percentage terms) by dividing housing spending by GDP and multiplying by 100.

Year	Housing Spending/GDP	Housing Spending Share
2000	0.05	5 percent
2010	0.06	6 percent
2020	0.07	7 percent
2030	0.08	8 percent

Housing spending as a share of GDP has increased from 5 percent to 8 percent over this 30 period.

b. Now suppose you are given data for the same time period on the overall price level and the price of housing:

Year	Overall Price	Housing Price
2000	1.00	.80
2010	1.10	.99
2020	1.21	1.21
2030	1.33	1.46

You can calculate the relative price of housing by dividing the price of housing by the overall price level:

Year	Relative Price of Housing
2000	0.80
2010	0.90
2020	1.00
2030	1.10

The relative price of housing has increased over this period.

2. We have learned that economic variables can be depicted by using either time-series graphs or scatter plots. We will use both to uncover the correlation between housing spending as a share of GDP and the relative price of housing in the fictional economy described above.

a. The movements in housing spending as a share of GDP and the relative price of housing can be shown by using time-series plots. In the first panel of Figure 1.4, the housing spending share is on the vertical axis and time (the year) is on the horizontal axis. The curve is upward-sloping, indicating that housing spending as a share of GDP has increased over this period. The second panel of Figure 1.4 depicts the relative price of housing on the vertical axis and the year on the horizontal axis. This curve is also upward-sloping, indicating that the relative price of housing has also increased over this period.

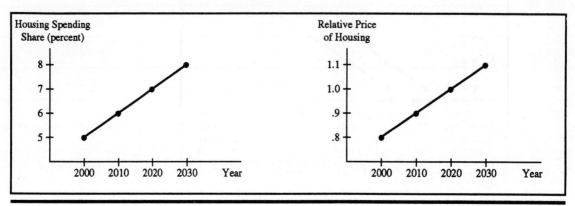

Figure 1.4

b. The relation between the housing spending share and the relative price of housing can be illustrated by using a scatter plot. In Figure 1.5, the relative price of housing is on the vertical axis and the housing spending share is on the horizontal axis. Each dot represents a different year, and the curve, which has a positive slope, is drawn by connecting the dots. The housing spending share and the relative price of housing are positively related; one increases when the other increases.

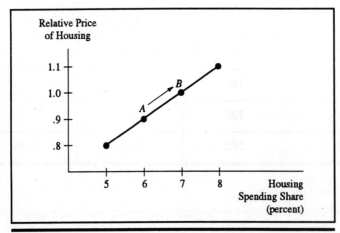

Figure 1.5

c. Changes in the value of one of the variables on the axes cause movement along a curve. In this example, if the relative price of housing increases from 0.9 to 1.0, the housing spending share increases from 6 percent to 7 percent. This is shown as a movement from point *A* to point *B* in Figure 1.5.

d. Changes in the value of variables not depicted on the axes cause shifts in the curve. In this example, suppose that something causes the housing spending share to increase by 1 percent at each relative price of housing. This is illustrated in Figure 1.6 as a shift of the curve marked "Original" to the right, to the curve marked "New."

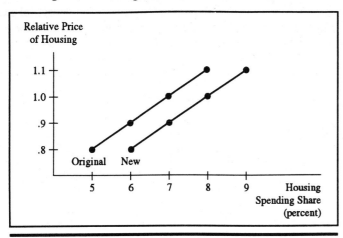

Figure 1.6

Worked Problems

1. Consider the following data for a fictional economy, starting in the year 2000:

Year	GDP	Food Spending	Overall Price	Food Price
2000	1,000	100	1.00	1.00
2010	2,000	180	1.20	1.32
2020	4,000	320	1.40	1.68
2030	8,000	560	1.60	2.08

GDP and food spending are in billions of dollars.

a. Calculate food spending as a share of GDP (in percentage terms) and the relative price of food.

b. What has happened to the food spending share and the relative price of food over this period?

Answers

a. *Food spending as a share of GDP equals food spending divided by GDP multiplied by 100. The relative price of food equals the price of food divided by the overall price level.*

Year	Food Spending Share	Relative Price of Food
2000	10 percent	1.00
2010	9 percent	1.10
2020	8 percent	1.20
2030	7 percent	1.30

b. *The food spending share has decreased and the relative price of food has increased during this period.*

2. Using the data for the economy in Worked Problem 1:

a. Draw a scatter plot to illustrate the relation between food spending as a share of GDP and the relative price of food. Are the two variables positively or negatively related?

b. Suppose that the relative price of food rises from 1.1 to 1.2. Is this a movement along the curve or a shift of the curve? Illustrate your answer.

c. Suppose that something causes the food spending share to decrease by 1 percent at each relative price of food. Is this a movement along the curve or a shift of the curve? Illustrate your answer.

Answers

a. *The scatter plot, with the relative price of food on the vertical axis and the food spending share on the horizontal axis, is shown in Figure 1.7. The curve is downward-sloping, indicating that the two variables are negatively related.*

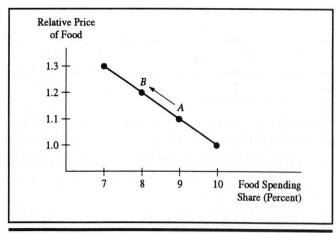

Figure 1.7

b. *The increase in the relative price of food is a movement along the curve; it is depicted by a movement from point A to point B in Figure 1.7. The food spending share falls from 9 percent to 8 percent.*

c. *The decrease in the food spending share by 1 percent at each relative price of food is a shift of the curve; it is depicted in Figure 1.8 by a shift of the curve marked "Original" to the left, to the curve marked "New."*

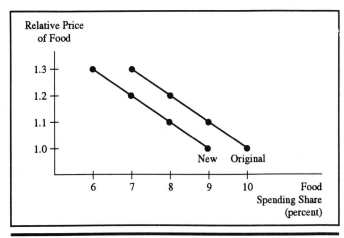

Figure 1.8

Practice Problems

1. Consider the following data for a fictional economy, starting in the year 2000:

Year	GDP	Automobile Spending	Overall Price	Automobile Price
2000	1,000	30	1.00	1.00
2010	2,000	70	1.20	1.10
2020	4,000	160	1.44	1.21
2030	8,000	360	1.73	1.33

GDP and automobile spending are in billions of dollars.

a. Calculate automobile spending as a share of GDP (in percentage terms) and the relative price of automobiles.

b. What has happened to the automobile spending share and the relative price of automobiles over this period?

2. Consider the following data for a fictional economy, starting in the year 2000:

Year	GDP	Clothing Spending	Overall Price	Clothing Price
2000	1,000	30	1.00	0.900
2010	2,000	70	1.10	1.045
2020	4,000	160	1.20	1.200
2030	8,000	360	1.30	1.365

GDP and clothing spending are in billions of dollars.

a. Calculate clothing spending as a share of GDP (in percentage terms) and the relative price of clothing.

b. What has happened to the clothing spending share and the relative price of clothing over this period?

3. Using the data for the economy in Practice Problem 1:

a. Draw a scatter plot to illustrate the relation between automobile spending as a share of GDP and the relative price of automobiles. Are the two variables positively or negatively related?

b. Suppose the relative price of automobiles falls from 0.92 to 0.84. Is this a movement along the curve or a shift of the curve? Illustrate your answer.

4. Using the data for the economy in Practice Problem 2:

a. Draw a scatter plot to illustrate the relation between clothing spending as a share of GDP and the relative price of clothing. Are the two variables positively or negatively related?

b. Suppose that something causes the clothing spending share to increase by 1/2 percent at each relative price of clothing. Is this a movement along the curve or a shift of the curve? Illustrate your answer.

CHAPTER TEST

1. Individuals or groups of individuals who share the same living quarters are called
   a. firms.
   b. households.
   c. governments.
   d. groups.

2. Private organizations that produce goods and services are called
   a. firms.
   b. households.
   c. governments.
   d. groups.

3. An arrangement through which exchanges of goods or services between people take place is called
   a. a firm.
   b. an industry.
   c. a market.
   d. an economic model.

4. When the movements in one variable bring about the movements in another variable, this is called
   a. causation.
   b. correlation.
   c. relationship.
   d. connection.

5. Two variables have a positive correlation if
   a. they move in opposite directions.
   b. they move in the same direction.
   c. one decreases when the other increases.
   d. one increases when the other decreases.

6. Which of the following is a central theme in economics?
   a. Causation
   b. Abundance
   c. Scarcity
   d. *Ceteris paribus*

7. Which of the following is an assumption that allows economists to use models for prediction?
   a. Causation
   b. Abundance
   c. Scarcity
   d. *Ceteris paribus*

8. The development of a new model in economics begins with
   a. an hypothesis statement
   b. observation of something that can't be explained by existing models
   c. an economic assumption
   d. a rejection of an older model

9. Macroeconomics focuses on
   a. the whole national economy.
   b. the behavior of individual firms.
   c. the behavior of households.
   d. markets.

10. Which of the following is most likely to be studied by a microeconomist?
    a. Inflation of the general price level
    b. Unemployment in the economy
    c. Employment of labor in furniture production
    d. The growth rate of aggregate output

11. Which of the following makes recommendations about what the government should do?
    a. Positive economics
    b. Negative economics
    c. Experimental economics
    d. Normative economics

12. The total value of all goods and services made in a country during a specified period of time is called
    a. supply.
    b. gross domestic product.
    c. demand.
    d. net domestic product.

13. The general increase in prices over time is called
    a. inflation.
    b. the inflation rate.
    c. the overall price level.
    d. the relative price level.

14. If a curve has a positive slope, then
    a. the two variables are negatively related.
    b. the two variables are positively related.
    c. one variable increases when the other decreases.
    d. the curve slopes down from left to right.

Use the following table for questions 15, 16, and 17.

Year	GDP	Food Spending	Overall Price	Food Price
2000	2,000	120	1.00	1.00
2010	4,000	200	1.20	1.44
2020	8,000	340	1.40	1.70
2030	16,000	640	1.60	2.10

GDP and food spending are in billions of dollars.

15. What is food spending as a share of GDP (in percentage terms) in the year 2010?
    a. 3 percent
    b. 6 percent
    c. 10 percent
    d. 5 percent

16. What is food spending as a share of GDP (in percentage terms) in the year 2030?
    a. 4 percent
    b. 5 percent
    c. 10 percent
    d. 8 percent

17. What is the relative price of food in the year 2010?
    a. 1.00
    b. 1.10
    c. 1.20
    d. 1.30

Use Figure 1.9 for questions 18 and 19.

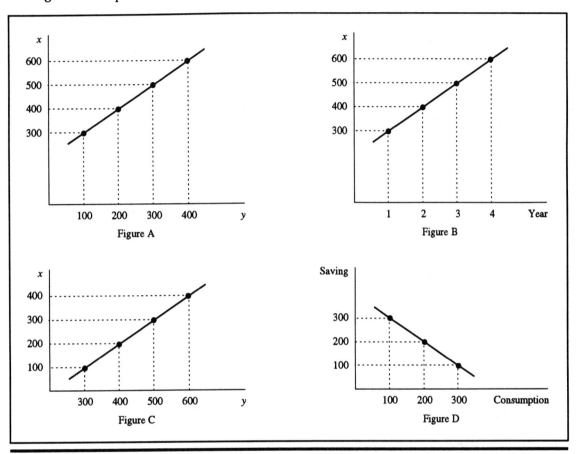

Figure 1.9

18. Which of the figures is a time-series graph?
    a. Figure A
    b. Figure B
    c. Figure C
    d. Figure D

19. What is the slope of the curve in Figure D?
    a. 3
    b. 2
    c. 0
    d. 1

Use Figure 1.10 for question 20.

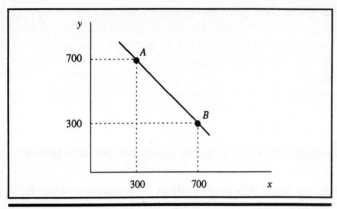

Figure 1.10

20. Movement from point *A* to point *B* is
    a. an upward movement along the curve.
    b. a downward movement along the curve.
    c. an upward shift of the curve.
    d. a downward shift of the curve.

ANSWERS TO THE REVIEW QUESTIONS

Fill-in Questions

1. Households
2. firms
3. market
4. labor, capital
5. economic model
6. positive correlation
7. law of demand
8. *ceteris paribus*
9. microeconomics, macroeconomics
10. Normative
11. gross domestic product
12. Inflation
13. Cartesian coordinate system
14. time-series graph
15. scatter plot

True-False Questions

1. **True**. They produce goods and services such as national defense and education.
2. **False**. Labor and capital are called factors of production.
3. **False**. Economic models are always simplifications of reality.
4. **False**. Correlation does not imply causation.
5. **False**. According to the law of supply, when the price of a good increases, people will provide more of that good.
6. **True**. Microeconomics studies the behavior of individual firms, households, and markets.
7. **True**. Macroeconomics focuses on the whole national, or even world, economy.
8. **True**. GDP is usually specified for one year.
9. **True**. Health-care spending was 10.8 percent of U.S. GDP for 1995.
10. **False**. Health-care spending is three times as large as spending on automobiles.

11. **True**. Although health-care spending and GDP have both been rising, health-care spending has been increasing more quickly than GDP.
12. **True**. The price of health care has risen more rapidly than the overall price level.
13. **False**. The value of the variable is on the vertical axis, and time is on the horizontal axis.
14. **False**. Variables depicted by a linear relationship can be either positively or negatively related.
15. **False**. Changes in the value of one of the variables on the two axes causes a movement along the curve, not a shift of the curve.

Short-Answer Questions

1. A market is an arrangement through which exchange of goods and services between people takes place.

2. Households supply their labor to the firms that employ them. The resources used by firms to produce goods and services are called capital.

3. Correlation means that two variables move together, either in the same direction or in opposite directions. Causation means that the movements in one variable bring about, or cause, the movements in another variable.

4. Scarcity is a central theme in economics because if people could have everything they wanted, there would be no economic problems.

5. The *ceteris paribus* assumption is that, when making a prediction of the effect of one variable on another, all other variables are unchanged.

6. Experimental economics is a new and growing branch of economics in which researchers conduct economic experiments in laboratory settings.

7. In the context of public policy making, positive economics describes or explains what the government does. Normative economics makes recommendations about what the government should do.

8. Health-care spending has grown more rapidly than the rest of the U.S. economy, and the price of health care has increased more than most other prices.

9. Health-care spending as a share of GDP can be calculated by dividing health-care spending by GDP and multiplying by 100.

10. The overall price level is a measure of the average price of all the goods and services in GDP.

11. Inflation is the general increase in prices over time. The inflation rate is the percentage increase in the overall price level from one year to the next.

12. The relative price of health care is calculated by dividing the price of health care by the overall price level.

13. A dual scale can be used when more than one variable is plotted on the same graph and the scales of measurement of the variables are very different.

14. The two variables are positively related if the slope is positive and negatively related if the slope is negative.

15. Changes in the values of variables that are depicted on the axes cause movements along a curve, whereas changes in the values of other variables cause shifts of the curve.

SOLUTIONS TO THE PRACTICE PROBLEMS

1. a. The automobile spending share and the relative price of automobiles are:

Year	Automobile Spending Share	Relative Price of Automobiles
2000	3.0 percent	1.00
2010	3.5 percent	0.92
2020	4.0 percent	0.84
2030	4.5 percent	0.77

   b. The automobile spending share has increased and the relative price of automobiles has decreased over this period.

2. a. The clothing spending share and the relative price of clothing are:

Year	Clothing Spending Share	Relative Price of Clothing
2000	3.0 percent	0.90
2010	3.5 percent	0.95
2020	4.0 percent	1.00
2030	4.5 percent	1.05

   b. The clothing spending share and the relative price of clothing have both increased during this period.

3. a. The scatter plot is drawn in Figure 1.11. The curve is downward-sloping, indicating that the two variables are negatively related.

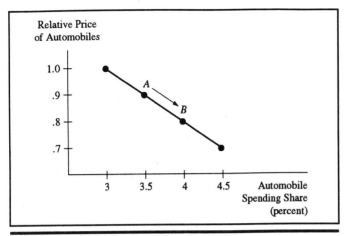

Figure 1.11

b. This is a movement along the curve; it is depicted by a movement from point *A* to point *B* in Figure 1.11.

4. a. The scatter plot is drawn in Figure 1.12. The curve is upward-sloping, indicating that the two variables are positively related.

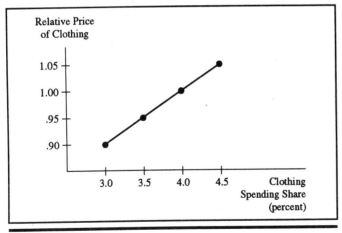

Figure 1.12

b. This is a shift of the curve; it is depicted in Figure 1.13 by a shift of the curve marked "Original" to the right, to the curve marked "New."

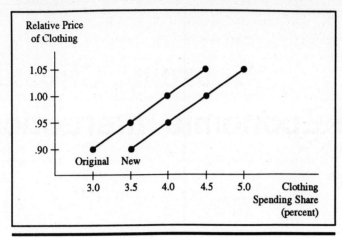

Figure 1.13

ANSWERS TO THE CHAPTER TEST

1. b	6. c	11. d	16. a
2. a	7. d	12. b	17. c
3. c	8. b	13. a	18. b
4. a	9. a	14. b	19. d
5. b	10. c	15. d	20. b

CHAPTER 2

Scarcity, Choice, and Economic Interaction

CHAPTER OVERVIEW

Economic interactions involve scarcity and choice. Time and income are limited, and people choose among alternatives every day. In this chapter, we study the choices people make when faced with a scarcity of resources and the economic interactions among people when they make their choices. We begin by looking at scarcity, choice, and interaction for individuals. We study consumer and producer decisions, learn about the gains from trade, and see how the same principles that guide interactions between individuals can be used to study interactions between countries. We then look at scarcity and choice for the economy as a whole, and introduce the production possibilities curve. We conclude by studying two alternative economic systems, the market economy and the command economy. We look at some of the key differences between market economies and command economies, and focus on the role of prices. This chapter completes our broad overview of economics. In the next chapter, we consider the most frequently used model in economics: the basic supply and demand model.

CHAPTER REVIEW

1. **Scarcity** is a situation in which people's wants exceed their resources. Scarcity is a fact of life; wants are unlimited, but resources are not. Because of scarcity, people must make a **choice**—to forgo, or give up, one thing in favor of another.

2. **Economic interaction** between people occurs when they trade or exchange goods and services with each other. Economic interactions occur in **markets**, arrangements where buyers and sellers can interact with each other, and within **organizations** such as families, firms, universities, and governments.

3. Because resources are limited, individual consumers face budget constraints that force them to make choices among different items that they want. Budget constraints can involve money (you want to buy dinner and football tickets but can't afford both) or time (you have both an economics test and a physics test tomorrow, and you need to allocate your remaining study time between them).

4. The **opportunity cost** of a choice is the value of the forgone alternative that was not chosen. In the above examples, the opportunity cost of football tickets is dinner, and the opportunity cost of studying economics is not doing as well in the physics test.

5. Economic interactions often involve **gains from trade**. Suppose that you can afford season tickets for either football or basketball, but not both, and that you would prefer attending half of the football games and half of the basketball games to attending all of either. If you could find someone with similar preferences to trade tickets with, you would both be better off. Gains from trade can occur in markets, such as a ticket agency, or in organizations, such as a family or a college dormitory.

6. Individual producers also face scarcity and choice; you cannot produce unlimited goods with limited time and resources. Gains from trade allow people to **specialize** in what they are good at. If a guitarist and a drummer form a rock group, **division of labor** allows each to concentrate on playing one instrument.

7. One person or group of people has a **comparative advantage** in producing one good relative to another good if they can produce with comparatively less time, effort, or resources than another person can produce that good. In the above example, production can be increased if the guitarist plays the guitar and the drummer plays the drums, rather than both trying to play both instruments. (There is one subtle aspect of the idea of comparative advantage: Even if the guitarist plays both the guitar and the drums better than the drummer, the guitarist will be able to play one instrument, presumably the guitar, and the drummer will be able to play the other instrument, presumably the drums, *comparatively* better than the other musician.)

8. **International trade** occurs when individuals who live in different countries trade with each other. There are gains from international trade for the same reasons that there are gains from trade within a country: By trading, people can either better satisfy their preferences for goods or better utilize their comparative advantage.

9. **Multilateral trade** is trade in which more than two people participate. Multilateral trade requires a **medium of exchange**, a generally acceptable item that people can buy and sell goods for, such as money. Different countries use different forms of money. The **exchange rate** is the price of one money in terms of another.

10. **Production possibilities** represent the alternative choices of goods that the economy can produce. Consider an economy that produces two goods, steel and food. If it produces more of one, it must produce less of the other. The opportunity cost of producing more steel is the value of the forgone food. The idea of **increasing opportunity costs** is that as steel production rises, the value of the forgone food increases. The rate of decline in food production increases as we produce more steel.

ZEROING IN

1. The **production possibilities curve** is a graphical representation of the idea of production possibilities. We will see how to construct the production possibilities curve, what causes a movement along the curve, and what causes the curve to shift.

   a. Figure 2.1 depicts the production possibilities curve for steel and food. Steel is on the vertical axis, and food is on the horizontal axis. Both are measured in tons. If the economy devotes all of its resources to either steel or food production, it can produce the maximum amount of one and none of the other. The production possibilities curve slopes downward and is bowed out from the origin. The curve is bowed out because the opportunity cost of producing food increases as more food is produced. As more resources are shifted from steel to food production, each additional ton of food means a greater loss of steel produced.

   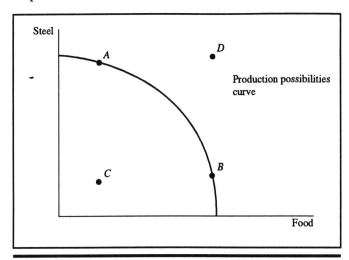

   Figure 2.1

   b. The production possibilities curve shows three situations. Points on the curve are *efficient* because they represent the maximum amount that can be produced with available resources. Production of food can be raised only by lowering production of steel, such as by moving from point *A* to point *B*. Points inside the production possibilities curve, such as point *C*, are *inefficient*. Using the same resources, the economy could produce more steel, more food, or both. Points outside the production possibilities curve, such as point *D*, are *impossible*. The economy does not have the resources to produce those quantities of steel and food.

   c. We discussed the distinction between movements along a curve and shifts of the curve in Chapter 1. In this context, a change in the production of one of the variables on the axes is a movement along the curve. For example, an increase in steel production is a movement from point *B* to point *A* in Figure 2.1. **Economic growth** causes an outward shift in the production possibilities curve. When there is economic growth, more resources are available, and more goods and services can be produced. The effects of economic growth are illustrated in Figure 2.2. The production possibilities curve shifts out from the curve labeled "Original" to the curve labeled "Growth."

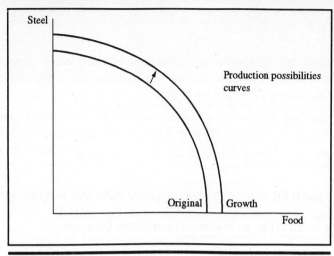

Figure 2.2

2. Every economy focuses on three essential questions: *what* are the goods and services to be produced, *how* are these goods and services to be produced, and *for whom* are the goods and services to be produced? In a *market economy*, these decisions are made by consumers, firms, governments, and other organizations interacting in markets. In a command economy, these decisions are made through a central plan by those who control the government. A command economy is also called a centrally planned economy. One of the most important economic events of recent years has been the attempt by the countries of Eastern Europe, the former Soviet Union, and China to make the transition from command economies to market economies.

3. There are a number of important characteristics that distinguish market economies from command economies, and we consider some of these differences.

    a. **Freely determined prices**, set by individuals and firms, are an essential characteristic of a market economy. In a command economy, most prices are set by the government. **Property rights**, the legal authority to keep or sell property, provide **incentives** for invention and specialization and are another key element of a market economy. Competitive markets and freedom to trade at home and abroad also characterize market, but not command, economies.

    b. The role of government in a market economy is a subject of much debate among economists. It is generally agreed that the government should provide for defense, help establish property rights, and keep the overall price level stable, but modern governments do much more. **Market failure** is a situation in which the market economy does not provide good enough answers to the three questions posed above—what, how, and for whom—and in which there is a role for government in improving the market outcome. However, when the government, even in the case of market failure, does worse than the market would have done if left on its own, there is **government failure**.

    c. Many of the economic interactions in market economies take place within organizations, such as firms, households, and universities, instead of in markets. A **transfer price** is a price that one department of an organization must pay to receive goods or services from another department in the same organization. One important reason why organizations are created is that they reduce market **transaction costs**, the costs of buying and selling. These costs include the cost of finding a buyer or a seller and the cost of reaching agreement on a price.

    d. Prices play three important roles in a market economy. They serve as *signals* about what should be produced and consumed when there are changes in tastes or technology, they provide *incentives* to people to alter their production or consumption, and they affect the *distribution of income*.

ACTIVE REVIEW

Fill-in Questions

1. _____ is a situation in which people's wants exceed their resources.

2. Economic interactions occur in _____ and within _____.

3. Individual consumers with limited resources face _____.

4. The _____ of a choice is the value of the forgone alternative that was not chosen.

5. When both participants are made better off by an economic interaction, there are

   _____.

6. Specialization in production results in _____.

7. One person or group of people has a(n) _____ in producing one good relative to another good when they can produce that good with comparatively less time, effort, or resources than another person can produce that good.

8. _____ occurs when individuals who live in different countries trade with each other.

9. The _____ is the price of one money in terms of another.

10. _____ represent the alternative choices of goods that the economy can produce.

11. The graphical depiction of production possibilities is called the _____.

12. _____ causes an outward shift in the production possibilities curve.

13. The two major types of economies are _____ economies and
    _____ economies.

14. A(n) _____ is the price that one department of an organization must pay to receive goods or services from another department in the same organization.

15. In a market economy, prices serve as _____, provide _____, and affect the _____.

True-False Questions

T   F   1. Scarcity is a characteristic of a command economy, but not of a market economy.

T   F   2. Individual consumers face budget constraints because of limited resources.

T   F   3. Budget constraints always involve money.

T   F   4. Gains from trade occur only in markets.

T   F   5. If Canada produces two goods with less resources than the United States, there can be no comparative advantage in those two goods.

T   F   6. Multilateral trade requires a medium of exchange.

T   F   7. Production possibilities represent the best choice of goods for the economy to produce.

T   F   8. The production possibilities curve slopes downward.

T   F   9. The production possibilities curve is linear.

T   F   10. Points on the production possibilities curve are efficient.

T   F   11. Points inside the production possibilities curve are inefficient.

T   F   12. A market economy is also called a centrally planned economy.

T   F   13. In recent years, Eastern Europe, the former Soviet Union, and China have moved away from central planning.

T   F   14. Freely determined prices and property rights are characteristics of centrally planned economies.

T   F   15. One reason why organizations are created is that they eliminate market failure.

Short-Answer Questions

1. What must people do because of scarcity?

2. When do economic interactions between occur?

3. Where do economic interactions occur?

4. What are opportunity costs?

5. What is comparative advantage?

6. Why are there gains from international trade?

7. Why are there increasing opportunity costs?

8. Why is the production possibilities curve bowed out?

9. What are the three situations defined by the production possibilities curve?

10. Why are points outside the production possibilities curve characterized as impossible?

11. How does economic growth affect the production possibilities curve?

12. What are the three essential questions faced by every economy?

13. Name four characteristics of market, but not command, economies.

14. What is the difference between market failure and government failure?

15. What are the three roles of prices in a market economy?

WORKING IT OUT

1. We have studied the idea of production possibilities and the production possibilities curve by using graphs. We will first consider the same two concepts using numerical examples, and then see how we can combine graphs and numbers.

   a. Suppose that the production possibilities for steel and food are given by:

Choice	Steel	Food
A	0	100
B	25	95
C	50	85
D	75	50
E	100	0

   Both steel and food are measured in tons. Increasing opportunity costs are illustrated by moving down the table. As we move from row to row, steel production increases by the same amount, 25 tons. The decline in food production, in contrast, gets larger, going from 5 tons between the first and second rows to 50 tons between the fourth and fifth rows. Each extra 25 tons of steel requires a loss of more and more food.

   b. The production possibilities curve for these numbers is depicted in Figure 2.3, with steel on the vertical axis and food on the horizontal axis. Both axes are measured in tons. The production possibilities curve is constructed by plotting pairs of points, labeled points *A* through *E*, for steel and food, and then connecting the dots. Since we do not know exactly how much food can be produced in between the 25-ton intervals for steel, we use straight lines to connect the dots.

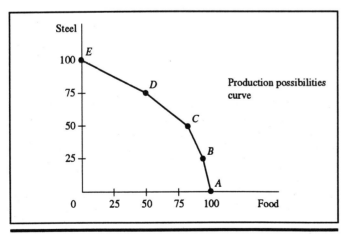

Figure 2.3

2. We have learned that economic growth shifts out the production possibilities curve. We will illustrate this with a numerical example. Suppose that economic growth allows us to produce more goods, so that the new production possibilities for steel and food are given by:

Choice	Steel	Food
A	0	125
B	25	120
C	50	110
D	75	90
E	100	50
F	125	0

The new production possibilities curve, labeled "Growth," is drawn with the original production possibilities curve in Figure 2.4. The new curve is farther away from the origin than the original curve at all points, indicating that more can be produced. For example, food production of 90 tons and steel production of 75 tons was impossible with the original production possibilities curve. After growth, that point is on the new production possibilities curve, and is therefore efficient.

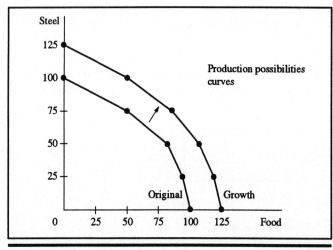

Figure 2.4

Worked Problems

1. Suppose that you must allocate your time between studying economics and studying physics. The percentage of time you spend studying economics and the grades you will get on the two exams are as follows:

Percent of Time Studying Economics	Economics Grade	Physics Grade
100	80	0
80	75	30
60	65	50
40	50	65
20	30	75
0	0	80

Draw the production possibilities curve. How does this example illustrate increasing opportunity costs?

Answer

The production possibilities curve is drawn in Figure 2.5. The example illustrates increasing opportunity costs because, as you move down the table or the curve, each additional point on your physics grade comes at a cost of more and more points on your economics grade.

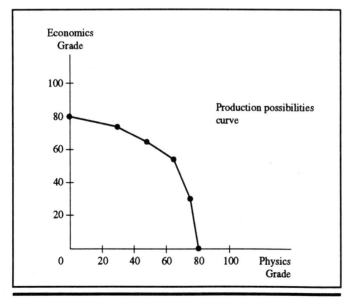

Figure 2.5

2. Now suppose that, by using the study guide for *Economics*, you are able to improve your choices as follows:

Percent of Time Studying Economics	Economics Grade	Physics Grade
100	100	0
80	95	30
60	85	50
40	70	65
20	40	75
0	0	80

a. Draw the new production possibilities curve, and describe how the new curve is related to the old curve.

b. Characterize an economics grade of 70 and a physics grade of 65 under the original and the new production possibilities curves.

Answers

a. *The new production possibilities curve, labeled "Study guide," and the original curve are depicted in Figure 2.6. Using this study guide raises your economics grade at each percent of time, above zero, spent studying economics, but it does not help your physics grade. Although the new curve is above the original curve, it tilts out rather than shifts out.*

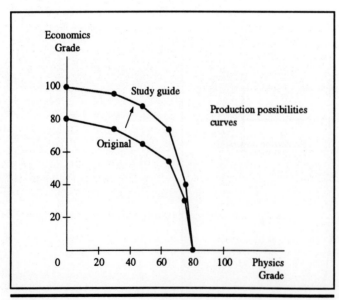

Figure 2.6

b. An economics grade of 70 and a physics grade of 65 was impossible to attain with the original production possibilities curve, but is now efficient.

Practice Problems

1. Suppose that the production possibilities for steel and food are given by:

Choice	Steel	Food
A	0	100
B	25	90
C	50	70
D	75	40
E	100	0

Both steel and food are measured in tons. Draw the production possibilities curve. How does this example illustrate increasing opportunity costs?

2. Suppose that economic growth allows us to produce more goods, so that the new production possibilities for steel and food are given by:

Choice	Steel	Food
A	0	120
B	25	115
C	50	105
D	75	90
E	100	60
F	125	0

a. Draw the new production possibilities curve, and describe how the new curve is related to the old curve.

b. Characterize the production of 75 tons of steel and 40 tons of food under the original and the new production possibilities curves.

3. Suppose that you must allocate your time between studying economics and studying physics. The percentage of time you spend studying economics and the grades you will get on the two exams are as follows:

Percent of Time Studying Economics	Economics Grade	Physics Grade
100	90	0
80	88	40
60	80	70
40	70	80
20	40	88
0	0	90

Draw the production possibilities curve. How does this example illustrate increasing opportunity costs?

4. Now suppose that, by using the study guide for *Economics*, you are able to improve your choices as follows:

Percent of Time Studying Economics	Economics Grade	Physics Grade
100	100	0
80	96	40
60	90	70
40	80	80
20	50	88
0	0	90

a. Draw the new production possibilities curve, and describe how the new curve is related to the old curve.

b. Characterize an economics grade of 80 and a physics grade of 70 under the original and the new production possibilities curves.

CHAPTER TEST

1. A situation in which people's wants exceed their resources is called
   a. abundance.
   b. choice.
   c. scarcity.
   d. allocation.

2. When one person or group of people can produce one good relative to another good with comparatively less time, effort, or resources than another person can produce that good, this is called
   a. comparative advantage.
   b. specialization.
   c. opportunity cost.
   d. division of labor.

3. Because resources are limited, individual consumers face
   a. opportunity costs.
   b. budget constraints.
   c. production possibilities.
   d. economic interactions.

4. Which of the following represents the alternative choices of goods that the economy can produce?
   a. Opportunity costs
   b. Economic interactions
   c. Budget constraints
   d. Production possibilities

5. The value of the alternative that was not chosen is called
   a. the marginal cost of the choice.
   b. the average cost of the choice.
   c. the opportunity cost of the choice.
   d. the gain from the choice.

6. When more than two people engage in trade, it is called
   a. international trade.
   b. multilateral trade.
   c. gains from trade.
   d. comparative advantage.

7. The price of one money in terms of another is called the
   a. opportunity cost.
   b. exchange rate.
   c. interest rate.
   d. inflation rate.

8. The production possibilities curve
   a. slopes downward and is bowed out from the origin.
   b. slopes upward and is bowed out from the origin.
   c. slopes downward and is bowed in toward the origin.
   d. slopes upward and is bowed in toward the origin.

9. Points outside the production possibilities curve are
   a. efficient.
   b. inefficient.
   c. impossible.
   d. possible.

10. Economic growth causes
    a. an inward shift in the production possibilities curve.
    b. an outward shift in the production possibilities curve.
    c. an upward movement on the production possibilities curve.
    d. a downward movement on the production possibilities curve.

11. Which of the following is *not* one of the essential questions that an economy focuses on?
    a. What are the goods and services to be produced?
    b. When are the goods and services to be produced?
    c. How are the goods and services to be produced?
    d. For whom are the goods and services to be produced?

12. Which of the following is *not* one of the characteristics of a market economy?
    a. Freely determined prices
    b. Property rights
    c. Competitive markets
    d. Centrally planned production

13. The price that one department of an organization must pay to receive goods or services from another department in the same organization is called a(n)
    a. transfer price.
    b. transaction cost.
    c. opportunity cost.
    d. transaction price.

14. Which of the following is *not* one of the important roles of prices in a market economy?
    a. They serve as signals.
    b. They provide incentives.
    c. They form preferences.
    d. They affect the distribution of income.

Use the following table for questions 15 and 16.

Suppose that the production possibilities for guns and flowers are given by:

Choice	Guns	Flowers
A	0	100
B	25	90
C	50	70
D	75	40
E	100	0

15. If all of the economy's resources were devoted to the production of flowers, the amount of guns that would be produced is
    a. 100.
    b. 75.
    c. 0.
    d. 50.

16. If the economy is currently producing 50 guns and 60 flowers, then
    a. it is at an efficient level of production.
    b. an efficient level of production can be achieved by producing 20 more flowers.
    c. an efficient level of production can be achieved by producing less flowers and more guns.
    d. an efficient level of production can be achieved by producing 10 more flowers.

Use Figure 2.7 for questions 17, 18, and 19.

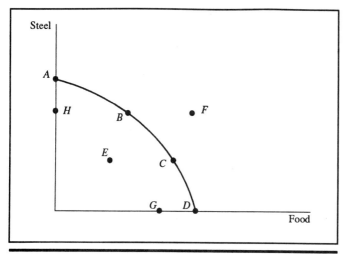

Figure 2.7

17. If the economy devotes all of its resources to steel production, it will be producing at point
    a. *A.*
    b. *B.*
    c. *H.*
    d. *G.*

18. Point *F* in Figure 2.7 represents
    a. an efficient production level.
    b. an inefficient production level.
    c. an impossible production level.
    d. a possible production level.

19. If the economy is currently producing at point *E*, then
    a. it is utilizing its resources efficiently.
    b. it is utilizing its resources inefficiently.
    c. it is on its production possibilities curve.
    d. it is beyond its production possibilities curve.

Use Figure 2.8 for question 20.

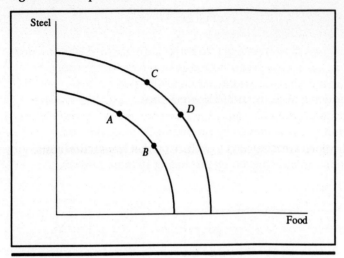

Figure 2.8

20. An economy experiences economic growth when it moves
   a. from point *A* to point *B*.
   b. from point *A* to point *C*.
   c. from point *D* to point *C*.
   d. from point *D* to point *B*.

ANSWERS TO THE REVIEW QUESTIONS

Fill-in Questions

1. Scarcity
2. markets, organizations
3. budget constraints
4. opportunity cost
5. gains from trade
6. division of labor
7. comparative advantage
8. International trade
9. exchange rate
10. Production possibilities
11. production possibilities curve
12. Economic growth
13. market, command
14. transfer price
15. signals, incentives, distribution of income

True-False Questions

1. **False.** Because wants are unlimited but resources are not, scarcity is a characteristic of all economies.
2. **True.** If resources were unlimited, there would be no constraints.
3. **False.** Budget constraints can also involve time.
4. **False.** Gains from trade can also occur within organizations.
5. **False.** The United States will still produce one of the goods with *relatively* less resources than Canada, leading to a *comparative* advantage in that good.
6. **True.** Multilateral trade requires a generally acceptable item that people can buy and sell goods for.

7. **False**. Production possibilities represent the alternative choices of goods that the economy can produce.
8. **True**. As more of one good is produced, less of the other can be produced.
9. **False**. The production possibilities curve is bowed out.
10. **True**. They represent the maximum amount that can be produced with available resources.
11. **True**. Using the same resources, the economy could produce more of both goods.
12. **False**. A command economy is also called a centrally planned economy.
13. **True**. They are making the transition from command economies to market economies.
14. **False**. Freely determined prices and property rights are characteristics of market, not centrally planned, economies.
15. **False**. One reason why organizations are created is to reduce market transaction costs.

Short-Answer Questions

1. Because of scarcity, people must make choices to forgo one thing in favor of another.

2. Economic interactions between people occur when they trade or exchange goods or services with each other.

3. Economic interactions occur in markets and within organizations.

4. The opportunity cost of a choice is the value of the forgone alternative that was not chosen.

5. One person or group of people has a comparative advantage in producing one good relative to another good if they can produce that good with comparatively less time, effort, or resources than another person can produce that good.

6. There are gains from international trade because by trading, people can either better satisfy their preferences for goods or better utilize their comparative advantage.

7. There are increasing opportunity costs because as the production of one good increases, the value of the forgone good increases.

8. The production possibilities curve is bowed out because of increasing opportunity costs.

9. Points on the production possibility curve are efficient, those inside the curve are inefficient, and those outside the curve are impossible.

10. They are called impossible because the economy does not have the resources to produce outside the production possibilities curve.

11. Economic growth shifts out the production possibilities curve.

12. Every economy must determine what are the goods and services to be produced, how are these goods and services to be produced, and for whom are the goods and services to be produced.

13. Freely determined prices, property rights, competitive markets, and freedom to trade at home and abroad characterize market, but not command, economies.

14. Market failure is a situation in which there is a role for the government in improving the market outcome. Government failure occurs when the government, even in the case of market failure, does worse than the market would have done if left on its own.

15. Prices serve as signals about what should be produced and consumed when there are changes in tastes or technology, they provide incentives to people to alter their production or consumption, and they affect the distribution of income.

SOLUTIONS TO THE PRACTICE PROBLEMS

1. The production possibilities curve is drawn in Figure 2.9. The example illustrates increasing opportunity costs because, as you move down the table or up the curve, each additional 25 tons of steel comes at a higher cost in food production.

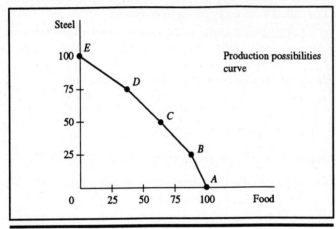

Figure 2.9

2. a. The new production possibilities curve, labeled "Growth," is drawn with the original production possibilities curve in Figure 2.10. The new curve shifts out from the old curve.

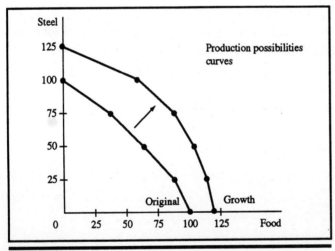

Figure 2.10

   b. Production of 75 tons of steel and 40 tons of food was efficient under the original production possibilities curve. It is inefficient under the new curve.

3. The production possibilities curve is drawn in Figure 2.11. Each additional point on your physics grade comes at a cost of more and more points on your economics grade.

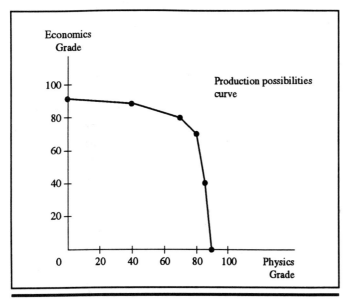

Figure 2.11

4. a. The new production possibilities curve, labeled "Study guide," and the original curve are depicted in Figure 2.12. The new curve is above the original curve, but it tilts out rather than shifting out.

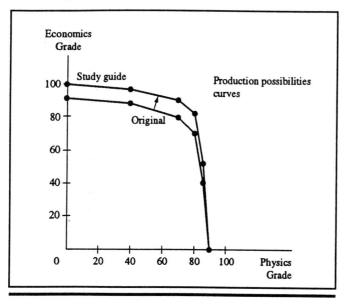

Figure 2.12

   b. An economics grade of 80 and a physics grade of 70 was efficient with the original production possibilities curve, but is now inefficient.

ANSWERS TO THE CHAPTER TEST

1. c	6. b	11. b	16. d
2. a	7. b	12. d	17. a
3. b	8. a	13. a	18. c
4. d	9. c	14. c	19. b
5. c	10. b	15. c	20. b

CHAPTER 3

The Supply and Demand Model

CHAPTER OVERVIEW

If people are left to choose for themselves what to consume and produce, what will society consume and produce? In this chapter, you will be introduced to the most important tool that economists have developed to answer this question. This is the supply and demand model of a market. It starts with a description of buyers' behavior and a description of sellers' behavior, and how their choices respond to changes in the economic environment. We will learn that neither buyers alone nor sellers alone but both together determine how much will be bought and sold, and at what price. We will also see that when buyers and sellers respond to changes in the economic environment, the quantity bought and sold and the price are likely to change too. In this way, a price change both signals to consumers and suppliers that something important has happened in the economy, and provides them with an incentive to make the right adjustment to their new circumstances. Finally, we will see that interfering with the interaction of buyers and sellers in the marketplace, even with the best of intentions, can frequently make things worse.

CHAPTER REVIEW

1. Remember that economics is, first and foremost, concerned with explaining how people behave. To understand how buyers and sellers interact with each other, we need three things: a description of buyers' behavior, a description of sellers' behavior, and a description of how they deal with each other.

2. **Demand** is the economist's term for the relationship between the **price** of a particular good and the amount of that good that consumers want to buy, which is called **quantity demanded**. It is important to distinguish between these two concepts. Quantity demanded is an *amount*; it is measured in pounds, or gallons, or haircuts. Demand is a *relationship* (a function, in mathematical terms); it gives an amount for each possible price, not a single amount.

3. The demand relationship can be represented in several ways. One is in the form of a table of numbers that gives the amount that consumers want to buy (quantity demanded) at different prices; this kind of table is called a **demand schedule**. Another is in the form of a graph of the amounts that consumers want to buy (quantity demanded) at different prices; this is called a

demand curve. When graphing a demand curve, it is important to put the quantity demanded on the horizontal axis and the price on the vertical axis.

4. The **law of demand** says that the demand relationship is a negative relationship; that is, the amount of a good that people wish to buy goes down as the price goes up, all other things being equal. More people will buy, and those who are buying will buy more, at lower prices because at the lower price the good looks more attractive compared to the alternatives than it did before. Remember the *ceteris paribus* condition, however. If other variables are changing at the same time that the price is falling, you can't tell what the relationship is between price and the amount that people want to buy.

5. Changes in other variables that affect the amount that people want to buy lead to a *shift in demand*. That is, they change the amount that people want to buy (quantity demanded) at each and every price. Among the most important variables that can shift the demand for a product are *consumers' preferences, consumers' information, consumers' incomes, the number of consumers in the population, consumers' expectations of future prices*, and *the price of related goods*.

6. Changes in consumers' preferences can clearly change the amount that people want to buy. If consumers decide that a product is more or less desirable, they will obviously want to buy more or less of it at each price. Be careful to distinguish this effect from consumers' desire to buy more when the price falls. In that case, their tastes have not changed (and the demand curve has not shifted); instead, consumers now find it more affordable to indulge their tastes.

7. When people learn more about a good, they may change the amount that they want to buy at every price. Additional information about the benefits of a good will increase demand for it, and additional information about the harm from consuming a good will reduce demand for it.

8. When consumers' incomes increase, they can afford to buy more things, and demand for most goods will increase. Those goods are called **normal goods**. However, the demand for some goods will fall when consumers become richer and can afford better; these are called **inferior goods**. For example, students with low incomes may buy a lot of ramen noodles, because they are a low-cost food. When these students graduate and start full-time jobs, they may buy less ramen and more pizza (or steak if they get a really good job). In that case, ramen is an inferior good, whereas pizza is a normal good.

9. Since demand is the relationship between the price of a good and the amount that *all* consumers want to buy, a change in the number of consumers is likely to change the amount that people want to buy at many prices. Therefore, the demand curve shifts when the number of consumers changes.

10. The demand for a good will shift when the price of a good that is a **substitute** for it changes. If the substitute becomes less expensive, it becomes relatively more attractive, and some consumers will switch. For example, if the price of crab falls and all other things remain equal, consumers as a group (although perhaps not every consumer) will want to buy less lobster. If the price of Corvettes increases and all other things remain equal, then consumers will want to buy more Camaros. Generally, demand for a good increases when the price of a substitute rises, and demand for a good decreases when the price of a substitute falls. The demand for a good is also shifted by changes in the price of a **complement,** a good that tends to be consumed together with another good. For example, if the price of playing a round of golf rises, the demand for golf carts will be reduced. If the price of coffee falls, the demand for coffee creamer increases. Generally, demand for a good decreases when the price of a complement rises, and demand for a good increases when the price of a complement falls.

11. Finally, demand will also respond to consumers' expectations of changes in the price of that good and of changes in other variables. For example, if consumers think they will be wealthier in the near future, they will start making additional purchases right now. Think about the graduating senior who just got that great job offer; isn't she already driving a new car? Similarly, if people believe that the price of something is going to change, their demand for it may change right away. For example, in December 1973, Johnny Carson's monologue joke on the *Tonight* show about the possibility of a toilet paper shortage led to such a large increase in the demand for toilet paper that in some places it really did become hard to find.

12. Changes in variables other than the price of the good in question *shift* the demand curve for that good. Changes in the price of the good in question, all other things being equal, result in consumers *moving along* the demand curve, but don't shift the demand curve. This is an important distinction to draw; don't confuse the two.

13. **Supply** is the economist's term for the relationship between the price of a good and the amount of that good that firms are willing to sell, which is called **quantity supplied**. As with demand, it is important to distinguish between these two concepts. Quantity supplied is an *amount*; it is measured in tons, or barrels, or shirts cleaned. Supply is a *relationship* or function; it gives an amount for each possible price, not a single amount.

14. Like the demand relationship, the supply relationship can be represented in several ways. One is in the form of a table of numbers that gives the amount that firms are willing to sell (quantity supplied) at different prices; this kind of table is called a **supply schedule**. Another is in the form of a graph of the amount that firms are willing to sell (quantity supplied) at different prices; this is called a **supply curve**. When graphing a supply curve, it is important to put the quantity supplied on the horizontal axis and the price on the vertical axis.

15. The **law of supply** says that all other things being equal, the higher the price, the more firms will be willing to supply. Thus, the price and the quantity supplied are positively related. More firms will wish to sell and the firms that are selling will wish to sell more when the price rises because producing this product looks more profitable than the alternatives. Again, remember the *ceteris paribus* condition; if other variables that affect the amount that firms wish to sell are changing at the same time that the price is changing, the quantity supplied can either rise or fall.

16. When other variables that affect the amount that producers are willing to sell change, this leads to a *shift* in supply. That is, those changes alter the amount that firms are willing to sell (quantity supplied) at each and every price. Among the most important variables that can shift the supply of a product are *technology, the price of goods used in production, the number of firms in the market, expectations of future prices,* and *government taxes, subsidies, and regulations.*

17. Technology refers to the ability to utilize other goods in order to produce the good or service. This can mean being able to utilize a chair, scissors, and someone's time and skill to produce a haircut, or being able to utilize complex equipment, silicon, and many people's time and skills to produce microchips. When knowledge improves in such a way that producers can produce the same amount of a good with fewer inputs, the cost of producing that good falls. Producing it becomes more attractive, all other things being equal, and the quantity supplied will increase at each and every price.

18. Similarly, if the price of the goods used in the production of a good falls, then the cost of producing that good falls. Again, producing that good becomes more profitable, all other things being equal, and firms will wish to sell more of it. This results in a rightward shift of the supply curve. Conversely, if the price of one or more inputs used in producing something rises, then firms will find it less profitable to produce that good, and will be willing to sell less at each and every price, shifting the entire supply curve to the left.

19. Since the supply curve shows the amount that *all* of the producers together are willing to supply at different prices, an increase in the number of suppliers will increase that total, and shift the supply curve to the right. Conversely, a decline in the number of sellers will reduce the total amount offered for sale at each and every price. This would lead to a leftward shift of the supply curve.

20. If firms expect that the price of their output is going to increase in the future, they will wish to delay selling their output until that price increase occurs. This results in less being offered for sale at any current price and a leftward shift of the supply curve. If the price of the goods that they sell is expected to fall in the future, sellers will want to sell more now; this increases supply and shifts the supply curve to the right.

21. Taxes imposed by the government raise firms' costs of production and, like increases in input prices, make selling the product less attractive. Subsidies to producers, on the other hand, lower the costs of production and make sales more attractive. Thus, taxes shift the supply curve to the left (decreasing supply), and subsidies shift the supply curve to the right (increasing supply). Government regulations can also increase the costs of production—for example, by requiring the installation of pollution control equipment or additional safety testing of the product. These regulations will have the effect of decreasing supply.

22. As with the demand curve, it is important to distinguish *shifts* of the supply curve from *movements along* the supply curve. Changes in variables other than the price of the good in question shift the supply curve for that good. Changes in the price of the good in question, all other things being equal, result in firms moving along the supply curve, but do not shift the supply curve.

23. The demand curve describes how much consumers *want* to purchase at different prices, and the supply curve describes how much producers *want* to sell at different prices. In order to determine how much of a good actually gets bought (and sold), we need to understand how these two groups interact with each other. Economists believe that when consumers and producers get together, they will put pressure on the price that brings it to the level at which the amount that consumers want to purchase is just the amount that producers want to sell. This situation is called an *equilibrium*, because the quantity supplied and the quantity demanded are in balance. How much will be traded and the price at which those purchases take place can be determined from the numbers in the supply and demand schedules, or from a diagram that includes both the supply curve and the demand curve.

24. A **shortage** of a good occurs when, at the current price, consumers want to purchase more of the good than producers want to sell. In that case, we would expect some producers to take advantage of the situation by trying to get more from those who want to buy, and those consumers who are willing to pay more to try to outbid other consumers. This will cause the price to rise. Some consumers will decide that they are no longer willing to buy at the higher prices, and some producers will decide that they are willing to sell more at the higher prices. Eventually the price increases will bring the quantity supplied and the quantity demanded together, and there will be no further upward pressure on the price.

25. A **surplus** of a good, on the other hand, occurs when producers want to sell more units of the good than consumers want to purchase at the current price. When there is a surplus, we would expect producers to start lowering the price to get their products sold. The surplus results in a falling price, which will cause some producers to decide that they no longer want to sell as much and some consumers to decide that they want to buy more. When the price falls to a level at which the quantity supplied equals the quantity demanded, there will be no further downward pressure on the price.

26. Thus, **market equilibrium**, a situation with neither upward nor downward pressure on the price, occurs when the quantity supplied equals the quantity demanded at the current price. We call the price at which this occurs the **equilibrium price**, and the quantity that gets bought and sold at that price the **equilibrium quantity**. If we have the supply and demand schedules for a good, we can find the equilibrium price by finding the price at which the quantity supplied equals the quantity demanded. If we have a supply and demand diagram that graphs the same information, we can find the equilibrium price and equilibrium quantity by finding where the supply curve and the demand curve cross. Look over to the vertical axis from the point at which the curves cross to find the equilibrium price, and look down to the horizontal axis from that point to find the equilibrium quantity.

27. Suppose a market is in equilibrium, and one or more of the variables that affect supply and demand change. As a result, either the demand curve or the supply curve or both will shift. At the original equilibrium price, there will now be either a shortage or a surplus (depending on which way the curves have shifted and by how much), and pressure on the price will lead to a new equilibrium price and quantity. For example, if an increase in income leads to an increase (rightward shift) in demand, then there will be a shortage at the original equilibrium price, and the price will be forced up to a new equilibrium. A decrease in input prices leading to an increase (rightward shift) in supply will cause a surplus at the original equilibrium price, and the price will fall until a new equilibrium is reached. In this way, the equilibrium price and quantity respond to changes in variables that affect consumers' demand and producers' supply.

28. Governments sometimes put limits on the quantity that can be bought or sold. These limits are called **quotas**. They reduce the supply and raise the equilibrium price.

29. Governments often impose **price controls** in the form of **price ceilings** (maximum prices) to prevent prices from rising to levels that they feel are unfair to consumers or **price floors** (minimum prices) to prevent prices from falling to levels that are viewed as unfair to suppliers. For example, **rent controls** are laws that put a ceiling on how high the price of rental housing can rise, while the **minimum wage** set by the federal government puts a floor below which wages (the price of labor inputs) cannot fall. When prices are prevented from rising or falling to their equilibrium levels, shortages or surpluses can persist, and other ways must be found to ration the goods. These often have undesirable features: People waste valuable time waiting in lines to make their purchases or take their chances on an illegal black market.

ZEROING IN

1. a. The key to understanding and being able to use demand and supply diagrams is being able to distinguish between *shifts* of the demand and supply curves and *movements along* them. To see the difference, imagine yourself riding a bicycle on a flat road and think about the relationship between how fast your pedals turn and how fast the bike goes. This is a positive relationship; turning the pedals slowly (say, once every second) makes the bike go slowly, and turning the pedals quickly (say, three times a second) makes the bike go faster. If you were to draw a graph showing how fast the pedals turn on the vertical axis and the speed of the bike on the horizontal axis, the graph would slope upward, something like Figure 3.1.

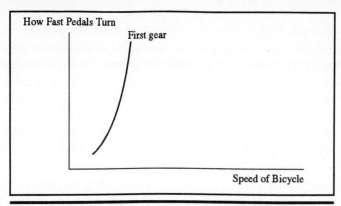

Figure 3.1

b. Now suppose you shift the gears on the bicycle to a higher gear. The relationship between how fast you turn the pedals and how fast the bicycle goes is still a positive one: The faster you turn the pedals, the faster the bike goes. But turning the pedals at the once-per-second low speed now makes the bike go faster than it did in low gear, and turning the pedals at the three-times-per-second high speed also makes the bike go faster than it did in low gear. If you were to graph the relationship between how fast you turn the pedals and how fast the bike goes in the higher gear, you would get a new upward-sloping line to the right of the first line, as in Figure 3.2. For a ten-speed bicycle, there would be ten different lines, one for each gear.

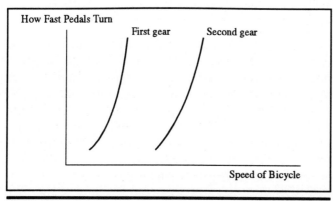

Figure 3.2

c. Whatever gear you are in, you move *along* the line corresponding to that gear by turning the pedals faster or more slowly, or changing the value on the vertical axis. When you shift gears, you *shift* to a different line, and how fast you go on that line depends on how fast you choose to turn the pedals. The same is true of supply and demand curves. For a given set of levels of the other things that affect the supply of or demand for a good, you move *along* the curves when the price of that good (which is on the vertical axis) changes. When one of the other variables that affects supply or demand changes, you *shift* to a new supply or demand curve, and what quantity will be supplied or demanded on that curve depends on what price is chosen.

2. a. The next most important issue is being able to separate the things that shift the demand curve from the things that shift the supply curve. Since households demand goods and services, the variables that shift demand curves are generally things that affect households: their income, their preferences or tastes, their beliefs or expectations, and their number. Also remember that a demand curve shows how much of *one particular* product consumers wish to buy at different prices for that product. Since the answer to that question is likely to depend on

whatever else consumers are buying, the prices of *other* products affect buyers' decisions and hence shift the demand curve.

  b. Firms supply goods and services, and so the variables that shift supply curves are generally things that affect firms: the prices they pay for inputs, including any taxes they pay or subsidies they receive from the government, their knowledge about how to produce (i.e., technology), their beliefs about profitability, and their number.

3. a. It is also important to remember that supply and demand curves shift *left* (decrease) or *right* (increase), not down or up. The reason for this is that quantity is always on the horizontal axis and price is always on the vertical axis. When consumers' income rises, the quantity that consumers wish to buy increases (if the good in question is a normal good) no matter what the price is, and an increase in quantity is shown as a movement to the *right*, as in Figure 3.3.

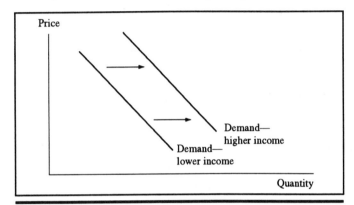

Figure 3.3

  b. This point doesn't seem very important when you look at shifts in demand curves, since a leftward shift looks like an upward shift (although the right answer is still that demand curves shift right for increases and left for decreases). But if you don't keep this straight when thinking about increasing or decreasing supply, you will get things wrong. An increase in supply because input prices fall moves the supply curve to the *right*, which looks like a shift downward, as in Figure 3.4. This is still an increase because at each and every price, the amount that firms wish to sell has increased.

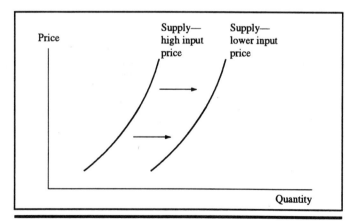

Figure 3.4

4. Finally, it is worth keeping in mind how the market adjusts from an initial equilibrium to a new equilibrium when something changes that shifts either supply or demand or both. It's not merely that one or both of the curves move and there is a new point at which they cross. The supply and demand analysis is intended to capture the behavior of real people. Suppose that the market for small cars is initially in equilibrium, and that because of rising gas prices consumers now want to buy more small cars. Car dealers find their inventory of small cars on the lot declining; they also find that they can charge a higher price for small cars without hurting sales. Thus, small car prices start to rise. This means more profits for firms that sell small cars, and they respond by increasing the number of small cars that they produce for sale. Thus, the quantity supplied rises. At the same time, the rising price of small cars deters some buyers who wanted a new small car at the initial price, but are not so excited about the prospect at a higher price. The price continues to rise until the dealers find that further price increases hurt business by driving too many customers away. At that point, the new equilibrium has been established; the new equilibrium price is higher, and the quantity bought and sold at that price is higher as well.

ACTIVE REVIEW

Fill-in Questions

1. _____ is the relationship between the price of a good and the quantity that consumers want to buy. The amount that consumers want to buy is called _____.

2. A demand schedule is a table of numbers showing _____ and _____. When these numbers are graphed, the resulting line is called a(n) _____.

3. The _____ states that as the price of a good falls (all else remaining equal), the _____ will _____. Therefore, demand curves slope _____.

4. Changes in the price of a good, all other things being equal, lead to _____ the demand curve for that good.

5. Shifts in the demand curve for a good are caused by changes in anything that affects the amount consumers want to buy *except* the _____ of that good.

6. Demand reflects, among other things, consumers' preferences. When consumers' tastes change, the demand curve _____.

7. When consumers' incomes rise, they will want to buy more of all _____ goods and less of all _____ goods.

8. When the price of a substitute for a good rises, the demand for that good _____;
    as a result, the demand curve for that good shifts to the _____. When the price of
    a(n) _____ rises, on the other hand, demand for the good in question
    _____, and the demand curve shifts to the _____.

9. If consumers expect that the price of a good will fall in the future, they will wish to buy
    _____ of it today. This results in a(n) _____ in demand.

10. The relationship between the _____ of a good and the quantity that producers
    are willing to sell is known as _____. The amount that producers wish to sell is
    called _____.

11. The _____ is a graph of the _____ of a good and the
    _____.

12. The law of supply states that as the price of a good rises (all else remaining equal), firms will
    wish to sell _____ of that good. As a result, _____ slope upward.

13. Changes in the _____ of a good lead to _____ the supply curve.
    Changes in anything else that affects the amount that firms wish to sell leads to a(n)
    _____ in the supply curve.

14. The ability to produce goods and services is known as _____. When
    improvements in this ability lead to savings in the amounts of inputs required to produce a given
    amount of output, the _____ shifts to the right.

15. When the prices of inputs rise, production becomes more _____. Firms will wish
    to sell _____ of the good, and the supply curve will shift to the
    _____. The same thing happens when government imposes
    _____ or _____ that raise the cost of production.

16. Entry by new firms means that _____ will be offered for sale at every price. This
    causes a(n) _____ shift of the _____.

17. A market is said to be in _____ when the amount that _____
    want to buy at the current price just equals the amount that _____ wish to
    _____.

18. If the price is above the _____, the quantity _____ will exceed the quantity _____. This results in a(n) _____, and we would expect to see _____ pressure on the price.

19. Conversely, if the price is below the _____ price, the quantity _____ will be less than the quantity _____, and a(n) _____ will occur. In this case, the price can be expected to _____.

20. Government restrictions on prices, such as _____ that prevent prices from rising to their equilibrium levels or _____ that prevent prices from falling, lead to _____ or surpluses.

True-False Questions

T F 1. Price is determined by the interaction of households and firms.

T F 2. When beans cost 69 cents a can, consumers in Oskaloosa wish to purchase 357 cans per month, so we would say that at this price, demand is 357 cans per month.

T F 3. The law of demand states that, all other things being equal, as price rises, demand falls.

T F 4. When T-shirts cost $17.50 apiece, consumers bought 336 T-shirts. After the price fell to $15.00, consumers purchased 472 of them. We would say that quantity demanded rose by 136 units.

T F 5. The law of demand implies that demand curves slope downward.

T F 6. Country club memberships and golf balls are complementary goods.

T F 7. Inferior goods refers to poor-quality, low-cost products.

T F 8. When incomes rise, the demand for normal goods increases.

T F 9. Supply shows how much firms wish to sell at different prices.

T F 10. As the price rises, quantity supplied rises, according to the law of supply.

T F 11. When the price of computer chips falls, lowering the cost of producing computers, the supply of computers can be expected to rise.

T F 12. The equilibrium price in a market is the price that equates supply and demand.

T F 13. A shortage occurs when demand is greater than supply.

T F 14. A falling price will eliminate a surplus by reducing quantity supplied and increasing quantity demanded.

T F 15. If supply increases and demand remains unchanged, the equilibrium quantity will increase and the equilibrium price will rise.

Short-Answer Questions

1. Why do consumers wish to buy more at lower prices? How is this reflected in the demand curve?

2. What is the difference between demand and quantity demanded?

3. Why does the demand for a good fall when the price of a substitute falls?

4. List four things that cause demand curves to shift, and explain how changes in them affect demand. What is the only thing that causes movement along the demand curve?

5. Why do firms wish to supply less at lower prices? How is this reflected in the supply curve?

6. Why does the supply of a good increase when the prices of the inputs used to produce it fall?

7. List four things that cause supply curves to shift, and explain how changes in them affect supply. What is the only thing that causes movement along the supply curve?

8. Explain how an increase in price eliminates a shortage.

9. Explain why people's behavior should cause the price to settle at the equilibrium price.

10. What happens to the equilibrium price and quantity if demand and supply both increase at the same time? Show your answer with a diagram, and explain.

WORKING IT OUT

1. Remember that changes in the *price* of a good do not shift its demand or supply curve but represent different points on the supply or demand curve. When price changes, you move *along* the demand or supply curve. Figure 3.5 shows the demand curve for Swiss cheese. When the price falls from $1.50 per pound to $1.25 per pound, and all other things remain the same, the demand curve does not change, but the amount that consumers want to buy increases from 1,250 pounds per day to 1,575 pounds per day. The arrow in Figure 3.5 shows the movement along the demand curve.

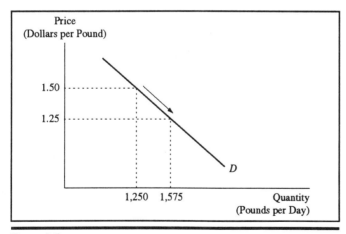

Figure 3.5

2. Changes in *anything else* that affects how much consumers want to buy or firms want to sell shift the demand and supply curves. To know which curve shifts, you need to know what other variable is changing. Is it something that affects consumers' well-being? Then it shifts the demand curve. Is it something that affects producers' profits? Then it shifts the supply curve.

3. The other thing that is central to understanding the supply and demand model is knowing how to combine supply and demand shifts to predict changes in the equilibrium price and quantity. Remember that supply and demand show the amounts that producers *want* to sell and consumers *want* to buy at different prices. The model also predicts that the price will eventually settle down at the equilibrium level, where the amount consumers want to buy just equals the amount that producers want to sell. When something changes either the supply or the demand, price will adjust to a new equilibrium level.

Worked Problems

1. Figure 3.6 shows the demand curve for whitewall tires. Currently the price of tires is $45 per tire. If the price of tires falls to $40 per tire (and all other things remain the same), what happens to the demand for tires and the quantity of tires demanded

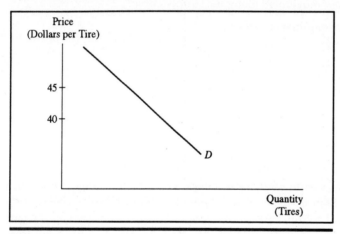

Figure 3.6

Answer

Nothing happens to the demand for tires. None of the variables that affect how much consumers want to buy other than the price have changed (remember, "all other things remain the same"). The demand curve remains where it was. Since the price of tires has fallen, however, consumers will wish to purchase more tires. The quantity of tires demanded will increase, and we move downward along the demand curve to the new, higher quantity demanded, as shown in Figure 3.7.

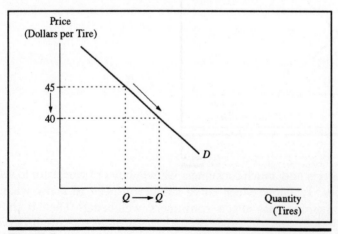

Figure 3.7

2. Suppose the demand curve for whitewall tires is still the one shown in Figure 3.6, but now suppose that the price of *blackwall* tires rises from $35 per tire to $40 per tire. What happens to the demand for whitewall tires?

Answer

It seems believable that at least some people who are currently buying blackwall tires view whitewall tires as substitutes. When the price of blackwall tires rises, those consumers will find the blackwall tires a less attractive purchase just because they're more expensive, and will switch from blackwalls to whitewalls. This will happen no matter what the price of whitewalls is currently; the demand for whitewalls will increase at each and every possible price. The increase in the price of a substitute (blackwalls) increases the demand for this good (whitewalls), and the demand curve shifts to the right (not up), as in Figure 3.8.

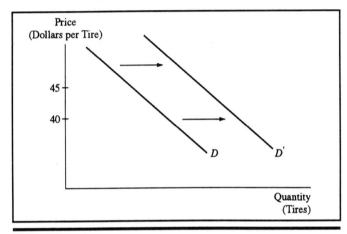

Figure 3.8

3. Figure 3.9 shows the market for peach daiquiris in Greenwich. At first, the market is in equilibrium, with the price of peach daiquiris at $2.50 per drink and 175 drinks being purchased each week. Now suppose that, because of bad weather in Georgia, the price of peaches rises sharply. What happens to the supply and demand for peach daiquiris, and what happens to the equilibrium price and quantity?

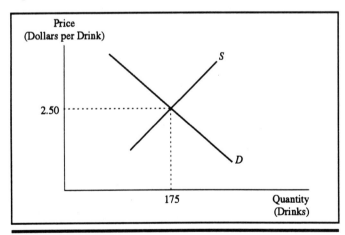

Figure 3.9

Answer

First, we need to know what happens to the supply and demand for peach daiquiris. Nothing happens to the demand; none of the variables that affect the amount that consumers want to buy have changed. However, peaches are an important ingredient in peach daiquiris, and an increase in their price increases the cost of making the drink. Producers will find it less profitable to sell peach daiquiris, and some will choose to stop selling them. The increase in the price of an input decreases the supply of the good and shifts the supply curve to the left, as shown in Figure 3.10.

At the original equilibrium price of $2.50, consumers still want to purchase 175 drinks each week, but producers now want to sell fewer drinks. There is a shortage of peach daiquiris at this price, and there will be upward pressure on the price. Producers will find that they can still sell all the drinks that they want to sell at $2.50 even if they raise the price to a higher price; in fact, at the higher price, producers want to sell somewhat more drinks, and they find that they can. At that price, some consumers find that peach daiquiris are not worth the extra outlay, and they switch to strawberry margaritas. Thus, while the demand for peach daiquiris hasn't changed, the quantity demanded falls as the price rises. From Figure 3.10, we can see that when the price rises to the new equilibrium (at $2.75), the quantity demanded falls to exactly the amount that producers want to sell at that price on the new supply curve (145).

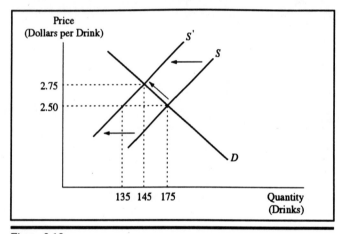

Figure 3.10

Practice Problems

1. Figure 3.11 shows the supply curve for jellybeans. Currently the price of jellybeans is $1.00 a pound. If the price of jellybeans rises to $1.25 a pound (and all other things remain the same), what happens to the supply of jellybeans and the quantity of jellybeans supplied?

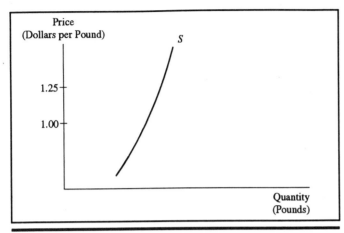

Figure 3.11

2. Figure 3.12 shows the demand for denim skirts. If the price of denim skirts rises from $27 to $32, what happens to the demand for denim skirts, and what happens to the quantity of denim skirts demanded?

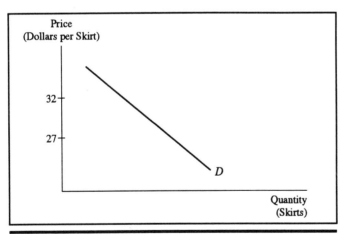

Figure 3.12

3. Suppose the demand for whitewall tires is as shown in Figure 3.6, and suppose that, because of rumors of increasing instability in the Mideast, consumers believe that the price of gasoline is going to increase dramatically and remain at that higher level for a long time. What happens to the demand for whitewall tires?

4. Suppose the supply of jellybeans is as shown in Figure 3.11, and suppose the price of sugar, which is a major ingredient in jellybeans, rises from $1.50 per pound to $1.78 per pound. What happens to the supply of jellybeans?

5. Figure 3.13 shows the supply and demand curves for the market for running suits in Portland. The market is initially in equilibrium at a price of $75 and 1,750 suits sold per year. Suppose that, because of an improving local economy, incomes in Portland rise significantly. What happens to the supply and demand for running suits, and what happens to the equilibrium price and quantity?

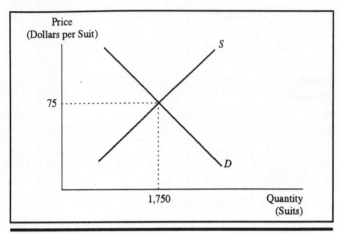

Figure 3.13

6. Figure 3.14 shows the supply and demand curves for the market for tofu in San Leandro, California. The market is initially in equilibrium at a price of $1.50 per container and 450 containers consumed per month. Suppose that, simultaneously, consumers become concerned about soybean pesticide residue in tofu and the state government eases regulations on the disposal of soybean wastes, which lowers the cost of producing tofu. What happens to the supply and demand for tofu, and what happens to the equilibrium price and quantity?

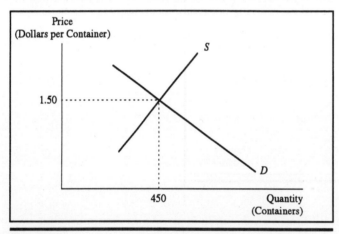

Figure 3.14

CHAPTER TEST

1. Potatoes would be classified as an inferior good if
   a. people at all levels of income consumed them.
   b. other food was more nutritious.
   c. more were consumed as incomes fell.
   d. fewer were consumed when the price of bread fell.

2. The demand curve for fresh swordfish is downward-sloping. Suddenly the price of swordfish rises from $8 per pound to $10 per pound. This will cause
   a. the demand curve to shift to the left.
   b. the demand curve to shift to the right.
   c. quantity demanded to increase.
   d. quantity demanded to decrease.

3. A leftward shift in the supply of Swiss watches might be due to
   a. an increase in the wages of Swiss watchmakers.
   b. an increase in the tax on imported watches.
   c. the introduction of cost-saving robots in the watch industry.
   d. increased popularity of foreign watches.

4. The supply curve for children's books is upward-sloping. A decrease in the price of children's books, all other things being equal, will lead to
   a. an increase in the quantity of children's books supplied.
   b. an increase in the supply of children's books.
   c. producers wishing to sell fewer children's books.
   d. a decrease in the supply of children's books.

   Use Figure 3.15 to answer the next three questions. The diagram refers to the demand for and supply of baseball caps. The baseball cap market is initially in equilibrium at point *A*. Assume that baseball caps are a normal good.

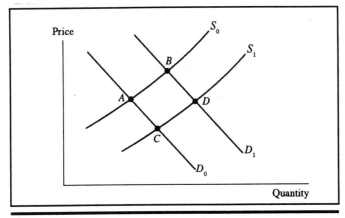

Figure 3.15

5. The baseball cap market moves from point *A* to a new equilibrium at point *B*. There has been
   a. an increase in demand and an increase in supply.
   b. an increase in demand and an increase in quantity supplied.
   c. an increase in quantity demanded and an increase in quantity supplied.
   d. an increase in quantity demanded and an increase in supply.

6. A movement from point *A* to point *C* might have been caused by
   a. a tightening of worker safety regulations in the production of baseball caps.
   b. a decrease in the price of cowboy hats (a substitute for baseball caps).
   c. a decrease in the cost of the cloth used in the baseball cap industry.
   d. increased income.

7. The discovery that wearing a hat reduces dandruff would be likely to move the market from point *A* to
   a. point *B*.
   b. point *C*.
   c. point *D*.
   d. none of the above; this discovery would have no effect on the equilibrium.

8. Which of the following is likely to cause an increase in the demand for gasoline?
   a. An increase in the price of cars
   b. A decrease in the price of gasoline
   c. An increase in subway and bus fares
   d. A decrease in the price of crude oil

9. You observe that the price of houses and the number of houses purchased both rise over the course of a year. You conclude that
   a. the demand for houses has increased.
   b. the demand curve for houses must be upward-sloping.
   c. the supply of houses has increased.
   d. housing construction costs must be decreasing.

10. An increase in supply is shown by
    a. shifting the supply curve up.
    b. shifting the supply curve to the left.
    c. shifting the supply curve to the right.
    d. moving upward along the supply curve.

11. An increase in the price of hamburgers could be explained by all of the following *except*
    a. stricter government controls in the meatpacking industry.
    b. a fall in the price of pickles.
    c. producers' expectations that beef prices will rise in the future.
    d. an increase in vegetarianism.

12. A market is said to be in equilibrium when
    a. supply equals demand.
    b. there is downward pressure on the price.
    c. the amount consumers wish to buy at the current price equals the amount producers wish to sell at that price.
    d. all buyers are able to find sellers willing to sell to them at the current price.

Use the following supply and demand schedules to answer the next four questions.

Price	Quantity Supplied	Quantity Demanded
$3	30	75
$4	40	70
$5	50	65
$6	60	60
$7	70	55
$8	80	50

13. When the price is $4, this market has
    a. a shortage of 45 units.
    b. a shortage of 30 units.
    c. a surplus of 30 units.
    d. a surplus of 25 units.

14. There is a surplus of 30 units when the price equals
    a. $5.
    b. $6.
    c. $7.
    d. $8.

15. This market is in equilibrium when the price equals
    a. $5.
    b. $6.
    c. $7.
    d. $8.

16. Suppose that the supply for this product shifts so that 15 fewer units are supplied at each price. The new equilibrium price will be
    a. $5.
    b. $6.
    c. $7.
    d. $8.

17. If wine and cheese are complements, then an increase in the price of wine will
    a. cause an increase in the price of cheese.
    b. cause a decrease in the demand for wine.
    c. cause less cheese to be demanded at each price.
    d. cause a rightward shift in the demand curve for cheese.

18. If both supply and demand increase simultaneously, the equilibrium
    a. price must rise and the equilibrium quantity must fall.
    b. price must rise and the equilibrium quantity may either rise or fall.
    c. quantity must rise and the equilibrium price may either rise or fall.
    d. price must fall and the equilibrium quantity may either rise or fall.

19. Which of the following would *not* eliminate a shortage of a good?
    a. A fall in the number of consumers
    b. A fall in the price of a substitute for the good
    c. A fall in the price of a complement for the good
    d. An increase in the price of the good

20. Demand for a product could increase for all of the following reasons *except*
    a. an increase in consumer incomes.
    b. a fall in the price of the product.
    c. an expected increase in the price of the product in the future.
    d. an increase in the price of a substitute.

ANSWERS TO THE REVIEW QUESTIONS

Fill-in Questions

1. Demand; quantity demanded
2. price; quantity demanded; demand curve
3. law of demand; quantity demanded; rise; downward
4. movement along
5. price
6. shifts
7. normal; inferior
8. rises; right; complement; falls; left
9. less; decrease
10. price; supply; quantity supplied
11. supply curve; price; quantity supplied
12. more; supply curves
13. price; movement along; shift
14. technology; supply curve
15. costly; less; left; taxes; regulations
16. more; rightward; supply curve
17. equilibrium; consumers; producers; sell
18. equilibrium price; supplied; demanded; surplus; downward
19. equilibrium; supplied; demanded; shortage; increase
20. price ceilings; price floors; shortages

True-False Questions

1. **True.** Household behavior (demand) and producer behavior (supply) determine price.
2. **False.** Quantity demanded is 357 cans per month. Demand is not an amount.
3. **False.** When price rises, quantity demanded (not demand) falls.
4. **True.** This statement distinguishes between demand and quantity demanded properly.
5. **True.** Since the law of demand says that quantity demanded is inversely related to price, it implies that demand curves slope downward.
6. **True.** When country club dues (the price of country club memberships) rise, some people decide not to join, and they do something other than golf for entertainment (e.g., they take up tennis). This reduces the demand for golf balls; fewer golf balls will be purchased no matter what their price is.
7. **False.** Inferior goods are goods that consumers want to buy less of when their incomes rise. They may be perfectly well-made products.
8. **True.** This is the definition of a normal good.
9. **True.** This is the definition of supply.
10. **True.** This is what the law of supply says.
11. **True.** Computer chips are an input into the production of computers. When their price falls, producing computers becomes less costly, and hence more profitable, so firms will increase the amount they wish to sell, no matter what the current price is. Thus, supply rises.
12. **False.** The equilibrium price equates quantity supplied and quantity demanded.

13. **False**. A shortage occurs when quantity demanded (not demand) exceeds quantity supplied (not supply).

14. **True**. A surplus occurs when quantity supplied exceeds quantity demanded at the current price. As the price falls, the amount consumers wish to purchase (quantity demanded) will rise, and the amount firms wish to sell (quantity supplied) will fall. This eliminates the surplus.

15. **False**. If supply increases and demand remains unchanged, the equilibrium quantity will increase, but the price will fall as consumers move downward along the demand curve.

Short-Answer Questions

1. When the price of a good falls (all other things being equal), the good becomes a more desirable alternative than other products. Less has to be given up in order to consume the product than before, and consumers will generally wish to consume more of it. This inverse relationship between the price and the quantity demanded is reflected in the negative (downward) slope of the demand curve.

2. Quantity demanded is the amount that consumers wish to purchase. It is measured in units of product (pounds, gallons, haircuts, etc.). The amount that customers wish to buy depends on many things. Demand is the relationship between one of those things (the price of the good) and the quantity demanded.

3. When the substitute becomes less expensive, it looks more attractive and some consumers will switch.

4. Changes in any of the following will cause a shift in the demand curve: consumers' preferences, consumers' information, consumers' income, consumers' expectations of future prices, the number of consumers in the population, and the price of closely related goods. A change in the price of the good is the only thing that leads to movement along the demand curve.

5. Fewer firms will wish to sell, and the firms that are selling will wish to sell less, when the price falls because producing this product looks less profitable than the alternatives. This direct relationship between the price and the quantity supplied is reflected in the positive (upward) slope of the supply curve.

6. If the prices of the goods used in the production of a good fall, then the cost of producing that good falls. Producing that good becomes more profitable, all other things being equal, and firms will wish to sell more of it. This results in a rightward shift of the supply curve.

7. Changes in any of the following will cause a shift in the supply curve: technology, the price of goods used in production, the number of firms in the market, expectations of future prices, and government taxes, subsidies, and regulations. A change in the price of the good is the only thing that leads to movement along the supply curve.

8. When there is a shortage, quantity demanded is greater than quantity supplied at the current price. As the price rises, quantity demanded falls as we move upward along the demand curve, whereas quantity supplied rises as we move upward along the supply curve. If the price continues to rise, eventually quantity demanded and quantity supplied are equal, and the shortage has been eliminated.

9. When there are either shortages or surpluses, there will be pressure on the price to move in the direction that eliminates the shortage or surplus. In the event of a shortage, producers find that they can raise the price and still sell everything they wish to sell. Consumers who are unable to find the product they want to buy will start offering a higher price for it. The increase in price will induce suppliers to offer more, and will also reduce the amount that buyers wish to

purchase. In the event of a surplus, producers will find themselves unable to sell everything they wish to, and will lower the price to sell their output. Consumers will find that they can negotiate discounts successfully. The decrease in price will lead buyers to purchase more, and will lead suppliers to wish to sell less. In this way, shortages and surpluses are eliminated, and the price moves toward the equilibrium level.

10. When both supply and demand increase (shift rightward) at the same time, the equilibrium quantity will increase. The equilibrium price can either rise or fall, depending on whether the shift of supply or demand is greater. For example, in the first panel of Figure 3.16, while both supply and demand increase, the shift of demand is greater and the new equilibrium price is higher. In the second panel of Figure 3.16, the shift of supply is greater and the new equilibrium price is lower. In both cases, the new equilibrium quantity is larger.

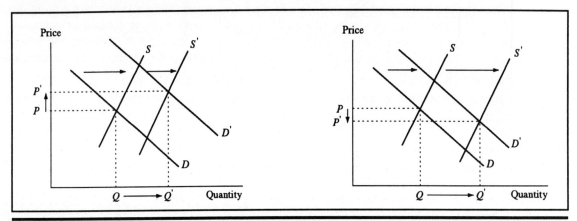

Figure 3.16

SOLUTIONS TO THE PRACTICE PROBLEMS

1. The *supply* of jellybeans is unchanged. None of the variables that affect how much producers want to sell other than the price have changed (remember, "all other things remain the same"). The supply curve remains where it was. Since the price of jellybeans has risen, however, producers wish to sell more of them. The quantity of jellybeans supplied increases, and we move upward along the supply curve to the new, higher quantity supplied, as shown in Figure 3.17.

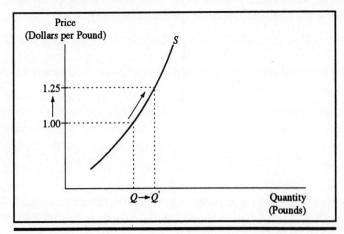

Figure 3.17

2. Nothing happens to the *demand* for denim skirts. The price of denim skirts has changed, but none of the other variables that affect how many skirts consumers wish to buy have changed. Since the price has risen, consumers will wish to buy fewer denim skirts, and the quantity demanded falls. We move upward along the demand curve, as shown in Figure 3.18.

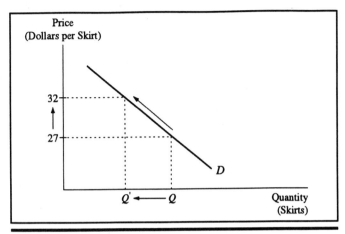

Figure 3.18

3. Tires and gasoline are complements; the more you drive, the more gasoline you purchase and the more tires you purchase. If consumers expect that gasoline is going to be much more expensive in the future, they will probably expect to be doing less driving in the future. In that case, there will be reduced demand for new tires; the old tires will last longer if they aren't going to be driven on as much. The increase in the price of a complement (gasoline) decreases the demand for this good (whitewall tires), and the demand curve shifts to the left (not down), as in Figure 3.19.

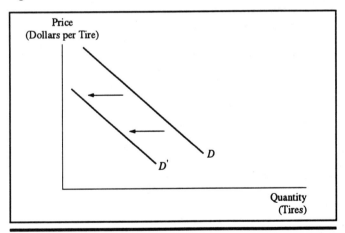

Figure 3.19

4. The increase in the price of sugar raises the cost of producing jellybeans and makes producing them less profitable. Some producers find that they can no longer continue to make a living selling jellybeans, and they stop producing them. This will happen no matter what the price of jellybeans is currently; the supply of jellybeans will decrease at each and every possible price. The increase in the price of an input (sugar) decreases the supply of this good (jellybeans), and the supply curve shifts to the *left* (not down), as in Figure 3.20.

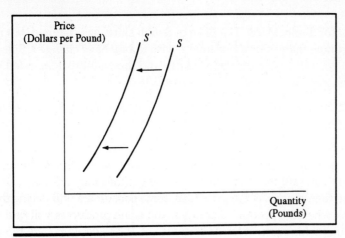

Figure 3.20

5. First, what happens to the supply and demand for running suits? Since none of the (nonprice) variables that affect the amount that producers want to sell have changed, nothing happens to the supply. It is likely, however, that running suits are a normal good; when peoples' incomes rise, they do more of their running in track suits and less in old sweats. At any price of running suits, the increase in income will result in consumers wanting to buy more of them. Demand increases, and the demand curve shifts to the right, as shown in Figure 3.21.

At the original equilibrium price of $75, consumers now want to purchase more running suits per year, but producers still want to sell 1,750 per year. There is a shortage of running suits at this price, and there will be upward pressure on the price. Producers will find that they can still sell 1,750 suits per year if they raise the price; in fact, at higher prices, producers want to sell more suits, and they find that they can. At that price, some consumers find that running suits are not worth the extra outlay, and they stick to their old sweatshirts. Thus, while the supply of running suits has not changed, the quantity supplied rises as the price rises. From Figure 3.21, we can see that when the price rises to its new equilibrium level, the quantity supplied rises to a level that is exactly the amount that consumers want to buy at that price on the new demand curve.

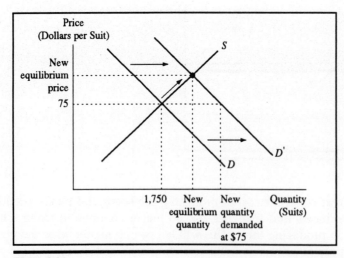

Figure 3.21

6. First, what happens to the supply and demand for tofu? The decreased regulation lowers the cost of producing tofu, and makes producing it more profitable. Some producers find that they can now make a living selling tofu, and they enter production. Others expand their operations. This will happen no matter what the price of tofu is currently; the supply of tofu will increase at each and every possible price. The supply curve shifts to the right, as in Figure 3.22. At the same time, the change in consumers' tastes decreases the quantity of tofu demanded, no matter what the price; the demand curve shifts to the left, as in Figure 3.22.

At the original price of $1.50, producers now wish to sell more tofu per month, but consumers now wish to buy less tofu per month. There is a surplus of tofu, and there will be downward pressure on the price. Producers will find that they cannot sell all the tofu they wish to, and will start offering discounts to move their stock. As the price falls, some consumers will decide that it is worth taking some health risk when the product is cheaper, and some producers will find that, eased regulation notwithstanding, selling tofu at lower prices is not as profitable as they thought. Thus, the quantity demanded rises as we move along the new demand curve and the quantity supplied falls as we move along the new supply curve, until the two are brought into balance. In Figure 3.22, this occurs at a new equilibrium price of $1.10 per container and a new equilibrium quantity of 500 containers per month. Notice, however, that if the increase in supply had been smaller and the decrease in demand had been larger, the new equilibrium quantity could have been smaller than the initial equilibrium quantity. When demand decreases and supply increases, all you can say for certain is that the equilibrium price will fall.

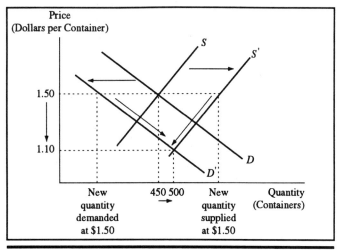

Figure 3.22

ANSWERS TO THE CHAPTER TEST

1. c	6. c	11. d	16. c
2. d	7. a	12. c	17. c
3. a	8. c	13. b	18. c
4. c	9. a	14. d	19. c
5. b	10. c	15. b	20. b

CHAPTER 4

Elasticity and Its Uses

CHAPTER OVERVIEW

One of the most practical uses of economic analysis is to predict the effects of changes in underlying conditions or policies on the prices and production of different goods and services. In this chapter, you will learn a useful way to measure the responsiveness of one economic variable to another, called elasticity. Elasticity can be used in many settings; here, we will use it to explore the sensitivity of quantity demanded to changes in the price of the good, in income, and in the prices of other closely related goods. We will also use elasticity to explore the sensitivity of quantity supplied to price. Finally, we will see how useful the concept is in answering different questions through supply and demand analysis.

CHAPTER REVIEW

1. *Elasticity* is a very general concept. It refers to a measure of the sensitivity of one economic variable to changes in another economic variable in percentage terms. There are many different pairs of variables between which we can calculate an elasticity. Here, we will focus on some of the elasticities that are most useful in economics.

2. The **price** elasticity of demand, sometimes referred to as the elasticity of demand or even just the elasticity when the meaning is clear from the context, measures the responsiveness of quantity demanded to price. It answers the question, "By what percentage will quantity demanded change for every percent that price changes, holding all else equal?" If you know the quantity demanded at two different prices on a demand curve or demand schedule, you can calculate how large that price change is in percentage terms, and by how much quantity demanded changes in response to that price change, also in percentage terms. The price elasticity of demand is defined as the percentage change in quantity demanded divided by the percentage change in the price, or

    $$\text{Price elasticity of demand} = \frac{\text{percentage change in quantity demanded}}{\text{percentage change in price}}$$

    This tells us by what percentage quantity demanded changed for each percentage point change in price.

3. Remember that to calculate the elasticity of demand, you need to know two points on the *same* demand curve. Price elasticity measures the responsiveness of quantity demanded to a change in price, *holding all else equal.*

4. To calculate the percentage change in quantity demanded, we take the number of units by which the quantity changed and divide by the quantity. Similarly, we take the number of dollars by which the price changed and divide by the price to calculate the percentage change in price. So, using symbols,

$$e_d = \frac{\Delta Q_d}{Q_d} \div \frac{\Delta P}{P}$$

where e_d represents the price elasticity of demand and Δ means "change in."

5. Since the demand curve slopes downward, an increase in the price causes a decrease in the quantity demanded. Thus, the elasticity of demand is a negative number; when $\Delta P/P$ is positive, $\Delta Q_d/Q_d$ is negative. Economists usually ignore the negative sign and just talk about the absolute value of the price elasticity of demand.

6. Since elasticities measure changes in percentage terms, you get the same answer no matter what units quantity and price are measured in—elasticity is a **unit-free measure**. The advantage of this is that you can easily compare the responsiveness of quantity demanded to price for different goods. It also means that the elasticity will not change if you use different units of measurement—say, six-packs instead of bottles. A 10-six-pack increase in consumption is not the same as a 10-bottle increase, but a 10 percent increase in the number of six-packs is also a 10 percent increase in the number of bottles.

7. The elasticity of demand is not the same thing as the *slope* of the demand curve. The slope of the demand curve is the change in price divided by the change in quantity demanded, or $\Delta P/\Delta Q$, and it depends on the units chosen to measure price and quantity. Changing the units that quantity is measured in, for example, will change the slope of the demand curve. If a 25-cent increase in the price of soft drinks causes a 6,000-bottle reduction in the quantity of soft drink demanded, it causes only a 1,000-six-pack reduction. But if consumption was originally 60,000 bottles (or 10,000 six-packs), the price increase causes a 10 percent reduction either way you measure soft drinks.

8. Goods for which the price elasticity of demand is greater than 1 are said to have an **elastic demand**. That is, a 1 percent change in the price causes a more than 1 percent change in quantity demanded. Goods for which the price elasticity of demand is less than 1, so that a 1 percent change in the price causes a *less* than 1 percent change in quantity demanded, are said to have an **inelastic demand**. Goods with a price elasticity of demand of exactly 1 are called **unit elastic**.

9. Since elasticities are unit-free, we can compare the elasticities of demand for different goods. When one good has a larger elasticity of demand than another, we say that the former has a demand curve that is **relatively elastic** compared with the demand curve of the latter, and that the latter has a demand curve that is relatively inelastic compared to that of the former. The use of the word *relatively* signals that we are comparing the elasticities of different goods. We would say this even if both goods had inelastic demands (elasticities less than 1) or elastic demands (elasticities greater than 1).

10. When the quantity demanded is completely unresponsive to the price, the demand curve is a vertical line, and we say that the demand is **perfectly inelastic**. When the demand curve is a horizontal line, consumers are not willing to buy any of the good if the price rises even a little bit above that price. In this case, even the smallest change in price would cause a total reduction in quantity demanded, and we say that demand is **perfectly elastic**.

11. Since a vertical demand curve is perfectly inelastic and a horizontal demand curve is perfectly elastic, it is tempting to think that flatter demand curves are more elastic than steeper demand curves. This is frequently wrong; remember that the slope of the demand curve is not the same thing as its elasticity. The only time that comparing the slopes of two demand curves gives the correct comparison of their elasticities is when you start from the same price and quantity on both curves and the same units of measurement are used on the axes. In this special case, for small changes in the price away from the common level of price and quantity, the flatter demand curve does have a higher elasticity than the steeper one. The reason for this is that the level of price and quantity with which absolute changes are compared to get percentage changes are the same on both curves. If the quantities of both goods start at the same level, then the good that has a larger absolute change in the quantity demanded must also have a larger percentage change.

12. When calculating percentage changes in price and quantity, we need to divide the absolute change in price or quantity by the level of price or quantity. However, if the price or quantity change being looked at is big enough, we will get different answers depending on whether we divide by the starting price or quantity, or by the ending price or quantity. For example, when price rises from $1.00 to $1.50, that's a 50 percent increase based on the $1.00 starting price, but only a 33 percent increase based on the $1.50 ending price. Neither of these is "right" or "wrong," but we need some standard way of doing things to avoid confusion. The economists' convention is to use the *average*, or *midpoint*, of the starting price (or quantity) and the ending price (or quantity) for calculating percentage changes. Using that convention, the price increase from $1.00 to $1.50 is a 40 percent increase, because 50 cents is 40 percent of $1.25, the average of $1.00 and $1.50.

13. When the price elasticity of demand is calculated using the average of the starting and ending prices and quantities, the *midpoint formula* is used. To calculate elasticity using the midpoint formula, you need to know two points on the demand curve: the old price and quantity (P_{old} and Q_{old}) and the new price and quantity (P_{new} and Q_{new}). The elasticity of demand is given by

$$\frac{\text{Price elasticity}}{\text{of demand}} = \frac{\text{change in quantity}}{\text{average of old and new quantity}} \div \frac{\text{change in price}}{\text{average of old and new price}}$$

$$= \frac{Q_{new} - Q_{old}}{(Q_{new} + Q_{old})} \div \frac{P_{new} - P_{old}}{(P_{new} + P_{old})/2}$$

14. Revenue is the total amount of money that consumers pay and producers receive when some amount of a good is sold at some price. If Q units are sold at a price of P per unit, then revenue is the product of price and quantity, or $P \times Q$.

15. When the price rises, the quantity demanded falls, and so revenue can change as well. But it's not obvious which way revenue will change when the price rises. Two things are occurring at the same time: Each unit that is sold is selling for more, which increases revenue; but fewer units get sold, which decreases revenue. The price elasticity of demand tells us which of these two effects is stronger, and therefore tells us whether revenue will rise or fall when the price rises. When demand is inelastic (elasticity of demand is less than 1), the percentage decrease in quantity will be less than the percentage increase in price, and so revenue will rise as the price rises. When

demand is elastic (elasticity of demand is greater than 1), the percentage decrease in quantity will be larger than the percentage increase in price, and so revenue will fall as the price rises. And when demand is unit elastic (elasticity of demand is equal to 1), the percentage decrease in quantity is exactly equal to the percentage increase in price, and revenue will not change when price rises. This explains why grain farmers are worse off when they all share a bumper crop; since the demand for grain is inelastic, the increased quantity sold is more than offset by falling prices.

16. Several variables determine whether the elasticity of demand for a good is large or small. The most important of these is whether there are good substitutes for the product. If there are, changes in price will cause consumers to switch to the substitutes, and the quantity demanded will fall dramatically; in this case, the elasticity of demand will be high. If, on the other hand, good substitutes are not available, consumers will continue to buy as the price rises, and demand will have a lower elasticity.

17. The price elasticity of demand will be higher for goods on which people spend a large fraction of their income. Changes in the price of something that you spend a lot on have big effects on your buying power, necessitating big adjustments. Changes in the price of something that represents only a small part of your income have little effect on what you can buy, and so only small changes in the amount you buy are needed.

18. People will respond more to price changes that are expected to be temporary than to long-lasting price changes, and so the price elasticity of a temporary change will tend to be high. If a price decrease is going to last a long time, there is no hurry to take advantage of the low price. Similarly, if a price increase is expected to persist, you might as well go on buying now, because the good will still be more expensive later on.

19. If a price changes permanently, the price elasticity of demand is likely to be lower immediately after the price change than after some time has passed. In the *short run*, people have only limited opportunities to adjust their consumption, but in the *long run*, more adjustments are possible. For example, when the price of home heating oil rises, in the short run people with oil heat can turn down their thermostats and wear sweaters, but they still have to heat their houses. In the long run, however, more new homes will be built with electric or natural gas heating, and the change in the quantity of oil demanded will be larger.

20. So far, we have been thinking about the price elasticity of demand. Price certainly is an important determinant of quantity demanded, but remember that there are other variables that also affect the amount that consumers want to buy. When those variables change, the demand curve shifts. We can also use the concept of elasticity to measure the responsiveness of quantity demanded to these changes.

21. One of the most important variables (other than price) that affects consumer demand is consumer income. The **income elasticity of demand** is the percentage change in quantity demanded divided by percentage change in income, holding all else (including the price) constant. That is,

$$\text{Income elasticity of demand} = \frac{\text{percentage change in quantity demanded}}{\text{percentage change in income}}$$

Recall that when income rises, consumers wish to buy more of all normal goods and less of all inferior goods. Thus, for normal goods the income elasticity of demand will be positive, whereas inferior goods will have negative income elasticities of demand.

22. The prices of other closely related goods also affect the amount that consumers want to buy. The **cross-price elasticity of demand** measures the responsiveness of quantity demanded of one good to a change in the price of a different good, again measured in percentage terms. That is,

$$\text{Cross-price elasticity of supply} = \frac{\text{percentage change in quantity demanded of } X}{\text{percentage change in price of } Y}$$

where X and Y are two different goods. Recall that when the price of a substitute for some good rises, the demand for the good increases. Therefore, the cross-price elasticity of demand for a substitute is positive. When the price of a complement to some good rises, the demand for the good decreases. Thus, the cross-price elasticities of demand for complementary goods are negative.

23. We can also apply the elasticity concept to the responsiveness of quantity supplied to price. The **price elasticity of supply** measures this. It is defined as the percentage change in the quantity supplied divided by the percentage change in the price, or

$$\text{Price elasticity of supply} = \frac{\text{percentage change in quantity supplied}}{\text{percentage change in price}}$$

24. A vertical supply curve is **perfectly inelastic** because any change in price will lead to no response in the quantity supplied, and the elasticity of supply is therefore zero. A horizontal supply curve is **perfectly elastic**. The slightest decrease in price reduces the supply to zero.

ZEROING IN

1. From the applications in the chapter, you can see that the elasticity concept is quite general. We can talk about the parking fine elasticity of parking tickets, or the tax rate elasticity of cigarette sales. Remember that elasticity just means responsiveness of one variable to changes in another, in percentage terms.

2. The main formula to learn in this chapter is the midpoint formula. In the section above, this was given for the price elasticity of demand. It also applies when calculating other elasticities, such as the price elasticity of supply. To calculate that elasticity using the midpoint formula, you need to know two points on the supply curve: the old price and quantity (P_{old} and Q_{old}) and the new price and quantity (P_{new} and Q_{new}). The price elasticity of supply is given by

$$\frac{\text{Price elasticity}}{\text{of supply}} = \frac{\text{change in quantity supplied}}{\text{average of old and new quantity}} \div \frac{\text{change in price}}{\text{average of old and new price}}$$

$$= \frac{Q_{new} - Q_{old}}{(Q_{new} + Q_{old})/2} \div \frac{P_{new} - P_{old}}{(P_{new} + P_{old})/2}$$

So, if firms wish to supply 560 units when the price is $13 per unit, and are willing to supply 640 units if the price rises to $17 per unit, then if we call the first price and quantity the old point on the supply curve and the second price and quantity the new point, we have

$$\frac{\text{Price elasticity}}{\text{of supply}} = \frac{\text{change in quantity supplied}}{\text{average of old and new quantity}} \div \frac{\text{change in price}}{\text{average of old and new price}}$$

$$= \frac{640 - 560}{(640 + 560)/2} \div \frac{17 - 13}{(17 + 13)/2} = \frac{80}{600} \div \frac{4}{15} = \frac{1}{2}$$

3. It's common to think that a demand curve has *a* price elasticity of demand, the way an object has *a* weight. This isn't right, however; the same demand curve can have different elasticities of demand depending on which prices and quantities you start from and finish at. To see this, look at the following demand schedule, which is graphed as a demand curve in Figure 4.1.

Price	Quantity Demanded
10	0
8	40
6	80
4	120
2	160
0	200

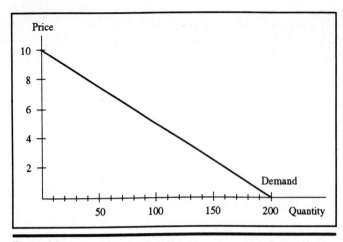

Figure 4.1

If we calculate the elasticity of demand using 10 as the starting price (and 0 as the starting quantity) and 8 as the ending price (and 40 as the ending quantity), we get

$$\text{Price elasticity of demand} = \frac{\text{change in quantity demanded}}{\text{average of old and new quantity}} \div \frac{\text{change in price}}{\text{average of old and new price}}$$

$$= \frac{40 - 0}{(40 + 0)/2} \div \frac{8 - 10}{(8 + 10)/2} = \frac{40}{20} \div \frac{-2}{9} = 9 \text{ (ignoring the minus sign)}$$

But if we calculate the elasticity of demand using 4 as the starting price (and 120 as the starting quantity) and 2 as the ending price (and 160 as the ending quantity), we get

$$\text{Price elasticity of demand} = \frac{\text{change in quantity demanded}}{\text{average of old and new quantity}} \div \frac{\text{change in price}}{\text{average of old and new price}}$$

$$= \frac{160 - 120}{(160 + 120)/2} \div \frac{2 - 4}{(2 + 4)/2} = \frac{40}{120} \div \frac{-2}{3} = \frac{3}{7}$$

In each case, the price falls by \$2 and the quantity demanded rises by 40 units, so why does the elasticity come out differently? The key is remembering that elasticity uses *percentage* changes. In the first case, the price fell from 10 to 8, which is only a 22 percent change (based on the average price of 9), whereas in the second case, the price fell from 4 to 2, which is a 67 percent change (based on the average price of 3). Similarly, in the first case, quantity demanded rose from 0 to 40, which is a 200 percent increase (based on the average of 20), whereas in the second case, quantity demanded rose from 120 to 160, which is only a 29 percent increase (based on the average of 140). So in the first case, a small percentage change in price led to a large percentage change in quantity demanded, whereas in the second case, a larger percentage change in price led to a smaller percentage change in quantity demanded. In percentage terms, quantity demanded is much more responsive to price in the first case than in the second, and the elasticity of demand shows this.

4. When you read about how elasticities are used in economic analysis, you will see that often the main issue is whether revenue will rise or fall with an increase in the price, which in turn hinges on whether demand is elastic or inelastic. Remember that revenue is simply $P \times Q$. When P rises,

Q falls; the question is, how fast? Elasticity gives you the answer; when demand is elastic, the percentage fall in quantity is greater than the percentage rise in price. When demand is inelastic, the percentage fall in quantity is less than the percentage increase in price. You can remember how this affects revenue by the following:

Elastic demand: $P\uparrow$ means $Q\downarrow$, so $P \times Q\downarrow$.

Inelastic demand: $P\uparrow$ means $Q\downarrow$, so $P \times Q\uparrow$.

ACTIVE REVIEW

Fill-in Questions

1. _____ is the general concept of measuring the responsiveness of one economic variable to another in _____ terms.

2. The price elasticity of demand measures the responsiveness of _____ to price.

3. To calculate the price elasticity of demand, you need to know _____ points on the _____ demand curve.

4. Since the demand curve slopes _____, the elasticity of demand has a(n) _____ sign. However, economists often ignore this, and treat elasticity as a(n) _____ number.

5. When you calculate elasticities, you will get the same answer no matter what _____ the prices and quantities are measured in; this means that elasticities for different goods can be compared. The same cannot be said about measuring responsiveness by the _____ of the demand curve.

6. When the price elasticity of demand for a good is greater than 1, we say that the demand is _____. Demand is said to be _____ when the elasticity of demand is less than _____.

7. Since elasticities are _____, we can compare the elasticities of demand for _____ different goods. For example, if the elasticity of demand for peas were 2.5 and the elasticity of demand for carrots were 3.1, we would say that the demand for peas was _____ compared to the demand for carrots. However, we would still say that both of these goods had _____ demands.

8. When demand is completely unresponsive to changes in price, the elasticity of demand is _____, and the demand curve is a(n) _____ line. We would describe this demand curve as _____.

9. When the demand curve is horizontal, a tiny price increase will lead to a very large percentage change in quantity demanded. We say that such a demand curve is _____.

10. Percentage changes in price and quantity are calculated by comparing absolute changes to a base amount. When the bases used for comparison are the averages of the starting and ending quantity and of the starting and ending price, the elasticity is calculated using the _____ formula.

11. When demand is elastic, price and revenue move in _____ direction(s); that is, an increase in price leads to a(n) _____ in revenue. On the other hand, when demand is inelastic, price and revenue move in _____ direction(s).

12. The elasticity of demand for a product will be larger if many good _____ for that good exist, if consumers spend a(n) _____ of their income on it, or if changes in price are expected to be _____.

13. The _____ elasticity of demand measures the responsiveness of _____ to changes in consumer income, holding all else equal. Normal goods will have _____ income elasticities, whereas _____ will have _____ income elasticities.

14. The _____ elasticity of demand measures the responsiveness of quantity demanded to changes in the _____ of another product. These elasticities will be _____ for substitutes and _____ for complementary goods.

15. The elasticity of supply measures the responsiveness of _____ to changes in the price. It will be _____ in the long run, when firms have more time to adapt to _____ changes.

True-False Questions

T F 1. The concept of elasticity has only limited applicability, since it refers only to the responsiveness of quantity demanded to price.

T F 2. The price elasticity of demand is the same as the slope of the demand curve.

T F 3. Elasticity of demand is calculated using percentage changes in both price and quantity.

T F 4. The steeper the demand curve, the less elastic the demand.

T F 5. Elasticities of demand have a minus sign to remind us that demand curves slope downward.

T   F   6. It makes no sense to compare elasticities for different goods, since that is like comparing apples and oranges.

T   F   7. If the percentage change in quantity demanded is less than the percentage change in price that caused it, demand is inelastic.

T   F   8. If a 5 percent increase in the price of tea causes a larger percentage decrease in the quantity of tea demanded in Indianapolis than it causes in the quantity of tea demanded in London, we would say that the demand for tea in Indianapolis is elastic.

T   F   9. When the demand for a product is perfectly elastic, its demand curve is downward-sloping.

T   F   10. A rise in the price of a good will always result in a decrease in the amount spent on that good.

T   F   11. If the income elasticity of demand for fast-food cheeseburgers is negative, we know that cheeseburgers must have many close substitutes.

T   F   12. The elasticity of demand will be lower if the change in price is only temporary, since no one pays much attention to temporary things.

T   F   13. The cross-price elasticity of demand for tennis racquets with respect to the price of golf clubs is likely to be positive, indicating that the two goods are substitutes.

T   F   14. The elasticity of supply is the ratio of the percentage change in quantity supplied to the percentage change in price, all else equal.

T   F   15. Perfectly elastic supply is represented by a vertical supply curve.

Short-Answer Questions

1. How would you calculate the temperature elasticity of people on the beach? What information would you need to know?

2. How do you calculate the price elasticity of demand using the midpoint formula?

3. What is the difference between elastic demand and inelastic demand?

4. If the demand curve has unit elastic demand, what happens to revenue when price falls 3 percent?

5. The City Council proposes raising parking fees in order to provide additional funds for the city bus system. What must the council be assuming about the elasticity of demand for parking?

6. List three things that tend to make the demand for a good more elastic.

7. Why is the long-run elasticity of demand for gasoline likely to be greater than the short-run elasticity of demand?

8. Explain the difference between the price elasticity of demand and the cross-price elasticity of demand.

9. What is the sign of the cross-price elasticity of demand for complementary goods? Explain.

10. Why is the elasticity of supply low if firms' production decisions are based on their expectations of future prices?

WORKING IT OUT

1. It is important to be able to use the midpoint formula correctly to calculate elasticities. To calculate an elasticity of demand, you need to know the quantity demanded at two different prices, when all else remains equal. To calculate an income elasticity of demand, you need to know the quantity demanded at two income levels, with all else equal. Then you need to apply the midpoint formula correctly.

2. It is actually very easy to find the revenue that is collected by sellers of a good (which is also the expenditure on that good by consumers) by looking at the demand curve. For each price, the demand curve tells us how much will be bought—for every P, the demand curve gives us a Q. Look at Figure 4.2; suppose the price is P_1 dollars per unit, and the resulting quantity is therefore Q_1 units. Revenue (in dollars) is the number of units sold times the number of dollars for which each one sells, or $P_1 \times Q_1$. This is the area of the rectangle in Figure 4.2 that has P_1 as its height and Q_1 as its base (since the area of a rectangle is the base times the height).

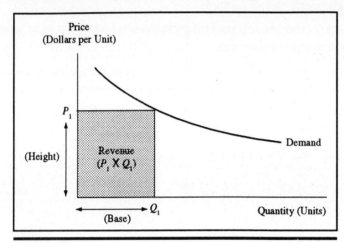

Figure 4.2

Worked Problems

1. Using the data from Table 4.1 on the demand for burgers and pizzas, calculate the price elasticity of demand for burgers.

TABLE 4.1				
Quantity of Burgers	**Quantity of Pizzas**	**Price of Burgers**	**Price of Pizzas**	**Weekly Income**
750	300	$2.50	$8.00	$150
900	150	$2.00	$9.00	$170
850	250	$2.50	$10.00	$150
800	300	$2.00	$9.00	$190
550	200	$3.00	$8.00	$150

Answer

First, you need to find two points on the same demand curve for burgers. The first row and the fifth row give you this: The price of pizza (a closely related good) and income are the same in these two rows. The only things that are different are the price and quantity of burgers (and the quantity of pizza, but that's not part of the demand curve for burgers). So if we let P_{old} be $2.50 and Q_{old} be 750, and let P_{new} be $3.00 and Q_{new} be 550, then the midpoint formula says that

$$\begin{aligned} \text{Price elasticity} \atop \text{of demand} = \frac{\text{change in quantity supplied}}{\text{average of old and new quantity}} \div \frac{\text{change in price}}{\text{average of old and new price}} \end{aligned}$$

$$= \frac{550 - 750}{(550 + 750)/2} \div \frac{3.00 - 2.50}{(3.50 + 2.50)/2} = \frac{-200}{650} \div \frac{0.50}{3.00} = \frac{24}{13}$$

2. Using Figure 4.3, what is the revenue when the price is $6 per unit? What area in Figure 4.3 corresponds to this revenue? What happens to revenue if the price falls to $5 per unit? Is the demand curve elastic or inelastic at $6 per unit?

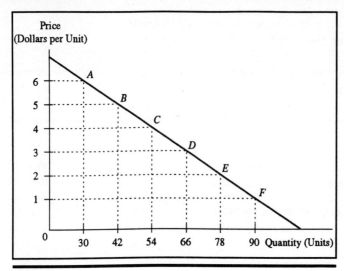

Figure 4.3

Answer

At $6 per unit, 30 units are demanded, so the revenue would be $6 per unit × 30 units, or $180. The area that gives this revenue is the area of the rectangle whose corners are $6–A–30–0. If the price falls to $5 per unit, the quantity demanded rises to 42 units, and revenue rises to $210. Since the price decrease leads to a revenue increase, we know that the demand curve must be elastic at this price.

Practice Problems

1. Using the data from Table 4.1, find the price elasticity of demand for pizza.

2. Using the data from Table 4.1, find the income elasticity of demand for burgers.

3. Using the data from Table 4.1, find the cross-price elasticity of demand for burgers with respect to the price of pizza.

4. Using Figure 4.3, what is the revenue when the price is $3 per unit? What area on Figure 4.3 corresponds to this revenue? What happens to revenue if the price rises to $4 per unit? Is the demand curve elastic or inelastic at $3 per unit?

5. Calculate the price elasticity of demand (using the midpoint formula) as the price rises from $3 per unit to $4 per unit in Figure 4.3, and verify your answer to the last part of question 4.

CHAPTER TEST

1. The price elasticity of demand shows us
   a. how steep the demand curve is.
   b. how fast demand responds to price.
   c. how much demand shifts when income changes.
   d. how quantity demanded responds to price changes.

2. In order to calculate the price elasticity of demand, you need to know
    a. two prices and two quantities demanded.
    b. the slope of the demand curve.
    c. the equilibrium price and quantity in the market.
    d. the quantity demanded at two different prices, all else equal.

3. Price elasticities are measured in percentage terms because
    a. it makes students' lives more complicated.
    b. the resulting measure is unit-free.
    c. it gives a more accurate answer.
    d. the answer is always negative that way.

4. The price elasticity of demand is given by the formula
    a. $e_d = \dfrac{\Delta Q_d}{Q_d} \div \dfrac{\Delta P}{P}$

    b. $e_d = \dfrac{\Delta Q_d}{Q_d}$

    c. $e_d = \dfrac{\Delta Q_d}{Q_d} \times \dfrac{\Delta P}{P}$

    d. $e_d = \dfrac{\Delta P}{P} \div \dfrac{\Delta Q_d}{Q_d}$

5. Demand is elastic when the elasticity of demand is
    a. greater than 0.
    b. greater than 1.
    c. less than 1.
    d. less than 0.

6. When the price of gasoline rises 10 percent, the quantity of gasoline purchased falls by 8 percent. The demand for gasoline is
    a. perfectly elastic.
    b. unit elastic.
    c. elastic.
    d. inelastic.

7. The demand for heart transplants does not respond to the price of the operation. This means that the demand for heart transplants is
    a. perfectly elastic.
    b. perfectly inelastic.
    c. inelastic, but not perfectly inelastic.
    d. elastic, but not perfectly elastic.

8. The elasticity of demand for salt is 0.5, and the elasticity of demand for cigarettes is 0.8. We can say that
    a. the demand for salt is relatively inelastic.
    b. the demand for salt is relatively elastic.
    c. the demand for salt is elastic.
    d. the demand for cigarettes is relatively inelastic.

9. Each month, 300 pairs of shoelaces are purchased at a price of $1.30 per pair. When the price rises to $1.50 per pair, the quantity demanded falls to 250 pairs per month. Using the midpoint formula, the elasticity of demand for shoelaces is
   a. 14/11.
   b. 2/77.
   c. 11/14.
   d. 2/11.

10. The Campus Cinema discovered that when it charged $3 for the afternoon matinee, it took in $360 per showing, but when it lowered the price to $2, it took in $480 per showing. This implies that the elasticity of demand for afternoon matinee movies is
    a. 3/5.
    b. 5/3.
    c. 5/2.
    d. 12/18.

11. We know that the demand for a product is elastic if
    a. when price rises, revenue rises.
    b. when price rises, revenue falls.
    c. when price rises, quantity demanded rises.
    d. when price falls, quantity demanded rises.

12. If a product has an inelastic demand, then
    a. we are probably thinking about the long-run demand curve.
    b. it has many close substitutes.
    c. an increase in the price leads to an increase in revenue.
    d. it probably represents a large proportion of consumer expenditures.

13. Which of the following products is likely to have the most elastic demand?
    a. Nike running shoes
    b. Running shoes
    c. Shoes
    d. Things you wear on your feet

14. Which of the following goods is likely to have the least elastic demand?
    a. Meals at restaurants
    b. Vacation travel
    c. Bubblegum
    d. College educations

15. When the price of gasoline rises, people immediately cut back on unnecessary trips. If the price of gasoline stays high, people eventually replace their cars with more fuel-efficient models. As a result,
    a. the long-run demand for gasoline falls.
    b. the short-run demand for gasoline is less elastic than the long-run demand.
    c. the short-run demand for gasoline is more elastic than the long-run demand.
    d. the price of gasoline is forced down to its original level.

16. It is not obvious whether VCRs and cable TV are substitutes or complements. Some people may view a VCR and rented videos as a substitute for cable, whereas others may use their VCR to tape movies from the cable broadcasts. If you knew that the cross-price elasticity of demand between VCRs and cable TV was negative, however, you would know that
    a. VCRs and cable TV are substitutes.
    b. VCRs and cable TV are complements.
    c. VCRs and cable TV are inferior goods.
    d. VCRs and cable TV have inelastic demands.

17. If the income elasticity of demand for boots is 0.2, a 10 percent increase in consumer income will lead to a
    a. 20 percent increase in the demand for boots.
    b. 20 percent decrease in the demand for boots.
    c. 2 percent increase in the demand for boots.
    d. 0.2 percent increase in the demand for boots.

18. Harold Woodyson, the movie star, makes two movies each year, for which he is paid $1 million each. Harold tells his agent, Dewey Cheatham, that if he were paid $2 million per movie, he'd be willing to make an additional movie each year. Harold's elasticity of movie supply is
    a. 2/3.
    b. 2/5.
    c. 3/5.
    d. 4/15.

19. Since the fish that are caught each day go bad very quickly, the daily catch will be offered for sale no matter what price it brings. As a result, we know that
    a. the daily supply curve for fish slopes upward.
    b. the daily supply curve for fish is perfectly inelastic.
    c. the daily supply curve for fish is perfectly elastic.
    d. the daily supply curve for fish is a horizontal line at today's price.

20. The size of the price elasticity of demand depends on
    a. the availability of substitutes for the item.
    b. whether the item represents a large fraction of income.
    c. whether the price change is permanent or temporary.
    d. all the above factors.

ANSWERS TO THE REVIEW QUESTIONS

Fill-in Questions

1. Elasticity; percentage
2. quantity demanded
3. two; same
4. downward; minus; positive
5. units; slope
6. elastic; inelastic; 1
7. unit-free; relatively inelastic; elastic
8. zero; vertical; perfectly inelastic
9. perfectly elastic
10. midpoint
11. opposite; decrease; the same
12. substitutes; large fraction; temporary
13. income; quantity demanded; positive; inferior goods; negative
14. cross-price; price; positive; negative
15. quantity supplied; larger; price

True-False Questions

1. **False**. Elasticity can be used to measure the responsiveness of the relationship between any two economic variables.
2. **False**. Slope is not unit-free; it depends on how the price and quantity are measured.
3. **True**.
4. **False**. Slope and elasticity are not the same thing. Only when you start at the same price and quantity on both demand curves and the same units are used on the axes do we know that the steeper demand curve has a lower elasticity, and this is true only for small price changes from the common starting point.
5. **False**. Although price elasticities of demand are technically negative numbers, economists often ignore the minus sign.
6. **False**. Since elasticities are unit-free, they can be compared across goods.
7. **True**. If the percentage change in quantity demanded is less than the percentage change in price, then the former divided by the latter is less than 1, and demand is inelastic.
8. **False**. We would say that the demand for tea in Indianapolis is *relatively* elastic compared to the demand for tea in London, but we don't know from this information whether the demand for tea in either location is elastic or inelastic.
9. **False**. When the demand for something is perfectly elastic, its demand curve is a horizontal line.
10. **False**. Revenue, which is the amount spent on the good, will rise when the price rises if the demand is inelastic.
11. **False**. The income elasticity of demand doesn't tell us about substitutes; it tells us whether goods are normal goods or inferior goods.
12. **False**. When price changes are expected to be temporary, consumers will respond more quickly in order to take advantage of the limited opportunity to save or to avoid the limited extra cost.
13. **True**. When the price of golf clubs rises, some people will take up tennis instead, and the demand for tennis racquets will rise. The positive cross-price elasticity shows that the two goods are substitutes.
14. **True**. This is the definition of the price elasticity of supply.
15. **False**. The vertical supply curve is inelastic: a higher price cannot bring about a higher quantity supplied.

Short-Answer Questions

1. To calculate the temperature elasticity of people on the beach, you would need to know how many people were on the beach on two days when the only thing that was different was the temperature. You would then calculate the percentage change in the number of people on the beach (based on the average) and the percentage change in temperature, and divide the former by the latter to find out what percentage change in people on the beach you get for each percentage point change in temperature.

2. To calculate the price elasticity of demand using the midpoint formula, you need to know two points on the demand curve: the old price and quantity (P_{old} and Q_{old}) and the new price and quantity (P_{new} and Q_{new}). The elasticity of demand is given by

$$\text{Price elasticity of demand} = \frac{\text{change in quantity demanded}}{\text{average of old and new quantity}} \div \frac{\text{change in price}}{\text{average of old and new price}}$$

$$= \frac{Q_{new} - Q_{old}}{(Q_{new} + Q_{old})/2} \div \frac{P_{new} - P_{old}}{(P_{new} + P_{old})/2}$$

3. Elastic demand refers to a demand curve with an elasticity greater than 1; a 1 percent change in price causes a more than 1 percent change in quantity demanded. Inelastic demand refers to a demand curve with an elasticity less than 1; a 1 percent change in price causes a less than 1 percent change in quantity demanded.

4. When the demand curve has unit elastic demand (elasticity equal to 1), revenue doesn't change when the price falls 3 (or any other) percent.

5. The City Council must think that the demand for parking is inelastic; if it is not, the increase in parking fees will lead to such a large decrease in the amount of parking that revenue will fall and there will be less funds for the bus system.

6. Any three of the following: there are many good substitutes; the good represents a large fraction of consumers' spending; price changes are expected to be temporary; and consumers have lots of time to adjust to the price changes.

7. In the short run, people can respond to an increase in the price of gasoline by taking fewer trips, carpooling, riding the bus more often, and so forth. In the long run, they can do all those things *plus* buying a more fuel-efficient car the next time they buy a car, moving closer to town to shorten their commute, and so on. In the long run, people have additional opportunities to adjust their consumption, and so the long-run elasticity will be greater than the short-run elasticity.

8. The price elasticity of demand measures the responsiveness of the quantity of a good that is demanded to a change in *that* good's price, holding all else equal. The cross-price elasticity of demand measures the responsiveness of the quantity of a good that is demanded to changes in the price of *another* good, holding all else equal.

9. The sign of the cross-price elasticity of demand is negative. When two goods are complements, an increase in the price of one of the goods will decrease the quantity demanded of that good and will decrease the quantity demanded of the other (so that quantity demanded at every price will fall). Thus, whatever the price of the complementary (second) good, an increase in the price of the first good leads to a decrease in the quantity demanded of the second.

10. If firms' production decisions are based on their expectations of future prices, they will not want to supply more or less if the current price changes. They will respond only to changes in what they think the future price will be.

SOLUTIONS TO THE PRACTICE PROBLEMS

1. In this case, you need to find two points on the same demand curve for pizza. The first row and the third row give you this: The price of burgers and income are the same in these two rows. The only things that are different are the price and quantity of pizzas (and the quantity of burgers, but that's not part of the demand curve for pizzas). So if we let P_{old} be $8.00 and Q_{old} be 300, and let P_{new} be $10.00 and Q_{new} be 250, then the midpoint formula says that

$$\frac{\text{Price elasticity}}{\text{of demand}} = \frac{\text{change in quantity demanded}}{\text{average of old and new quantity}} \div \frac{\text{change in price}}{\text{average of old and new price}}$$

$$= \frac{250 - 300}{(250 + 300)/2} \div \frac{10.00 - 8.00}{(10.00 + 8.00)/2} = \frac{-50}{275} \div \frac{2.00}{9.00} = \frac{9}{11} \quad \text{(ignoring the minus sign)}$$

2. In this case, you need to find two points where the only things that have changed are income and the quantity of burgers (and possibly the quantity of pizzas). The second row and the fourth row give you this; the prices of burgers and pizzas are the same in these two rows. So if we let I_{old} be $170 and Q_{old} be 900, and let I_{new} be $190 and Q_{new} be 800, then the midpoint formula says that

$$\frac{\text{Income elasticity}}{\text{of demand}} = \frac{\text{change in quantity demanded}}{\text{average of old and new quantity}} \div \frac{\text{change in income}}{\text{average of old and new income}}$$

$$= \frac{800 - 900}{(800 + 900)/2} \div \frac{190 - 170}{(190 + 170)/2} = \frac{-100}{850} \div \frac{20}{180} = \frac{-18}{17}$$

Here we can't ignore the minus sign; it tells us that burgers are an inferior good. When income rises, the quantity of burgers demanded falls.

3. In this case, we want to find out how the quantity of burgers responds to a change in the price of pizzas, all else equal, so we return to the first and third rows, where the only things that are different are the price of pizza and the quantities of pizzas and burgers. Let P_{old} be $8.00 and Q_{old} be 750, and let P_{new} be $10.00 and Q_{new} be 850; then the midpoint formula says that

$$\frac{\text{Cross-price elasticity}}{\text{of demand}} = \frac{\text{change in burgers demanded}}{\text{average of old and new quantity}} \div \frac{\text{change in pizza price}}{\text{average of old and new price}}$$

$$= \frac{850 - 750}{(850 + 750)/2} \div \frac{10.00 - 8.00}{(10.00 + 8.00)/2} = \frac{100}{800} \div \frac{2.00}{9.00} = \frac{9}{16}$$

Here, the sign of the cross-price elasticity is positive, which tells us that burgers and pizzas are substitutes. An increase in the price of pizzas leads to an increase in the demand for burgers.

4. At $3 per unit, 66 units are demanded, so the revenue would be $3 per unit × 66 units, or $198. The area that gives this revenue is the area of the rectangle whose corners are $3–D–66–0. If the price rises to $4 per unit, the quantity demanded falls to 54 units, and revenue rises to $216. Since the price increase leads to a revenue increase, we know that demand must be inelastic at this price.

5. Using the midpoint formula,

$$\text{Price elasticity of demand} = \frac{\text{change in quantity demanded}}{\text{average of old and new quantity}} \div \frac{\text{change in price}}{\text{average of old and new price}}$$

$$= \frac{54 - 66}{(54 + 66)/2} \div \frac{4 - 3}{(4 + 3)/2} = \frac{-12}{60} \div \frac{1}{3.50} = \frac{7}{10} \text{ (ignoring the minus sign)}$$

Since the elasticity is less than 1, we have verified that demand is indeed inelastic at $3 per unit.

ANSWERS TO THE CHAPTER TEST

1. d	6. d	11. b	16. b
2. d	7. b	12. c	17. c
3. b	8. a	13. a	18. c
4. a	9. a	14. c	19. b
5. b	10. b	15. b	20. d

(CHAPTERS 1– 4)
Introduction to Economics and Its Foundations

1. In Economics, the term *household* refers to
   a. housing developments.
   b. two or more people living together.
   c. consumers.
   d. individuals who are related to each other and who live in the same dwelling.

2. The mechanism that enables exchanges to take place between people is called a(n)
   a. firm.
   b. market.
   c. government.
   d. HMO.

3. Economic analysis that explains what happens in the economy and why, without making policy recommendations, is called
   a. normative analysis.
   b. positive analysis.
   c. market analysis.
   d. subjective analysis.

4. Economic analysis that involves policy recommendations is called
   a. normative analysis.
   b. positive analysis.
   c. market analysis.
   d. command analysis.

5. Economic models
   a. need to be the same as the phenomena they describe.
   b. require either algebra or graphs.
   c. are complicated, since human behavior is complicated.
   d. are not complicated, since the behavior they describe is not complicated.
   e. are simplifications of the phenomena they attempt to explain.

6. Ceteris paribus means
   a. "all other things equal."
   b. "all variables are independent."
   c. "all relationships are inverse."
   d. that no other assumptions are being made.

7. The problem of scarcity
   a. is a problem only for poor countries.
   b. is faced by all economies.
   c. is not faced by free market economies.
   d. is eliminated as the economy grows.

8. When an economy is operating on its production possibilities curve, more production of one good means less production of another because
   a. resources are limited.
   b. resources are not perfectly adaptable to alternative uses.
   c. wants are limited.
   d. wants are unlimited.

9. If a resource is unlimited, then
   a. it has low opportunity costs.
   b. it is scarce.
   c. it is not scarce.
   d. people have enough money to pay for it.

10. The exchange rate is
    a. the percentage change in exports from one year to the next.
    b. the price of one money in terms of another.
    c. the amount of trade going on between two countries.
    d. the rate of production in one country compares to the rate of production in another.

11. An essentail characteristic of the market economy is
    a. freely determined prices.
    b. an asbsence of property rights.
    c. prices set by the government.
    d. lack of competition.

12. In an economic interaction between two people, there are gains from trade if
    a. the two people trade involuntarily.
    b. neither person has any incentive to trade.
    c. reallocation makes one of the two people better off and the other worse off.
    d. the trade reallocates goods between the two people in a way that they both prefer.

13. Economic interactions within organizations take place at
    a. market prices.
    b. transaction prices.
    c. transfer prices.
    d. transfer costs.

14. A situation in which the market does not lead to an efficient economic outcome and in which there is a potential role for government is referred to as
    a. government failure.
    b. market failure.
    c. a competitive market.
    d. economic growth.

15. The negative relationship between price and quantity demanded, other things being equal, is considered to be
    a. true only in market-based economies.
    b. sometimes true in all economies.
    c. never true in heavily regulated economies.
    d. universally true for all economies.

16. The law of demand states that
    a. there is a direct relationship between price and quantity supplied.
    b. as price increases, quantity demanded increases.
    c. there is an inverse relationship between price and quantity demanded.
    d. there is an inverse relationship between price and quantity supplied.

17. A complement is a good
    a. that provides some of the same uses or enjoyment as another good.
    b. for which demand increases when income rises and decreases when income falls.
    c. that tends to be consumed together with another good.
    d. for which demand decreases when income rises and increases when income falls.

18. Which of the following is an example of two goods that are substitutes for each other?
    a. Bicycle and bike helmet
    b. Rollerblades and knee pads
    c. Hat and gloves
    d. Cobblestones and brick paving

    19. The law of supply are positively related
    b. the higher the price, the smaller the quantity that will be sold.
    c. price and quantity supplied are inversely related.
    d. price and quantity demanded are inversely related. states that
    a. price and quantity supplied

20. When both supply and demand shift at the same time,
    a. the change in equilibrium price cannot be predicted, but the change in equilibrium can be predicted.
    b. the change in equilibrium price can be predicted but the change in equilibrium quantity cannot be predicted.
    c. neither change in equilibrium price nor the change in equilibrium quantity can be predicted.
    d. the change in equilibrium quantity cannot be predicted, and the change in equilibrium price cannot be predicted.

21. Which of the following is *not* an example of a government price control?
    a. Price ceiling
    b. Price floor
    c. Minimum wage
    d. Milk shortage

22. The labor supply and demand model predicts that minimum wage
    a. has no effect on employment.
    b. is a cause of unemployment among skilled workers.
    c. is a cause of unemployment among less skilled workers.
    d. ends up hurting all members of society.

23. Elasticity is a measure of
    a. how quickly a particular market reaches equilibrium.
    b. the change in income associated with increased education.
    c. the responsiveness of one variable to a change in another variable.
    d. the effect of an increase in the number of consumers in a particular market.

24. If a good represents a large portion of consumers' income, then the price elasticity of demand will be
    a. low.
    b. high.
    c. the same as when it represents a small portion of peoples' income.
    d. inelastic.

25. For a substitute, the cross-price elasticity of demand
    a. is the same as for a complement.
    b. is inversely related.
    c. is negative.
    d. is positive.

26. For demand to be inelastic, it must be the case that
    a. the percentage change in quantity demanded is greater that the associated percentage change in price.
    b. the percentage change in quantity demanded is less that the associated percentage change in price.
    c. the percentage change in quantity demanded is equal to the associated percentage change in price.
    d. quantity demanded must change with a change in price.

27. Because the price elasticity of demand is very low for agricultural products,
    a. increases and decreases in supply result in large price changes.
    b. increases and decreases in supply result in small price changes.
    c. increases in supply result in large price changes while decreases in supply result in small price changes.
    d. increases in supply result in small price changes while decreases in supply result in large price changes.

28. The most important factor determining the price elasticity of supply is
    a. the degree to which firms are able to adjust their inputs to production.
    b. the availability of substitutes for the item.
    c. the original quantity supplied.
    d. the popularity of the item.

29. The price elasticity of supply is
    a. greater in the short run than in the long run.
    b. the same in the short run as it is in the long run.
    c. greater in the long run than in the short run.
    d. not all that useful for determining how much prices will change when there is a change in demand.

30. The term *unit elastic demand* refers to
    a. a situation in which the elasticity of one good is greater than the elasticity of another good.
    b. demand for which price elasticity is greater than 1.
    c. demand for which price elasticity equals 1.
    d. demand for which price elasticity is less than 1.

Answers to Sample Test

1. c	7. b	13. c	19. a	25. d
2. b	8. a	14. b	20. d	26. b
3. b	9. c	15. d	21. d	27. a
4. a	10. b	16. c	22. c	28. a
5. e	11. a	17. c	23. c	29. c
6. a	12. d	18. d	24. b	30. c

Introduction to Macroeconomics

Macroeconomics is the study of long-term economic growth and short-term economic fluctuations. Part 2 in *Principles of Macroeconomics* as a whole, and then goes on to consider how to measure the economy. Thus, these two chapters serve as preparation for the study of long-run economic growth in Part 3 and fluctuations in total production in Part 4.

Chapter 5 provides a preview of macroeconomics and introduces the elements that comprise economic growth theory and economic fluctuations theory. Important concepts such as gross domestic product (GDP), inflation, unemployment, and the interest rate are also discussed. Chapter 6 examines how production of goods and services in the whole economy is measured, focusing on the spending, income, and production approaches to measuring GDP. A second important topic covered in the chapter involves measuring the price level and the inflation rate.

CHAPTER 5

A Preview of Macroeconomics

CHAPTER OVERVIEW

Macroeconomics is the study of economic growth and economic fluctuations—how the economy grows and changes over time. The topics of macroeconomics—inflation, unemployment, interest rates, exchange rates—are the subject of newspaper headlines and television stories. The study of macroeconomics entails understanding how they all relate to one another. This chapter, as indicated by its title, provides a preview of this enterprise. We introduce the two basic concepts of macroeconomics, long-term economic growth and short-term economic fluctuations. We study unemployment, inflation, and interest rates, and see how they are related to growth and fluctuations. We consider how the government can use macroeconomic policies to promote economic growth and smooth economic fluctuations. Remember that this chapter is only a preview. It introduces a number of concepts and a lot of terminology, and you should not expect to master it all just yet. Try to see the big picture here; details and more complete understanding will come later.

CHAPTER REVIEW

1. **Real gross domestic product (GDP)** is the total value of all goods and services produced in the economy during a specified period of time, usually a year or a quarter. It is called *real* because the measure of production is adjusted for the increase in prices over the same time period. Real GDP is also called *output* or *production*. Real GDP divided by the population is called *real GDP per capita*; it measures average production per person.

2. **Economic growth** describes increases in real GDP. It is measured by the annual *economic growth rate*, the percentage increase in real GDP each year. For countries with a growing population, real GDP per capita grows more slowly than real GDP. Over the past two centuries, growth in real GDP per capita has greatly increased living standards.

3. In the United States, real GDP per capita doubled during the last 40 years. However, economic growth was higher from the mid-1950s to the mid-1970s than it was from the mid-1970s to the mid-1990s. This *economic growth slowdown* also occurred in many other countries. Reversing the economic growth slowdown is a major—and, as we will see, very difficult—goal of macroeconomic policy.

4. **Economic fluctuations**, also called **business cycles**, are short-run movements around an economy's long-run economic growth path. A **recession** is a fall in real GDP that lasts for 6 months or more. There have been 15 recessions in the United States since the 1920s, the last occurring in 1990–1991. A **peak** is the highest point in the business cycle before the start of a recession, and a **trough** is the lowest point at the end of a recession. An **expansion** is the period between recessions, from the trough to the next peak. The start of an expansion, when the economy is emerging from the recession, is called a **recovery**.

5. A *depression* is an extremely large recession. The period 1929–1932, when real GDP fell by one-third, is called the *Great Depression*. The recent recessions of the mid-1970s, early 1980s, and early 1990s are not comparable in severity to the Great Depression.

6. The *labor force* consists of those people who are either working or looking for work. If you are out of work and looking for work, you are unemployed, and the **unemployment rate** is the number of unemployed people as a percentage of the labor force. The unemployment rate rises during recessions and falls during expansions. The labor force is not constant. The *labor force participation rate*, the number of people in the labor force as a percentage of the working-age population, falls in recessions and rises in recoveries.

7. The **inflation rate** is the increase in the general price of goods and services in the economy, measured as a percentage per year. The consumer price index is the most widely used measure of inflation. A decline in inflation is called *disinflation*, while negative inflation, a fall in the price level, is called *deflation*.

8. Inflation is also characterized by long-term trends and short-term fluctuations. First, inflation in the United States has been positive during every year since 1955. Second, U.S. inflation rose from 3 to 4 percent per year in the mid-1960s to double digits, 10 percent per year or higher, in 1980, then returned to 3 to 4 percent per year in the mid-1980s through the mid 1990s. The rise of inflation in the late 1970s is called the *Great Inflation*. Third, inflation is closely related to the business cycle. Inflation increases during booms and decreases in recessions and recoveries. Higher inflation has occurred prior to every recession in the United States in the past 40 years.

9. The **interest rate** is the amount charged to borrow money, expressed as a percent of the amount borrowed. There are many different interest rates, such as the *mortgage interest rate*, the *Treasury bill interest rate*, and the *savings deposit interest rate*. The *federal funds rate* is the interest rate that banks change each other on overnight loans. The **real interest rate** is the interest rate minus the *expected rate of inflation*, the rate of inflation that people expect to occur. The term **nominal interest rate** is sometimes used to refer to an interest rate that is not adjusted for inflation.

10. **Potential GDP** is the average or normal level of real GDP. Despite the use of the word *potential*, it is not the maximum attainable level of real GDP. The growth rate of potential GDP represents the long-run growth rate for the economy. Real GDP falls below potential GDP in recessions and rises above potential GDP in booms.

11. **Aggregate supply** is the total of all goods and services produced in the economy. Aggregate supply is determined by **labor**, the total number of hours workers are available to work; **capital**, the total available amount of factories, land, and machines; and **technology**, the available knowledge, which can be combined to produce real GDP. Potential GDP is, in turn, determined by aggregate supply.

12. **Aggregate demand** is the total demand for goods and services in the economy. Demand in the whole economy can be divided into demand by four groups—consumers, business firms, government, and foreigners—and aggregate demand is the sum of these four demands.

ZEROING IN

1. *Macroeconomic theory* consists of economic growth theory and economic fluctuations theory. Later in the text we will develop each theory in a great deal of detail. Here, in the spirit of a preview, we will illustrate each theory with one diagram.

   a. The goal of *economic growth theory* is to explain the long-term upward rise of real GDP over time. Figure 5.1 presents a very stylized picture of economic growth for the United States during the past 40 years. The line represents potential GDP, and so booms and recessions have been smoothed out. The figure is drawn using a *ratio scale* so that constant growth of potential GDP is depicted as a straight line. The potential GDP line is steeper from 1955 to 1973 than it is from 1973 to 1997, indicating that economic growth was higher during the first 20 years than during the second 20 years. This depicts the economic growth slowdown.

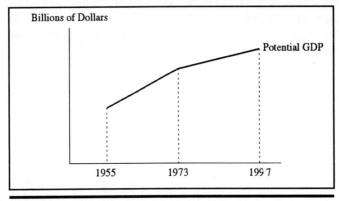

Figure 5.1

   b. *Economic fluctuations theory* attempts to explain short-run movements around the long-run growth path. Figure 5.2 depicts a stylized picture of an economic fluctuation for the United States. The economy was in an expansion until 1990, a recession during 1990–1991, and a recovery through 1997. The cycle of expansion, peak, recession, trough, and recovery is an important feature of economic fluctuations.

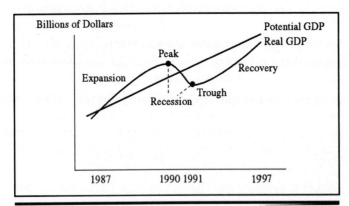

Figure 5.2

2. Economic growth is the focus of Part 3 of the text. Understanding economic growth involves learning about both economic growth theory and how macroeconomic policies can affect growth.

   a. The **production function** is the heart of economic growth theory. According to the production function, real GDP is a function of labor, capital, and technology. In symbols, the production function is written as:

   $$Y = F(L, K, T)$$

   where Y is real GDP, L is labor, K is capital, and T is technology. The symbol F represents a function and means that Y is determined by L, K, and T. How does this relate to growth theory? If real GDP is determined by labor, capital, and technology, then real GDP growth must be determined by the growth of labor, the growth of capital, and the growth of technology. From a different angle, the slowdown in real GDP growth in the 1970s must have been caused by a slowdown in the growth of labor, capital, or technology.

   b. **Labor productivity** is defined as real GDP per hour of work in the economy as a whole. Labor productivity is often simply called *productivity*. Although productivity has risen over time, there has been a slowdown in productivity growth in the United States since the early 1970s. Put differently, although productivity growth has been positive, it was higher in the 1950s and 1960s than it was in the 1970s and 1980s. The growth rate of productivity is determined by the growth of capital and the growth of technology. Although the growth of labor increases output, it does not affect output per hour of work.

   c. *Supply side economic policies* are government policies that attempt to increase long-term economic growth. These policies focus on increasing the available supply of labor, capital, and technology. Supply side policies can affect growth by changing the *incentives* for business firms to invest in capital or to hire more workers, for workers to work harder or to enter the labor force, and for researchers to invent new technologies. Providing funds for education is another important policy by which the government aims to increase productivity and growth.

   d. *Fiscal policy* is government policies concerning spending, taxing, and borrowing. Fiscal policy affects long-term economic growth by affecting the incentives of workers and firms. *Monetary policy* is government policy concerning the money supply and control of inflation. Monetary policy affects long-term economic growth because the inflation rate in the long run depends on the growth rate of the money supply. In the long run, countries with low and stable inflation have higher economic growth than countries with high and variable inflation.

3. As with economic growth, understanding economic fluctuations, the focus of Part 4 of the text, involves learning about both economic fluctuations theory and how macroeconomic policies affect business cycles.

   a. Most theories of economic fluctuations emphasize *changes in aggregate demand*. Why do fluctuations in aggregate demand cause fluctuations in real GDP? Business firms, faced with short-run changes in the demand for their products, adjust their production to meet these short-run fluctuations. If demand declines, firms lay off workers and use their capital at less than full capacity, whereas if demand increases, firms hire more workers and use their capital more intensively.

   b. The theory of economic fluctuations describes business cycles as fluctuations of real GDP around potential GDP. Although potential GDP is not constant, most economists place more emphasis on the role of aggregate demand than on changes in potential GDP to explain short-run economic fluctuations.

ACTIVE REVIEW

Fill-in Questions

1. Real _____ is the total of all goods and services produced in the economy during a specified period of time.

2. Real GDP divided by the population is called _____.

3. The _____ is the percentage increase in real GDP each year.

4. _____ or _____ are short-run movements around an economy's long-run economic growth path.

5. A(n) _____ is a fall in real GDP that lasts for six months or more.

6. A(n) _____ is the highest point in the business cycle before the start of a recession.

7. A(n) _____ is an extremely large recession.

8. The _____ is the number of unemployed people as a percentage of the labor force.

9. _____ is the increase in the general price of goods and services in the economy.

10. The _____ is the amount charged to borrow money, expressed as a percent.

11. _____ GDP is the average or normal level of real GDP.

12. The total supply of all goods and services in the economy is called _____.

13. According to the production function, real GDP is a function of _____, _____, and _____.

14. Fiscal policy is government policy concerning _____, _____, and _____.

15. Monetary policy is government policy concerning the _____.

True-False Questions

T F 1. Real GDP per capita in the United States has not increased since World War II.

T F 2. Economic growth in the United States has increased since the mid-1970s.

T F 3. A recession is a decrease in the economic growth rate.

T   F   4. The recession of 1990–1991 was so severe that it can be characterized as a depression.

T   F   5. In recent years, inflation in the United States has been greater than zero.

T   F   6. The federal funds rate is the interest rate on Treasury bills.

T   F   7. Potential GDP is not the maximum attainable level of real GDP.

T   F   8. Aggregate demand is determined by labor, capital, and technology.

T   F   9. One goal of economic fluctuations theory is to explain the economic growth slowdown.

T   F   10. The growth rate of productivity in the United States has decreased since the early 1970s.

T   F   11. Supply side economic policies are government policies that attempt to smooth out short-run economic fluctuations.

T   F   12. In the long run, economic growth is unrelated to inflation.

T   F   13. According to economic fluctuations theory, potential GDP fluctuates around real GDP.

T   F   14. Economic fluctuations are caused by changes in aggregate demand.

T   F   15. Fiscal and monetary policy have little effect on economic fluctuations.

Short-Answer Questions

1. What are two other names for real gross domestic product (GDP)?

2. Describe the phases of a business cycle.

3. What happens to the labor force participation rate over the business cycle?

4. What is the difference between disinflation and deflation?

5. What is the Great Inflation?

6. What happens to inflation during the business cycle?

7. What is the real interest rate?

8. Describe the relationship between real GDP and potential GDP during economic fluctuations.

9. According to the production function, what caused the slowdown in real GDP growth in the 1970s?

10. What determines the growth rate of productivity?

11. How can fiscal policy affect long-run economic growth?

12. How can monetary policy affect long-term economic growth?

13. What is the relation between inflation and economic growth in the long run?

14. Why do fluctuations in aggregate demand cause fluctuations in real GDP?

15. How do business firms increase their production in response to an increase in demand?

WORKING IT OUT

1. If real GDP grows by 10 percent per year, how long does it take for it to double? Your first thought might be 10 years, since adding 10 percent per year would add up to 100 percent. But you would be wrong; compound growth makes the process faster.

   a. Suppose the real GDP of a country that initially has real GDP of $100 billion grows by 10 percent per year. In year 1, real GDP is $110 (we will suppress the "billion"). In year 2, adding 10 percent to $110 gives $121. In year 3, it is $133.1; in year 4, $146.4; in year 5, $161.1; in year 6, $177.2; in year 7, $194.9; in year 8, $214.4; in year 9, $235.8; and in year 10, $259.4. Because of compounding, it takes between 7 and 8 years, instead of 10, for real GDP to double. Another way to look at this is to see that, after 10 years, real GDP increases by 160 percent, not 100 percent.

   b. The formula for compound growth is:

   $$\text{(Initial level)} \times (1 + g)^n = \text{level at end of } n \text{ years}$$

   where g is the annual growth rate stated as a fraction. In the above example, the 10 percent growth rate stated as a fraction is .1, so that:

   $$\$100 \times (1.1)^{10} = \$100 \times 2.594 = \$259.4$$

   You need a hand calculator with a key that does y^x to do this calculation.

   c. The compound growth formula can be inverted to calculate growth rates from initial and final income levels:

   $$g = \frac{\text{Level at end of } n \text{ years}^{1/n}}{\text{(initial level)}} - 1$$

   In the above example, since growth is constant, we can calculate the growth rate using any year. Choosing year 7,

   $$g = (194.9/100)^{1/7} - 1 = (1.949)^{1/7} - 1 = 1.10 - 1 = .1$$

   As above, you need a hand calculator with a key that does y^x.

   d. Calculating growth rates after one year is much easier.

   $$g = \frac{\text{Level at end of 1 year}}{\text{(initial level)}} - 1$$

   In the above example,

   $$g = (110/100) - 1 = 1.1 - 1 = .1$$

2. Plotting growing variables involves a few subtleties. Let's consider real GDP in problem 1, which we know is growing at 10 percent per year:

Year	Real GDP (Billions)
0	$100.0
1	$110.0
2	$121.0
3	$133.1
4	$146.4
5	$161.1
6	$177.2
7	$194.9
8	$214.4
9	$235.8
10	$259.4

In Figure 5.3, these data are plotted on a ratio or logarithmic scale, where equal percentage changes in the variable have the same vertical distance. On a ratio scale, a variable that grows at a constant rate is depicted as a straight line. Ratio scales are very useful for plotting growing variables; they were also used in Figures 5.1 and 5.2.

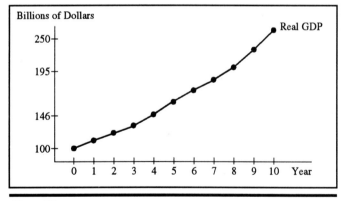

Figure 5.3

Worked Problems

1. Suppose that an economy with per capita GDP of $2,000 grows at a rate of 2 percent per year.

   a. What is per capita GDP after 1 year?

   b. What is per capita GDP after 10 years?

   c. What is per capita GDP after 100 years?

Answers

a. *Although you don't need the formula for compound growth to solve this part, using it is good practice. The formula for compound growth is:*

   (Initial level) $\times (1 + g)^n$ = level at end of n years

   With 2 percent stated as a fraction = .02 and n = 1,

   $2,000 $\times (1.02)$ = $2,040

b. *Using the compound growth formula, after 10 years:*

   $2,000 $\times (1.02)^{10}$ = $2,000 $\times 1.219$ = $2,438

c. *Again using the compound growth formula, after 100 years:*

   $2,000 $\times (1.02)^{100}$ = $2,000 $\times 7.245$ = $14,489

2. Suppose that real GDP for an economy is as follows:

Year	Real GDP (Billions)
0	$5,000
1	$5,250
2	$5,510
3	$5,680
4	$5,630
5	$5,560
6	$5,730
7	$6,020
8	$6,330

   a. What is the growth rate of potential GDP?

   b. Using a ratio scale, plot real GDP and potential GDP.

   c. Identify the expansion, peak, recession, trough, and recovery.

Answers

a. *The growth rate of potential GDP is the long-run growth rate of the economy. To determine the long-run growth rate g, use the compound growth formula between the initial (year 0) and final (year 8) levels. Using the formula:*

$$g = \frac{6,330^{1/8}}{(5,000)} - 1 = (1.266)^{1/8} - 1 = 1.03 - 1 = .03$$

The growth rate of potential GDP is 3 percent per year.

b. *With a ratio scale, the constant growth of potential GDP is depicted as a straight line. Figure 5.4 illustrates this and also shows the fluctuations of real GDP around potential GDP.*

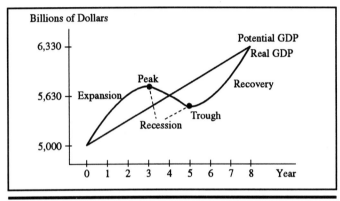

Figure 5.4

c. *The economy starts in an expansion that peaks in year 3. A recession occurs as real GDP falls, with a trough in year 5. The recovery begins in year 6 and continues through year 8.*

Practice Problems

1. Suppose that an economy with real GDP of $300 billion per year grows at a rate of 4 percent per year.

   a. What is real GDP after 1 year?

   b. What is real GDP after 5 years?

   c. What is real GDP after 10 years?

2. Suppose that an economy with per capita GDP of $1,000 grows at a rate of 3 percent per year.

   a. What is per capita GDP after 1 year?

   b. What is per capita GDP after 10 years?

   c. What is per capita GDP after 50 years?

3. Suppose that real GDP for an economy is as follows:

Year	Real GDP (Billions)
0	$6,000
1	$6,300
2	$6,610
3	$6,550
4	$6,420
5	$6,480
6	$6,610
7	$6,810
8	$7,030

a. What is the growth rate of potential GDP?

b. Using a ratio scale, plot real GDP and potential GDP.

c. Identify the expansion, peak, recession, trough, and recovery.

4. Suppose that real GDP for an economy is as follows:

Year	Real GDP (Billions)
0	$5,000
1	$4,900
2	$5,050
3	$5,350
4	$5,780
5	$6,240
6	$6,610
7	$6,910
8	$6,840

a. What is the growth rate of potential GDP?

b. Using a ratio scale, plot real GDP and potential GDP.

c. Identify the expansion, peak, recession, trough, and recovery.

CHAPTER TEST

1. The growth in real GDP per capita
   a. is slower than the growth in real GDP for countries with a growing population.
   b. is faster than the growth in real GDP for countries with a growing population.
   c. is about the same as the growth in real GDP for countries with a growing population.
   d. has greatly decreased living standards over the past two centuries.

2. Economic growth describes
   a. increases in the labor force.
   b. increases in real GDP.
   c. increases in inflation.
   d. increases in interest rates.

3. A fall in real GDP that lasts 6 months or more is called
   a. an expansion.
   b. a peak.
   c. an economic growth slowdown.
   d. a recession.

4. The highest point in the business cycle before the start of a recession is called
   a. a trough.
   b. a peak.
   c. a recovery.
   d. an expansion.

5. Which of the following groups of people are *not* considered part of the labor force?
   a. People who are unemployed
   b. People who are working
   c. People who are not working and are looking for work
   d. People who are not working and are not looking for work

6. The unemployment rate
   a. is always rising.
   b. is always falling.
   c. rises during recessions and falls during expansions.
   d. falls during recessions and rises during expansions.

7. The labor force participation rate is the number of people
   a. unemployed as a percentage of the labor force.
   b. unemployed as a percentage of the working-age population.
   c. employed as a percentage of the labor force.
   d. in the labor force as a percentage of the working-age population.

8. A fall in the price level is called
   a. a growth slowdown.
   b. deflation.
   c. disinflation.
   d. inflation.

9. Inflation
   a. increases during booms and decreases during recessions and recoveries.
   b. decreases during booms and increases during recessions and recoveries.
   c. increases during booms and recoveries and decreases during recessions.
   d. decreases during booms and recoveries and increases during recessions.

10. The real interest rate is the interest rate minus
    a. the federal funds rate.
    b. the Treasury bill interest rate.
    c. the mortgage interest rate.
    d. the expected inflation rate.

11. Real GDP
    a. is the normal or average level of production for an economy.
    b. is the maximum attainable level of production for an economy.
    c. is the total of all goods and services produced in an economy during a specified period of time.
    d. rises above potential GDP in recessions and falls below potential GDP in booms.

12. The goal of economic growth theory is to explain
    a. short-run movements around the long-run growth path.
    b. the short-term upward rise of real GDP over time.
    c. the long-term upward rise of real GDP over time.
    d. the long-term downward fall of real GDP over time.

13. Government policies that focus on increasing the available supply of labor, capital, and technology are
    a. supply side economic policies.
    b. fiscal policies.
    c. monetary policies.
    d. demand side economic policies.

14. Fiscal policy
    a. is government policy concerning the money supply.
    b. is government policy concerning money demand.
    c. is government policy concerning spending, taxing, and borrowing.
    d. affects long-term economic growth because inflation in the long run depends on the growth rate of the money supply.

15. Theories of economic fluctuations emphasize
    a. the inflation rate.
    b. the interest rate.
    c. aggregate supply.
    d. aggregate demand.

16. Economic fluctuations theory
    a. postulates that business cycles are due to changes in potential GDP.
    b. postulates that business cycles are due to changes in inflation.
    c. describes business cycles as fluctuations of real GDP around potential GDP.
    d. describes business cycles as fluctuations of potential GDP around real GDP.

17. Suppose that an economy with per capita GDP of $4,000 grows at a rate of 5 percent per year. What is the per capita GDP after 2 years?
    a. $4,200
    b. $4,400
    c. $4,410
    d. $4,500

Use Figure 5.5 for question 18.

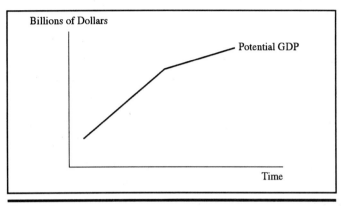

Figure 5.5

18. Figure 5.5 illustrates a(n)
    a. recession.
    b. recovery.
    c. expansion.
    d. economic growth slowdown.

Use Figure 5.6 for questions 19 and 20.

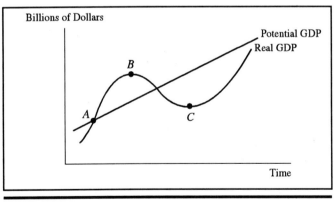

Figure 5.6

19. Point C on Figure 5.6 illustrates
    a. an expansion.
    b. a trough.
    c. a peak.
    d. a recovery.

20. Movement from point *A* to point *B* on Figure 5.6 illustrates
    a. an expansion.
    b. a trough.
    c. a peak.
    d. a recovery.

ANSWERS TO THE REVIEW QUESTIONS

Fill-in Questions

1. gross domestic product (GDP)
2. real GDP per capita
3. economic growth rate
4. Economic fluctuations; business cycles
5. recession
6. peak
7. depression
8. unemployment rate
9. Inflation
10. interest rate
11. Potential
12. aggregate supply
13. labor; capital; technology
14. spending; taxing; borrowing
15. money supply and the control of inflation

True-False Questions

1. **False**. Real GDP per capita has doubled during the last 40 years.
2. **False**. There has been an economic growth slowdown in the United States since the mid-1970s.
3. **False**. A recession is a fall in the level, not just the growth rate, of real GDP.
4. **False**. The recession of the early 1990s was not comparable in severity to the Great Depression.
5. **True**. Inflation in the United States has been positive during every year since 1955.
6. **False**. The federal funds rate is the interest rate on overnight loans between banks.
7. **True**. Potential GDP is the average or normal level of real GDP.
8. **False**. Labor, capital, and technology determine aggregate supply.
9. **False**. Economic fluctuations theory attempts to explain short-run movements around the long-run growth path. The economic growth slowdown is a long-term decrease in the economic growth rate.
10. **True**. There has been a slowdown in productivity growth since the early 1970s.
11. **False**. Supply side economic policies attempt to increase long-run economic growth.
12. **False**. Countries with low inflation have higher long-run economic growth than countries with high inflation.
13. **False**. Real GDP fluctuates around potential GDP.
14. **True**. Changes in aggregate demand cause economic fluctuations.
15. **False**. Macroeconomics policy has a huge effect on economic fluctuations.

Short-Answer Questions

1. Real GDP is also called output or production.
2. Starting with an expansion, the economy attains its peak. Then real GDP falls, initiating a recession. Once the economy reaches bottom, at the trough, a recovery occurs.
3. The labor force participation rate falls in recessions and rises in recoveries.
4. Disinflation is a decline in the inflation rate. Deflation, or negative inflation, is a fall in the price level.
5. The Great Inflation is the rise of inflation in the United States in the late 1970s.

6. Inflation rises during booms and decreases in recessions and recoveries.
7. The real interest rate is the interest rate minus the expected rate of inflation.
8. Real GDP rises above potential GDP in booms and falls below potential GDP in recessions.
9. The economic growth slowdown was caused by a slowdown in the growth of labor, capital, or technology.
10. The growth rate of productivity is determined by the growth of capital and the growth of technology.
11. Fiscal policy can affect growth by changing the incentives for firms and workers.
12. Monetary policy can affect growth by keeping inflation low and stable.
13. In the long run, countries with low and stable inflation have higher economic growth than countries with high and variable inflation.
14. In response to fluctuations in aggregate demand, business firms adjust their production, causing fluctuations in real GDP.
15. If demand increases, firms hire more workers and use their capital more intensively.

SOLUTIONS TO THE PRACTICE PROBLEMS

1. a. Real GDP = $300 \times (1.04)$ = $312 billion.

   b. Real GDP = $300 \times (1.04)^5$ = $365 billion.

   c. Real GDP = $300 \times (1.04)^{10}$ = $440 billion.

2. a. Per capita GDP = $1,000 \times (1.03)$ = $1,030.

   b. Per capita GDP = $1,000 \times (1.03)^{10}$ = $1,344.

   c. Per capita GDP = $1,000 \times (1.03)^{50}$ = $4,384.

3. a. Using the compound growth formula:

   $$g = (7,030/6,000)^{1/8} - 1 = (1.172)^{1/8} - 1 = 1.02 - 1 = .02$$

   The growth rate of potential GDP is 2 percent per year.

   b. Using a ratio scale, Figure 5.7 shows potential GDP as a straight line and the fluctuations of real GDP around potential GDP.

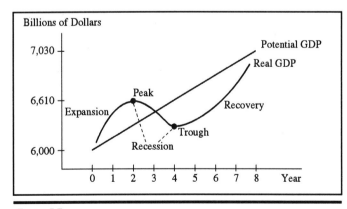

Figure 5.7

   c. The economy starts in an expansion that peaks in year 2. A recession occurs as real GDP falls, with a trough in year 4. The recovery begins in year 5 and continues through year 8.

4. a. Using the compound growth formula:

$$g = (6{,}840/5{,}000)^{1/8} - 1 = (1.368)^{1/8} - 1 = 1.04 - 1 = .04$$

The growth rate of potential GDP is 4 percent per year.

b. Using a ratio scale, Figure 5.8 shows potential GDP as a straight line and the fluctuations of real GDP around potential GDP.

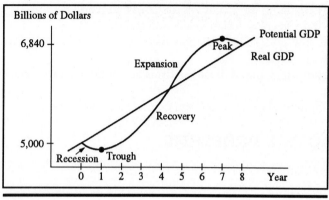

Figure 5.8

c. The economy starts in a recession that ends with a trough in year 1. A recovery occurs as real GDP rises, with an expansion culminating in a peak in year 7. Another recession begins in year 8.

ANSWERS TO THE CHAPTER TEST

1. a	6. c	11. c	16. c
2. b	7. d	12. c	17. c
3. d	8. b	13. a	18. d
4. b	9. a	14. c	19. b
5. d	10. d	15. d	20. a

CHAPTER 6

Measuring the Macroeconomy

CHAPTER OVERVIEW

Accurate measurement of growth and fluctuations is essential for making economic decisions. Although we looked at how the economy grows and fluctuates over time in Chapter 5, it is not enough to be able to say that the economy has entered a growth slowdown or is in a recession; we want to know how much growth has fallen or how bad the recession is. In this chapter, we learn how to measure the macroeconomy. We study gross domestic product (GDP) in detail and learn about the spending, income, and production approaches to its measurement. We then consider a country's saving, investment, and net exports, and see how they are related. We learn about the difference between real and nominal GDP, and see how to measure inflation. Measurement of GDP is not perfect, and we consider some of the problems. Finally, we look at international comparisons of GDP and see how fluctuating exchange rates make cross-country comparisons difficult.

CHAPTER REVIEW

1. *Gross domestic product (GDP)* is a measure of all the goods and services newly produced in a country during some period of time. The definition contains a number of important concepts. First, both goods—such as automobiles and computers—and services—such as health care and legal services—are included. Second, GDP includes only newly produced goods and services. Sales of used cars, for example, are not included. Also excluded are **intermediate foods**, which are goods that undergo further processing before being sold to consumers; intermediate foods are part of **final goods**; which are counted as part of GDP. Third, only goods and services produced within the borders of a country are included. The location of the production, not the ownership, is what matters. Fourth, GDP is always measured during a specified period of time, usually one year.

2. There are three ways to measure GDP, all reported in the **national income and product accounts**. The *spending* approach measures the total amount that people spend on goods and services made in America. The *income* approach measures the total income that is earned by all workers and businesses. The *production* approach measures the total of all the goods and services as they are produced. We consider each of the three approaches in turn.

3. The *spending* approach to measuring GDP divides spending into four categories: consumption, investment, government purchases, and net exports. GDP is the total of spending on the four categories.

a. **Consumption** consists of purchases of final goods and services, ranging from automobiles to college tuition, by individuals. Consumption is the largest category of GDP—it accounts for 69 percent of GDP in the United States.

b. **Investment** includes three types of spending. **Business fixed investment** is purchases of final goods by business firms, including building a new factory or purchasing a new computer. **Residential investment** is the purchase of new houses and apartment buildings. Even though most new houses are purchased by consumers, they are still counted as part of investment because they provide long-term services. **Inventory investment** is the change in inventories, goods that have been produced but not yet sold.

c. **Government purchases** consist of spending by federal, state, and local governments on new goods and services. Government outlays also include *transfer payments*, such as social security and unemployment benefits, and interest on the debt; these are not included in GDP.

d. **Net exports** are **exports**, what Americans sell to foreigners, minus **imports**, what Americans buy from foreigners. Net exports are also called the **trade balance**. Exports are included separately in GDP because they are produced in the United States but are not part of consumption, investment, or government purchases. Imports are subtracted to get GDP because they are part of consumption and investment spending but, not being produced in the United States, should not be included in GDP.

4. The income approach to measuring GDP adds up the income received by workers and businesses for producing the goods that make up GDP. This includes labor income, capital income, depreciation, indirect business taxes, net income of foreigners, and the statistical discrepancy.

a. **Labor income**, which consists of wages, salaries, and fringe benefits, is the largest component of income. **Capital income**—profits, rental payments, and interest payments—is the next largest.

b. **Depreciation** is the amount by which factories and machines wear out each year. Much of investment spending goes to replace worn-out factories and equipment, and that spending is included in GDP. Investment, which is sometimes called **gross investment**, minus depreciation equals **net investment**. Spending to replace depreciated factories and machines is not included in capital income, however, because firms subtract depreciation to compute profits. Since depreciation is included in GDP but not in capital income, it must be added as a separate category.

c. **Indirect business taxes** consist mainly of sales taxes. Like depreciation, they are included in GDP but not in firms' profits and need to be added as a separate category. *Net income of foreigners* equals income earned by foreigners in the United States minus income earned by Americans abroad. This is also part of GDP, but it is not included in labor and capital income, and so it is added as another category. Finally, because data on income and spending are collected in different ways, the **statistical discrepancy** ensures that GDP is the same using either measure.

d. **National income** is the sum of labor income and capital income. **Personal income** is a measure of the income paid directly to individuals.

5. The production approach to measuring GDP adds up the production of each firm or industry in the economy. When using this method, it is important to avoid double counting goods, such as automobile tires, which are final goods for one firm but intermediate goods for another. **Value added** is the value of a firm's output less the value of the intermediate goods used in production. Measuring GDP by production involves counting the value added, not the final sales, at each level of production, which avoids double counting.

6. For an individual, saving equals income less consumption. For a country, government purchases must also be accounted for. **National saving**, the sum of all saving in the economy, equals income less consumption less government purchases. At any time, some people, whose income is greater than their consumption, are saving, while others, who consume more than their income, are *dissaving*. Middle-aged people generally save, while the young and the old either save very little or dissave.

7. The budget surplus is the difference between the government's receipts from taxes and its expenditures. When expenditures exceed receipts, as has been the case for the United States in recent years, there is a budget deficit. When there is a budget surplus, the government saves, and when there is a budget deficit, the government dissaves.

8. Gross domestic product (GDP) measures goods and services at their current prices. When there is inflation and prices increase, GDP rises even if the quantity of goods and services produced is unchanged. **Real GDP** is a measure of production that corrects for inflation. It measures what GDP would have been if prices were constant. GDP is sometimes called **nominal GDP**. If there is inflation, as there has been in the United States over the last 40 years, nominal GDP grows faster than real GDP.

9. The **GDP deflator** is the measure of the **price level** that is used to compute real GDP. More precisely, the GDP deflator equals nominal GDP divided by real GDP. The GDP deflator is a measure of the price of all goods and services in GDP: consumption, investment, government purchases, and net exports. The **consumer price index (CPI)** is another measure of the price level. It is the price of a fixed collection of consumer goods and services in a given year divided by the price of the same collection in some base year. The **chain weighted price index** is a third measure of prices. Unlike the CPI, it is not based on a fixed quantity of goods and services in some base year. The quantities in the index change each year, and the percentage changes in the index are "chained" together.

10. The use of fixed weights is an important reason why economists believe that the CPI overstates inflation. By not allowing quantities to change when prices change, the CPI puts too much weight on items with rising prices and too little weight on items with falling prices. The result is that measured inflation is greater than actual inflation.

11. Making international comparisons of GDPs involves several difficulties. Although GDP for the United States is calculated in dollars, GDP for other countries is calculated in their currencies. Using the market exchange rate between currencies is misleading because the market exchange rate is not a good guide to price differences between countries. The **purchasing power parity exchange rate**, which is defined as the amount of foreign currency required to buy the same amount of goods that can be bought with one dollar, provides a better basis for comparison.

ZEROING IN

1. How can you tell what is counted, and what is not counted, as part of GDP? The first step is to remember the definition. GDP is a measure of all the goods and services newly produced in a country during some period of time.

   a. *Goods and services.* GDP is not just a measure of tangible goods like dishwashers and televisions. Services such as banking and tourism are a very important part of GDP.

   b. *Newly produced.* When an automobile is manufactured, it is counted as part of GDP. Whether it remains with the original owner until it falls apart or is sold ten times in the next five years does not affect GDP; only newly produced goods are counted.

   c. *In a country.* The location of the production is what matters for GDP, not the ownership. Honda Accords produced in Ohio count toward U.S., not Japanese, GDP. Similarly, IBM computers manufactured in Malaysia do not add to the GDP of the United States; they count toward the GDP of Malaysia.

   d. *Measure.* GDP can include only what can be measured. Child care by parents and relatives does not count toward GDP, but day care does. Illegal activities do not count toward GDP.

2. One of the most confusing parts of this chapter is the meaning of investment. Economists define *investment* as the purchase of new factories, houses, or equipment. To everybody else, investment is putting away money for the future, perhaps in the stock market. This doesn't mean that economists are right and everybody else is wrong; it simply means that you need to be careful with your use of language.

3. Although GDP is the most comprehensive measure of economic activity, it is not perfect. We discuss some of its shortcomings:

   a. Collection of data on GDP is a big job, and it takes time. *Revisions in GDP* are the changes in GDP as new data become available. Some of these revisions are quite large and can change our perception of how the economy is performing.

   b. There are a number of important *omissions from GDP.* Home production is not included in GDP because the transactions are not recorded in markets. Illegal activity, also called the *underground economy*, is omitted for the same reason. Improvements in the quality of goods and services are difficult to measure. A $3,000 personal computer in 1995 is a vastly different good from a $3,000 personal computer in 1985, yet they count exactly the same toward GDP. Finally, leisure activity is not included in GDP.

   c. GDP is not a complete measure of the well-being of individuals. Life expectancy, infant mortality, and environmental quality, among others, also measure how a country is performing over time.

ACTIVE REVIEW

Fill-in Questions

1. _____ is a measure of the value of all the goods and services newly produced in a country during some period of time.

2. GDP can be measured by the _____, _____, and _____ approaches.

3. The spending approach divides spending into _____, _____, _____, and _____.

4. _____ is the largest category of GDP.

5. The three types of investment spending are _____, _____, and _____.

6. _____ consist of spending by federal, state, and local governments on new goods and services.

7. Net exports are _____ minus _____.

8. The two largest components of income are _____ and _____ income.

9. Gross investment minus _____ equals net investment.

10. _____ is the value of a firm's output minus the value of the intermediate goods used in production.

11. National saving equals _____ minus _____ minus _____.

12. When the government's expenditures exceed its receipts, there is a(n) _____.

13. _____ is a measure of production that corrects for inflation.

14. Three measures of the price level are the _____, the _____, and the _____.

15. The _____ is the amount of foreign currency required to buy the same amount of goods that can be purchased with one dollar.

True-False Questions

T   F   1. Haircuts are not included in GDP.

T   F   2. Sales of used textbooks are not part of GDP.

T   F   3. When General Motors builds a truck in Brazil, this adds to U.S. GDP.

T   F   4. If a woman marries her nanny, who becomes a stay-at-home husband, GDP falls.

T   F   5. Legalization of marijuana would increase GDP.

T   F   6. All government outlays are part of GDP.

T F   7. Capital income (profits, rental payments, and interest payments) is the largest component of income.

T F   8. GDP can be measured by counting final sales at each level of production.

T F   9. The spending, income, and production approaches to GDP all add up to the same value.

T F   10. People usually save throughout their lifetimes.

T F   11. In recent years, there has been positive government saving in the United States.

T F   12. Nominal GDP always grows faster than real GDP.

T F   13. Investing in the stock market adds to GDP.

T F   14. Much of the data that make up GDP is not quickly available in its final form.

T F   15. GDP is a complete measure of the well-being of a country.

Short-Answer Questions

1. What determines GDP, the location or the ownership of the production?

2. What is the spending approach to measuring GDP?

3. Why is residential investment counted as part of investment instead of consumption?

4. Why does GDP include net exports instead of simply exports?

5. How is GDP calculated by the income approach?

6. What is the difference between gross and net investment?

7. What is the production approach to measuring GDP?

8. With the production approach, why is value added counted instead of final sales?

9. How can GDP increase if production of goods and services is constant?

10. What is the difference between nominal and real GDP?

11. What is the GDP deflator?

12. Why do economists believe that the CPI overstates inflation?

13. What exchange rate should be used when making international comparisons of GDP?

14. Why are home production and illegal activities omitted from GDP?

15. Why do personal computers cause difficulties in measuring GDP?

WORKING IT OUT

1. The spending approach to measuring GDP can be illustrated using algebra. It is important that you familiarize yourself with these terms and equations now, because they will be used a great deal later.

    a. According to the spending approach, GDP is the sum of consumption, investment, government purchases, and net exports. Let Y stand for GDP, C for consumption, I for investment, G for government purchases, and X for net exports. In symbols:

    $$Y = C + I + G + X$$

    GDP is computed by adding up consumption, investment, government purchases, and net exports.

    b. We earlier defined national saving as income minus consumption minus government purchases. Since GDP can be measured by income as well as by spending or production, we let Y stand for income too. Call national saving S and use, as above, C for consumption and G for government purchases. In symbols:

    $$S = Y - C - G$$

    c. We can use these two equations to derive a formula for national saving. Start with the expression for GDP, $Y = C + I + G + X$, and subtract consumption (C) and government purchases (G) from both sides:

    $$Y - C - G = I + X$$

    Now look at the last two equations. In the first, $Y - C - G = S$, and in the second, $Y - C - G = I + X$. Therefore:

    $$S = I + X$$

    In words, national saving equals investment plus net exports.

    d. Manipulating the equation one more time,

    $$X = S - ,$$

    or, in words, net exports equals national saving minus investment. When saving is greater than investment, net exports are positive and there is a trade surplus. When saving is less than investment, net exports are negative and there is a trade deficit.

2. The relationship among real GDP, nominal GDP, and the GDP deflator can also be illustrated using algebra.

    a. The GDP deflator was defined to equal nominal GDP divided by real GDP. Written as an equation:

    $$\text{GDP deflator} = \frac{\text{nominal GDP}}{\text{real GDP}}$$

    This expression can be manipulated to provide a formula for real GDP:

    $$\text{Real GDP} = \frac{\text{nominal GDP}}{\text{GDP deflator}}$$

    Alternatively, nominal GDP can be written:

    $$\text{Nominal GDP} = \text{GDP deflator} \times \text{real GDP}$$

b. Inflation is positive when the price level is increasing. Since the GDP deflator is a measure of the price level, inflation means that the GDP deflator is growing over time. From the formula for the GDP deflator, it can be growing only if the numerator, nominal GDP, is rising faster than the denominator, real GDP. This is another way of showing that when there is inflation, nominal GDP grows faster than real GDP.

Worked Problems

1. Suppose you are given the following information about the economy, with the values in billions of dollars.

Consumption	$5,000
Investment	$2,000
Government purchases	$1,000
Net exports	$1,000

a. What is GDP?
b. What is national saving?

Answers

a. *Using the spending approach, GDP equals consumption plus investment plus government purchases plus net exports. In equation form:*

$$Y = C + I + G + X$$

Substituting the values:

$$Y = \$5,000 + \$2,000 + \$1,000 + \$1,000 = \$9,000 \text{ billion}$$

b. *National saving equals income minus consumption minus government purchases. Written as a formula:*

$$S = Y - C - G$$

Substituting the values, including the value of income (GDP) calculated above:

$$S = \$9,000 - \$5,000 - \$1,000 = \$3,000 \text{ billion}$$

Saving can also be calculated as the sum of investment and net exports:

$$S = I + X$$

Substituting values:

$$S = \$2,000 + \$1,000 = \$3,000 \text{ billion}$$

The answer, that saving = $3,000 billion, is the same either way.

2. Suppose that the economy is characterized by the following information, with values in billions of dollars:

Year	Nominal GDP	Real GDP
2000	$5,000	$5,000
2001	$6,000	$5,455
2002	$7,200	$6,000

   a. What is the GDP deflator for the three years?

   b. Which is growing faster, nominal or real GDP?

Answers

   a. *The GDP deflator equals nominal GDP divided by real GDP. For the year 2000, the GDP deflator = $5,000/$5,000 = 1.00. For the year 2001, the GDP deflator = $6,000/$5,455 = 1.10. For the year 2002, the GDP deflator = $7,200/$6,000 = 1.20.*

   b. *Since the GDP deflator is increasing over time, there is inflation. When there is inflation, nominal GDP grows faster than real GDP.*

Practice Problems

1. Suppose you are given the following information about the economy, with the values in billions of dollars.

Consumption	$6,000
Investment	$2,000
Government purchases	$1,000
National saving	$1,000

   a. What are net exports? Is there a trade surplus or a trade deficit?

   b. What is GDP?

2. Suppose you are given the following information about the economy, with the values in billions of dollars.

Consumption	$4,000
Net exports	$2,000
Government purchases	$1,000
National saving	$4,000

a. What is investment?

b. What is GDP?

3. Suppose that the economy is characterized by the following information, with values for real GDP in billions of dollars:

Year	GDP Deflator	Real GDP
2000	.90	$6,000
2001	1.00	$6,000
2002	1.10	$6,000

What is nominal GDP for the three years? What is happening in the economy?

4. Suppose that the economy is characterized by the following information, with values for nominal GDP in billions of dollars:

Year	GDP Deflator	Nominal GDP
2000	1.25	$8,000
2001	1.25	$8,500
2002	1.25	$9,000

What is real GDP for the three years? What is happening in the economy?

CHAPTER TEST

1. Which of the following would *not* be included in the measurement of gross domestic product (GDP) for the United States?
   a. New Honda Accords produced in the United States
   b. Used Ford Broncos sold in the United States
   c. Health care and legal services
   d. Computers and software products

2. When calculating GDP, what matters is
   a. the location of production only.
   b. the ownership of production only.
   c. both the location and the ownership of production.
   d. neither the location nor the ownership of production.

3. The production approach to calculating GDP measures
   a. the total amount people spend on goods and services made in the United States.
   b. the total amount people spend on goods and services made in the United States and abroad.
   c. the total income that is earned by workers and businesses.
   d. the total of all goods and services produced.

4. The income approach to calculating GDP measures
   a. the total amount people spend on goods and services made in the United States.
   b. the total amount people spend on goods and services made in the United States and abroad.
   c. the total income that is earned by workers and businesses.
   d. the total of all goods and services produced.

5. The spending approach to calculating GDP divides spending into four categories:
   a. income, production, investment, and consumption.
   b. consumption, income, production, and net imports.
   c. consumption, investment, imports, and exports.
   d. consumption, investment, government purchases, and net exports.

6. Which of the following accounts for the largest portion of GDP?
   a. Investment
   b. Net exports
   c. Consumption
   d. Government expenditures

7. Net investment equals
   a. gross investment plus depreciation.
   b. gross investment minus depreciation.
   c. net business fixed investment plus residential investment plus inventory investment.
   d. net business fixed investment plus residential investment plus financial investment.

8. Which of the following is *not* a component of income?
   a. Labor income
   b. Depreciation
   c. Transfer payments
   d. Indirect business taxes

9. The largest component of income is
   a. capital income.
   b. labor income.
   c. depreciation.
   d. transfer payments.

10. Value added is
    a. used to measure GDP under the spending approach.
    b. the final sales value of a firm's output.
    c. the value of a firm's output plus the value of intermediate goods used in production.
    d. the value of a firm's output minus the value of intermediate goods used in production.

11. National saving equals
    a. income minus consumption.
    b. income plus consumption.
    c. income minus consumption minus government purchases.
    d. income plus consumption plus government purchases.

12. When the government's expenditures exceed the government's receipts from taxes,
    a. there is a budget deficit.
    b. there is a budget surplus.
    c. there is a balanced budget.
    d. the government saves.

13. If there is inflation,
    a. nominal GDP grows faster than real GDP.
    b. nominal GDP grows faster than the GDP deflator.
    c. real GDP grows faster than nominal GDP.
    d. real GDP grows faster than the GDP deflator.

14. The GDP deflator equals
    a. real GDP divided by nominal GDP.
    b. nominal GDP divided by real GDP.
    c. nominal GDP plus real GDP.
    d. nominal GDP minus real GDP.

15. The measure of the price level that is the price of a fixed collection of consumer goods and services in a given year divided by the price of the same collection in some base year is
    a. the GDP deflator.
    b. the chain weighted price index.
    c. the purchasing power parity exchange rate.
    d. the consumer price index.

16. National saving equals
    a. $I - X$.
    b. $I + X$.
    c. $X - I$.
    d. $I + C$.

17. When saving is less than investment,
    a. net exports are positive, and there is a trade deficit.
    b. net exports are positive, and there is a trade surplus.
    c. net exports are negative, and there is a trade deficit.
    d. net exports are negative, and there is a trade surplus.

18. Which of the following is *not* omitted from GDP?
    a. Home production
    b. Illegal activities
    c. Leisure activities
    d. Legal services

Use the following table for questions 19 and 20.

Suppose you are given the following information about the economy (values in billions of dollars).

Consumption	$6,000
Investment	$2,000
Government purchases	$1,000
National saving	$3,000

19. What are net exports?
    a. $1,000 billion
    b. $2,000 billion
    c. $3,000 billion
    d. $4,000 billion

20. What is GDP?
    a. $3,000 billion
    b. $4,000 billion
    c. $10,000 billion
    d. $12,000 billion

ANSWERS TO THE REVIEW QUESTIONS

Fill-in Questions

1. Gross domestic product (GDP)
2. spending; income; production
3. consumption; investment; government purchases; net exports
4. Consumption
5. business fixed investment; residential investment; inventory investment
6. Government purchases
7. exports; imports
8. labor income; capital income
9. depreciation
10. Value added
11. income; consumption; government purchases
12. budget deficit
13. Real GDP
14. GDP deflator; consumer price index; chain weighted price index
15. purchasing power parity exchange rate

True-False Questions

1. **False**. Haircuts are a service and are part of GDP.
2. **True**. The textbook was included in GDP when it was new; it is not counted again.
3. **False**. Building a truck in Brazil adds to Brazilian GDP. It does not matter who owns the truck.
4. **True**. Child care counts toward GDP only when it is a market activity.
5. **True**. Illegal activities are not included in GDP.
6. **False**. A large part of government outlays is for transfer payments, which are not included in GDP.
7. **False**. Labor income (wages, salaries, and fringe benefits) is the largest component of income.
8. **False**. GDP is measured by counting value added, not final sales.
9. **True**. GDP is the same however it is measured.
10. **False**. Most saving is done by the middle-aged. The young and the old either save very little or dissave.
11. **False**. When there is a budget deficit, as has been the case for the United States, the government dissaves.
12. **False**. Nominal GDP grows faster than real GDP if there is inflation.
13. **False**. Buying stocks is not a form of investment, and therefore is not part of GDP.
14. **True**. Revisions to GDP can be quite large.
15. **False**. Many other factors, such as life expectancy, infant mortality, and environmental quality, measure how a country is performing over time.

Short-Answer Questions

1. The location determines GDP. The ownership is irrelevant.
2. The spending approach measures the total amount that people spend on goods and services.
3. Residential investment provides long-term services, and so it is counted with investment rather than consumption.
4. Imports need to be subtracted when computing GDP because they are included in consumption and investment spending, but they are not produced in the United States.
5. In the income approach, the income received by workers and businesses for producing the goods that make up GDP is added up.
6. Net investment equals gross investment minus depreciation.
7. In the production approach, the production of each firm or industry in the economy is added up.
8. Counting value added avoids double-counting goods that are final goods for one firm but intermediate goods for another.
9. When there is inflation, GDP increases even if production is unchanged.
10. Real GDP adjusts nominal GDP for changing prices.
11. The GDP deflator, the measure of the price level that is used to compute real GDP, equals nominal GDP divided by real GDP.
12. By using fixed weights that do not allow quantities to change when prices change, the CPI puts too much weight on items with rising prices and too little weight on items with falling prices.
13. The purchasing power parity exchange rate should be used when making international comparisons of GDP.
14. Home production and illegal activities are not recorded in markets, and so they cannot be counted as part of GDP.
15. Goods whose quality is improving rapidly over time, such as personal computers, cause problems in measuring GDP.

SOLUTIONS TO THE PRACTICE PROBLEMS

1. a. Net exports (X) = saving (S) - investment (I). Using the values:

    $X = \$1,000 - \$2,000 = -\$1,000$

    Since net exports are negative, there is a trade deficit.

    b. The formula for GDP is $Y = C + I + G + X$. Using the values:

    $Y = \$6,000 + \$2,000 + \$1,000 - \$1,000 = \$8,000$ billion

2. a. Investment (I) = saving (S) - net exports (X). Using the values:

    $I = \$4,000 - \$2,000 = \$2,000$ billion

    b. The formula for GDP is $Y = C + I + G + X$. Using the values:

    $Y = \$4,000 + \$2,000 + \$1,000 + \$2,000 = \$9,000$ billion

3. Nominal GDP = GDP deflator × real GDP. Using the values, nominal GDP = \$5,400 in the year 2000, \$6,000 in the year 2001, and \$6,600 in the year 2002. Because of inflation, nominal GDP is growing even though real GDP is constant.

4. Real GDP = nominal GDP/GDP deflator. Using the values, real GDP = \$6,400 in the year 2000, \$6,800 in the year 2001, and \$7,200 in the year 2002. With constant prices, there is no inflation. Real and nominal GDP grow at the same rate.

ANSWERS TO THE CHAPTER TEST

1. b	6. c	11. c	16. b
2. a	7. b	12. a	17. c
3. d	8. c	13. a	18. d
4. c	9. b	14. b	19. a
5. d	10. d	15. d	20. c

(CHAPTERS 5, 6)
Introduction to Macroeconomics

1. Real GDP is
   a. a measure of the economy's potential.
   b. the amount of all goods and services produced during a specific time period adjusted for the general increase in prices.
   c. another term for inflation.
   d. the total of all goods and services produced during a specific time period.

2. Economic growth describes
   a. increases in inflation.
   b. increases in GDP.
   c. increases in interest rates.
   d. increases in real GDP.

3. There was an economic growth slowdown for the United States because economic growth
   a. was higher from the mid-1930s to the mid-1950s than it was from the mid-1950s to the mid-1970s
   b. was higher from the mid-1940s to the mid-1960s than it was from the mid-1960s to the mid-1980s
   c. was higher from the mid-1950s to the mid-1970s than it was from the mid-1970s to the mid-1990s
   d. was higher from the mid-1970s to the mid-1980s than it was from the mid-1980s to the mid-1990s

4. Economic fluctuations are also called
   a. business cycles.
   b. recessions.
   c. expansions.
   d. recoveries.

5. A depression is
   a. a moderate expansion.
   b. a very large recession.
   c. a moderate recession.
   d. a very large expansion.

6. Which of the following groups of people are *not* considered part of the labor force?
   a. People who are unemployed
   b. People who are working part time
   c. People who are *not* working and are looking for work
   d. People who are not working and are *not* looking for work

7. Inflation
   a. increases during booms and recoveries and decreases in recessions.
   b. increases during booms and decreases in recessions and recoveries.
   c. increases during recessions and decreases in booms and recoveries.
   d. increases during booms and recessions and decreases in recoveries.

8. The real interest rate is the interest rate minus the
   a. the unemployment rate.
   b. expected rate of employment.
   c. inflation rate.
   d. expected rate of inflation.

9. Potential GDP
   a. is the same as real GDP.
   b. is always above real GDP.
   c. is the average or normal level of real GDP.
   d. is the maximum attainable level of real GDP.

10. Which of the following does *not* determine aggregate supply?
    a. Labor
    b. Demand
    c. Capital
    d. Technology

11. Which of the following would *not* be included in the measurement of GDP for the United States?
    a. Legal and health-care services
    b. Computer and software products
    c. New Ford Broncos produced in Germany
    d. New Honda Accords produced in the United States

12. The three ways to measure GDP are the
    a. spending, income, and consumption approaches.
    b. spending, income, and investment approaches.
    c. spending, income, and government purchases approaches.
    d. spending, income and net exports approaches.
    e. spending, income and production approaches.

13. The spending approach to calculating GDP divides spending into four categories:
    a. consumption, investment, government purchases, and net exports.
    b. consumption, investment, government purchases, and net imports.
    c. consumption, investment, government imports, and exports.
    d. consumption, investment, income, and net exports.

14. For a hypothetical economy in a given year, consumption equaled $355, investment equaled $124, government spending equaled $175, exports equaled $65, and imports equaled $59. What was the value of GDP?
    a. $654
    b. $660
    c. $719
    d. $778

15. National income
    a. is the sum of labor income and capital income.
    b. is the sum of labor income and personal income.
    c. is the sum of capital income and personal income.
    d. equals personal income.

16. Measuring GDP by production involves counting the
    a. final sales of each firm's output.
    b. value added of each firm's output.
    c. income of each firm's output.
    d. depreciation of each firm's output.

17. When a government's expenditures are less than the government's receipts from taxes,
    a. the government dissaves.
    b. there is a budget deficit.
    c. there is a budget surplus.
    d. there is a balanced budget.

18. If there is inflation,
    a. nominal GDP grows faster than real GDP.
    b. nominal GDP grows faster than the GDP deflator.
    c. real GDP grows faster than nominal GDP.
    d. nominal GDP and real GDP grow at the same rate.

19. The measure of the price level that measures the price of a fixed collection of consumer goods and services in a year compared to some base year is
    a. the GDP deflator.
    b. the chain weight price index.
    c. the purchasing power parity exchange rate.
    d. the consumer price index.

20. The purchasing power parity exchange rate
    a. is the same as the market exchange rate.
    b. is the amount of foreign currency required to buy the same amount of goods that can be bought with one dollar.
    c. is the exchange rate minus the rate of inflation.
    d. is the exchange rate minus the domestic interest rate.

Answers

1. b	5. b	9. c	13. a	17. c
2. d	6. d	10. b	14. b	18. a
3. c	7. b	11. c	15. a	19. d
4. a	8. d	12. d	16. b	20. d

PART 3

Long-Run Fundamentals and Economic Growth

We introduced a large number of macroeconomic concepts in part 2, and now we begin to analyze and understand these concepts. In order to abstract from the complications inherent in short-run economic fluctuations, we first study the economy in the long run. Chapter 7 focuses on unemployment and employment. It considers why unemployment in normal times is so high, and it introduces the natural employment rate. Chapter 8 discusses investment and the interest rate and shows how GDP can be divided into consumption, investment, government, and net exports shares.

Economic growth holds the key to economic well-being. Economic growth theory helps us understand why the standard of living has increased dramatically in the United States over the last two centuries and also to understand why the gap between rich and poor nations has not narrowed over the last 30 years. Increasing labor productivity is the key to increasing economic growth. In Chapter 9, we study the aggregate production function and the growth accounting formula and see how technological progress is necessary to understand the dramatic economic growth over the past two centuries.

Chapter 10 describes the monetary system. In the first part of the chapter, we learn about the functions of money, how it is defined, and the role of banks in creating money. Then we study the quantity equation, the relationship between money growth and inflation, the Philips curve, the relationship between inflation and unemployment, and the effects of inflation on productivity growth.

CHAPTER 7

Unemployment and Employment

CHAPTER OVERVIEW

In normal times, when the economy is neither in a boom nor in a recession, the unemployment rate is about 6 percent. Why are over 7 million workers unemployed on any given day in the United States? This chapter examines the causes of unemployment and explains why the natural unemployment rate, unemployment in normal times, seems so high. We first study measures and trends in employment and unemployment, how the two concepts are defined, and how patterns of employment and unemployment are evolving over time. We then focus on the nature of unemployment—who becomes unemployed and for how long. You will then learn about the determination of employment and unemployment, how economic theory can explain unemployment, and why the unemployment rate is always greater than zero. The experience of Europe, where the long-term unemployment rate is over 10 percent, is contrasted with that of the United States. We focus on the determinants of the natural unemployment rate in this chapter and consider unemployment resulting from recessions when we study economic fluctuations.

CHAPTER REVIEW

1. The **natural unemployment rate** is the rate of unemployment when the economy is in normal times, neither in a recession nor in a boom, and real GDP is equal to potential GDP. The natural unemployment rate is not a constant, and economists do not know its precise value. For the United States, it is now somewhere near 6 percent, up from about 5 percent in the 1950s. Some economists believe that the natural unemployment rate has been falling and is actually now around 5.5 percent. For some European countries, the natural unemployment rate is now about 10 percent or even higher. Unemployment above the natural rate during and immediately following recessions, such as occurred in the United States during 1990–1992, is called **cyclical unemployment**.

2. There are two aspects of unemployment in normal times. **Frictional unemployment** occurs as workers either change jobs or enter the labor force and are unemployed for a time until they find work. Most frictional unemployment is short term. In contrast, **structural unemployment** occurs when workers are unemployed for a long time, six months or more, either because they have insufficient skills or because shifts in tastes or technology cause their skills to no longer be in demand.

3. Understanding how to measure unemployment requires learning a few definitions. The **working-age population** consists of those people age 16 and above (and not in jail or in a hospital). Out of the working-age population, you are *employed* if you have a job, *unemployed* if you do not have a job and are looking for work, and *not in the* **labor force** if you do not have a job and are not looking for work. In the United States, employment and unemployment are measured by the **current population survey**.

4. Some of these definitions can get tricky. You are counted as employed if you have a job outside the home or a paid job inside the home, but not if you have an unpaid job inside the home. You are also counted as employed if you are a **part-time worker**, working as little as 1 hour per week. On the other hand, *discouraged workers*, who have stopped looking for work because they cannot find a job, are out of the labor force and are not counted as unemployed. Full-time college students, who are not employed and are not looking for work, are also neither employed nor unemployed; they are out of the labor force.

5. The **unemployment rate** is the ratio of unemployed workers to the labor force. Although the natural unemployment rate has been fairly steady for the United States, the unemployment rate has fluctuated, reaching a post-World War II high of about 10 percent in 1982 following the 1981–1982 recession. The **labor force participation rate** is the ratio of people in the labor force to the working-age population. It has increased from about 62 percent in the mid-1970s to about 66 percent now, mainly because of more women entering the labor force. The **employment-to-population ratio** is the ratio of employed workers to the working-age population. It has increased from about 57 percent in 1976 to about 62 percent in 1993, again mainly because of more women in the labor force.

6. **Aggregate hours**, the total number of hours worked by all workers, is the most comprehensive measure of labor input to the production of real GDP. Aggregate hours are the number of hours worked per employed worker times the number of employed workers. When the total number of hours worked is measured, rather than, as with employment, the total number of employed workers, part-time workers do not count as much as full-time workers. Aggregate hours grew at about 1 percent per year in the 1980s, and that growth rate is expected to continue in the 1990s.

7. Why do people become unemployed? The many reasons can be divided into three broad categories. **Job losers** are people who have lost their previous job, **job leavers** are those who have quit their previous job, and **new entrants** and re-entrants have either just entered the labor force or are re-entering the labor force and are looking for work. **Seasonal unemployment** is the increase in unemployment each June, when students graduate and enter the labor force, as well as the decrease in unemployment around the holiday season, when many employers hire extra workers.

8. **Job vacancies** are the jobs that firms are trying to fill. Unemployment and job vacancies can exist simultaneously because the available jobs may require different skills, be at a different location, or pay lower wages than the former jobs of the unemployed workers.

9. When we think about unemployment, we view long-term structural unemployment very differently from the short-term unemployment associated with changing jobs. About 50 percent of unemployment is very short term, less than 5 weeks. Another 35 percent of unemployed workers have been unemployed for between 5 weeks and 6 months, and the remaining 15 percent have been unemployed for more than 6 months—the truly long-term unemployed.

10. Unemployment rates are very different for different groups of people in the United States. Unemployment is lowest for adult men and women, and is very high for teenagers. In 1996, with the overall unemployment rate equal to 5.4 percent, the unemployment rate for teenagers was about 18 percent and the unemployment rate for black teenagers was nearly 37 percent.

ZEROING IN

1. What determines employment and unemployment? A good starting point is to look at the demand for labor and the supply of labor. In Figure 7.1, the real wage (the price of labor) is on the vertical axis and the quantity of labor (measured by employment) is on the horizontal axis. The labor supply curve describes the behavior of workers; it is upward-sloping because workers are willing to supply more labor if the real wage (what they receive for working) is higher. The labor demand curve describes the behavior of firms; it is downward-sloping because firms are willing to hire more workers if the real wage (the cost of labor) is lower. The intersection of the labor supply curve and the labor demand curve determines the equilibrium real wage that equates the quantity of labor supplied with the quantity of labor demanded.

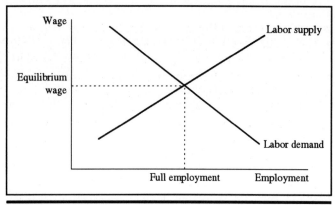

Figure 7.1

2. What is wrong with Figure 7.1? The intersection of the labor supply curve and the labor demand curve determines employment, but what about unemployment? According to the figure, there should be no unemployment, a prediction contrary to the facts. There are several explanations for why the unemployment rate is always greater than zero.

   a. **Job rationing** is a situation in which workers are willing to take jobs at the wage that firms are paying, but there are not enough jobs available at that wage. Job rationing is illustrated in Figure 7.2. Suppose that the wage is higher than the wage that would equate the quantity of labor supplied with the quantity of labor demanded. At this wage, the number of workers demanded by firms, at A, is smaller than the number of workers willing to supply their labor, at B, and there is unemployment. The amount of unemployment is measured by the horizontal distance between the labor supply curve and the labor demand curve at the given wage, shown by the distance between A and B.

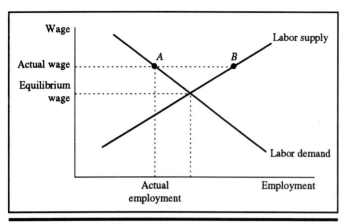

Figure 7.2

b. The job rationing story raises several questions. Why is the wage always too high to produce zero unemployment? Moreover, why doesn't the wage fall when there is unemployment? In most markets, a situation of excess supply causes the price to fall. Since the wage is the price of labor, and there is an excess supply of labor, why doesn't the wage fall by enough to equate the quantity of labor supplied with the quantity of labor demanded? Economists have proposed several explanations for why the wage might always be above the wage at the intersection of the labor supply curve and the labor demand curve.

c. The **minimum wage** is the lowest possible wage that employers can legally pay their employees. If the minimum wage is too high, it could price unskilled workers, such as many teenagers, out of the market, causing unemployment. **Insiders** versus **outsiders** is the theory that sometimes groups of workers who have jobs—the insiders—can prevent the wage from declining and thus prevent firms from hiring unemployed workers—the outsiders—at a lower wage. Labor unions and legislation preventing firms from firing workers without significant legal costs could create this situation. The theory of an **efficiency wage** is that firms will choose to pay workers an extra amount to encourage them to be more productive or efficient. Turnover will be lower when workers are paid more, and there will be less shirking. With efficiency wages, workers are paid more than the wage that equates the quantity of labor supplied with the quantity of labor demanded, and there is unemployment.

d. **Job search** is the second explanation for why unemployment is greater than zero. The labor market is never characterized by the static supply and demand curves in Figure 7.1. There is constant job creation and job destruction, and the curves are always shifting. In such a situation, some people will always be searching for a job. It is not necessarily to their advantage to take the first job that comes along, and they may turn down offers in the hope of finding a higher-paying job. While they are searching for a job, they are unemployed.

ACTIVE REVIEW

Fill-in Questions

1. The _____ is the rate of unemployment when the economy is in normal times.

2. Unemployment above the natural rate is called _____ unemployment.

3. Unemployment in normal times can be divided into _____ and _____ unemployment.

4. If you are part of the working-age population, you are classified as either _____, _____, or _____.

5. People who have stopped looking for work because they cannot find a job are called _____ workers.

6. The _____ is the ratio of unemployed workers to the labor force.

7. The _____ is the ratio of people in the labor force to the working-age population.

8. The _____ is the ratio of employed workers to the working-age population.

9. _____ is the total number of hours worked by all workers.

10. People who become unemployed are either _____, _____, or _____.

11. _____ are the jobs that firms are trying to fill.

12. The _____ is the price of labor.

13. Two explanations for why the unemployment rate is always greater than zero are _____ and _____.

14. The _____ is the lowest possible wage that employers can pay their employees.

15. The theory of _____ is that firms will choose to pay workers an extra amount to encourage them to be more productive.

True-False Questions

T   F   1. In normal times, the unemployment rate for the United States is about 6 percent.

T   F   2. Frictional and structural unemployment both occur during normal times.

T   F   3. If you are of working age, you are classified as either employed or unemployed.

T   F   4. If you are working part time but looking for a full-time job, you are classified as unemployed.

T   F   5. The unemployment rate fluctuates more than the natural unemployment rate.

T   F   6. Aggregate hours have been falling since 1980.

T   F   7. When a new college graduate begins to look for a job, she is counted as unemployed until she finds work.

T   F   8. Most unemployed workers stay unemployed for more than one year.

T   F   9. Since long-term unemployment represents only about 15 percent of unemployment, it is not a matter of concern for policymakers.

T   F   10. Unemployment rates are similar for different groups of people in the United States.

T   F   11. The natural unemployment rate is higher for most European countries than for the United States.

T   F   12. The intersection of the labor supply curve and the labor demand curve provides a good explanation of unemployment.

T   F   13. With job rationing, workers are unwilling to accept jobs at the prevailing wage.

T   F   14. The minimum wage is the wage paid to the lowest-paid worker in the firm.

T   F   15. Unemployment can be caused by job rationing or job search, but not both.

Short-Answer Questions

1. The unemployment rate for the United States in 1994 was about 6 percent. What was cyclical unemployment?

2. What is the difference between frictional and structural unemployment?

3. What is the difference between being unemployed and not being in the labor force?

4. Why are discouraged workers not counted as unemployed?

5. Why have the labor force participation rate and the employment-to-population ratio increased from the mid-1970s to today?

6. Why are aggregate hours a better measure of labor input to the production of real GDP than employment?

7. What is the difference between job losers and job leavers?

8. How can there be unemployment and job vacancies at the same time?

9. How is unemployment divided among short-term, medium-term, and long-term unemployment?

10. Describe the overall unemployment rate, the unemployment rate for teenagers, and the unemployment rate for black teenagers in 1996.

11. What is job rationing?

12. According to the job rationing story, why is the wage rate always above the wage at the intersection of the labor supply curve and the labor demand curve?

13. What is the insiders versus outsiders explanation for why wages don't fall when there is unemployment?

14. If workers are paid efficiency wages, why is there unemployment?

15. According to the job search explanation, why is there unemployment?

WORKING IT OUT

1. We have defined aggregate hours to be:

   Aggregate hours = (hours per employed worker) × (employment).

   Since employment, the number of employed workers, can be written as:

   Employment = (employment-to-population ratio) × (working-age population),

   we can rewrite our definition of aggregate hours:

   Aggregate hours = (hours per employed worker) × (employment-to-population ratio) ×

   (working-age population).

   We can use data on these three variables to compute aggregate hours and employment, and see how they change over time. If hours per employed worker are constant, aggregate hours will grow at the rate as employment. If hours per employed worker are increasing, aggregate hours will grow faster than employment. If hours per employed worker are decreasing, aggregate hours will grow more slowly than employment.

2. The job rationing explanation for unemployment can be illustrated by using numbers and graphs. Suppose you are given the following data on the labor demand curve and the labor supply curve:

Labor Demand Curve		Labor Supply Curve	
Wage	Employment	Wage	Employment
10	180	10	220
9	190	9	210
8	200	8	200
7	210	7	190
6	220	6	180

where wages are in dollars per hour and employment is in millions of workers.

a. The first step is to determine the equilibrium wage and the level of full employment. As shown in Figure 7.3, the labor demand curve is downward-sloping and the labor supply curve is upward-sloping. The equilibrium wage, determined by the intersection of the labor demand curve and the labor supply curve, is the wage that equates the quantity of labor supplied and the quantity of labor demanded, or the wage at which employment is equal on the two curves. At the intersection of the two curves, the wage is $8 per hour and full employment is 200 million.

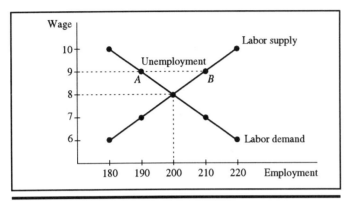

Figure 7.3

b. Now suppose that the actual wage is $9 per hour. This wage, as shown in Figure 7.3, is too high to produce full employment. The actual level of employment is the quantity of labor demanded, which is determined by the labor demand curve and is 190 million. The quantity of labor supplied, determined by the labor supply curve, is 210 million. Unemployment is the difference between the quantity of labor supplied and the quantity of labor demanded. It is the horizontal distance between *A* and *B* and equals 20 million. Note that unemployment is the difference between the quantity of labor supplied and the quantity of labor demanded at the given wage, not the difference between the quantity of labor demanded at the given wage and the level of full employment at the equilibrium wage.

Worked Problems

1. Suppose you are given the following data:

Year	Hours per Employed Worker	Employment-to-Population Ratio	Working-Age Population
2000	1,700	.60	200
2010	1,800	.70	210

where hours per employed worker are for the year and the working-age population is in millions.

a. Calculate employment and aggregate hours for the years 2000 and 2010.

b. Calculate the growth rate of aggregate hours and employment. Are aggregate hours growing faster than, slower than, or at the same rate as employment?

Answers

a. *Employment = (employment-to-population ratio) × (working-age population). In the year 2000, employment = (.60) × (200) = 120 million. In 2010, employment = (.70) × (210) = 147 million. Aggregate hours = (hours per employed worker) × (employment). In the year 2000, aggregate hours = (1,700) × (120) = 204,000 million, or 204 billion. In 2010, aggregate hours = (1800) × (147) = 264,600 million, or 264.6 billion.*

b. *The growth rate of aggregate hours for the decade between 2000 and 2010 is (264.6 - 204)/204 = .297, or 29.7 percent. The growth rate of employment is (147 - 120)/120 = .225, or 22.5 percent. Because hours per employed worker are increasing, aggregate hours are growing faster than employment.*

2. Suppose you are given the following data:

Labor Demand Curve		Labor Supply Curve	
Wage	**Employment**	**Wage**	**Employment**
10	130	10	205
9	140	9	190
8	150	8	175
7	160	7	160
6	170	6	145

where wages are in dollars per hour and employment is in millions of workers. Graph the labor demand curve and the labor supply curve. What are the equilibrium wage and the level of full employment? If the actual wage equals $9 per hour, what is the level of unemployment?

Answer

The labor demand curve and the labor supply curve are graphed in Figure 7.4, with the labor demand curve downward-sloping and the labor supply curve upward-sloping. The equilibrium wage, determined at the intersection of the labor demand curve and the labor supply curve, is $7 per hour, and full employment is 160 million workers. If the actual wage equals $9 per hour, unemployment is the difference between the quantity of labor supplied and the quantity of labor demanded, and equals 50 million workers.

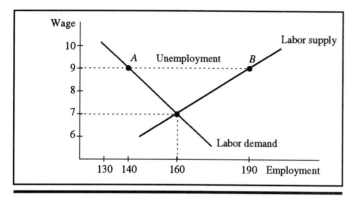

Figure 7.4

Practice Problems

1. Suppose you are given the following data:

Year	Hours per Employed Worker	Employment-to-Population Ratio	Working-Age Population
2000	1,500	.50	120
2010	1,400	.60	140

   where hours per employed worker are for the year and the working-age population is in millions.

   a. Calculate employment and aggregate hours for the years 2000 and 2010.

   b. Calculate the growth rate of aggregate hours and employment. Are aggregate hours growing faster than, slower than, or at the same rate as employment?

2. Suppose you are given the following data:

Year	Hours per Employed Worker	Employment-to-Population Ratio	Working-Age Population
2000	1,900	.55	170
2010	1,900	.65	180

where hours per employed worker are for the year and the working-age population is in millions.

a. Calculate employment and aggregate hours for the years 2000 and 2010.

b. Calculate the growth rate of aggregate hours and employment. Are aggregate hours growing faster, slower, or at the same rate as employment?

3. Suppose you are given the following data:

Labor Demand Curve		Labor Supply Curve	
Wage	Employment	Wage	Employment
10	125	10	150
9	140	9	140
8	155	8	130
7	170	7	120
6	185	6	110

where wages are in dollars per hour and employment is in millions of workers. Graph the labor demand curve and the labor supply curve. What are the equilibrium wage and the level of full employment? If the actual wage equals $10 per hour, what is the level of unemployment?

4. Suppose you are given the following data:

Labor Demand Curve		Labor Supply Curve	
Wage	Employment	Wage	Employment
10	210	10	270
9	220	9	260
8	230	8	250
7	240	7	240
6	250	6	230

where wages are in dollars per hour and employment is in millions of workers. Graph the labor demand curve and the labor supply curve. What are the equilibrium wage and the level of full employment? If the actual wage equals $7 per hour, what is the level of unemployment?

CHAPTER TEST

1. The natural rate of unemployment for the United States is about
   a. 0 percent.
   b. 4 percent.
   c. 6 percent.
   d. 10 percent.

2. The natural rate of unemployment is the rate of unemployment when the economy is
   a. in a recession.
   b. in a boom.
   c. in either a recession or a boom.
   d. in neither a recession nor a boom.

3. Unemployment that occurs during and immediately following a recession is called
   a. natural unemployment.
   b. cyclical unemployment.
   c. frictional unemployment.
   d. structural unemployment.

4. What are the two types of unemployment that occur in normal times?
   a. Frictional and structural unemployment
   b. Frictional and cyclical unemployment
   c. Structural and cyclical unemployment
   d. Cyclical and seasonal unemployment

5. Unemployment that occurs when workers either change jobs or enter the labor force is called
   a. structural unemployment.
   b. frictional unemployment.
   c. seasonal unemployment.
   d. cyclical unemployment.

6. Unemployment that occurs when workers have insufficient skills or their skills are no longer in demand is called
   a. structural unemployment.
   b. frictional unemployment.
   c. seasonal unemployment.
   d. cyclical unemployment.

7. Which of the following are considered part of the working-age population?
   a. People in jail
   b. People in the hospital
   c. People over the age of 16, but in school
   d. People under the age of 16

8. If an individual does not have a job but is looking for work, then he or she is considered
   a. a discouraged worker.
   b. not in the labor force.
   c. unemployed.
   d. employed.

9. An individual who has stopped looking for work because he or she cannot find a job is considered
   a. a discouraged worker.
   b. in the labor force.
   c. unemployed.
   d. employed.

10. The unemployment rate is
    a. the number of unemployed workers divided by the number of people in the working-age population.
    b. the number of unemployed workers divided by the number of people in the labor force.
    c. the number of people in the labor force divided by the number of people in the working-age population.
    d. the number of people in the working-age population divided by the number of people in the labor force.

11. The labor force participation rate is
    a. the number of unemployed workers divided by the number of people in the working-age population.
    b. the number of unemployed workers divided by the number of people in the labor force.
    c. the number of people in the labor force divided by the number of people in the working-age population.
    d. the number of people in the working-age population divided by the number of people in the labor force.

12. What percentage of unemployment is long-term unemployment?
    a. 15 percent
    b. 25 percent
    c. 35 percent
    d. 50 percent

13. The unemployment rate for teenagers in the United States is
    a. about the same as the unemployment rate for adults.
    b. lower than the unemployment rate for adults.
    c. about 6 percent.
    d. about 20 percent.

14. The labor supply curve
    a. describes the behavior of firms.
    b. describes the behavior of workers.
    c. is downward-sloping.
    d. is horizontal.

15. Which of the following is *not* an explanation for why the actual wage rate may always be above the equilibrium wage rate?
    a. The minimum wage
    b. Job vacancies
    c. The insiders versus outsiders theory
    d. The efficiency wages theory

Use the following table for questions 16 and 17.

Suppose you are given the following data:

Year	Hours per Employed Worker	Employment-to-Population Ratio	Working-Age Population
2000	1,000	.50	100
2010	1,200	.60	120

where hours per employed worker are for the year and the working-age population is in millions.

16. What is employment in the year 2000?
    a. 50 million
    b. 72 million
    c. 500 million
    d. 720 million

17. What are aggregate hours in the year 2010?
    a. 50 billion
    b. 60 billion
    c. 72 billion
    d. 86.4 billion

Use Figure 7.5 for questions 18 to 20.

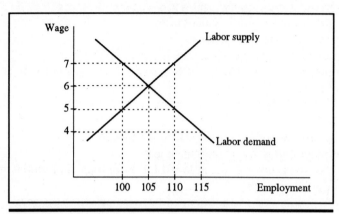

Figure 7.5

18. What is the equilibrium wage rate?
    a. $4 per hour
    b. $5 per hour
    c. $6 per hour
    d. $7 per hour

19. What is the level of full employment?
    a. 100 million
    b. 105 million
    c. 110 million
    d. 115 million

20. If the actual wage equals $7, what is the level of unemployment?
    a. 0 million
    b. 5 million
    c. 10 million
    d. 15 million

ANSWERS TO THE REVIEW QUESTIONS

Fill-in Questions

1. natural unemployment rate
2. cyclical
3. frictional; structural
4. employed; unemployed; not in the labor force
5. discouraged
6. unemployment rate
7. labor force participation rate
8. employment-to-population ratio
9. Aggregate hours
10. job losers; job leavers; new entrants and re-entrants
11. Job vacancies
12. real wage
13. job rationing; job search
14. minimum wage
15. efficiency wages

True-False Questions

1. **True**. The natural unemployment rate for the United States is 6 percent.
2. **True**. They are the two parts of the natural unemployment rate.
3. **False**. You can also be classified as not in the labor force.
4. **False**. You are counted as employed if you are working, whether part or full time.
5. **True**. Although the natural unemployment rate is fairly steady, the unemployment rate fluctuates over the business cycle.
6. **False**. Aggregate hours grew at about 1 percent per year in the 1980s, and that growth rate is expected to continue in the 1990s.
7. **True**. She would be a new entrant and would be classified as unemployed.
8. **False**. About 85 percent of unemployment is for six months or less.
9. **False**. When 15 percent of 7 million workers are unemployed for more than six months, it is a matter of great concern for policymakers.
10. **False**. Unemployment is lowest for adult men and women, and is very high for teenagers.
11. **True**. The natural unemployment rate is over 10 percent for most European countries, compared with 6 percent for the United States.
12. **False**. At the intersection of the labor supply and labor demand curves, there is no unemployment, a prediction that is contrary to the facts.
13. **False**. Under job rationing, workers are willing to accept jobs at the prevailing wage, but not enough are available.
14. **False**. The minimum wage is the lowest possible wage that employers can legally pay their employees.
15. **False**. The job rationing and job search explanations are complementary. Unemployment can be caused by either or both.

Short-Answer Questions

1. Since the natural unemployment rate for the United States is also about 6 percent, cyclical unemployment was zero in 1994.
2. Frictional unemployment occurs when workers either change jobs or enter the labor force. Structural unemployment occurs when workers are unemployed for a long time.
3. You are unemployed if you do not have a job and are looking for work. You are not in the labor force if you do not have a job and are not looking for work.
4. Discouraged workers have stopped looking for work, and so they are not in the labor force.
5. The increase in both statistics is mainly due to more women entering the labor force.
6. In computing aggregate hours, unlike employment, part-time workers do not count as much as full-time workers.
7. Job losers are people who have lost their previous job; job leavers are people who have quit their previous job.
8. Unemployment and job vacancies can exist simultaneously because the available jobs may require different skills, be at a different location, or pay lower wages than the former jobs of the unemployed workers.
9. About 50 percent of unemployment is for less than 5 weeks, another 35 percent is for between 5 weeks and 6 months, and the remaining 15 percent is for more than 6 months.
10. The overall unemployment rate was 5.4 percent, the unemployment rate for teenagers was about 18 percent, and the unemployment rate for black teenagers was nearly 37 percent in 1996.
11. Job rationing is a situation in which workers are willing to take jobs at the wage that firms are paying, but there are not enough jobs available at that wage.

12. Minimum wage laws, insiders versus outsiders, and efficiency wages are several explanations of why wages are too high to produce zero unemployment.

13. The insiders versus outsiders explanation is that sometimes groups of workers who have jobs—the insiders—can prevent the wage from declining and thus prevent firms from hiring unemployed workers—the outsiders—at a lower wage.

14. With efficiency wages, workers are paid more than the wage that equates the quantity of labor supplied with the quantity of labor demanded, and so there is unemployment.

15. With constant job creation and job destruction, there will always be people searching for jobs, and they are counted as unemployed while they are looking.

SOLUTIONS TO THE PRACTICE PROBLEMS

1. a. In the year 2000, employment = (.50) × (120) = 60 million. In 2010, employment = (.60) × (140) = 84 million. Aggregate hours in the year 2000 = (1,500) × (60) = 90,000 million, or 90 billion. In 2010, aggregate hours = (1,400) × (84) = 117,600 million, or 117.6 billion.

    b. The growth rate of aggregate hours = 30.6 percent. The growth rate of employment = 40 percent. Because hours per employed worker are decreasing, aggregate hours are growing more slowly than employment.

2. a. In the year 2000, employment = (.55) × (170) = 93.5 million. In 2010, employment = (.65) × (180) = 117 million. Aggregate hours in the year 2000 = (1,900) × (93.5) = 177,650 million, or 177.65 billion. In 2010, aggregate hours = (1,900) × (117) = 222,300 million, or 222.3 billion.

    b. The growth rate of both aggregate hours and employment = 25.1 percent. Because hours per employed worker are constant, aggregate hours are growing at the same rate as employment.

3. The labor demand curve and the labor supply curve are graphed in Figure 7.6. The equilibrium wage is $9 per hour, and full employment is 140 million workers. If the actual wage equals $10 per hour, unemployment equals 25 million workers.

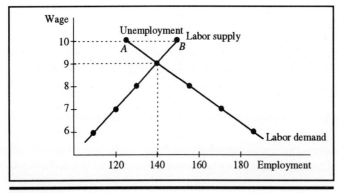

Figure 7.6

4. The labor demand curve and the labor supply curve are graphed in Figure 7.7. The equilibrium wage is $7 per hour, and full employment is 240 million workers. If the actual wage also equals $7 per hour, there is zero unemployment.

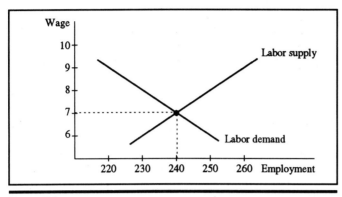

Figure 7.7

ANSWERS TO THE CHAPTER TEST

1. c	6. a	11. c	16. a
2. d	7. c	12. a	17. d
3. b	8. c	13. d	18. c
4. a	9. a	14. b	19. b
5. b	10. b	15. b	20. c

CHAPTER 8

Investment in New Capital

CHAPTER OVERVIEW

Increasing labor productivity is the key to raising long-run economic growth and improving living standards. Raising employment, as we saw in Chapter 7, increases real GDP but does not affect productivity. In order to improve productivity, we must either increase capital, the subject of this chapter, or increase technological know-how, which we will discuss in the next chapter. How is capital increased? Capital is the accumulation of past investment, and so we focus on the causes of investment in order to understand capital accumulation. We study investment as a share of GDP and learn how the interest rate affects consumption, investment, and net exports. We then learn how to determine the equilibrium interest rate and see how changes in government purchases and shifts in consumption affect investment. We consider the appropriate size of the government and see how the size of the government is related to economic growth.

CHAPTER REVIEW

1. **Capital** is the factories, equipment, and other productive resources used to produce the goods and services that make up real GDP. **Investment** consists of purchases of goods by businesses for use in production and purchases of new residences by households. In order for capital to increase, there must be investment.

2. *Gross investment* is the actual amount of purchases of new goods by businesses each year. *Depreciation* is the amount of capital that wears out each year. *Net investment* is gross investment minus depreciation. When we use the term *investment* or the symbol *I*, we mean gross investment, and it is gross investment that is included in GDP. It is only net investment, however, that is added to the stock of capital.

3. **Public infrastructure investment** consists of government purchases, such as highways and schools, that contribute to the economy's productive potential. Although public infrastructure investment is classified as part of government purchases instead of part of investment, it is an important component of capital accumulation. A central feature of the economic plan that contributed to President Clinton's election in 1992 was an increase in public infrastructure investment. *Gross private domestic investment* is a more specific term for investment that makes it clear that *I* does not include public infrastructure investment.

4. The **consumption share** of GDP is consumption C divided by GDP, or C/Y. It is the proportion of GDP that is used for consumption. The consumption share is negatively related to the interest rate. A higher interest rate encourages saving, decreasing consumption.

5. The **investment share** of GDP is investment I divided by GDP, or I/Y. It is the proportion of GDP that is used for investment. The investment share is also negatively related to the interest rate. A higher interest rate increases the cost of borrowing, making it more expensive for a firm to build a new factory or buy a new computer. When mortgage interest rates rise, it becomes more expensive to purchase new houses, and so the residential component of investment falls. The investment share is more sensitive to interest rates than the consumption share.

6. The **net exports share** of GDP is net exports X divided by GDP, or X/Y. It is the proportion of GDP that is used for net exports. The net exports share is also negatively related to the interest rate. A higher interest rate in the United States raises the exchange rate because it makes dollar-denominated assets more attractive than foreign assets. The higher exchange rate makes domestic goods more expensive and foreign goods cheaper, reducing exports and increasing imports. With lower exports and higher imports, net exports, which are exports minus imports, decline. Thus a higher interest rate decreases net exports. The net exports share is also more sensitive to interest rates than the consumption share. The net exports share can be positive, zero, or negative. When the net exports share is positive, there is a trade surplus. When the net exports share is negative, there is a trade deficit.

7. The **government purchases share** of GDP is government purchases G divided by GDP, or G/Y. It is the proportion of GDP that is used for government purchases. Since government purchases are not affected by the interest rate, the government purchases share is not related to the interest rate.

8. The *nongovernment share* of GDP is the sum of the consumption, investment, and net exports shares. The nongovernment share is negatively related to the interest rate because each of its components, the consumption, investment, and net exports shares, is negatively related to the interest rate. The interest rate adjusts to ensure that the government and nongovernment shares add up to 100 percent of GDP. Equivalently, the interest rate adjusts to ensure that the sum of the consumption, investment, government purchases, and net exports shares equals 1.

9. The *real interest rate* is the nominal interest rate, the interest rate on loans, minus the expected inflation rate. It is the real interest rate, not the nominal interest rate, that determines how real GDP is divided among consumption, investment, government purchases, and net exports. In addition, it is important to remember that it takes time for consumers and firms to completely respond to a change in the interest rate. The division of real GDP into shares is applicable to the long run, three years or more, not to short-run fluctuations.

10. When the government purchases share of GDP increases, the nongovernment share decreases by the same amount. Since the nongovernment share is negatively related to the interest rate, the interest rate must rise. Furthermore, since each component of the nongovernment share is negatively related to the interest rate, the consumption, investment, and net exports shares all fall. The decline in investment resulting from an increase in government purchases is called **crowding out**. The process is reversed when the government purchases share of GDP decreases. The interest rate falls, and the consumption, investment, and net exports shares rise.

11. What is the appropriate size of the government? Although economics cannot completely answer that question, there are economic growth arguments for both smaller and larger government. Some economists argue that the smaller the government, the better. A higher government share lowers the investment share, reducing capital formation and decreasing long-term economic growth. Others believe that public infrastructure investment—roads, education, etc.—is essential for economic growth and that spending on public infrastructure investment should be increased.

12. The size of the government is determined by both economic and political factors. The 1960s and 1970s saw a substantial increase in the size of the government. The 1980 election of President Reagan was in part due to a reaction against this increase and a widespread belief that, except for defense, the government was spending too much. The trend appeared to shift again with President Clinton's election in 1992, given his emphasis on public infrastructure investment. It is not clear, however, how much the trend has really shifted. Between concern over the deficit and preoccupation with health-care reform, no plan to increase public-sector investment has been approved by Congress.

ZEROING IN

1. The division of real GDP between government and nongovernment shares and the determination of the **equilibrium interest rate** are two of the most important topics in this chapter. We now focus on using graphs to further our understanding.

   a. The consumption, investment, and net exports shares are depicted in Figure 8.1. The real interest rate is on the vertical axis, and the shares, as a percent of GDP, are on the horizontal axis. Although all three are negatively related to the interest rate, the fact that consumption is less sensitive to the interest rate than investment and net exports is shown by the steeper slope of the consumption share line. Note that the consumption and investment shares are always positive, whereas the net exports share can be positive or negative.

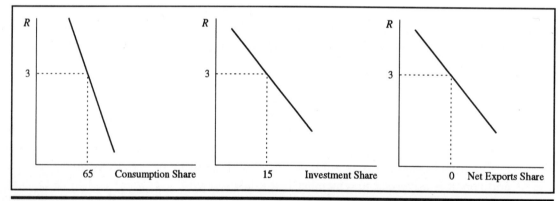

Figure 8.1

   b. The nongovernment share, which is determined by adding up the consumption, investment, and net exports shares, is illustrated in Figure 8.2. The nongovernment share depends negatively on the interest rate. Because the shares are expressed as a percent of GDP, the government purchases share, which is not shown, is 100 minus the nongovernment share. If the shares were expressed as fractions, the government purchases share would be 1 minus the nongovernment share.

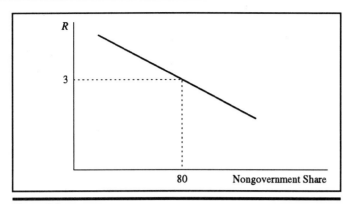

Figure 8.2

c. The equilibrium interest rate is determined by the division of GDP into the government purchases share and the nongovernment share. In Figure 8.2, a non-government share of 80 percent of GDP produces a real interest rate of 3 percent. Looking back at Figure 8.1, the 3 percent interest rate divides the nongovernment share into consumption, investment, and net exports shares.

2. What happens when the share of government purchases increases? As shown in Figure 8.3, an increase in the government purchases share of GDP from 20 to 25 percent lowers the nongovernment share from 80 to 75 percent. The smaller nongovernment share raises the real interest rate from 3 to 4 percent, reducing the consumption, investment, and net exports shares.

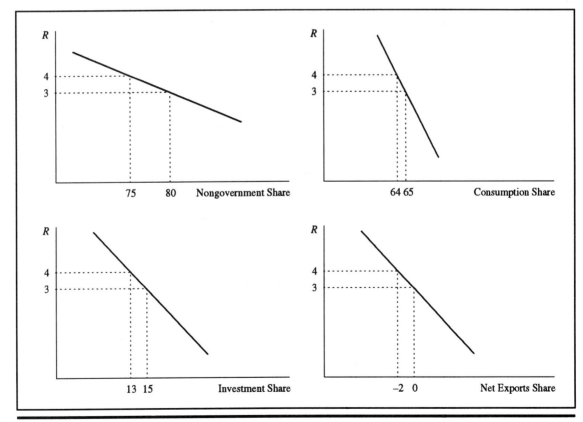

Figure 8.3

3. The saving investment approach is an alternative method of determining the equilibrium interest rate. The interest rate determined using the saving investment approach is exactly the same as that obtained by dividing GDP into shares.

   a. *National saving* is defined as aggregate income minus consumption minus government purchases, or

   $$S = Y - C - G$$

   The **national saving rate**, the ratio of national saving to GDP, is obtained by dividing both sides by Y,

   $$\frac{S}{Y} = 1 - \frac{C}{Y} - \frac{G}{Y}$$

   The national saving rate equals 1 minus the consumption share minus the government purchases share. When the interest rate rises, the national saving rate increases because the consumption share falls. Thus the national saving rate is positively related to the interest rate.

   b. From the identity $Y = C + I + G + X$, we know that national saving equals investment plus net exports,

   $$S = I + X$$

   An alternative expression for the national saving rate is obtained by dividing both sides by Y,

   $$\frac{S}{Y} = \frac{I}{Y} - \frac{X}{Y}$$

   The national saving rate equals the investment share plus the net exports share.

   c. The determination of the equilibrium interest rate is shown in Figure 8.4. The real interest rate is on the vertical axis, and the share of GDP (in percent) is on the horizontal axis. The line S/Y is upward-sloping because the national saving rate is positively related to the interest rate. The line $I/Y + X/Y$ is downward-sloping because both the investment share and the net exports share are negatively related to the interest rate. The intersection of the two lines, where the national saving rate equals the investment share plus the net exports share, determines the equilibrium interest rate.

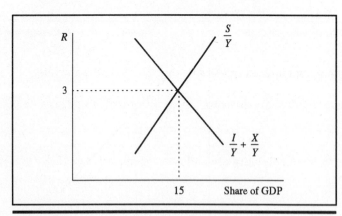

Figure 8.4

ACTIVE REVIEW

Fill-in Questions

1. _____ is the factories, equipment, and other productive resources used to produce the goods and services that constitute real GDP.

2. Purchases of goods by businesses for use in production and purchases of new residences by households are called _____.

3. _____ is the actual amount of purchases of new goods by businesses each year.

4. _____ is the amount of capital that wears out each year.

5. Gross investment minus depreciation is _____.

6. _____ investment consists of government purchases that contribute to the economy's productive potential.

7. Investment is also called _____ investment.

8. The _____ of GDP is consumption divided by GDP.

9. The investment share of GDP is _____ related to the interest rate.

10. The net exports share of GDP can be _____, _____, or _____.

11. The _____ of GDP is the proportion of GDP that is used for government purchases.

12. The nongovernment share of GDP is the sum of the _____, _____, and _____ shares.

13. The _____ is the nominal interest rate minus the expected inflation rate.

14. The decline in investment caused by an increase in government purchases is called _____.

15. The _____ is the sum of the investment and net exports shares of GDP.

True-False Questions

T   F   1. In order for capital to increase, there must be investment.

T   F   2. All investment represents an addition to the capital stock.

T   F   3. Public infrastructure investment is part of gross, but not net, investment.

T   F   4. The consumption share of GDP is negatively related to the interest rate.

T   F   5. The investment share of GDP is negatively related to the interest rate.

T   F   6. The net exports share of GDP is negatively related to the interest rate.

T   F   7. The government purchases share of GDP is negatively related to the interest rate.

T   F   8. The nongovernment share of GDP is negatively related to the interest rate.

T   F   9. The nominal interest rate determines how real GDP is divided into shares.

T   F   10. Consumers and firms fully adjust their spending to changes in the real interest rate very quickly.

T   F   11. When the government purchases share of GDP rises, the nongovernment share falls by the same amount.

T   F   12. The decline in consumption resulting from an increase in government purchases is called crowding out.

T   F   13. After President Clinton was elected in 1992, Congress quickly passed a program to increase public-sector investment.

T   F   14. National saving equals income minus consumption.

T   F   15. The national saving rate is positively related to the interest rate.

Short-Answer Questions

1. What are the two major categories of investment?

2. What is the relationship among gross investment, net investment, and depreciation?

3. Which is included in GDP, gross or net investment?

4. What is gross private domestic investment?

5. Why is the consumption share of GDP less sensitive to interest rates than the investment and net exports shares?

6. Why does a higher interest rate in the United States raise the exchange rate?

7. What mechanism ensures that the sum of the consumption, investment, government purchases, and net exports shares of GDP equals 1?

8. What is the relationship between the real interest rate and the nominal interest rate?

9. Why do the consumption, investment, and net exports shares all fall when the government purchases share of GDP increases?

10. What is the economic growth argument for a smaller government?

11. What is the economic growth argument for a larger government?

12. How is the equilibrium interest rate determined?

13. What are the two expressions for the national saving rate?

14. According to the saving investment approach, how is the equilibrium interest rate determined?

15. What is the relationship between the interest rate determined by dividing GDP into shares and the interest rate determined by the saving investment approach?

WORKING IT OUT

1. Suppose that you are given data on consumption, investment, government purchases, and net exports. From the identity

$$Y = C + I + G + X$$

you can determine GDP. In order to determine the shares of GDP, divide both sides by Y:

$$1 = \frac{C}{Y} + \frac{I}{Y} \quad \frac{G}{Y} + \frac{X}{Y}$$

The sum of the consumption, investment, government purchases, and net export shares must equal 1. If any one of the shares increases, the sum of the other three must decline by the same amount. The nongovernment share can be calculated by adding the consumption, investment, and net exports shares. The national saving rate is determined by adding the investment and net export shares.

2. We have analyzed the effects of an increase in the government purchases share of GDP and seen how the interest rate rises and the consumption, investment, and net exports shares decline. The same technique can be used to consider the effects of shifts in consumption, investment, and net exports. We will focus on investment.

   a. Suppose that the desire to invest rises at every interest rate, perhaps as a result of a change in the tax law designed to stimulate investment. This is shown in Figure 8.5 as a shift of the investment share line to the right. Because the nongovernment share is the sum of the consumption, investment, and net exports shares, the nongovernment share line also shifts to the right. Now comes the subtle part. Even though the *nongovernment share line* shifts to the right, the *nongovernment share* of GDP does not change. Government purchases are not affected by the increased desire to invest. With long-run GDP unchanged, the government purchases share is also not changed. Since the government purchases share does not change, the nongovernment purchases share does not change.

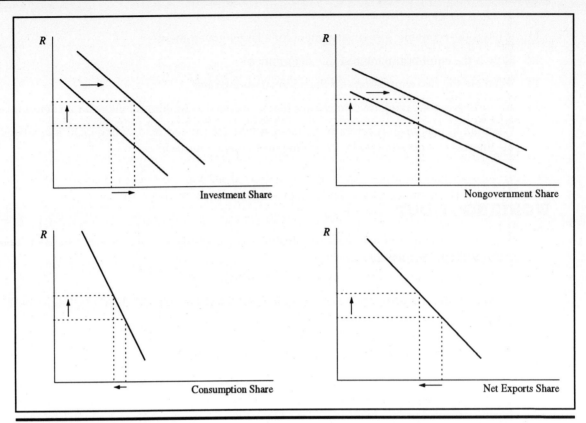

Figure 8.5

b. Since the nongovernment share line shifts to the right, but the nongovernment share is unchanged, the interest rate must rise, as shown in Figure 8.5. The higher interest rate decreases the consumption share and the net exports share. The investment share rises. Thus an increase in the desire to invest increases the interest rate, raises the investment share, and lowers the consumption and net export shares.

Worked Problems

1. Suppose that consumption = 3,400, investment = 800, government purchases = 700, and net exports = 100.

   a. Calculate GDP. What are the consumption, investment, government purchases, and net exports shares of GDP?

   b. What are the nongovernment share of GDP and the national saving rate?

   c. Suppose that government purchases decrease to 600 and GDP does not change. What are the new government purchases and nongovernment shares of GDP?

Answers

   a. *To calculate GDP, use the identity*

   $$Y = C + I + G + X = 3,400 + 800 + 700 + 100 = 5,000$$

   To determine the shares, divide the values for consumption, investment, government purchases, and net exports by the value for GDP:

   Consumption share = C/Y = 3,400/5,000 = .68

   Investment share = I/Y = 800/5,000 = .16

   Government purchases share = G/Y = 700/5,000 = .14

   Net exports share = X/Y = 100/5,000 = .02

   Note that the sum of the four shares = .68 + .16 + .14 + .02 = 1.

   b. *The nongovernment share is the sum of the consumption, investment, and net exports shares, .68 + .16 + .02 = .86. The nongovernment share can also be calculated as 1 minus the government purchases share, 1 - .14 = .86. The national saving rate equals the investment share plus the net exports share, .16 + .02 = .18.*

   c. *If government purchases decrease to 600 and GDP does not change, the new government purchases share equals 600/5,000 = .12. The nongovernment share is 1 - .12 = .88.*

2. Suppose that the government purchases share of GDP decreases. Using diagrams, illustrate what happens to the consumption, investment, and net exports shares of GDP.

Answer

The lower government purchases share of GDP raises the nongovernment share of GDP, illustrated by a movement along the nongovernment share line in Figure 8.6. The interest rate falls. The consumption, investment, and net exports shares all rise.

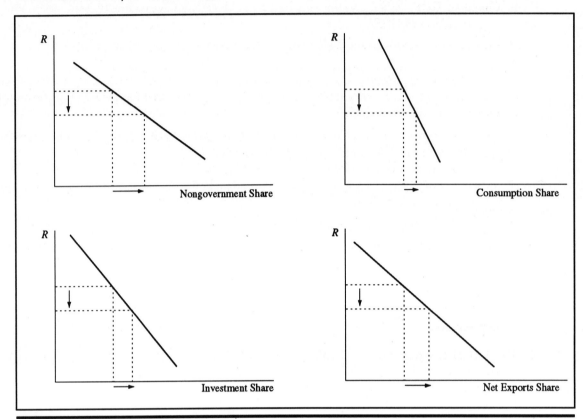

Figure 8.6

Practice Problems

1. Suppose that consumption = 2,800, investment = 600, government purchases = 800, and net exports = -200.

    a. Calculate GDP. What are the consumption, investment, government purchases, and net exports shares of GDP?

    b. What are the nongovernment share of GDP and the national saving rate?

    c. Suppose that government purchases increase to 1,000 and GDP does not change. What are the new government purchases and nongovernment shares of GDP?

2. Suppose that consumption = 7,200, investment = 900, government purchases = 1,600, and net exports = 300.

   a. Calculate GDP. What are the consumption, investment, government purchases, and net exports shares of GDP?

   b. What are the nongovernment share of GDP and the national saving rate?

   c. Suppose that government purchases decrease to 1,200 and GDP does not change. What are the new government purchases and nongovernment purchases shares of GDP?

3. Suppose that net exports rise at every level of the interest rate, perhaps caused by an increase in foreign demand for U.S. automobiles. Using diagrams, show what happens to the consumption and investment shares of GDP.

4. Suppose that consumption falls at every level of the interest rate. Using diagrams, show what happens to the investment and net exports shares of GDP.

CHAPTER TEST

1. Purchases of goods by businesses for use in production and purchases of new residences by households are called
   a. capital.
   b. net investment.
   c. investment.
   d. depreciation.

2. The factories, equipment, and other productive resources used to produce the goods and services that constitute real GDP are called
   a. capital.
   b. net investment.
   c. gross investment.
   d. depreciation.

3. Government purchases, such as highways and schools, that contribute to the economy's productive potential are called
   a. public infrastructure investment.
   b. gross private domestic investment.
   c. gross investment.
   d. net investment.

4. The consumption share of GDP
   a. is positively related to the interest rate.
   b. is negatively related to the interest rate.
   c. is not related to the interest rate.
   d. increases when the interest rate increases.

5. The investment share of GDP
   a. is positively related to the interest rate.
   b. is negatively related to the interest rate.
   c. is not related to the interest rate.
   d. decreases when the interest rate decreases.

6. A higher interest rate
   a. decreases net exports.
   b. increases net exports.
   c. does not change net exports.
   d. decreases imports.

7. When the net exports share is positive,
   a. there is a trade deficit.
   b. there is a trade surplus.
   c. there is no trade deficit or surplus.
   d. the economy is experiencing crowding out.

8. Which of the following is *not* related to the interest rate?
   a. The consumption share of GDP
   b. The investment share of GDP
   c. The net exports share of GDP
   d. The government purchases share of GDP

9. The nongovernment share of GDP is
   a. the proportion of GDP that is used for government purchases.
   b. the sum of the consumption, investment, and net exports shares.
   c. the investment share minus the consumption share.
   d. the investment share minus the net exports share.

10. Which of the following is the *least* sensitive to interest rates?
    a. The investment share of GDP
    b. The net exports share of GDP
    c. The consumption share of GDP
    d. The nongovernment share of GDP

11. The nominal interest rate minus the expected inflation rate is called the
    a. real interest rate.
    b. expected interest rate.
    c. interest rate on loans.
    d. real inflation rate.

12. The sum of the consumption, investment, government purchases, and net exports shares equals
    a. zero.
    b. one.
    c. one-half
    d. one-fourth.

13. Which of the following determines how real GDP is divided among consumption, investment, government purchases, and net exports?
    a. The nominal interest rate
    b. The real interest rate
    c. The real inflation rate
    d. The expected inflation rate

14. An economy experiences crowding out when
    a. consumption declines because of an increase in government purchases.
    b. net exports decline because of an increase in government purchases.
    c. investment declines because of an increase in government purchases.
    d. imports decline because of an increase in government purchases.

15. Which of the following is national saving?
    a. Investment minus consumption
    b. Investment minus government purchases
    c. Investment plus government purchases
    d. Investment plus net exports

16. The national saving rate is
    a. the ratio of national saving to consumption.
    b. the ratio of national saving to investment.
    c. the ratio of national saving to GDP.
    d. the ratio of national saving to government purchases.

17. The national saving rate is
    a. negatively related to the interest rate.
    b. positively related to the interest rate.
    c. not related to the interest rate.
    d. negatively related to investment.

    Use Figure 8.7 for question 18.

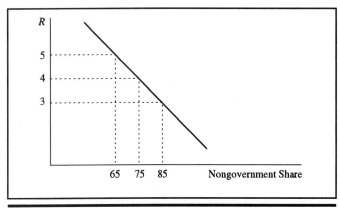

Figure 8.7

18. What is the government purchases share of GDP when the interest rate is 4 percent?
    a. 25 percent
    b. 15 percent
    c. 35 percent
    d. 20 percent

Use Figure 8.8 for question 19.

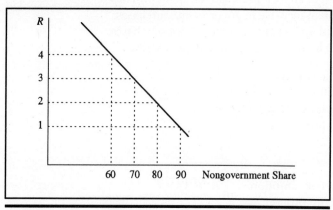

Figure 8.8

19. What is the equilibrium interest rate when the government purchases share of GDP is 30 percent?
    a. 1 percent
    b. 2 percent
    c. 3 percent
    d. 4 percent

Use Figure 8.9 for question 20.

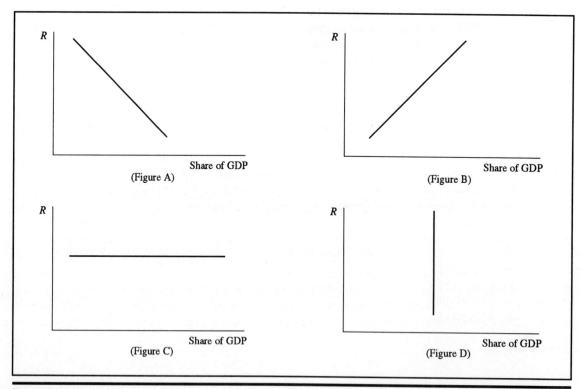

Figure 8.9

20. Which of the above figures appropriately represents the national saving rate line?
    a. Figure A
    b. Figure B
    c. Figure C
    d. Figure D

ANSWERS TO THE REVIEW QUESTIONS

Fill-in Questions

1. Capital
2. investment
3. Gross investment
4. Depreciation
5. net investment
6. Public infrastructure
7. gross private domestic
8. consumption share
9. negatively
10. positive; zero; negative
11. government purchases share
12. consumption; investment; net exports
13. real interest rate
14. crowding out
15. national saving rate

True-False Questions

1. **True**. Investment is purchases that add to or replace the stock of capital.
2. **False**. Only net investment adds to the capital stock.
3. **False**. Public infrastructure investment is part of government purchases.
4. **True**. Higher interest rates encourage saving, decreasing consumption.
5. **True**. Higher interest rates increase the cost of borrowing, making it more expensive to build new factories, buy new equipment, and purchase new houses, thus decreasing investment.
6. **True**. Higher U.S. interest rates raise the exchange rate, making domestic goods more expensive and foreign goods cheaper, and thus decreasing net exports.
7. **False**. The government purchases share is not affected by the interest rate.
8. **True**. The nongovernment share is the sum of the consumption, investment, and net exports shares, all of which are negatively related to the interest rate.
9. **False**. The real interest rate determines how real GDP is divided into shares.
10. **False**. The division of real GDP into shares is applicable to the long run, three years or more, not to short-run fluctuations.
11. **True**. The government purchases and nongovernment shares of GDP must sum to 1.
12. **False**. Crowding out is the decline in investment, not consumption, caused by an increase in government purchases.
13. **False**. No plan to increase public-sector investment has been approved by Congress.
14. **False**. National saving equals income minus consumption minus government purchases.
15. **True**. When the interest rate rises, the national saving rate increases because the consumption share falls.

Short-Answer Questions

1. The two major categories of investment are purchases of goods by businesses for use in production and purchases of new residences by households.
2. Net investment is gross investment minus depreciation.
3. Gross investment is included in GDP.
4. Gross private domestic investment is another term for investment that makes it clear that investment does not include public infrastructure investment.
5. Changes in the interest rate, either through the cost of borrowing or through the exchange rate, have a strong effect on investment and net exports. The effects of interest rates on consumption, through encouraging or discouraging saving, are much weaker.
6. A higher interest rate in the United States raises the exchange rate because it makes dollar-denominated assets more attractive than foreign assets.
7. The interest rate adjusts to ensure that the sum of the four shares equals 1.
8. The real interest rate is the nominal interest rate minus the expected inflation rate.
9. The higher government purchases share lowers the nongovernment share, raising the interest rate. Since each component of the nongovernment share is negatively related to the interest rate, the consumption, investment, and net exports shares all fall.
10. The economic growth argument for a smaller government is that a higher government share lowers the investment share, reducing capital formation and decreasing long-term economic growth.
11. The economic growth argument for a larger government is that spending on public infrastructure investment should be increased in order to promote economic growth.
12. The equilibrium interest rate is determined by the division of GDP into the government purchases share and the nongovernment share.
13. The national saving rate equals 1 minus the consumption share minus the government purchases share, which is equivalent to the sum of the investment share plus the net exports share.
14. According to the saving investment approach, the equilibrium interest rate is the rate at which the national saving rate equals the investment share plus the net exports share of GDP.
15. The two methods determine the same interest rate.

SOLUTIONS TO THE PRACTICE PROBLEMS

1. a. GDP = 2,800 + 600 + 800 - 200 = 4,000. The consumption share = 2,800/4,000 = .70, the investment share = 600/4,000 = .15, the government purchases share = 800/4,000 = .20, and the net exports share = -200/4,000 = -.05.

   b. The nongovernment share = .70 + .15 - .05 = .80. The national saving rate = .15 - .05 = .10.

   c. The new government purchases share = 1,000/4,000 = .25. The nongovernment share = 1 - .25 = .75.

2. a. GDP = 7,200 + 900 + 1,600 + 300 = 10,000. The consumption share = 7,200/10,000 = .72, the investment share = 900/10,000 = .09, the government purchases share = 1,600/10,000 = .16, and the net exports share = 300/10,000 = .03.

    b. The nongovernment share = .72 + .09 + .03 = .84. The national saving rate = .09 + .03 = .12.

    c. The new government purchases share = 1,200/10,000 = .12. The nongovernment share = 1 - .12 = .88.

3. The net exports share line shifts to the right, causing the same shift in the nongovernment share line. With unchanged government purchases and constant GDP, the nongovernment share does not change, raising the interest rate. The consumption and investment shares fall. These effects are illustrated in Figure 8.10.

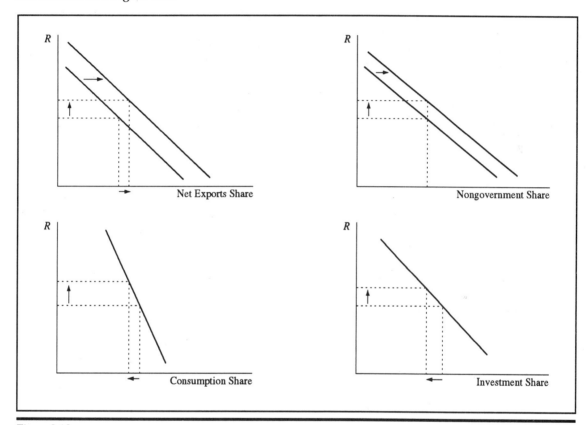

Figure 8.10

4. The consumption share line shifts to the left, causing the same shift in the nongovernment share line. With unchanged government purchases and constant GDP, the nongovernment share does not change, lowering the interest rate. The investment and net exports shares rise. These effects are illustrated in Figure 8.11.

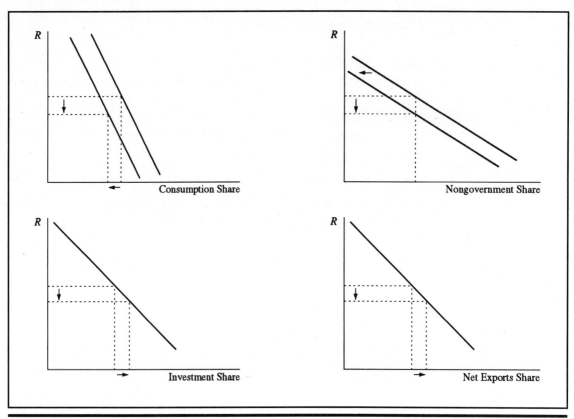

Figure 8.11

ANSWERS TO THE CHAPTER TEST

1. c	6. a	11. a	16. c
2. a	7. b	12. b	17. b
3. a	8. d	13. b	18. a
4. b	9. b	14. c	19. c
5. b	10. c	15. d	20. b

CHAPTER 9

Technology and Economic Growth

CHAPTER OVERVIEW

What caused the dramatic increase in economic growth over the last 200 years? Why has economic growth slowed down in the last two decades? We have studied labor in Chapter 7 and capital in Chapter 8. In this chapter, we study technology, the key to understanding the growth process. We first demonstrate that labor alone, or even labor and capital, cannot explain the miracle of economic growth during the past two centuries. We then show how to combine labor, capital, and technology to create the modern theory of economic growth, and learn about the aggregate production function and the growth accounting formula. We apply the growth accounting formula to understand such diverse topics as the productivity slowdown in the United States, the demise of the former Soviet Union, and the differences in economic performance between Singapore and Hong Kong. Finally, we study policies to improve technological progress and see how they might restore higher productivity growth in the United States.

CHAPTER REVIEW

1. **Technology** is anything that raises the amount of real GDP that can be produced with a given amount of capital and labor. *Technological progress* is an improvement in technology between two dates. **Technological change** is simply the change in the existing technology, but since technology is usually increasing, this term is often used synonymously with technological progress. **Labor-saving technological change** means that fewer workers are needed to produce the same amount of output. **Capital-saving technological change** means that fewer machines are needed to produce the same amount of output.

2. Technological change occurs when new ideas are developed into new products that increase production. This process has several stages: **invention** is the discovery of new knowledge or a new principle; **innovation** is when the invention is brought into application with a new product, and **diffusion** is the spreading of the innovation throughout the economy.

3. The organization of a firm is also part of technology, for the organization helps determine how much the firm produces from its labor and capital. Specialization of workers, called **division of labor,** adds to productivity. **Learning by doing,** the process by which workers become more proficient with experience, is part of the reason why specialization increases productivity.

4. Two special qualities of technology help us understand how much technology will be produced. **Nonrivalry** means that one person's use of the technology does not reduce the amount that another person can use. My use of computer software to write this study guide does not affect your use of the same software to write a term paper. **Nonexcludability** means that the owner of the technology cannot prevent other people from using it. Continuing with the example, the software that I'm using contains many features originally developed by other programs. **Intellectual property laws** provide for patents, copyrights, and trademarks, which determine in part the degree of nonexcludability.

5. The **growth accounting formula** enables economists to estimate the relative contributions of capital and technology to economic growth. The formula states that the growth rate of real GDP per hour of work equals 1/3 times the growth rate of capital per hour of work plus the growth rate of technology. The growth of capital per hour is multiplied by 1/3 because capital income plus depreciation for the U.S. economy as a whole is about 1/3 of aggregate income.

6. The *productivity slowdown* in the United States since the mid-1970s can be analyzed by the growth accounting formula. The slowdown in the growth of real GDP per hour of work is largely attributable to a slowdown in the growth rate of technology. Although the growth rate of capital per hour of work has also slowed down, this has been of secondary importance.

7. If economic policy is to help reverse the productivity slowdown, it must provide incentives for technological progress. There have been a number of proposals for technology policy.

   a. The education and training of workers is called **human capital**. If education can be improved, more human capital can improve the production of technology. Proposals to reform education, especially in mathematics and science at the primary and secondary levels, are designed to raise human capital and increase productivity growth.

   b. Increased funding for **research and development** (R&D) would positively affect technological progress. There is much controversy, however, over whether the gov-ernment should directly support research in certain industries at the expense of others. Critics of such a policy, called *industrial policy*, argue that the private sector provides a better allocation mechanism than the government. A *tax credit for research* would be another way to increase research and development. Other proposals include relaxing the antitrust laws to permit firms to cooperate in applied research and improving intellectual property laws to give inventors a more certain claim to the property rights from their inventions. **Patents,** for which an inventor must apply to the Patent and Trademark Office of the federal government, indicate that an invention is original—and give the inventor exclusive rights to its use for 17 years. Patents give inventors an inducement to invent.

8. The former Soviet Union experienced high rates of growth in the 1970s and early 1980s. Most of that was due to increases in capital per worker, not to technological change, and it could not be sustained. Hong Kong and Singapore both had high rates of growth in the 1970s and 1980s, but for very different reasons. For Hong Kong, the growth rate of technology contributed almost 35 percent, and the growth rate of capital per worker about 65 percent, of the growth rate of output. For Singapore, the output growth was almost entirely attributable to the growth rate of capital per worker.

9. Although the growth accounting formula separates the effects of capital and technology on productivity growth, it is not always possible to separate them in practice. It may be necessary to invest in new capital in order to take advantage of a new technology. *Embodied technological change* requires new capital, whereas *disembodied technological change* does not require new capital in order to be implemented.

ZEROING IN

1. Why is technological progress necessary in order to explain economic growth? The first step is to show that labor alone cannot produce economic growth. This theory was originally proposed by the eighteenth-century British economist Thomas Malthus, and its predictions were so pessimistic that they gave economics the name the "dismal science."

   a. Consider an economy with fixed capital and fixed technology, such as a farm with fixed acreage and equipment, so that labor is the only variable input to production. The production function for such an economy is shown in Figure 9.1, with output on the vertical axis and labor input on the horizontal axis. The curvature of the production function illustrates **diminishing returns to labor**—the greater the number of workers used in producing output, the less the additional output that comes from each additional worker.

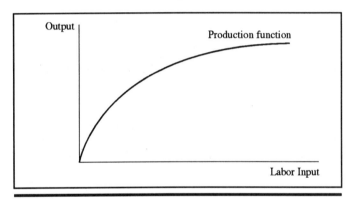

Figure 9.1

   b. The **subsistence line** is depicted along with the production function in Figure 9.2. Along the subsistence line, output per worker just equals what is needed to live. Above the subsistence line, people have more than enough to survive, and so population and labor input rise. Below the subsistence line, people do not have enough to survive, and so population and labor input fall.

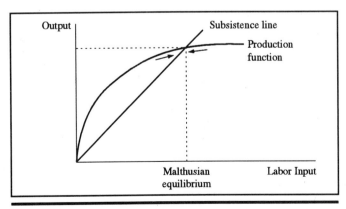

Figure 9.2

c. The **Malthusian equilibrium** is shown in Figure 9.2 as the intersection of the production function and the subsistence line. To the left of the Malthusian equilibrium, labor input is increasing. To the right of the Malthusian equilibrium, labor input is declining. There is no long-term economic growth; real GDP always moves toward the subsistence level of output. The Malthusian prediction is also called the **iron law of wages** because the total amount that workers could receive is limited to the subsistence level of output.

2. The next step is to add capital to the economy. But this will only be part of the story. Although growth of capital can produce economic growth, it cannot account for the sustained growth over the last 200 years.

   a. The production function with variable capital is illustrated in Figure 9.3. As in Figure 9.1, output is on the vertical axis and labor input is on the horizontal axis. With more capital, the production function shifts up. More output can be produced at every level of labor input.

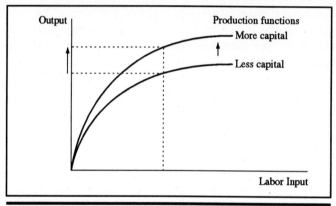

Figure 9.3

   b. Figure 9.4 shows how capital growth can keep the economy out of the Malthusian equilibrium. Suppose the economy starts at point *A*. If there is no capital growth, the population expands and the economy moves toward the subsistence line at point *B*. But with capital growth, the production function shifts up, and, even with population growth, the economy stays above the subsistence level at point *C*.

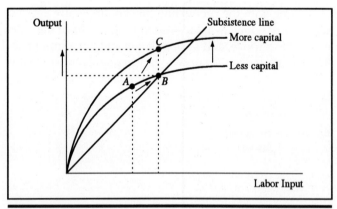

Figure 9.4

c. In an economy with positive net investment, capital is continually growing, and so the predictions of this model are not as dismal as the Malthusian predictions. But there are also *diminishing returns to capital*; each additional amount of capital results in a smaller addition to output. If we keep adding equal increments of capital, the production function shifts up at a decreasing rate, limiting productivity growth.

3. We have shown that a model that allows only for labor growth cannot produce economic growth and that adding capital growth is not sufficient to explain the growth explosion of the last 200 years. Our final step is to include technological progress.

a. We need to develop a different, although related, diagram. Figure 9.5 shows the **productivity curve**, with productivity (Y/L) on the vertical axis and capital per hour of work (K/L) on the horizontal axis. The productivity curve illustrates diminishing returns to capital; each additional amount of capital per hour of work causes a smaller increase in productivity.

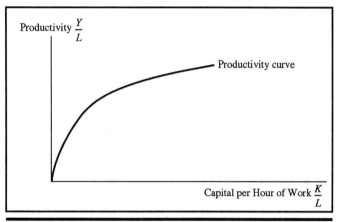

Figure 9.5

b. An increase in capital per hour of work, as shown in Figure 9.6, causes a movement along the productivity curve and an increase in productivity. Because of diminishing returns to capital, however, productivity does not rise by as much as capital per hours of work increases.

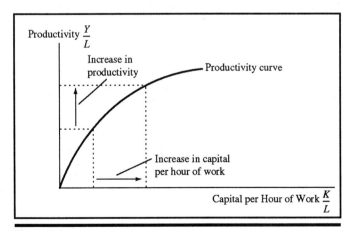

Figure 9.6

c. Technological progress, as shown in Figure 9.7, shifts the productivity curve up. Even with a constant level of capital per hour of work, productivity increases. With continual technological progress, as in the last two centuries, the productivity curve always shifts up. Sustained economic growth can be achieved.

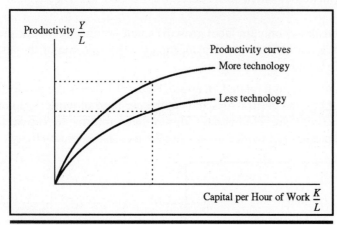

Figure 9.7

d. Technological progress that increases capital per hour of work, as shown in Figure 9.8, causes both a shift in the productivity curve and a movement along the productivity curve. Productivity increases for both reasons.

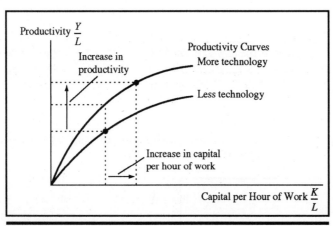

Figure 9.8

ACTIVE REVIEW

Fill-in Questions

1. _____ is anything that raises the amount of real GDP that can be produced with a given amount of capital and labor.

2. Technological _____ or _____ is an improvement in technology between two dates.

3. _____ means that fewer workers are needed to produce the same amount of output.

4. The three stages of technological change are _____, _____, and _____.

5. The process by which workers become more proficient with experience is called _____.

6. Two special features of technology are _____ and _____.

7. Intellectual property laws provide for _____, _____, and _____.

8. The _____ estimates the relative contributions of capital and technology to economic growth.

9. The education and training of workers is called _____.

10. _____ occurs when the government directly supports research in certain industries at the expense of others.

11. _____ technological change requires new capital in order to be implemented.

12. With _____ returns to labor, each additional amount of labor results in a smaller addition to output.

13. The _____ equilibrium is the intersection of the production function and the subsistence line.

14. The Malthusian prediction that GDP converges toward the subsistence level of output is called the _____.

15. The _____ depicts the relation between productivity and capital per hour of work.

True-False Questions

T   F   1. In the process of technological change, innovation precedes diffusion.

T   F   2. The organization of a firm is part of technology.

T   F   3. Specialization of workers is called division of capital.

T   F   4. Intellectual property laws affect the degree of nonrivalry of technology.

T   F   5. The growth accounting formula enables economists to estimate the relative contributions of labor and capital to economic growth.

T   F   6. The productivity slowdown is a slowdown in the growth of real GDP per hour of work.

T   F   7. The high rates of growth in the former Soviet Union during the 1970s were due to technological progress.

T   F   8. Hong Kong and Singapore have experienced high rates of growth for similar reasons.

T   F   9. The effects of capital and technology on economic growth cannot always be separated in practice.

T   F   10. In an economy with fixed capital and fixed technology, the production function will exhibit diminishing returns to labor.

T   F   11. Labor alone cannot produce economic growth.

T   F   12. Unlike labor, capital is not subject to diminishing returns.

T   F   13. Capital growth is not sufficient to fully explain economic growth.

T   F   14. The productivity curve illustrates diminishing returns to capital.

T   F   15. Technological progress raises productivity.

Short-Answer Questions

1. What is the difference between labor-saving and capital-saving technological change?

2. What is meant by nonrivalry?

3. What is meant by nonexcludability?

4. What is the growth accounting formula?

5. What has caused the productivity slowdown in the United States since the mid-1970s?

6. How can economic policy help reverse the productivity slowdown?

7. Why is improving education important for technological progress?

8. Name four proposals for increasing research and development.

9. What is the difference between embodied and disembodied technological change?

10. What is the Malthusian prediction?

11. Why is economics sometimes called the "dismal science"?

12. How does capital growth keep the economy out of the Malthusian equilibrium?

13. Why is capital growth incapable of accounting for sustained productivity growth?

14. What is the effect on the productivity curve of technological progress that increases capital per hour of work?

15. How does technological change allow the economy to achieve sustained economic growth?

WORKING IT OUT

1. The growth accounting formula is one of the most important topics in this chapter. It is also very simple.

   a. The formula can be written as follows:

      (Growth rate of real GDP per hour of work) = 1/3(growth rate of capital

      per hour of work) + (growth rate of technology)

      For example, if the growth rate of capital per hour of work is 3 percent per year and the growth rate of technology is 2 percent per year, then the growth rate of real GDP per hour of work is $[(1/3) \times 3] + 2 = 1 + 2 = 3$ percent per year.

   b. The formula can be rewritten to determine the growth rate of technology from productivity growth and the growth rate of capital:

      (Growth rate of technology) = (growth rate of real GDP per hour

      of work) - 1/3(growth rate of capital per hour of work)

      Continuing with the same example, if the growth rate of real GDP per hour of work is 3 percent per year and the growth rate of capital per hour of work is 3 percent per year, the growth rate of technology is $3 - [(1/3) \times 3] = 3 - 1 = 2$ percent per year.

2. Using the productivity curve, we can show the effects of technological progress on productivity growth.

   a. Figure 9.9 depicts the economy's original equilibrium at point A, the point on the productivity curve (original) consistent with the amount of capital per hour of work. Technological progress which does not change the level of capital per hour of work shifts up the productivity curve. The new equilibrium is at point B. Technological progress which increases capital per hour of work causes both a shift up and a movement along the productivity curve. The new equilibrium is at point C.

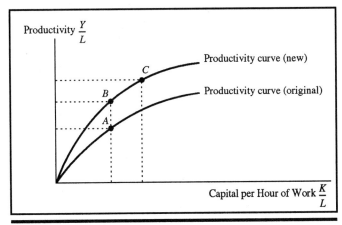

Figure 9.9

b. The economy is always undergoing technological progress, and so the productivity line is always shifting up. So what is meant by the productivity slowdown? Even though there has been technology growth in the United States during the past 20 years, technology has grown more slowly than between the end of World War II and the mid-1970s. The productivity function, while still shifting up, is shifting up at a slower rate than before, causing productivity, while growing, to grow at a slower rate. In other words, productivity growth is slowing down.

Worked Problems

1. a. Suppose that the growth rate of capital per hour of work is 1.5 percent per year and the growth rate of technology is 2 percent per year. What is the growth rate of real GDP per hour of work?

   b. Suppose that technology growth falls to 1 percent per year. How large is the productivity slowdown?

Answers

a. *According to the growth accounting formula, the growth rate of real GDP per hour of work = [(1/3) × 1.5] + 2 = .5 + 2 = 2.5 percent per year.*

b. *If technology growth falls to 1 percent per year, the growth rate of real GDP per hour of work = [(1/3) × 1.5] + 1 = .5 + 1 = 1.5 percent per year. Productivity falls by 1 percent per year.*

2. Consider an economy in which the productivity curve is given by the following data:

Capital per Hour of Work (K/L)	Output per Hour of Work (Y/L)
10	13
20	21
30	27
40	31
50	33

Capital per hour of work and output per hour of work are measured in dollars.

a. Plot the productivity curve. What is the equilibrium if capital per hour of work (K/L) = 30?

b. Suppose that technological progress shifts the productivity curve up by $5 at each level of capital per hour of work and raises the level of capital per hour of work (K/L) to 40. Plot the new productivity curve. What is the new equilibrium?

Answers

a. The productivity function (original) is plotted in Figure 9.10, with output per hour of work (Y/L) on the vertical axis and capital per hour of work (K/L) on the horizontal axis. The equilibrium is determined at point A, with output per hour of work (Y/L) = 27 and capital per hour of work (K/L) = 30.

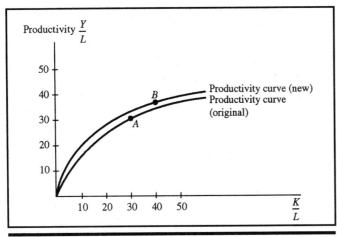

Figure 9.10

b. The new productivity curve is also plotted in Figure 9.10. The new equilibrium is at point B, with output per hour of work (Y/L) = 36 and capital per hour of work (K/L) = 40.

Practice Problems

1. a. Suppose that the growth rate of capital per hour of work is 2.7 percent per year and the growth rate of technology is 1 percent per year. What is the growth rate of real GDP per hour of work?

    b. Suppose that technology growth rises to 1.5 percent per year. How large is the increase in productivity?

2. a. Suppose that the growth rate of real GDP per hour of work is 2 percent per year and the growth rate of capital per hour of work is 3 percent per year. What is the growth rate of technology?

    b. If the growth rate of capital per hour of work rises to 4.5 percent per year and the growth rate of real GDP per hour of work is unchanged, what is the new growth rate of technology?

3. Consider an economy in which the productivity curve is given by the following data:

Capital per Hour of Work (K/L)	Output per Hour of Work (Y/L)
10	14
20	22
30	28
40	32
50	34

Capital per hour of work and output per hour of work are measured in dollars.

a. Plot the productivity curve. What is the equilibrium if capital per hour of work (K/L) = 40?

b. Suppose that negative technological change shifts the productivity curve down by $4 at each level of capital per hour of work. Plot the new productivity curve. What is the new equilibrium if capital per hour of work (K/L) is constant?

4. Consider an economy in which the productivity curve is given by the following data:

Capital per Hour of Work (K/L)	Output per Hour of Work (Y/L)
10	20
20	26
30	30
40	32
50	33

Capital per hour of work and output per hour of work are measured in dollars.

a. Plot the productivity curve. What is equilibrium if capital per hour of work (K/L) = 30?

b. Suppose that the level of capital per hour of work (K/L) increases to 40. What is the new equilibrium?

CHAPTER TEST

1. Anything that raises the amount of real GDP that can be produced with a given amount of capital and labor is called
   a. innovation.
   b. technology.
   c. invention.
   d. diffusion.

2. The discovery of new knowledge or a new principle is called
   a. innovation.
   b. technology.
   c. invention.
   d. diffusion.

3. An improvement in technology between two dates is called
   a. innovation.
   b. technology.
   c. invention.
   d. technological progress.

4. Spreading of an innovation throughout the economy is called
   a. diffusion.
   b. technological change.
   c. invention.
   d. technological progress.

5. When the owner of the technology cannot prevent other people from using it, it is called
   a. nonrivalry.
   b. learning by doing.
   c. nonexcludability.
   d. diffusion.

6. Which of the following is *not* one of the stages of technological change?
   a. Invention
   b. Innovation
   c. Diffusion
   d. Learning by doing

7. Which of the following enables economists to estimate the relative contributions of capital and technology to economic growth?
   a. The growth accounting formula
   b. Intellectual property laws
   c. Nonexcludability
   d. Productivity slowdown

8. Which of the following is *not* a way of increasing research and development?
   a. A tax credit for research
   b. Eliminating patents, copyrights, and trademarks
   c. Relaxing the antitrust laws
   d. Improving intellectual property laws

9. The process by which workers become more proficient is called
   a. learning by doing.
   b. increasing returns to labor.
   c. nonrivalry.
   d. decreasing returns to labor.

10. The high rates of growth in the 1970s and early 1980s in the former Soviet Union were mostly due to
    a. technological change.
    b. technological progress.
    c. increases in capital per worker.
    d. an industrial policy.

11. Each additional amount of labor results in a smaller addition to output; this is called
    a. increasing returns to capital.
    b. diminishing returns to capital.
    c. increasing returns to labor.
    d. diminishing returns to labor.

12. The education and training of workers is called
    a. technological change.
    b. technological progress.
    c. human capital.
    d. increasing returns to labor.

13. The Malthusian equilibrium occurs when the production function intersects the
    a. demand curve.
    b. supply curve.
    c. subsistence line.
    d. capital maintenance line.

14. Which of the following is the Malthusian prediction?
    a. There will always be long-term economic growth.
    b. Real GDP always moves toward the subsistence level of output.
    c. Growth of capital cannot produce economic growth.
    d. Growth of capital can produce economic growth.

15. Suppose that the growth rate of capital per hour of work is 1.8 percent per year and the growth rate of technology is 2.5 percent per year. What is the growth rate of real GDP per hour of work?
    a. 2.5 percent
    b. 2.3 percent
    c. 1.9 percent
    d. 3.1 percent

16. Suppose that the growth rate of real GDP per hour of work is 3 percent per year and the growth rate of capital per hour of work is 1.5 percent per year. What is the growth rate of technology?
    a. 2.0 percent
    b. 2.5 percent
    c. 3.0 percent
    d. 3.5 percent

Use the following table for questions 17 and 18.

Capital per Hour of Work (K/L)	Output per Hour of Work (Y/L)
5	18
10	22
15	26
20	30

Consider an economy in which the productivity curve is given by the data above, where capital per hour of work and output per hour of work are measured in dollars, and the original equilibrium is with $K/L = 10$ and $Y/L = 22$.

17. Suppose that technological progress shifts the productivity curve up by $4 at each level of capital per hour of work and raises the level of capital per hour of work (K/L) to 15. What is the new equilibrium?

    a. $K/L = 10$ and $Y/L = 22$
    b. $K/L = 10$ and $Y/L = 26$
    c. $K/L = 15$ and $Y/L = 26$
    d. $K/L = 15$ and $Y/L = 30$

18. Suppose that negative technological change shifts the productivity curve down by $4 at each level of capital per hour of work. What is the new equilibrium if capital per hour of work (K/L) is constant?

    a. $K/L = 5$ and $Y/L = 14$
    b. $K/L = 10$ and $Y/L = 18$
    c. $K/L = 15$ and $Y/L = 22$
    d. $K/L = 20$ and $Y/L = 26$

Use Figure 9.11 for question 19.

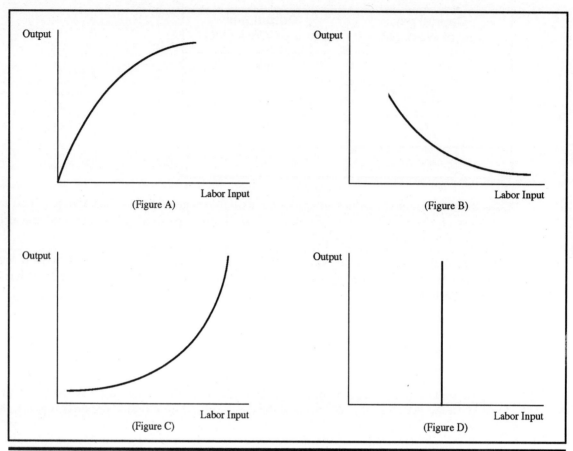

Figure 9.11

19. Which of the figures above appropriately represents a production function?
    a. Figure A
    b. Figure B
    c. Figure C
    d. Figure D

Use Figure 9.12 for question 20.

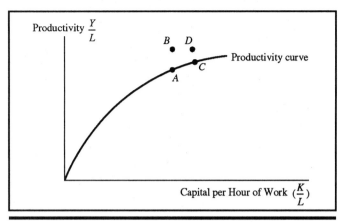

Figure 9.12

20. If the original equilibrium is at point A, which of the points on the graph represents technological progress which increases capital per hour of work?
    a. Point A
    b. Point B
    c. Point C
    d. Point D

ANSWERS TO THE REVIEW QUESTIONS

Fill-in Questions

1. Technology
2. change or progress
3. labor-saving technological change
4. invention; innovation; diffusion
5. learning by doing
6. nonrivalry; nonexcludability
7. patents; copyrights; trademarks
8. growth accounting formula
9. human capital
10. Industrial policy
11. Embodied
12. diminishing
13. Malthusian
14. iron law of wages
15. productivity curve

True-False Questions

1. **True.** Innovation, bringing an invention into application with a new product, comes before diffusion, the spreading of the innovation throughout the economy.
2. **True.** The organization helps determine how much a firm produces from its capital and labor.
3. **False.** Specialization of workers is called division of labor.
4. **False.** Intellectual property laws affect the degree of nonexcludability of technology. They do not affect nonrivalry.
5. **False.** The growth accounting formula measures the contributions of capital and technology to economic growth.
6. **True.** Productivity is output per hour of work, and so productivity growth is the growth of real GDP per hour of work.

7. **False**. Most of the growth in the former Soviet Union during the 1970s was due to increases in capital per worker.
8. **False**. Technology growth has been much more important for Hong Kong than for Singapore.
9. **True**. Although the growth accounting formula separates the effects of capital and technology on productivity growth, it is not always possible to separate them in practice.
10. **True**. If labor is the only variable input to production, each additional amount of labor will result in a smaller addition to output.
11. **True**. With fixed capital and fixed technology, labor growth will not produce economic growth.
12. **False**. With fixed labor and fixed technology, each additional amount of capital results in a smaller addition to output.
13. **True**. Although growth of capital can produce economic growth, it cannot account for the sustained growth over the last 200 years.
14. **True**. Each additional amount of capital per hour of work causes a smaller increase in productivity.
15. **True**. Technological progress shifts the productivity curve up, increasing productivity even with a constant level of capital per hour of work.

Short-Answer Questions

1. With labor-saving technological change, fewer workers are needed to produce the same amount of output. Capital-saving technological change means that fewer machines are needed to produce the same amount of output.
2. Nonrivalry means that one person's use of technology does not reduce the amount that another person can use.
3. Nonexcludability means that the owner of technology cannot prevent other people from using it.
4. The growth accounting formula states that the growth rate of real GDP per hour of work equals 1/3 times the growth rate of capital per hour of work plus the growth rate of technology.
5. The productivity slowdown is largely attributable to a slowdown in the growth rate of technology.
6. Economic policy can help reverse the productivity slowdown by providing incentives for technological progress.
7. If education can be improved, more human capital can improve the production of technology.
8. Industrial policy, a tax credit for research, relaxing antitrust laws, and improving intellectual property laws are four proposals for increasing research and development.
9. Embodied technological change requires new capital in order to be implemented, whereas disembodied technological change does not require new capital.
10. The Malthusian prediction is that real GDP always moves toward the subsistence level of output.
11. The Malthusian predictions were so pessimistic that they gave economics the name the "dismal science."
12. With capital growth, the production function shifts up, and, even with population growth, the economy stays above the subsistence level.
13. Because of diminishing returns to capital, adding equal increments of capital causes the production function to shift up at a decreasing rate, limiting productivity growth.
14. Technological progress that increases capital per hour of work causes both a shift in the productivity curve and a movement along the productivity curve.
15. With continual technological progress, the productivity curve always shifts up, and sustained economic growth can be achieved.

SOLUTIONS TO THE PRACTICE PROBLEMS

1. a. The growth rate of real GDP per hour of work = $[(1/3) \times 2.7] + 1 = .9 + 1 = 1.9$ percent per year.

    b. The new growth rate of real GDP per hour of work = $[(1/3) \times 2.7] + 1.5 = .9 + 1.5 = 2.4$ percent per year. Productivity increases by 1/2 percent per year.

2. a. The growth rate of technology = $2 - [(1/3) \times 3] = 2 - 1 = 1$ percent per year.

    b. The new growth rate of technology = $2 - [(1/3) \times 4.5] = 2 - 1.5 = .5$ percent per year.

3. a. The productivity curve (original) is plotted in Figure 9.13. the equilibrium is at point A, with output per hour of work (Y/L) = 32 and capital per hour of work (K/L) = 40.

    b. The new productivity curve is also plotted in Figure 9.13. The new equilibrium is at point B, with output per hour of work (Y/L) = 28 and capital per hour of work (K/L) = 40.

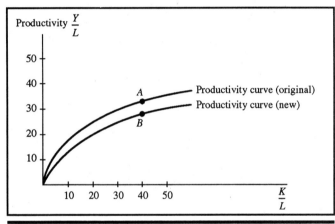

Figure 9.13

4. a. The productivity curve (original) is plotted in Figure 9.14. The equilibrium is at point *A*, with output per hour of work (Y/L) = 30 and capital per hour of work (K/L) = 30.

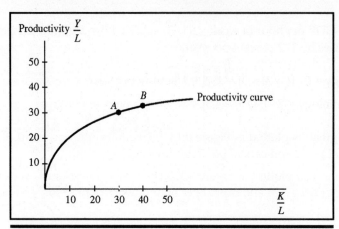

Figure 9.14

b. The new equilibrium is at point *B*, with output per hour of work (Y/L) = 32 and capital per hour of work (K/L) = 40.

ANSWERS TO THE CHAPTER TEST

1. b	6. d	11. d	16. b
2. c	7. a	12. c	17. d
3. d	8. b	13. c	18. b
4. a	9. a	14. b	19. a
5. c	10. c	15. d	20. d

CHAPTER **10**

The Monetary System and Inflation

CHAPTER OVERVIEW

Money is a vital component of economic activity. Without money, buyers and sellers would not make transactions unless they wanted each other's goods. This is almost impossible to imagine, and the economic system as we know it would cease to exist. In this chapter, we study the monetary system, the arrangement through which people carry out transactions with one another, and learn how the monetary system fits into the theory of economic growth. We first learn about the functions of money and how it is defined. Then we examine the role of banks in creating money and learn about the money multiplier. An important focus of this chapter is the relation between money growth and inflation, and we study the quantity equation. Finally, we learn about the Phillips curve, which describes the relation between inflation and unemployment, and study the effects of inflation on productivity growth.

CHAPTER REVIEW

1. **Money** is the part of a person's wealth that can be readily used for transactions. Money is not the same as wealth. Although the dollar bills in your wallet can be used to buy groceries, the equity in your house cannot. Money is therefore defined as the sum of **currency** (coin and **paper money**) and deposits at banks.

2. Should all deposits at banks be counted as money? **Checking deposits**, which can easily be used to make payments, obviously count because they can be readily used for transactions. The narrowest measure of the **money supply**, called **M1**, consists mainly of currency plus checking deposits. What about **time deposits** and **savings deposits**? Although you can't write a check on these accounts, you can withdraw the funds, so the answer is ambiguous. A broader measure of the money supply, called **M2**, is defined as M1 plus time and savings deposits. Most of money is held as deposits. Only about one-third of M1, and one-tenth of M2, consists of currency.

3. Money has three functions. One of its functions is as a **medium of exchange**, an item that people are willing to accept as payment for the goods they are selling. Money also serves as a **store of value** from one period to another. If you receive money as payment for your goods today, you will be able to use the money in the future to make purchases. Finally, money also serves as a **unit of account** because prices of goods are usually stated in units of money. You say that an apple costs 25 cents, not that an apple costs 8 grapes.

4. A **barter** system, in which goods are exchanged only for other goods, does not have a single medium of exchange. The advantage of a monetary system over a barter system is that a barter system requires a **coincidence of wants**; the person who wants to buy what you want to sell needs to have exactly what you want to buy in order to make transactions.

5. Many items have been used for money, including cigarettes and large stones. Although **commodity money** describes any monetary system in which money is linked to an item, or commodity, gold and silver are the most common forms of commodity money. The **gold standard** is a monetary system in which the price of gold in terms of money is fixed by the government. The United States was on the gold standard from 1879 until World War I.

6. The *central bank* is the part of the government that supplies currency. In the United States, the central bank is called the **Federal Reserve System**, or "Fed." The **Federal Open Market Committee (FOMC)** makes decisions about the supply of currency and deposits.

7. **Banks** are firms that channel funds from savers to investors by accepting deposits and making loans. They play an important role in the monetary system. Banks are sometimes called *commercial banks* to distinguish them from other *financial intermediaries*, a more general name for firms that "intermediate" between savers and investors. The **assets** of a bank are the **reserves** that commercial banks hold at the Fed, the **loans** that are made by banks to individual or firms, and the **bonds** that the banks hold. The **liabilities** of a bank are the deposits that individuals or firms have made.

8. Banks serve as creators of money. By law, commercial banks are required to hold a fraction of their deposits as reserves at the Fed; that fraction is called the **required reserve ratio**. Since reserves do not pay interest, banks have incentives to make loans or buy bonds with as much of their deposits as possible. Suppose a bank receives a deposit of $1 million. If the reserve ratio is 10 percent, it would deposit $100,000 at the Fed as reserves and make loans or buy bonds with the remaining $900,000. The people who receive the loans or sell the bonds will then deposit the $900,000 in their banks, which will in turn deposit 10 percent, or $90,000, as reserves and make loans or buy bonds with the remaining $810,000. These rounds of lending continue, and so deposits, and thus money, expand by much more than the initial $1 million.

9. The **monetary base** consists of currency plus reserves. When the Fed buys and sells bonds, it changes the amount of bank reserves. When the Fed buys bonds, reserves and loans rise. Through the rounds of lending described above, deposits expand. The **money multiplier** describes by how much a change in the monetary base changes the money supply.

10. Inflation is the rate of growth of the price level. In the long run, inflation is closely related to money growth. When money growth increases, inflation rises, and when money growth decreases, inflation falls. Countries with higher money growth have higher long-run inflation than countries with lower money growth.

11. *Hyperinflation* is extremely high inflation. The most common reason for hyperinflation is that governments run very large budget deficits and finance them by printing money. When inflation is used to finance budget deficits, it is called the *inflation tax*. We will explore the link between budget deficits, money creation, and inflation in Chapter 16.

12. The **Phillips curve** is a relationship between inflation and unemployment. At one time, this relationship led many economists to believe that lower unemployment could be achieved in the long run by having a higher inflation rate. We know today that this assumption is not correct. In the long run, the unemployment rate will be at its normal or natural level. Put differently, the long-run Phillips curve is vertical.

13. Inflation appears to be *negatively correlated* with economic growth; that is, countries with high inflation have low growth, and countries with low inflation have high growth. Why would this occur? High inflation rates are also associated with highly volatile inflation rates, which increases uncertainty. More uncertainty lowers investment in physical and human capital, which reduces productivity growth.

14. Inflation in the United States in the early 1990s fell to around 3 percent per year for several years. Should it be lowered further? One argument against further reducing inflation is that, because price indexes have fixed weights that do not reflect changes in spending patterns, inflation is measured with an *upward bias*, so that 2 percent inflation is essentially zero.

ZEROING IN

1. We have defined the money multiplier as the number that describes by how much a change in the monetary base changes the money supply. Let's look at that process in more detail.

    a. We need to review some definitions. Money is defined as currency plus deposits. If CU is currency and D is deposits, then $M = CU + D$. The monetary base is currency plus reserves. If MB is the monetary base and BR is the reserves that commercial banks hold at the Fed, then $MB = CU + BR$.

    b. The *reserve ratio* is the fraction of commercial bank deposits that the banks hold in the form of reserves at the Fed. If r is the reserve ratio, then reserves equal the reserve ratio times deposits, or $BR = rD$. At any time, people hold both currency and deposits. We define the **currency to deposit ratio**, denoted by k, to be the amount of currency divided by the amount of deposits; $k = CU/D$. Remember that currency is a fraction of deposits, so that k is less than 1. Multiplying both sides of the definition by deposits, $CU = kD$.

    c. We now derive the money multiplier, the link between the monetary base MB and money M. Start with the definition of money, $M = CU + D$, and substitute the equation for currency, $CU = kD$; you get $M = kD + D$ or $M = (k + 1)D$. Now take the definition of the monetary base, $MB = CU + BR$, and substitute the equation for currency, $CU = kD$, and the equation for reserves, $BR = rD$; you get $MB = kD + rD$ or $MB = (k + r)D$. Finally, divide the expression for money by the expression for the monetary base:

    $$\frac{1}{MB} = \frac{(k+1)D}{(k+r)D} = \frac{(k+1)}{(k+r)}$$

    The ratio $(k + 1)/(k + r)$ is the money multiplier, which is greater than 1 because the reserve ratio r is less than 1.

2. The relationship between money growth and inflation is one of the most important topics in this chapter. We will use the quantity equation of money to understand the relationship.

    a. The **quantity equation of money** describes the relationship between money and nominal GDP. Remember that nominal GDP is the price level times real GDP. The quantity equation is written: Money × velocity = price level × real GDP. **Velocity** is simply the term by which money is multiplied to get nominal GDP. Using growth rates, Money growth + velocity growth = inflation + real GDP growth.

b. The quantity equation is the key to understanding the long-run relationship between money growth and inflation. Along a long-run growth path, where real GDP growth equals potential GDP growth, an increase in money growth will increase inflation by the same amount (in percentage points) unless there is a change in velocity growth. In other words, higher money growth leads to higher inflation in the long run.

3. The history of the Phillips curve provides an interesting illustration of the interaction between economic theory and economic policy.

a. Following the "discovery" of the Phillips curve in 1958, many economists became convinced that the downward-sloping relationship between inflation and unemployment, depicted in Figure 10.1, represented an exploitable tradeoff between inflation and unemployment. By raising inflation, the government could permanently reduce unemployment.

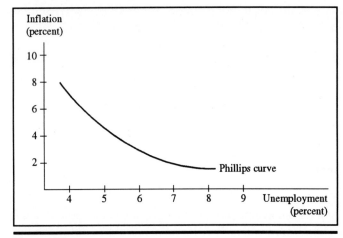

Figure 10.1

b. This belief contributed to the inflationary policies of the late 1960s and early 1970s. If the long-run Phillips curve was downward-sloping, higher inflation should have produced lower unemployment. What happened? Inflation rose, but unemployment didn't permanently fall. Figure 10.2 shows two years, 1967 and 1978, with unemployment at the normal 6 percent level. But inflation in 1978 was more than double inflation in 1967.

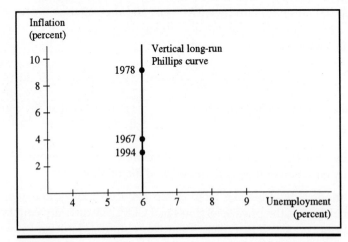

Figure 10.2

c. There is a silver lining in this cloud. Although reducing inflation in the 1980s had large short-run costs, there was no long-term effect on unemployment. Look again at Figure 10.2. In 1994, unemployment was at 6 percent and inflation was lower than it was in 1967.

d. The long-run Phillips curve is vertical.

ACTIVE REVIEW

Fill-in Questions

1. _____ is the part of a person's wealth that can readily be used for transactions.

2. Money is the sum of _____ and _____.

3. The three functions of money are as a(n) _____, a(n) _____, and a(n) _____.

4. In a(n) _____, goods are exchanged only for other goods.

5. A(n) _____ is required in order to make transactions in a barter system.

6. The _____ is a monetary system in which the price of gold in terms of paper money is fixed by the government.

7. The _____ makes decisions about the supply of currency and deposits.

8. The assets of a commercial bank are _____, _____, and _____.

9. _____ are firms that channel funds from savers to investors.

10. The fraction of deposits that commercial banks are required to hold as reserves at the Fed is called the _____.

11. The _____ equals currency plus reserves.

12. The _____ describes by how much the change in the monetary base changes the money supply.

13. _____ is extremely high inflation.

14. The _____ is a relationship between inflation and unemployment.

15. _____ is the term by which money is multiplied to get nominal GDP in the quantity equation.

True-False Questions

T F 1. Money is not the same as wealth.

T F 2. Over 50 percent of money consists of currency.

T F 3. Unlike a monetary system, a barter system does not have a single medium of exchange.

T F 4. Currency in the United States is an example of commodity money.

T F 5. When a bank receives a deposit, it cannot use that entire deposit to buy bonds or make loans.

T F 6. Banks attempt to hold as much reserves as possible.

T F 7. The money multiplier describes by how much a change in M1 changes M2.

T F 8. Money growth and inflation are not related in the long run.

T F 9. Inflation and unemployment are not related in the long run.

T F 10. The United States experienced hyperinflation in the late 1970s.

T F 11. Inflation appears to be negatively correlated with economic growth.

T F 12. Inflation in the United States in the early 1990s was high and variable.

T F 13. If the reserve ratio falls, the money multiplier rises.

T F 14. If the currency to deposit ratio falls, the money multiplier rises.

T F 15. The quantity equation of money describes the relationship between money and real GDP.

Short-Answer Questions

1. What is the difference between money and the monetary base?

2. What is the difference between M1 and M2?

3. What is the major disadvantage of a barter system?

4. During what period was the United States on the gold standard?

5. What is the central bank of the United States?

6. What are the assets and liabilities of commercial banks?

7. Define the currency to deposit ratio.

8. Along a long-run growth path, where real GDP growth equals potential GDP growth, what is the effect of an increase in money growth on inflation?

9. In the long run, how does inflation in countries with higher money growth differ from inflation in countries with lower money growth?

10. What is the inflation tax?

11. Why does inflation lower economic growth?

12. Why is inflation measured with an upward bias?

13. What is the quantity equation of money?

14. According to the quantity equation of money, what is the relationship between money growth and inflation along a long-run growth path?

15. Based on the unemployment rates for 1967, 1978, and 1994, what is the slope of the long-run Phillips curve?

WORKING IT OUT

1. The money multiplier is a number that indicates by how much a change in the monetary base changes the money supply. The formula for the money multiplier, derived above, is

$$\frac{(k+1)}{(k+r)}$$

   where k is the currency to deposit ratio and r is the reserve ratio.

   a. Suppose that all money is held as deposits, so that the currency to deposit ratio k equals zero, and the reserve ratio r equals 10 percent. The money multiplier is $1/.1 = 10$.

   b. Now suppose that the currency to deposit ratio is 20 percent, while the reserve ratio is still 10 percent. The money multiplier is $(.2 + 1)/(.2 + .1) = 1.2/.3 = 4$.

2. The quantity equation of money can be used both in levels, to describe the relationship between money and nominal GDP, and in growth rates, to describe the relationship between money growth and inflation.

   a. According to the quantity equation, money times velocity equals real GDP times the price level. Suppose you are given the following information:

Year	Money	Velocity	Real GDP	Price Level
2000	1,000		4,000	1.00

   By the quantity equation,

   $1,000 \times \text{velocity} = (4,000) \times (1.00)$

   $\text{Velocity} = 4,000/1,000 = 4$

   You can use the same technique to solve for any of the variables if you are given values for the other three variables.

b. Now consider data for two years:

Year	Money	Velocity	Real GDP	Price Level
2000	1,000	4	4,000	1.00
2010	1,100	4	4,200	

The inflation rate between the years 2000 and 2010 can be calculated in two ways. Using the quantity equation in levels for the year 2010,

Money × velocity = real GDP × price level

(1,100)(4) = 4,200 × price level

Price level = 4,400/4,200 = 1.05

Inflation = (1.05 - 1.00)/1.00 = .05 (5 percent)

Using the quantity equation in growth rates, Money growth + velocity growth = real GDP growth + inflation. Money growth is 10 percent, velocity growth is zero, and real GDP growth is 5 percent. By the quantity equation, 10 percent + 0 percent = 5 percent + inflation. Therefore, inflation is 5 percent.

Worked Problems

1. Suppose that the currency to deposit ratio k is 40 percent and the reserve ratio r is 10 percent.

   a. What is the money multiplier?

   b. Suppose that the reserve ratio increases to 12 percent. What is the new money multiplier?

Answers

   a. The money multiplier is (.4 + 1)/(.4 + .1) = 1.4/.5 = 2.8.

   b. When the reserve ratio rises, the money multiplier falls. The new money multiplier is (.4 + 1)/ (.4 + .12)/ = 1.4/.52 = 2.69.

2. Consider an economy described by the following information:

Year	Money	Velocity	Real GDP	Price Level
2000	1,000	4.00		1.00
2010	1,100	4.40	4,200	
2020	1,210	4.40	4,410	

   a. What is real GDP in the year 2000?

   b. What is inflation for the decades between 2000 and 2010 and between 2010 and 2020?

Answers

  a. *You need to use the quantity equation in levels to determine real GDP for the year 2000. By the quantity equation, 1,000 × 4.00 = real GDP × 1.00. Therefore, real GDP = 4,000.*

  b. *Although you can solve for inflation by first using the quantity equation in levels to compute the price level and then computing the inflation rates, it is easier to work in growth rates. Calculating growth rates:*

Decade	Money	Velocity	Real GDP	Inflation
2000 to 2010	10%	10%	5%	?
2010 to 2020	10%	0%	5%	?

The quantity equation in growth rates is money growth + velocity growth = real GDP growth + inflation. For the first decade, 10 percent + 10 percent = 5 percent + inflation. Therefore, inflation is 15 percent. For the second decade, 10 percent + 0 percent = 5 percent + inflation. Therefore, inflation is 5 percent.

Practice Problems

1. Suppose that the currency to deposit ratio k is 30 percent and the reserve ratio r is 10 percent.

   a. What is the money multiplier?

   b. Suppose that the currency to deposit ratio decreases to 25 percent. What is the new money multiplier?

2. Suppose that the currency to deposit ratio k is 15 percent and the reserve ratio r is 10 percent.

   a. What is the money multiplier?

   b. Suppose that the reserve ratio decreases to 8 percent. What is the new money multiplier?

3. Consider an economy described by the following information:

Year	Money	Velocity	Real GDP	Price Level
2000	4,000		8,000	1.00
2010	4,400	2.00		1.10
2020	5,280	2.00		1.32

   a. What is velocity in the year 2000?

   b. What is real GDP growth for the decades between 2000 and 2010 and between 2010 and 2020?

4. Consider an economy described by the following information:

Year	Money	Velocity	Real GDP	Price Level
2000		3.00	6,000	2.00
2100	6,000	3.30	7,800	
2200	9,000	3.96	9,360	

a. What is money in the year 2000?

b. What is inflation for the twenty-first and twenty-second centuries?

CHAPTER TEST

1. M1 is
   a. the broadest measure of money.
   b. currency plus time and savings deposits.
   c. currency plus checking, time, and savings deposits.
   d. currency plus checking deposits.

2. M2 is
   a. the narrowest measure of money.
   b. currency plus time and savings deposits.
   c. currency plus checking, time, and savings deposits.
   d. currency plus checking deposits.

3. About what percentage of M1 consists of currency?
   a. One-tenth
   b. One-third
   c. One-half
   d. Two-thirds

4. Which of the following is *not* a function of money?
   a. A medium of exchange
   b. A store of value from one period to the next
   c. A means of facilitating a barter system
   d. A unit of account

5. Which of the following is *not* considered part of the assets of a bank?
   a. Reserves held at the Fed
   b. Loans made to individuals and firms
   c. Bonds held by the bank
   d. Deposits made by individuals and firms

6. The monetary base consists of
   a. currency plus reserves.
   b. currency plus loans.
   c. currency plus bonds.
   d. reserves plus loans.

7. The money multiplier describes
   a. how much a change in loans changes bank assets.
   b. how much a change in money growth changes inflation.
   c. how much a change in money supply changes the monetary base.
   d. how much a change in the monetary base changes the money supply.

8. If money growth decreases, in the long run
   a. inflation increases.
   b. inflation increases, but at a decreasing rate.
   c. inflation decreases.
   d. inflation remains unchanged.

9. The Phillips curve shows the relationship between
   a. money growth and inflation.
   b. the monetary base and the money supply.
   c. inflation and unemployment.
   d. money and nominal GDP.

10. The long-run Phillips curve is
    a. horizontal.
    b. vertical.
    c. upward-sloping.
    d. downward-sloping.

11. Inflation is
    a. positively correlated with economic growth.
    b. negatively correlated with economic growth.
    c. uncorrelated with economic growth.
    d. either positively or negatively correlated with economic growth, depending on other factors.

12. The reserve ratio is the fraction of
    a. commercial bank deposits held in reserve at the Fed.
    b. commercial bank deposits held in reserve at a commercial bank.
    c. commercial bank assets held in reserve at the Fed.
    d. commercial bank assets held in reserve at a commercial bank.

13. The expression for the money multiplier is
    a. $\dfrac{(k + r)}{(k + 1)}$.

    b. $\dfrac{(k + 1)}{(k + r)}$.

    c. $\dfrac{(k - 1)}{(k + r)}$.

    d. $\dfrac{(k + r)}{(k - 1)}$.

14. The money multiplier is
    a. less than 0.
    b. between 0 and 1.
    c. equal to 1.
    d. greater than 1.

15. The money multiplier rises if
    a. the currency to deposit ratio rises.
    b. the currency to deposit ratio falls.
    c. the reserve ratio rises.
    d. the inflation rate rises.

16. The quantity equation of money describes the relationship between
    a. money and nominal GDP.
    b. money and real GDP.
    c. unemployment and inflation.
    d. the monetary base and the money supply.

17. Suppose the currency to deposit ratio is 5 percent and the reserve ratio is 10 percent. What is the money multiplier?
    a. 1/7
    b. 3/19
    c. 6 1/3
    d. 7

Use the following table for questions 18 to 20. Consider an economy described by the following information:

Year	Money	Velocity	Real GDP	Price Level
2000	2,000	2.2		1.1
2100	2,500	2.42	5,000	

18. What is real GDP in the year 2000?
    a. 2,000
    b. 3,000
    c. 4,000
    d. 5,000

19. What is the price level in the year 2100?
    a. 1.0
    b. 1.1
    c. 1.11
    d. 1.21

20. What is inflation in the twenty-first century?
    a. 1 percent
    b. 10 percent
    c. 11 percent
    d. 21 percent

ANSWERS TO THE REVIEW QUESTIONS

Fill-in Questions

1. Money
2. currency, deposits
3. medium of exchange, store of value, unit of account
4. barter system
5. coincidence of wants
6. gold standard
7. Federal Open Market Committee
8. reserves, loans, bonds
9. Banks
10. required reserve ratio
11. monetary base
12. money multiplier
13. Hyperinflation
14. Phillips curve
15. Velocity

True-False Questions

1. **True**. Money is only part of a person's wealth, that part that can be readily used for transactions.
2. **False**. Most money is held as deposits.
3. **True**. In a barter system, goods are exchanged directly for other goods.
4. **False**. Currency in the United States is not linked to any commodity.
5. **True**. Banks are required to hold a fraction of deposits as reserves at the Fed.
6. **False**. Because reserves do not pay interest, banks try to minimize their holdings of reserves.
7. **False**. The money multiplier describes by how much changes in the monetary base change the money supply.
8. **False**. In the long run, inflation is closely related to money growth.
9. **True**. In the long run, the unemployment rate equals its normal or natural level independent of the inflation rate.
10. **False**. Inflation in the United States during the late 1970s was about 10 percent per year. Hyperinflation consists of much higher rates.
11. **True**. Countries with high inflation have low growth, and countries with low inflation have high growth.
12. **False**. Inflation in the United States has been about 3 percent per year in the early 1990s.
13. **True**. If banks hold fewer reserves at the Fed, they buy more bonds and/or make more loans, increasing the money supply. This raises the money multiplier.
14. **True**. A fall in the currency to deposit ratio raises deposits. Banks buy bonds and make loans with most of these deposits, increasing the money multiplier and the money supply.
15. **False**. The quantity equation describes the relationship between money and nominal GDP.

Short-Answer Questions

1. Money is defined as currency plus deposits; the monetary base is currency plus reserves.
2. M1 is defined as currency plus checking deposits. M2 adds time and savings deposits.
3. A barter system requires a coincidence of wants in order for transactions to occur.
4. The United States was on the gold standard from 1879 until World War I.
5. The Federal Reserve System is the central bank of the United States.
6. The assets of commercial banks are reserves, loans, and bonds. Their liabilities are the deposits that individuals or firms have made.
7. The currency to deposit ratio is the amount of currency divided by the amount of deposits.
8. Along a long-run growth path, an increase in money growth will increase inflation by the same amount (in percentage points) unless there is a change in velocity growth.

9. Countries with higher money growth have higher long-run inflation than countries with lower money growth.
10. The inflation tax is inflation that is used to finance budget deficits.
11. High inflation increases uncertainty, lowering investment in physical and human capital and reducing productivity growth.
12. The price indexes used to measure inflation have fixed weights and do not incorporate changes in spending patterns.
13. The quantity equation of money is money times velocity equals the price level times real GDP.
14. According to the quantity equation, an increase in money growth will increase inflation by the same amount unless there is a change in velocity growth.
15. Unemployment was about 6 percent during 1967, 1978, and 1994 despite very different levels of inflation, indicating that the long-run Phillips curve is vertical.

SOLUTIONS TO THE PRACTICE PROBLEMS

1. a. The money multiplier is 3.25.

   b. The new money multiplier is 3.57.

2. a. The money multiplier is 4.60.

   b. The new money multiplier is 5.00.

3. a. In the year 2000, velocity = 2.0.

   b. Calculating growth rates:

Decade	Money	Velocity	Real GDP	Inflation
2000 to 2010	10%	0%	?	10%
2010 to 2020	20%	0%	?	20%

Using the quantity equation, real GDP growth is zero for both decades.

4. a. In the year 2000, money = 4,000.

   b. Calculating growth rates:

Century	Money	Velocity	Real GDP	Inflation
2000 to 2100	50%	10%	30%	?
2100 to 2200	50%	20%	20%	?

Using the quantity equation, inflation is 30 percent for the twenty-first century and 50 percent for the twenty-second century.

ANSWERS TO THE CHAPTER TEST

1. d	6. a	11. b	16. a
2. c	7. d	12. a	17. d
3. b	8. c	13. b	18. c
4. c	9. c	14. d	19. d
5. d	10. b	15. b	20. b

(CHAPTERS 7-10)
LONG-RUN FUNDAMENTALS
AND ECONOMIC GROWTH

1. Unemployment that occurs because people have insufficient skills is referred to as
   a. cyclical unemployment.
   b. frictional unemployment.
   c. natural unemployment.
   d. structural unemployment.

2. A 25-year-old woman who decides to stay home and take care of her family after unsuccessfully searching for a job for 2 years is considered
   a. a discouraged worker.
   b. unemployed.
   c. in the labor force.
   d. self employed.

3. Which of the following groups is likely to experience the highest rate of unemployment?
   a. Adult men
   b. Adult women
   c. Black teenagers
   d. White teenagers

Use Figure 1 for question 4.

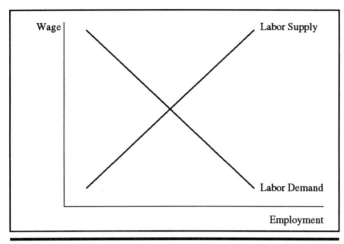

Figure 1

4. Using Figure 1, *ceteris paribus*, a leftward shift in the labor curve would cause
   a. both the real wage and the amount of labor employed to increase.
   b. both the real wage and the amount of labor employed to decrease.
   c. the real wage to increase and the amount of labor employed to decrease.
   d. the real wage to decrease and the amount of labor employed to increase.

5. Which of the following will cause unemployment during job search to decline?
   a. Lowering the minimum wage
   b. Reducing unemployment compensation
   c. Reducing the bargaining strength of labor
   d. Increasing unemployment compensation

6. The natural unemployment rate occurs when
   a. the economy is in normal times and real GDP is equal to potential GDP.
   b. the economy is in normal times and real GDP is greater than potential GDP.
   c. the economy is in normal times and real GDP is less than potential GDP.
   d. the economy is in recession.

7. On average, the percent of unemployed workers unemployed for more than 6 months is approximately
   a. 35 percent.
   b. 50 percent.
   c. 5 percent.
   d. 15 percent.

8. The theory of an efficiency wage is that firms will choose to pay workers an extra amount
   a. to encourage them to be more productive.
   b. to pay more than the minimum wage.
   c. to avoid unions.
   d. to minimize drugs.

9. The factories, equipment, and other productive resources used to produce good and services by businesses is referred to as
   a. capital.
   b. net investment.
   c. private sector expenditures.
   d. public infrastructure investment.

10. Which of the following best explains what will happen if the government purchases share of GDP falls?
   a. The consumption share of GDP will fall with it.
   b. The net exports share of GDP will fall with it.
   c. The investment share of GSP will fall with it.
   d. The investment, consumption, and/or net exports of GSP will rise.

11. Which of the following is the *least* sensitive to changes in the interest rate?
   a. The consumption share of GDP
   b. The net exports share of GDP
   c. The nongovernment share of GDP
   d. The investment share of GDP

12. The share of GDP available for nongovernment use is
   a. positively related to the real interest rate.
   b. negatively related to the real interest rate.
   c. positively related to the nominal interest rate.
   d. negatively related to the nominal interest rate.

13. Which of the following best explains what is meant by the term *crowding out?*
   a. An increase in consumption expenditures, by causing interest rates to rise, results in a decline in investment expenditures.
   b. An increase in investment, by causing interest rates to rise, results in a decline in government purchases.
   c. An increase in consumption expenditures, by causing interest rates to rise, results in a decline in government purchases.
   d. An increase in government purchases, by causing interest rates to rise, results in a decline in investment expenditures.

14. Which of the following statements is true?
   a. A higher exchange rate means cheaper exports and more expensive imports.
   b. A higher exchange rate means more expensive exports and cheaper imports.
   c. A higher exchange rate means more expensive exports and more expensive imports.
   d. A higher exchange rate means cheaper exports and cheaper imports.

15. The national savings rate
   a. equals the consumption share plus the net exports share.
   b. equals the consumption share plus the investment share.
   c. equals the investment share plus the net exports share.
   d. equals the nongovernment share.

16. To understand what causes productivity growth, which of the following should be focused on?
   a. The growth of labor and capital
   b. The growth of labor and technology
   c. The growth of capital and technology
   d. The growth of the labor force

Use Figure 2 for question 17.

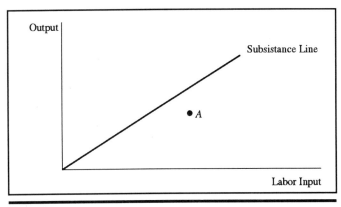

Figure 2

17. At point *A* in Figure 2,
    a. people have more than enough to survive, so the population and the labor force will increase.
    b. people have more than enough to survive, so the population and the labor force will decrease.
    c. people do not have enough to survive, so the population and the labor force will decrease.
    d. people do not have enough to survive, so the population and the labor force will increase.

18. The term that best describes what happens when fewer workers are needed to produce the same amount of output is
    a. creative destruction.
    b. diffusion.
    c. capital-saving technological change.
    d. labor-saving technological change.

19. Suppose that capital per hour of work grows by 2 percent and technology grows by 1 percent over a one-year interval. What is the growth rate of real GDP per hour of work?
    a. 0.67 percent
    b. 1.33 percent
    c. 1.67 percent
    d. 3.0 percent

20. Which of the following is the best example of disembodied technological change?
    a. Learning by doing
    b. A company replacing workers with robots
    c. A mortgage company using a new computer program to determine whether an applicant qualifies for a loan
    d. A local bagel bakery deciding to use the Thompson bagel machine

21. The Malthusian prediction is that real GDP
    a. will always be above the subsistence level of output.
    b. will always be below the subsistence level of output.
    c. will gravitate toward the subsistence level of output and remain there.
    d. can never be at the subsistence level of output.

22. The productivity slowdown in the United States since the mid-1970s is
    a. a decrease in the growth of real GDP per hour of work.
    b. a decrease in the growth of nominal GDP per hour of work.
    c. a decrease in the growth of real GDP.
    d. a decrease in the growth of nominal GDP.

23. Money is
    a. the same as wealth.
    b. the sum of coins and paper money.
    c. the sum of currency and deposits at banks.
    d. the sum of all assets and currency.

24. M2 is
    a. the narrowest measure of money.
    b. currency plus checking deposits.
    c. M1 plus deposits at the Fed.
    d. M1 plus time and savings deposits.

Use Table 1 for question 25.

Assets		Liabilities	
Loans	375	Deposits	500
Bonds	100		
Reserves	25		

TABLE 1

25. Table 1 shows the balance sheet (in millions of dollars) for Bank Inf. Assuming that the bank's reserves are what is required by law, the required reserve ratio is
    a. 5 percent.
    b. 10 percent.
    c. 25 percent.
    d. 75 percent.

26. Suppose the amount of reserves in the banking system equals $60 billion, the amount of deposits equals $802 billion, and the amount of currency equals $321 billion. Under these circumstances, the money multiplier would equal
    a. 0.36.
    b. 1.80.
    c. 2.80.
    d. 2.95.

Use Figure 3 for questions 27 and 28.

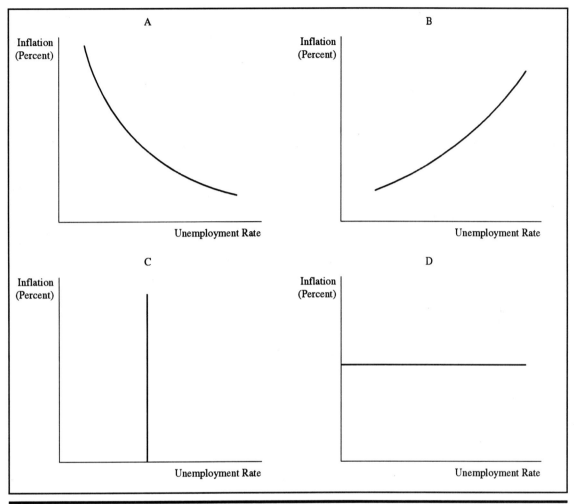

Figure 3

27. Which of the diagrams in Figure 3 represents the shape of a Philips curve that illustrates an exploitable tradeoff between inflation and unemployment?
    a. A
    b. B
    c. C
    d. D

28. Which of the diagrams in Figure 3 represents the shape of the Philips curve in the long run?
    a. A
    b. B
    c. C
    d. D

29. The quantity equation of money describes the relation between
    a. velocity and real GDP.
    b. velocity and nominal GDP.
    c. money and real GDP.
    d. money and nominal GDP.

30. Over the last 20 years, for the largest developed economies in the world
    a. there has been no correlation between the rate of growth of money and the rate of inflation.
    b. there has been a positive correlation between the rate of growth of money and the rate of inflation.
    c. there has been a negative correlation between the rate of growth of money and the rate of inflation.
    d. there has been both a positive and a negative correlation between the rate of growth of money and the rate of inflation.

ANSWERS

1. d	7. d	13. d	19. c	25. a
2. a	8. a	14. b	20. a	26. d
3. c	9. a	15. c	21. c	27. a
4. b	10. d	16. c	22. a	28. c
5. b	11. a	17. c	23. c	29. d
6. a	12. b	18. d	24. d	30. b

PART 4

Economic Fluctuations

Understanding economic fluctuations, the ups and downs of the economy over the business cycle, is as important as understanding long-term economic growth. Chapter 11 begins our study of economic fluctuations. We learn what happens as the economy first enters a recession or a boom, study some of the tools of analysis—the marginal propensity to consume and the consumption function—that will be used throughout the text, and see how these tools help forecast real GDP. In Chapter 12, we complete our study of the economy in the short run. We introduce the concept of the multiplier, a number that describes by how much increases in government purchases, investment, and net exports cause real GDP to rise, and see how the forward-looking consumption model makes the size of the multiplier uncertain.

The next two chapters explain how booms and recessions cause fluctuations in inflation, with the ultimate result that real GDP returns to potential GDP. Chapter 13 constructs the economic fluctuations model. We derive the aggregate demand/inflation (*ADI*) curve and the price adjustment (*PA*) line, and show how the equilibrium level of real GDP and inflation is determined by their intersection. In Chapter 14, the economic fluctuations model is used to study the effects of shocks to the economy, changes in aggregate expenditure, and changes in the monetary policy rule. The process of price adjustment, which provides the transition between short-run booms and recessions and long-run potential GDP, plays a particularly important role.

CHAPTER 11

The First Steps Toward Recession or Boom

CHAPTER OVERVIEW

In the last few chapters, we have studied long-term economic growth. We examined the roles of labor, capital, and technology, and looked at economic growth around the world. We now begin to study economic fluctuations, booms and recessions when real GDP departs from its long-run growth trend. In this chapter, we look at the initial movement of the economy as it enters a recession or boom. We consider why changes in aggregate demand first lead to changes in output and study the role of nominal rigidities. We learn about the marginal propensity to consume and the consumption function, and see how to find real GDP when consumption and income move together. Finally, we see how the tools that we acquire in this chapter can be used to forecast real GDP. In subsequent chapters, we will study the size of the initial step, look at what makes the boom or recession mild or severe, and examine the process by which the economy returns, over time, to potential GDP.

CHAPTER REVIEW

1. Economic fluctuations are temporary departures of real GDP from its long-run growth trend. These departures include recessions, periods when real GDP falls below potential GDP, and booms, times when real GDP rises above potential GDP. Economic fluctuations are also called business cycles.

2. Aggregate demand is the total amount that consumers, businesses, government, and foreigners are willing to spend on all goods and services in the economy. Changes in aggregate demand occur when any or all of these groups expand or cut back their spending plans. These changes range from the government spending more on health care, to foreigners buying more American computers, to consumers feeling more optimistic about the future and buying more holiday presents.

3. What happens if an increase in aggregate demand occurs? Suppose that the economy is in "normal times," neither in a recession nor in a boom, so that real GDP equals potential GDP. In theory, firms could respond to the greater demand for their goods either by expanding output or by raising prices. In practice, prices are sticky. Firms do not raise prices in the short run. Instead, they expand output, and the economy enters a boom. But prices are only sticky, not fixed

forever. Over time, if demand stays high, firms raise their prices, and the boom ends. If aggregate demand falls, the reverse occurs. In the short run, firms lower output instead of cutting prices, and the economy enters a recession. Over time, if demand stays low, prices fall, and the economy recovers.

4. An unwritten understanding between a firm and its customers not to change prices too frequently can be described as an **implicit contract**. Similar "contracts" exist between firms and their workers. Pay scales are typically adjusted once a year. If the firm sees the demand for its product decline, it does not immediately lower wages. In some cases, such as union contracts, these contracts are explicit rather than implicit.

5. This type of behavior, where wages and prices do not adjust immediately to changes in demand, is an example of **nominal rigidities** and is based on the **sticky price assumption**. This is simply another way of saying that wages and prices, both nominal variables, are fixed (rigid) in the short run, but they adjust over time. By contrast, the **flexible price assumption** would predict that a firm would raise its price immediately when demand increases and lower its price immediately when demand falls.

6. Not all economists subscribe to this explanation of economic fluctuations. An alternative explanation, advocated by economists who belong to the **real business cycle school**, is that business cycles are caused by fluctuations *in* potential GDP rather than by changes in aggregate demand that cause movements of real GDP *around* potential GDP. Although, in principle, short-run fluctuations in potential GDP are possible, the factors that underlie potential GDP growth— population, capital, and technology—do not seem to exhibit enough short-run variation to account for the magnitude of observed fluctuations in real GDP.

7. The **consumption function** describes how consumption depends on income. If you receive income, you can either consume or save. In its simplest form, the consumption function says that when income increases—for an individual, the United States, or the whole world—consumption also increases. At low levels of income, individuals borrow—they consume more than their income. At higher income levels, they save—they consume less than their income.

8. The **marginal propensity to consume**, MPC for short, measures *how much* consumption changes for a given change in income. It is defined as the change in consumption divided by the change in income. The MPC is about .60 for the U.S. economy. Thus when income goes up by $1,000, consumption rises by about $600.

9. **Disposable income** is the income that households receive in wages, dividends, and interest payments plus transfers minus taxes. It is the preferred measure of income for use in the consumption function because it measures what households have available to spend. Another form of income used in the consumption function is **aggregate income**, which is also equal to real GDP.

10. The simple consumption function ignores several important factors. Forward-looking theories of consumption explain why people smooth their consumption over time rather than let consumption fluctuate with month-to-month or year-to-year fluctuations in income. They also explain why people smooth their consumption over their entire lifetime. The simple consumption function also ignores the effects of interest rates and wealth on consumption.

11. A **forecast** of real GDP is a prediction of its future level. A short-run forecast would be a prediction of real GDP one year ahead. Economic forecasters use the identity that real GDP is the sum of consumption, investment, government purchases, and net exports ($Y = C + I + G + X$ in symbols) to predict future real GDP based on their predictions of the four categories of spending. A **conditional forecast** is a prediction of what real GDP will be under alternative assumptions about future government purchases. This can be used to make predictions about the effects on the economy of proposed changes in government spending.

12. If all business cycles were identical, they would be easy to forecast. Unfortunately, no two are alike. Some are short, lasting only a year or two, whereas others extend over a number of years. Some are deep, with fast growth (boom) or high unemployment (recession), whereas others are shallow. Although business cycles differ in both duration and intensity, they are all temporary. Over time, real GDP eventually returns to its long-run growth path.

ZEROING IN

1. When demand for a firm's product rises, the firm can either raise prices and sell the same amount at a higher price or increase production and sell more at the original price. Why do firms first respond to increases in demand by adjusting output instead of by raising prices?

   a. When demand increases, the first thing that the owner and/or manager of a firm notices is an increase in demand for the firm's product. Firms operate under **limited information**. First, they do not know whether the change is temporary or permanent. Second, they do not know whether the change affects the entire economy or is specific to their industry. Changing prices is costly. Catalogues need to be reprinted, advertising needs to be changed. If the increase in demand is temporary, firms risk losing some of their regular customers to competitors.

   b. In normal times, firms operate with excess capacity and underutilized equipment. Faced with an increase in demand, they will typically first respond by expanding production instead of by raising prices. The capacity utilization rate, the percent of firms' capacity used for production, is about 80 percent in normal times, falling to 70 percent or lower in recessions and rising to 90 percent or higher in booms.

2. How is income (GDP) determined?

   a. Income is determined when **spending balance** occurs. What is meant by spending balance? It means that two conditions hold simultaneously. These are the income-spending identity (income = consumption + investment + government purchases + net exports, $Y = C + I + G + X$) and the consumption function relating consumption to income.

   b. The easiest way to understand the concept of spending balance is by using a graph. Figure 11.1 puts spending on the vertical axis and income (real GDP) on the horizontal axis. Because income is always equal to spending, we draw a line, called the **45-degree line**, that depicts this equality. If you remember geometry, it is called the 45-degree line because it bisects the 90-degree angle formed by the two axes. If you've forgotten all your geometry, just think of the 45-degree line as those points on the diagram where income and spending are equal.

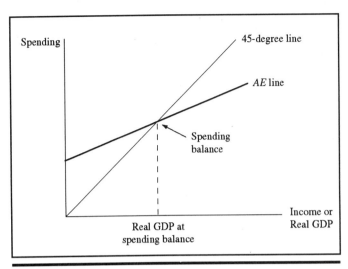

Figure 11.1

c. The **aggregate expenditure (AE) line** is also depicted in Figure 11.1. The AE line is the sum of $C + I + G + X$. According to the simple consumption function, consumption depends only on income, and the slope of the consumption function is the marginal propensity to consume (MPC). Although we haven't said much about investment, government purchases, and net exports, assume, for the moment, that they are constant. (In particular, assume that they do not depend on income.) Then the AE line, the sum of the consumption function and three constants, has the same slope, the MPC, as the consumption function.

d. Spending balance can now be defined as the intersection between the 45-degree line and the aggregate expenditure line. Along the 45-degree line, income equals spending. Along the AE line, consumption is determined by income according to the consumption function. Although either of these conditions can be satisfied by many values of real GDP, only one value, the point of spending balance, satisfies both.

3. What causes income (GDP) to increase or decrease?

   a. We have shown how spending balance is determined by the intersection of the 45-degree line and the aggregate expenditure line. We now look at shifts of the AE line and show how they affect the point of spending balance and the level of real GDP.

   b. What shifts the AE line? Remember how the AE line was constructed. First, the consumption function was used to relate consumption to income. Then, investment I, government purchases G, and net exports X were added to the consumption function to determine the AE line. Changes in the same three variables cause the AE line to shift. Increases in I, G, and X shift the AE line upward, and decreases in I, G, and X shift the AE line downward.

   c. This can be seen in Figure 11.2, in which the initial point of spending balance is where real GDP equals potential GDP. If the AE line shifts up, spending balance occurs at a point where output exceeds potential, and the economy is in a boom. If the AE line shifts down, spending balance occurs at a point where output is less than potential, and the economy is in a recession. These movements of the point of spending balance are called the first steps toward a boom or recession because, as we shall see in the next few chapters, they are not the end of the story.

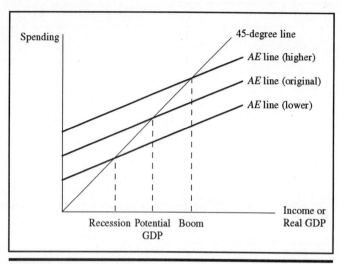

Figure 11.2

d. The same diagram can also be used to illustrate shifts of the point of spending balance toward, instead of away from, potential GDP. Suppose that the initial point of spending balance in Figure 11.2 occurs during a recession, with output below potential. An increase in government spending would shift the *AE* line up, moving the point of spending balance toward potential GDP. Depending on the size of the increase in *G*, the *AE* line could move by enough to shift the point of spending balance so that real GDP equals, or even exceeds, potential GDP. Increases in *I* or *X* would have the same effect. On the other hand, a decline in *G*, *I*, or *X* would move the point of spending balance down, further reducing real GDP and causing a greater recession.

ACTIVE REVIEW

Fill-in Questions

1. Economic _____ are temporary departures of real GDP from its long-run growth trend.

2. _____ is the total amount consumers, businesses, government, and foreigners are willing to spend on all goods and services in the economy.

3. Prices are called _____ because they do not change in the short run.

4. The _____ is the percentage of firms' capacity used for production.

5. A firm is said to operate under _____ information when it does not know whether changes in the demand for its product are temporary or permanent.

6. A(n) _____ is an unwritten understanding between a firm and its customers not to change prices too frequently.

7. Economists of the _____ school believe that economic fluctuations can be explained by movements in potential GDP.

8. The response of consumption to income is described by the _____.

9. The _____ measures how much consumption changes for a given change in income.

10. _____ income measures what households have available to spend.

11. _____ theories of consumption help explain why people smooth consumption over time.

12. The _____ identity is that income = consumption + investment + government purchases + net exports.

13. The _____ depicts the equality between income and spending.

14. The _____ line is the sum of consumption + investment + government purchases + net exports.

15. _____ occurs at the intersection of the 45-degree line and the aggregate expenditure line.

True-False Questions

T   F   1. When the economy is in neither a recession nor a boom, real GDP equals potential GDP.

T   F   2. The economy is in a boom if real GDP is less than potential GDP.

T   F   3. Booms and recessions never last more than a year or two.

T   F   4. Booms and recessions are temporary.

T   F   5. Business cycles are easy to forecast because they are so regular.

T   F   6. Prices are called sticky because they never change.

T   F   7. Firms normally operate at 100 percent of capacity.

T   F   8. Contracts can be either explicit or implicit.

T   F   9. Conditional forecasts are always more accurate than unconditional forecasts.

T   F   10. At low levels of income, individuals consume more than their income.

T   F   11. The marginal propensity to consume is the change in consumption divided by the change in income.

T   F   12. Spending balance occurs when income equals consumption.

T F   13. Spending balance occurs at the intersection of the 45-degree line and the aggregate expenditure line.

T F   14. Spending balance can occur only at potential GDP.

T F   15. The aggregate expenditure line shifts with changes in technology.

Short-Answer Questions

1. What are the two types of economic fluctuations?

2. What is another name for economic fluctuations?

3. Are economic fluctuations permanent?

4. What is real GDP in "normal times"?

5. What does it mean for prices to be sticky?

6. Why do firms first respond to changes in demand by adjusting output rather than changing prices?

7. What is the difference between a forecast and a conditional forecast of real GDP?

8. How do economists who belong to the real business cycle school explain economic fluctuations?

9. According to the simple consumption function, how is consumption determined?

10. What is measured by the marginal propensity to consume?

11. What does the simple consumption function ignore?

12. Which two conditions are satisfied at the point of spending balance?

13. Which two lines intersect at the point of spending balance?

14. What causes the aggregate expenditure (AE) line to shift?

15. What happens to the point of spending balance when the AE line shifts up?

WORKING IT OUT

1. The first concept that we will illustrate is how, using graphs, to determine the level of income (GDP) at the point of spending balance. Then we will show what happens to income if a component of aggregate expenditure, in this case net exports, increases.

    a. The first step is to draw a diagram, remembering to label the axes. In this case, illustrated in Figure 11.3, spending is on the vertical axis and income (real GDP) is on the horizontal axis.

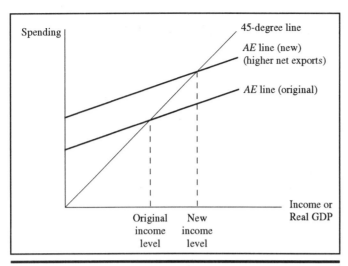

Figure 11.3

b. Spending balance occurs at the intersection of the 45-degree line and the aggregate expenditure line. As shown in Figure 11.3, the 45-degree line has a slope of 1, so that income equals spending. The AE line is also upward-sloping, but it is flatter than the 45-degree line. Their intersection determines the point of spending balance.

c. Income will change if something occurs that shifts the AE line. In this case, the increase in net exports shifts the AE line upward from AE (original) to AE (new). This determines a new point of spending balance at a higher level of income. This is also shown in Figure 11.3.

2. The point of spending balance can also be determined using tables. Suppose you are given the following information on the relation between income and consumption (in billions of dollars).

Income (Y)	Consumption (C)
0	500
1,000	1,000
2,000	1,500
3,000	2,000
4,000	2,500
5,000	3,000

Assume that investment I is $500 billion, government purchases G are $400 billion, and net exports X are $100 billion.

a. The first thing that you can determine is the marginal propensity to consume (MPC), which is the change in consumption divided by the change in income. Looking at the two columns of the table, you can see that whenever consumption increases by 500, income rises by $1,000. The MPC is the change in consumption, 500, divided by the change in income, 1,000, which is 500/1,000, or .50.

b. You can also determine the level of income at the point of spending balance, which occurs when income Y = consumption C + investment I + government purchases G + net exports X. Subtracting C from both sides of the equation, this can be written as $Y - C = I + G + X$. Since $I + G + X = 500 + 400 + 100 = 1,000$, the point of spending balance is where $Y - C = 1,000$. When $Y = 3,000$, $C = 2,000$, and $3,000 - 2,000 = 1,000$. Thus income is $3,000 billion at the point of spending balance.

Worked Problems

1. Draw a diagram with a 45-degree line and an aggregate expenditure (AE) line. What determines the point of spending balance? Assume that spending balance occurs when real GDP equals potential GDP. What happens to income if net exports decrease?

Answer

First, draw a diagram with spending on the vertical axis and income (real GDP) on the horizontal axis, as shown in Figure 11.4. The 45-degree line has a slope of 1, the AE line is upward-sloping but flatter than the 45-degree line, and their intersection determines the point of spending balance. The problem assumes that this point occurs when real GDP equals potential GDP. If net exports decrease, the AE line shifts downward from AE (original) to AE (new). This causes a decrease in income. Since income decreases to below potential GDP, this is a recession.

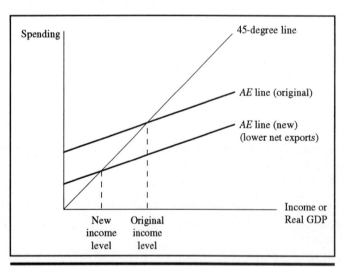

Figure 11.4

2. The following table shows the relationship between income and consumption (in billions of dollars).

Income (Y)	Consumption (C)
0	800
1,000	1,400
2,000	2,000
3,000	2,600
4,000	3,200
5,000	3,800

Assume that investment I is $400 billion, government purchases G are $300 billion, and net exports X are $100 billion.

a. What is the numerical value of the marginal propensity to consume?

b. What is the level of income at the point of spending balance?

Answers

a. *The marginal propensity to consume (MPC) is the change in consumption divided by the change in income. Whenever consumption increases by 600, income rises by 1,000. The MPC is 600/1,000, or .60.*

b. *Spending balance occurs when income = consumption + investment + government purchases + net exports. Since I + G + X = 800, the point of spending balance is where Y - C = 800. When Y = 4,000, C = 3,200, and 4,000 - 3,200 = 800. Thus income is $4,000 billion at the point of spending balance.*

Practice Problems

1. Draw a diagram with a 45-degree line and an aggregate expenditure (AE) line. What determines the point of spending balance? Assume that spending balance occurs when real GDP equals potential GDP. What happens to income if government purchases decrease?

2. Draw a diagram with a 45-degree line and an aggregate expenditure (AE) line. Assume that spending balance occurs when real GDP is below potential GDP. What happens to income if both investment and net exports increase?

3. Draw a diagram with a 45-degree line and an aggregate expenditure (AE) line. Assume that spending balance occurs when real GDP equals potential GDP. What happens to income if government purchases increase and net exports decrease by exactly the same amount?

4. The following table shows the relationship between income and consumption (in billions of dollars).

Income (Y)	Consumption (C)
0	500
1,000	1,000
2,000	1,500
3,000	2,000
4,000	2,500
5,000	3,000

Assume that investment I is $400 billion, government purchases G are $100 billion, and net exports X are $0 billion.

a. What is the numerical value of the marginal propensity to consume?

b. What is the level of income at the point of spending balance?

5. The following table shows the relationship between income and consumption (in billions of dollars).

Income (Y)	Consumption (C)
0	600
1,000	1,300
2,000	2,000
3,000	2,700
4,000	3,400
5,000	4,100

Assume that investment I is $500 billion, government purchases G are $300 billion, and net exports X are $100 billion.

a. What is the numerical value of the marginal propensity to consume?

b. What is the level of income at the point of spending balance?

6. The following table shows the relationship between income and consumption (in billions of dollars).

Income (Y)	Consumption (C)
0	400
1,000	1,200
2,000	2,000
3,000	2,800
4,000	3,600
5,000	4,400

Assume that investment I is $300 billion, government purchases G are $200 billion, and net exports X are -$100 billion.

a. What is the numerical value of the marginal propensity to consume?

b. What is the level of income at the point of spending balance?

CHAPTER TEST

1. Economic fluctuations
   a. never last more than 2 years.
   b. are all alike.
   c. are also called business cycles.
   d. are permanent departures of real GDP from potential GDP.

2. In "normal times,"
   a. real GDP equals consumption.
   b. real GDP equals investment.
   c. real GDP equals government purchases.
   d. real GDP equals potential GDP.

3. Firms respond to an increase in the demand for their goods in the short run by
   a. expanding output.
   b. raising prices.
   c. reducing output.
   d. cutting prices.

4. In normal times, the capacity utilization rate is about
   a. 60 percent.
   b. 70 percent.
   c. 80 percent.
   d. 90 percent.

5. Firms are said to operate with limited information because
   a. they do not know the size of their work force.
   b. they do not know the value of their capital stock.
   c. they do not know whether changes in demand are temporary or permanent.
   d. they do not know their capacity utilization rate.

6. Prices are called sticky because
   a. they never change.
   b. they adjust immediately to changes in demand.
   c. they are fixed in the short run but adjust over time.
   d. they can go up, but they never come down.

7. Economists who belong to the real business cycle school believe that
   a. economic fluctuations are caused by fluctuations in potential GDP.
   b. economic fluctuations are caused by fluctuations in real GDP.
   c. economic fluctuations are caused by changes in aggregate demand.
   d. economic fluctuations are caused by changes in government purchases.

8. The difference between a forecast and a conditional forecast of real GDP is
   a. that a forecast is made under alternative assumptions about government purchases.
   b. that a conditional forecast is made under alternative assumptions about government purchases.
   c. that a forecast is made under alternative assumptions about net exports.
   d. that a conditional forecast is made under alternative assumptions about net exports.

9. The simple consumption function describes
   a. how income depends on consumption.
   b. how income depends on interest rates.
   c. how consumption depends on income.
   d. how consumption depends on interest rates.

10. Spending balance occurs when
    a. $Y - C = I + G + X$.
    b. $Y - I = C + G + X$.
    c. $Y - G = C + I + X$.
    d. $Y - X = C + I + G$.

11. The 45-degree line depicts the equality of
    a. consumption and income.
    b. real GDP and potential GDP.
    c. income and spending.
    d. income and real GDP.

Questions 12 and 13 refer to the following table. (Income and consumption are in billions of dollars.)

Income (*Y*)	Consumption (*C*)
0	200
1,000	800
2,000	1,400
3,000	2,000
4,000	2,600
5,000	3,200

12. Using the above table, the marginal propensity to consume is
    a. .3.
    b. .6.
    c. .8.
    d. 1.0.

13. Suppose investment *I* is $300 billion, government purchases *G* are $200 billion, and net export *X* are $100 billion. At what level of income does spending balance occur?
    a. $1,000 billion
    b. $2,000 billion
    c. $3,000 billion
    d. $4,000 billion

14. The aggregate expenditure (*AE*) line is the sum of
    a. $C + I + G$.
    b. $C + I + X$.
    c. $C + I + G + X$.
    d. $C + I + G + Y$.

15. The slope of the aggregate expenditure line is
    a. the marginal propensity to consume.
    b. the marginal propensity to invest.
    c. the marginal propensity to export.
    d. the marginal propensity to save.

16. Which of the following causes an upward shift in the aggregate expenditure (*AE*) line?
    a. A decrease in investment
    b. A decrease in government purchases
    c. An increase in real GDP
    d. An increase in net exports

Use Figure 11.5 for questions 17, 18, and 19.

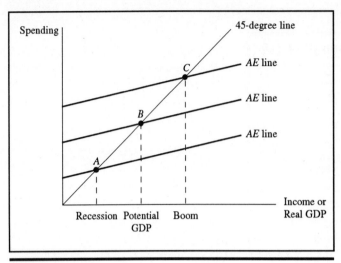

Figure 11.5

17. Starting from a point of spending balance with real GDP equal to potential GDP, a decrease in government purchases
    a. shifts the *AE* line up from *A* to *B*.
    b. shifts the *AE* line up from *B* to *C*.
    c. shifts the *AE* line down from *B* to *A*.
    d. leaves the *AE* line unchanged.

18. Starting from a point of spending balance with real GDP equal to potential GDP, an increase in net exports
    a. shifts the *AE* line up from *A* to *C*.
    b. shifts the *AE* line up from *B* to *C*.
    c. shifts the *AE* line down from *C* to *A*.
    d. leaves the *AE* line unchanged.

19. Starting from a point of spending balance with real GDP equal to potential GDP, an increase in investment matched by an equal decrease in net exports
    a. shifts the *AE* line up from *A* to *B*.
    b. shifts the *AE* line up from *B* to *C*.
    c. shifts the *AE* line down from *C* to *A*.
    d. leaves the *AE* line unchanged.

20. Starting from a point of spending balance with real GDP below potential GDP, an increase in government purchases
    a. increases real GDP to equal potential GDP.
    b. increases real GDP to above potential GDP.
    c. increases real GDP, but to a point that is still below potential GDP.
    d. increases real GDP, but we do not know whether a, b, or c is correct.

ANSWERS TO THE REVIEW QUESTIONS

Fill-in Questions

1. fluctuations
2. Aggregate demand
3. sticky
4. capacity utilization rate
5. imperfect
6. implicit contract
7. real business cycle
8. consumption function
9. marginal propensity to consume
10. Disposable
11. Forward-looking
12. income-spending
13. 45-degree line
14. aggregate expenditure
15. Spending balance

True-False Questions

1. **True**. Real GDP equals potential GDP in normal times.
2. **False**. When real GDP is less than potential GDP, the economy is in a recession.
3. **False**. Some business cycles last for a number of years.
4. **True**. Real GDP eventually returns to potential GDP.
5. **False**. Business cycles are difficult to forecast because no two are alike.
6. **False**. Prices are called sticky because they do not change in the short run.
7. **False**. In normal times, there is some unused capacity.
8. **True**. Union contracts are explicit, whereas unwritten understandings between a firm and its customers or workers are implicit.
9. **False**. The two types of forecasts cannot be compared in this manner.
10. **True**. At low levels of income, individuals borrow.
11. **True**. The MPC measures how much consumption changes when income changes.
12. **False**. Spending balance occurs when income equals spending and consumption is determined by income according to the consumption function.
13. **True**. Income equals spending along the 45-degree line, and the consumption function helps determine the aggregate expenditure line.
14. **False**. Spending balance can also occur during booms and recessions.
15. **False**. The aggregate expenditure line shifts with changes in government purchases, investment, taxes, and net exports.

Short-Answer Questions

1. Booms and recessions are the two types of economic fluctuations.
2. Another name for economic fluctuations is business cycles.
3. No, economic fluctuations are temporary. Real GDP returns over time to its long-run growth path.
4. In "normal times," real GDP equals potential GDP.
5. Prices are called sticky because they do not adjust in the short run when demand changes. In the long run, however, they do respond to changes in demand.
6. Firms have limited information. When demand changes, they do not always know why it has changed or whether the change is permanent. Therefore, firms, which normally operate with excess capacity, will adjust output rather than incur the costs involved in changing prices.
7. A forecast of real GDP is a prediction of its future level. A conditional forecast is a prediction of what real GDP will be under alternative assumptions about future government purchases.

8. Members of the real business cycle school believe that economic fluctuations are caused by fluctuations in potential GDP.
9. According to the simple consumption function, consumption is determined by income.
10. The marginal propensity to consume measures how much consumption changes for a given change in income.
11. The simple consumption function ignores the effects on consumption of forward-looking behavior, interest rates, and wealth.
12. The income-spending identity and the consumption function are satisfied at the point of spending balance.
13. The 45-degree line and the aggregate expenditure line intersect at the point of spending balance.
14. Changes in investment, government purchases, and net exports shift the *AE* line.
15. When the *AE* line shifts up, spending balance occurs at a higher level of income.

SOLUTIONS TO THE PRACTICE PROBLEMS

1. The point of spending balance is always at the intersection of the 45-degree line and the aggregate expenditure line. A decrease in government purchases shifts the *AE* line down, reducing income and causing a recession.

2. Increases in investment and net exports shift the *AE* line up, increasing income. The initial point of spending balance occurred at a level of income below potential GDP, but we do not know whether the increase in income is sufficient to raise real GDP up to, or even beyond, potential GDP.

3. An increase in government purchases would shift the *AE* line up, and the decrease in net exports would shift it down. Since the increase in *G* is equal to the decrease in *X*, the two effects cancel each other out. The *AE* line does not move, and income remains at potential GDP.

4. a. The marginal propensity to consume (MPC) = 500/1,000 = .50.

   b. At the point of spending balance, income (*Y*) = $2,000 billion.

5. a. The marginal propensity to consume (MPC) = 700/1,000 = .70.

   b. At the point of spending balance, income (*Y*) = $5,000 billion.

6. a. The marginal propensity to consume (MPC) = 800/1,000 = .80.

   b. At the point of spending balance, income (*Y*) = $4,000 billion.

ANSWERS TO THE CHAPTER TEST

1. c	6. c	11. c	16. d
2. d	7. a	12. b	17. c
3. a	8. b	13. b	18. b
4. c	9. c	14. c	19. d
5. c	10. a	15. a	20. d

CHAPTER **12**

The Uncertain Multiplier

CHAPTER OVERVIEW

You have learned that increases in government purchases, investment, and net exports cause income (real GDP) to rise. In this chapter, you'll learn by how much income rises. The question of by how much income rises when government spending increases has important implications for policy decisions such as the cuts in defense spending at the close of the cold war and the projected jump in health-care spending over the next few years. The most important concept introduced in this chapter is the multiplier, a number that determines by how much real GDP changes when government spending, investment, or net exports change. We study how to find the multiplier using both graphs and algebra, and see that the size of the multiplier is uncertain. We then look at the multiplier when net exports depend on income and the multiplier for a tax change. Finally, we study the forward-looking consumption model and learn more about why the multiplier is uncertain. This chapter completes our analysis of the economy in the short run. In the rest of Part 4, we discuss how the economy moves over time from the short-run fluctuations to its long-run growth path.

CHAPTER REVIEW

1. The **multiplier** is a number that represents how much real GDP changes when aggregate expenditure changes. Algebraically, it is the change in real GDP divided by the change in aggregate expenditure, or the ratio of the two changes. The change in aggregate expenditure may be caused by a number of factors; changes in government purchases, taxes, investment, and net exports are the most important.

2. When aggregate expenditure increases, real GDP rises by more than the change in expenditure. Algebraically, the change in real GDP exceeds the change in aggregate expenditure, or the ratio of the two changes is greater than 1. The *size of the multiplier*, which is the ratio of the two changes, is greater than 1.

3. Why is the multiplier greater than 1? Suppose that the government increases spending so that NASA can build a space station. If this were the end of the story, the change in real GDP would equal the change in aggregate expenditure, and the multiplier would be 1. But there is more. In order to build the space station, NASA hires additional workers and outside suppliers, and they spend part of their wages and payments. This spending goes to more people (grocery store owners, etc.), who in turn spend part of their payments on other goods. Through these *rounds of spending*, the total change in real GDP exceeds the initial change in aggregate expenditure, and the multiplier is greater than 1. These rounds of spending occur quickly—the total change in real GDP is achieved in about a year.

4. The *marginal propensity to consume (MPC)*, as you should remember from Chapter 11, is the change in consumption divided by the change in income. In the above example, the additional workers that NASA hires will spend more of their wages if their MPC is higher than if their MPC is lower. More generally, each round of spending will be greater if the MPC is higher. The greater the spending, the larger the total effect on real GDP. Thus the multiplier, which measures by how much income increases when aggregate expenditure rises, will be larger if the MPC is higher. Uncertainty about the value of the MPC is an important cause of uncertainty about the value of the multiplier.

5. The **marginal propensity to save (MPS)** is the change in saving divided by the change in income. Since any additional income that an individual receives must be either consumed or saved, the marginal propensity to consume plus the marginal propensity to save = 1, or MPS = 1 minus MPC. Since the multiplier is positively related to the MPC, the multiplier is greater the higher the MPC; since it is negatively related to the MPS, the multiplier is smaller the higher the MPS.

6. The **marginal propensity to import (MPI)** is the change in imports divided by the change in income. When U.S. income goes up, part of the increase is spent on foreign produced goods (automobiles, consumer electronics, etc.), and so the MPI is positive. Since most of the goods that are consumed when income rises are produced in the United States (not imported), the MPI is smaller than the MPC.

7. *Net exports* are exports minus imports. Although imports, as explained above, are positively related to U.S. income, exports are not related to U.S. income. (Exports are positively related to foreign income, not U.S. income.) Net exports, exports minus imports, are negatively related to income because exports are unrelated to income and imports are positively related.

8. The value of the multiplier is negatively related to the value of the MPI. When the MPI is higher, a larger part of the rounds of spending goes to foreign produced goods. Although this increases foreign income, it does not affect U.S. income, and so does not contribute to further rounds of spending.

9. The **twin deficits** are the budget deficit and the trade deficit. If government purchases are increased, the budget deficit, which is defined as government receipts minus government spending, will also increase. (Receipts are constant while spending rises.) The increase in government purchases also increases the trade deficit. First, the increase in government purchases raises income through the multiplier effect. Second, the increase in income raises imports because the MPI is positive. Third, net exports fall because exports are constant while imports rise, causing a trade deficit. Thus there is a relationship between the twin deficits in the short-run period covered in this chapter. An increase in government purchases causes both a budget deficit and a trade deficit.

10. The **tax rate** is the percentage of income that individuals are required to pay to the government, and taxes, or **tax revenue**, is the total amount that the government receives. Changes in tax rates can raise or lower potential GDP, and changes in tax revenue cause short-run departures of real GDP from potential GDP. Tax cuts raise disposable income, increasing consumption (by the MPC times the change in disposable income) and raising real GDP. The *multiplier for tax changes* is smaller than the multiplier for aggregate expenditure because the initial round of spending equals the MPC (< 1) times the change in disposable income rather than the full increase in aggregate expenditure.

11. The **balanced budget multiplier** is the ratio of the change in real GDP to a change in government purchases matched by a change in taxes. In other words, it describes by how much real GDP changes if the rise in government purchases is matched by an increase in taxes, so that

the budget deficit is unchanged (hence the term *balanced budget multiplier*). At first, you might think that the balanced budget multiplier would be zero, but you would be wrong. Remember that the multiplier for government purchases is greater than the multiplier for tax changes. The increase in government purchases raises income by more than the tax increase lowers income, so the balanced budget multiplier is positive. You can show algebraically that the balanced budget multiplier equals 1.

ZEROING IN

1. The most important concept for you to understand in this chapter is that of the multiplier. Remember that the multiplier represents how much income changes when aggregate expenditure changes. In the chapter review, we explained the concept of the multiplier intuitively through rounds of spending. Here we will provide a graphical illustration.

   a. The first step in graphing the multiplier is to set up the diagram. In Figure 12.1, with spending on the vertical axis and income (real GDP) on the horizontal axis, we draw the 45-degree line and the aggregate expenditure (*AE*) line. Note that the *AE* line slopes upward but is flatter than the 45-degree line.

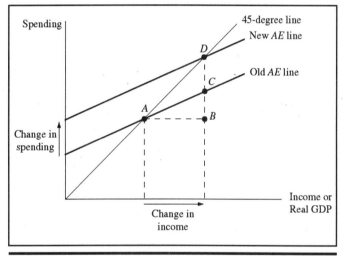

Figure 12.1

   b. An increase in aggregate expenditure shifts the *AE* line up from the old *AE* line to the new *AE* line. The point of spending balance, the intersection of the 45-degree line and the *AE* line, shifts from point *A* to point *D*. Income (real GDP) increases.

   c. The change in spending (aggregate expenditure) is the vertical distance between the old and new *AE* lines. Since the two lines are parallel, this can be measured at any point on the lines and equals the distance *CD*. (By the distance *CD*, we mean the distance from the point *C* to the point *D*.) The change in income is the horizontal distance between the two dotted lines, or *AB*. (Since the two dotted lines are also parallel, this can also be measured at any point.)

   d. How much does income increase? Because *ABD* forms a right triangle, the distance *AB*, the change in income, equals the distance *BD*. Remember that the distance *CD* is the change in spending. Since the distance *BD* is greater than the distance *CD*, the change in income is greater than the change in spending. The multiplier, which is the change in income divided by the change in spending, is greater than 1.

2. What determines the value of the multiplier? We will show that a lower marginal propensity to consume (MPC) and/or a higher marginal propensity to import (MPI) will lower the multiplier.

   a. The MPC and the MPI determine the slope of the aggregate expenditure (*AE*) line. The smaller the MPC and the larger the MPI, the flatter the *AE* line. This is illustrated in Figure 12.2.

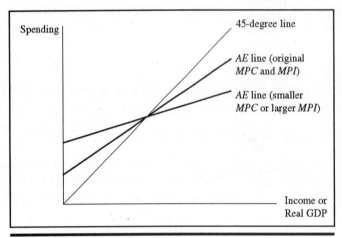

Figure 12.2

   b. With a flatter *AE* line, the multiplier is smaller. This is shown in Figure 12.3. Although the change in income, the distance *BD*, is greater than the change in spending, the distance *CD*, the ratio of *BD* divided by *CD* is smaller than with the steeper *AE* line in Figure 12.1. Therefore the multiplier in Figure 12.3, with a flatter *AE* line, although still greater than 1, is smaller than the multiplier in Figure 12.1.

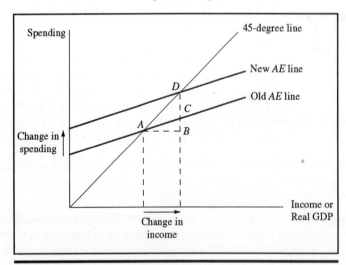

Figure 12.3

3. The simple consumption function, with a constant marginal propensity to consume (MPC), does not provide a satisfactory theory of consumption. Instead of being constant, the MPC, and therefore the multiplier, seems to change in different situations. The **forward-looking consumption model**, although more complicated than the consumption function, provides a way to understand how the MPC changes.

a. The forward-looking consumption model has its origins in two models developed in the 1950s: Milton Friedman's **permanent income model** and Franco Modigliani's **life-cycle model**. The forward-looking model used in the 1990s, however, has been developed tremendously since that time.

b. The central idea of the forward-looking model is that most people engage in **consumption smoothing**. Instead of allowing their consumption to vary with their income, which would be implied by a constant MPC, they spend less than their income (and save) in good years and spend more than their income (and dissave) in bad years. Suppose you were to win $1 million in a lottery. If your MPC was .90, would you spend $900,000 in the year that you won and then return to your old lifestyle, or would you spread the winnings over time? A constant MPC implies the former; consumption smoothing implies the latter.

c. Consumption smoothing is not perfect. One reason is that some people are **liquidity constrained**: They cannot borrow enough to completely smooth their consumption. One example is (virtually) every reader of this study guide. As a student, if you go to your local bank and say, "I want a loan so that I can increase my consumption while I'm in school up to the level that I'll be able to afford after I graduate and get a high-paying job," don't expect the banker to reply, "That's fine, we always approve consumption smoothing loans."

d. A striking implication of the forward-looking model is that, because people attempt to smooth their consumption, the MPC is very small for temporary changes in income and very large for permanent changes in income. Thus the multiplier for a *temporary tax cut*, which produces only a temporary change in income, is smaller than the multiplier for a *permanent tax cut*, which produces a permanent change in income. This explains the contrast between the low MPC for the one-year tax rebate of 1975, which was explicitly temporary, and the high MPC for the tax cuts of the early 1980s, which were explicitly permanent.

e. A final implication of the forward-looking model is that *anticipated tax changes* will have effects before the tax changes are actually enacted. Suppose you expect a tax increase in the future. According to the forward-looking model, you will begin to reduce your consumption now in anticipation of your expected lower income in the future. Although these effects are difficult to measure, estimates based on the **rational expectations assumption**, that people's predictions of the future are on average about the same as economic forecasters', suggest that the effects are large and significant.

ACTIVE REVIEW

Fill-in Questions

1. The _____ represents by how much real GDP changes when aggregate expenditure changes.

2. The multiplier is _____ than 1.

3. The _____ is the change in consumption divided by the change in income.

4. The _____ is the change in saving divided by the change in income.

5. The _____ is the change in imports divided by the change in income.

6. _____ are exports minus imports.

7. The twin deficits are the _____ and _____ deficits.

8. The _____ is the percentage of income that individuals are required to pay to the government.

9. The multiplier for tax changes is _____ than the multiplier for aggregate expenditure.

10. The _____ is the ratio of the change in real GDP to a change in government purchases matched by a change in taxes.

11. The _____ consumption model allows the marginal propensity to consume to change.

12. The origins of the forward-looking consumption model are the _____ and _____ models.

13. _____ occurs when people try to keep their consumption steady over time.

14. When people cannot borrow enough to completely smooth their consumption, they are said to be _____.

15. A temporary tax cut is also called a tax _____.

True-False Questions

T   F   1. The multiplier is the change in real GDP divided by the change in aggregate expenditure.

T   F   2. When government purchases increase by $100 billion, real GDP increases by more than $100 billion.

T   F   3. When government purchases increase by $100 billion, real GDP immediately increases by more than $100 billion.

T   F   4. The total effect on real GDP of a change in net exports is achieved in about a decade.

T   F   5. The marginal propensity to consume (MPC) and the multiplier are positively related.

T   F   6. The marginal propensity to import is positive.

T   F   7. Exports are positively related to U.S. income.

T   F   8. The budget and trade deficits are called the twin deficits because they are the same size.

T   F   9. Changes in tax rates and changes in tax revenues have different effects on real GDP.

T   F   10. The balanced budget multiplier is the multiplier when the government budget is balanced.

T   F   11. The forward-looking consumption model assumes that the MPC is constant.

T   F   12. Consumers are liquidity constrained if they cannot borrow all that they want.

T   F   13. According to the forward-looking model, the MPC is different for temporary and permanent changes in income.

T   F   14. According to the forward-looking model, people will spend a large proportion of a one-year tax rebate.

T   F   15. According to the consumption function, anticipated tax changes will have effects before the tax changes are enacted.

Short-Answer Questions

1. What factors cause aggregate expenditure to change?

2. How large is the multiplier?

3. Why is the multiplier greater than 1?

4. What is the relation between the marginal propensity to consume (MPC) and the marginal propensity to save (MPS)?

5. How does the multiplier depend on the MPS?

6. Why is the MPI smaller than the MPC?

7. What causes uncertainty about the value of the multiplier?

8. What is the relation between budget deficits and trade deficits in the short run?

9. Why is the multiplier for tax changes smaller than the multiplier for aggregate expenditure?

10. Why is the balanced budget multiplier positive?

11. What is the central idea of the forward-looking consumption model?

12. What are the origins of the forward-looking consumption model?

13. According to the forward-looking model, how do the multipliers for temporary and permanent tax cuts differ?

14. According to the forward-looking model, why do anticipated tax cuts have effects before the tax cuts are actually enacted?

15. What is the rational expectations assumption?

WORKING IT OUT

1. In Chapter 11, we used the 45-degree line and the consumption function to derive the point of spending balance. Here we will use the same concepts to derive the multiplier.

   a. Start with the identity that income equals spending,

   $$Y = C + I + G + X$$

   where Y is income, C is consumption, G is government purchases, and X is net exports. This is the algebraic version of the 45-degree line.

   b. The consumption function states that consumption consists of two parts. The first part, which we call c, does not depend on income. The second part consists of the marginal propensity to consume (MPC) times the level of income. Adding the two parts together,

   $$C = c + (\text{MPC} \times Y)$$

   The part of consumption that does not depend on income, c, is positive because at very low levels of income, people borrow rather than consume nothing.

   c. Assume (for the moment) that investment, government purchases, and net exports do not depend on income. Substitute the consumption function into the income = spending identity:

   $$Y = c + \text{MPC} \times Y + I + G + X$$

   Subtract $\text{MPC} \times Y$ from both sides of the equation:

   $$Y - \text{MPC} \times Y = c + I + G + X$$

   Gather terms involving Y:

   $$Y(1 - \text{MPC}) = c + I + G + X$$

   Divide both sides by $1 - \text{MPC}$ to get

   $$Y = \frac{1}{1 - \text{MPC}} (c + I + G + X)$$

   d. To derive the multiplier, we need to write the above equation in terms of changes. Using the Greek letter Δ to denote the change in a variable,

   $$Y\Delta = \frac{1}{1 - \text{MPC}} (\Delta I + \Delta G + \Delta X)$$

   where $\Delta c = 0$ because c is a constant. The multiplier

   $$\frac{1}{1 - \text{MPC}}$$

   is the number that shows how much income changes when any of the categories of aggregate expenditure, $I + G + X$, change. Note that the multipliers for investment, government spending, and net exports are identical.

2. The multiplier can also be derived using specific numerical values for the variables and the MPC.

   a. As above, start with the identity that income equals spending,

   $$Y = C + I + G + X$$

   Suppose that the consumption function is

   $$C = c + .8Y$$

   where the MPC = .8.

   b. Substitute C (from the consumption function) into the identity:

   $$Y = c + .8Y + I + G + X$$

   Subtract .8Y from both sides

   $$Y - .8Y = c + I + G + X$$

   Gather terms involving Y:

   $$Y(1 - .8) = c + I + G + X$$
   $$Y(.2) = c + I + G + X$$

   Divide both sides by .2 (or multiply both sides by 5):

   $$Y = 5(c + I + G + X)$$

   c. To complete the derivation, write the equation in terms of changes:

   $$\Delta Y = 5 (\Delta I + \Delta G + \Delta X)$$

   The multiplier equals 5.

   d. You can also use the formula to find the multiplier. With the MPC = .8,

   $$\frac{1}{1 - \text{MPC}} = \frac{1}{1 - 8} = \frac{1}{.2} = 5$$

   The multiplier again equals 5.

3. Another way to think about the multiplier is by starting with numbers instead of equations. In Chapter 11, we looked at this example to determine the point of spending balance.

Income (Y)	Consumption (C)
0	500
1,000	1,000
2,000	1,500
3,000	2,000
4,000	2,500
5,000	3,000

We will use the same values to derive the multiplier.

a. We first need to calculate the marginal propensity to consume. Remember that the MPC is the change in consumption divided by the change in income. In this example, $\Delta C/\Delta Y = 500/1{,}000 = .5$.

b. Now use the formula for the multiplier.

$$\frac{1}{1 - \text{MPC}} = \frac{1}{1 - 5} = \frac{1}{.5} = 2$$

The multiplier equals 2.

Worked Problems

1. Suppose that the consumption function is

   $$C = c + .8Y$$

   and the net export function is

   $$X = x - .2Y$$

   where the MPC = .8 and the marginal propensity to import (MPI) = .2. What is the multiplier?

Answer

Substitute the consumption and net export functions into the income = spending identity:

$$Y = c + .8Y + I + G + x - .2Y$$

Collecting and gathering terms,

$$Y - .8Y + .2Y = c + I + G + x$$

$$Y(1 - .8 + .2) = c + I + G + x$$

$$Y(.4) = c + I + G + x$$

Dividing both sides by .4 (multiplying by 2.5) and writing the result in change form,

$$Y = 2.5(c + I + G + x)$$

$$\Delta Y = 2.5(\Delta I + \Delta G)$$

The multiplier is 2.5. Because net exports depend on income, the formula $\dfrac{1}{1 - \text{MPC}}$, which is correct only if only consumption depends on income, is not applicable. The correct formula when both consumption and net exports depend on income is $\dfrac{1}{1 - \text{MPC} + \text{MPI}}$.

2. The following table shows the relationship among income, consumption, and net exports (in billions of dollars).

Income (*Y*)	Consumption (*C*)	Net Exports (*X*)
0	800	400
1,000	1,400	300
2,000	2,000	200
3,000	2,600	100
4,000	3,200	0
5,000	3,800	-100

What is the multiplier?

Answer

In order to calculate the multiplier, you first need to calculate the MPC and the MPI. The MPC = $\Delta C/\Delta Y$ = 600/1,000 = .6. Calculating the MPI is more subtle. When income increases by 1,000, net exports decrease by 100. Since exports do not depend on income, this means that imports must increase by 100. Thus the MPI = $\Delta Imports/\Delta Y$ = 100/1,000 = .1. The multiplier can now be calculated from the formula:

$$\frac{1}{1 - \text{MPC} + \text{MPI}} = \frac{1}{1 - .6 + .1} = \frac{1}{.5} = 2$$

Practice Problems

1. Suppose that the consumption function is

$C = c + .9Y$

where the MPC = .9. What is the multiplier?

2. Suppose that the consumption function is

$C = c + .9Y$

and the net export function is

$X = x - .3Y$

where the MPC = .9 and the MPI = .3. What is the multiplier?

3. The following table shows the relationship between income and consumption (in billions of dollars).

Income (*Y*)	Consumption (*C*)
0	800
1,000	1,500
2,000	2,200
3,000	2,900
4,000	3,600
5,000	4,300

What are the MPC and the multiplier?

4. The following table shows the relationship between income, consumption, and net exports (in billions of dollars).

Income (*Y*)	Consumption (*C*)	Net Exports (*X*)
0	900	500
1,000	1,500	300
2,000	2,100	100
3,000	2,700	-100
4,000	3,300	-300
5,000	3,900	-500

What are the MPC, the MPI, and the multiplier?

CHAPTER TEST

1. The multiplier is a number that represents
   a. how much real GDP changes when aggregate expenditure changes.
   b. how much consumption changes when aggregate expenditure changes.
   c. how much investment changes when aggregate expenditure changes.
   d. how much net exports change when aggregate expenditure changes.

2. The size of the multiplier
   a. is between zero and 1.
   b. is zero.
   c. is 1.
   d. is greater than 1.

3. The multiplier is
   a. positively related to the MPC and positively related to the MPI.
   b. negatively related to the MPC and negatively related to the MPI.
   c. positively related to the MPC and negatively related to the MPI.
   d. positively related to the MPI and negatively related to the MPC.

4. The marginal propensity to consume (MPC)
   a. is larger than the MPI.
   b. is smaller than the MPI.
   c. is equal to the MPI.
   d. can be larger than, smaller than, or equal to the MPI.

5. The marginal propensity to save (MPS) is
   a. the change in saving divided by the change in income.
   b. greater than 1.
   c. equal to 1 - MPI.
   d. positively related to the multiplier.

6. Net exports are
   a. exports minus taxes.
   b. exports adjusted for inflation.
   c. exports adjusted for depreciation.
   d. exports minus imports.

7. The marginal propensity to import is
   a. positive.
   b. greater than the MPC.
   c. the change in imports divided by the change in income.
   d. the change in imports divided by the change in exports.

8. In the short run, an increase in government purchases causes
   a. a budget deficit and a trade deficit.
   b. a budget deficit and a trade surplus.
   c. a budget surplus and a trade deficit.
   d. a budget surplus and a trade surplus.

9. The budget and trade deficits are called the twin deficits because
   a. they are identical.
   b. they are fraternal.
   c. they move in the same direction when government purchases change.
   d. they move in opposite directions when government purchases change.

10. The multiplier for tax changes
    a. is the change in real GDP divided by the change in taxes.
    b. is the change in potential GDP divided by the change in taxes.
    c. is greater than the multiplier for government expenditures.
    d. is equal to the multiplier for government expenditures.

11. The balanced budget multiplier is the ratio of the change in real GDP to a change in
    a. taxes.
    b. net exports.
    c. government purchases matched by a change in taxes.
    d. government purchases matched by a change in net exports.

12. Which of the following will lower the multiplier?
    a. A higher MPC
    b. A lower MPC
    c. A lower MPI
    d. A lower MPS

Use Figure 12.4 for questions 13–15.

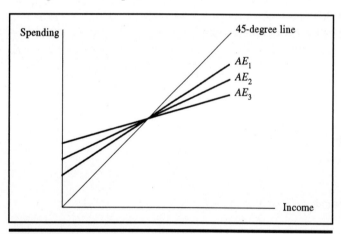

Figure 12.4

13. Order the multipliers associated with the three AE lines from largest to smallest.
    a. AE_1, AE_2, AE_3
    b. AE_1, AE_3, AE_2
    c. AE_3, AE_2, AE_1
    d. AE_3, AE_1, AE_2

14. If the MPC for AE_2 is .7, what could be the MPC for AE_1?
    a. .7
    b. .8
    c. 1.0
    d. 1.4

15. If the multiplier for AE_1 is 5, what could be the multipliers for AE_2 and AE_3?
    a. .8 for AE_2 and .6 for AE_3
    b. .6 for AE_2 and .8 for AE_3
    c. 5 for both AE_2 and AE_3
    d. 4 for AE_2 and 3 for AE_3

16. The forward-looking consumption model
    a. explains why the MPC changes in different situations.
    b. explains why the MPI changes in different situations.
    c. centers on the idea that most people engage in income smoothing.
    d. used in the 1990s has changed very little since its original development in the 1950s.

17. Individuals who engage in consumption smoothing
    a. have a constant MPC.
    b. spend less than their income in good years and more than their income in bad years.
    c. spend more than their income in good years and less than their income in bad years.
    d. gamble and play lotteries more than other people.

18. According to the forward-looking consumption model, individuals who win the lottery will
    a. spend all of their winnings immediately.
    b. save all of their winnings for retirement.
    c. adjust their spending to keep their MPC constant.
    d. adjust their spending to smooth their consumption.

19. According to the forward-looking consumption model, the multiplier for a temporary tax cut is
    a. larger than the multiplier for a permanent tax cut.
    b. smaller than the multiplier for a permanent tax cut.
    c. equal to the multiplier for a permanent tax cut.
    d. larger than the multiplier for aggregate expenditure.

20. According to the forward-looking consumption model, an anticipated tax cut will
    a. lower current consumption.
    b. lower current investment.
    c. raise current consumption.
    d. raise current investment.

ANSWERS TO THE REVIEW QUESTIONS

Fill-in Questions

1. multiplier
2. greater
3. marginal propensity to consume
4. marginal propensity to save
5. marginal propensity to import
6. Net exports
7. budget; trade
8. tax rate
9. smaller
10. balanced budget multiplier
11. forward-looking
12. permanent income; life cycle
13. Consumption smoothing
14. liquidity constrained
15. rebate

True-False Questions

1. **True**. The multiplier is the ratio of the two changes.
2. **True**. The multiplier is greater than 1.
3. **False**. The full multiplier effect on GDP is reached through rounds of spending.
4. **False**. The full multiplier effect is achieved in about a year.
5. **True**. The higher the MPC, the higher the multiplier.
6. **True**. When U.S. income goes up, part of the increase is spent on imported goods, and so the MPI is positive.
7. **False**. Exports are positively related to foreign income, not to U.S. income.
8. **False**. Although the budget and trade deficits are positively related, there is no reason for them to be the same size.
9. **True**. Changes in tax rates can affect potential GDP, whereas changes in tax revenues cause real GDP to differ from potential GDP in the short run.
10. **False**. It is the multiplier when the budget deficit is unchanged.
11. **False**. The forward-looking consumption model provides a way to understand how the MPC changes.
12. **False**. They are liquidity constrained if they cannot borrow enough to completely smooth their consumption.
13. **True**. Because people smooth their consumption, the MPC is much smaller for temporary than for permanent changes in income.
14. **False**. The MPC for a one-year tax rebate is very low.
15. **False**. This is an implication of the forward-looking model, not of the consumption function.

Short-Answer Questions

1. Changes in aggregate expenditure are caused by changes in government purchases, taxes, investment, and net exports.
2. Although the exact size of the multiplier depends on a number of factors, it is always greater than 1.
3. The multiplier is greater than 1 because the initial change in aggregate expenditure induces rounds of spending that cause the total change in real GDP to exceed the initial change in aggregate expenditure.
4. The MPS equals 1 minus the MPS, or MPC = 1 - MPS.
5. The multiplier is negatively related to the MPS.
6. The MPI is smaller than the MPC because most of the goods that are consumed when income rises are produced in the United States.
7. Uncertainty about the value of the MPC causes uncertainty about the value of the multiplier.
8. An increase in government purchases causes both a budget deficit and a trade deficit in the short run.
9. The multiplier for tax changes is smaller because the initial round of spending equals the MPC times the change in disposable income, not the full increase in aggregate expenditure.
10. The balanced budget multiplier is positive because the multiplier for government purchases is greater than the multiplier for tax changes.
11. The central idea of the forward-looking consumption model is that people attempt to smooth consumption over their lifetimes.
12. The permanent income and life cycle models of consumption are the origins of the forward-looking model.
13. The multiplier for temporary tax cuts is smaller than the multiplier for permanent tax cuts.

14. If you expect your taxes to be reduced in the future, you will increase your consumption now in anticipation of your expected higher future income.
15. The rational expectations assumption is that people's predictions of the future are on average about the same as economic forecasters'.

SOLUTIONS TO THE PRACTICE PROBLEMS

1. The multiplier $= \dfrac{1}{1-\text{MPC}} = \dfrac{1}{1-.9} = \dfrac{1}{.1} = 10.$

2. The multiplier $= \dfrac{1}{1-\text{MPC}+\text{MPI}} = \dfrac{1}{1-.9+.3} = \dfrac{1}{.4} = 2.5.$

3. The MPC $= .7.$

   The multiplier $= \dfrac{1}{1-\text{MPC}} = \dfrac{1}{1-.7} = \dfrac{1}{.3} = 3.33.$

4. The MPC $= .6$ and the MPI $= .2.$

   The multiplier $= \dfrac{1}{1-\text{MPC}+\text{MPI}} = \dfrac{1}{1-.6+.2} = \dfrac{1}{.6} = 1.67.$

ANSWERS TO THE CHAPTER TEST

1. a	6. d	11. c	16. a
2. d	7. c	12. b	17. b
3. c	8. a	13. a	18. d
4. a	9. c	14. b	19. b
5. a	10. a	15. d	20. c

CHAPTER 13

Aggregate Demand, and Price Adjustment

CHAPTER OVERVIEW

In our discussion of economic fluctuations, we first learned how the economy moves from potential GDP into a boom or recession. Next, in the material on the multiplier, we learned how much a change in aggregate expenditure, especially a change in government purchases, will move income away from potential. In this chapter, we construct the economic fluctuations model. We derive the aggregate demand/inflation (*ADI*) curve and the price adjustment (*PA*) line, and see how the equilibrium level of real GDP and inflation is given by the intersection of the *ADI* curve and the *PA* line. We learn what causes movements along the *ADI* curve, how changes in government purchases or the central bank's inflation target cause the *ADI* curve to shift, and how the *PA* line shifts in response to changes in expectations of inflation or changes in raw materials prices. The *ADI* curve and *PA* line will be used extensively in the rest of the text, so it is important that you learn to derive and manipulate them now.

CHAPTER REVIEW

1. The **aggregate demand/inflation (ADI) curve** is an inverse (negative) relation between inflation and real GDP. It is derived using two concepts that we will explain below. First, the level of real GDP at the point of spending balance is negatively related to the interest rate. Second, the interest rate is positively related to the inflation rate because of the central bank's policy rule.

2. The inflation rate is the annual rate of change in the overall price level. It is important to remember the distinction between the inflation rate, which is expressed as a percent, and the price level, which is expressed as a number. When inflation is positive, prices are rising. When inflation is negative, prices are falling. If inflation is positive but decreasing, prices are still rising, but at a slower rate.

3. At the point of spending balance, real GDP depends on aggregate expenditure. *Real GDP depends negatively on interest rates* because three of the components of aggregate expenditure, investment, net exports, and consumption, depend negatively on interest rates.

4. The *real interest rate* is the stated interest rate minus the expected rate of inflation. It is the correct measure of the effect of interest rates on investment, net exports, and consumption because it adjusts for inflation. If inflation is low and stable, as in the early 1990s, the real interest rate is not much different than the stated interest rate.

5. The *central bank* is the part of the government that controls monetary policy. Examples are the U.S. Federal Reserve System, the German Bundesbank, and the Bank of Japan. Most central banks set goals for inflation, called **target inflation rates**, which they try to maintain on average over the long run. The target inflation rate for the Fed and the Bundesbank is about 2 percent.

6. A **monetary policy rule** is a systematic response by the central bank to economic events. A particular policy rule is that the central bank raises the real interest rate whenever inflation rises. Since the real interest rate is the stated interest rate minus the expected rate of inflation, this means that the central bank must raise the stated interest rate by more than the rise in inflation. This policy rule provides a good description of the actions of the Federal Reserve in the late 1980s and 1990s.

7. The central bank does not control interest rates directly. It buys and sells bonds so that through the forces of supply and demand, interest rates are affected. In the United States, the Federal Reserve focuses on the **federal funds rate**, a very short-term interest rate on overnight loans between banks.

8. The **price adjustment (PA)** line depicts the inflation rate in the economy at any point in time. Like the *ADI* curve, it is drawn on a diagram with inflation on the vertical axis and real GDP on the horizontal axis. The price adjustment line has three important features:

   a. *The PA line is flat.* Firms and workers adjust their prices and wages so that inflation stays constant in the short run, even when real GDP changes.

   b. *The PA line moves over time when real GDP departs from potential GDP.* In normal times, when real GDP = potential GDP, inflation does not change. Firms and workers continue the previous wage and price increases. The *PA* line does not shift. In a boom, real GDP > potential GDP. Firms, seeing high demand for their products, raise their prices. Workers, seeing low unemployment, demand higher wages. Inflation increases. The *PA* line shifts up. In a recession, real GDP < potential GDP. Firms, seeing low demand for their products, lower their prices to retain market share. Workers, seeing high unemployment, lower their wage demands. Inflation decreases. The *PA* line shifts down.

   c. *The PA line shifts with changes in expectations or raw materials prices.* If firms and workers expect inflation to rise, they will raise their prices and wages to keep up with the expected inflation, causing the *PA* line to shift up. If inflation is expected to fall, the *PA* line will shift down. An increase in raw materials prices, such as an oil price increase, will raise firms' costs of production. This will cause firms to charge higher prices, shifting the *PA* line up.

9. Expectations of future inflation are an important reason why the price adjustment (*PA*) line is flat. Suppose that wages and prices have been rising at 5 percent per year for a long time, so that both current and expected inflation is 5 percent. When workers negotiate new contracts, they believe that a 5 percent annual wage increase will both make them as well off as before, because prices are also rising by 5 percent, and not change their wages relative to those of other workers, whose wages are also rising by 5 percent. Firms face a similar calculation. Suppose they agree to the 5 percent wage increase and then raise the price of their goods by 5 percent. They remain as well off as before, both relative to their costs, because wages are rising by 5 percent and relative to their competitors, who are also raising prices by 5 percent.

10. Staggered price and wage setting is another reason why the price adjustment (*PA*) line is flat. Wages and prices are not all set at the same time. They are staggered over different months and, in the case of three-year union contracts, different years. Since firms and workers care about prices and wages in other firms (and even other industries), this imparts a backward-looking component to price and wage decisions. This backward-looking component means that wages and prices change slowly over time.

ZEROING IN

1. Although no two business cycles are identical, there is a pattern in the movements of real GDP and inflation that characterizes most economic fluctuations. It is this relation between real GDP and inflation that the aggregate demand/inflation (*ADI*) curve and price adjustment (*PA*) line attempt to explain.

   a. A typical business cycle is illustrated in Figure 13.1. Although fictional, it illustrates many of the features of real-world economic fluctuations. The inflation rate (in percent) is on the vertical axis. The gap between real GDP and potential GDP (also in percent) is on the horizontal axis.

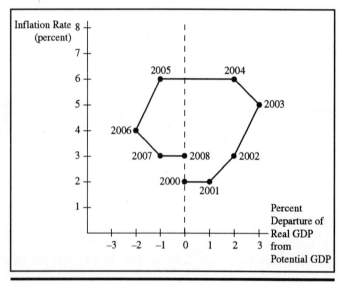

Figure 13.1

   b. The economy starts at potential GDP with 2 percent inflation in the year 2000. In 2001, aggregate expenditure increases (maybe caused by a tax cut or an increase in government spending), and the economy enters a boom with no change in inflation. In 2002 and 2003, the boom continues, with inflation rising.

   c. The higher inflation rate causes the Federal Reserve Board (following its policy rule) to raise interest rates, lowering real GDP in 2004 even though inflation continues to rise. Recession strikes in 2005, with GDP below potential as inflation stays high. Inflation falls in 2006 as the recession gets worse. Finally, in 2007, a recovery occurs, with inflation continuing to fall. The economy returns to potential GDP with a higher (3 percent) inflation rate in 2008.

d. The long-run impact of the change in policy is that real GDP returns to potential GDP. In other words, there is no long-run impact from inflation and the departures of real GDP from potential GDP. Although this example shows a slightly higher inflation rate at the end of the cycle than at the beginning, it could have been lower, the same, or even much higher, depending on the Fed's policy rule. In any case, real GDP would return to potential GDP.

2. Why does real GDP depend negatively on interest rates? The answer comes from an understanding of how investment, net exports, and consumption, three of the components of aggregate expenditure, depend negatively on interest rates.

a. Why is *investment negatively related to interest rates*? Recall that investment includes both the purchase of new equipment and factories by business firms and the purchase of new houses by households. Many of these purchases, both by firms and by households, are financed by borrowing, and higher interest rates make borrowing more expensive. This raises the cost of investment. With higher interest rates, firms and households are less likely to build new factories or buy new houses, and so investment is lower than it would have been with lower interest rates.

b. Why are *net exports negatively related to interest rates*? If the U.S. interest rate is high relative to foreign interest rates, U.S. financial assets become more attractive than foreign assets, and the U.S. exchange rate rises, or appreciates. When the U.S. exchange rate is high, U.S. goods are expensive relative to foreign goods. This decreases U.S. exports and increases U.S. imports, both of which decrease U.S. net exports. Thus a high interest rate causes net exports to decrease. Conversely, a low U.S. interest rate causes the dollar to falls or depreciate. U.S. goods become relatively cheap, causing exports to rise, imports to fall, and thus net exports to rise.

c. Why is *consumption negatively related to interest rates*? Although most of consumption, such as food, is purchased out of current income, consumer durables such as automobiles are financed by borrowing. High interest rates increase the cost of borrowing, lowering spending on those items.

d. These effects are illustrated in Figure 13.2. Recall that the aggregate expenditure (*AE*) line is constructed by adding up consumption, investment, net exports, and government spending. A lower interest rate raises the first three components of aggregate expenditure, shifting the *AE* line up. A higher interest rate lowers these three components, shifting the *AE* line down.

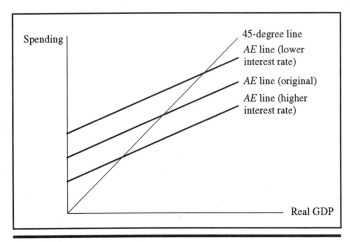

Figure 13.2

3. The monetary policy rule described above, that the central bank raises the real interest rate when inflation rises, is illustrated in Figure 13.3. At the inflation target of 2 percent, consistent with price stability, the interest rate equals its target of 4 percent. When inflation exceeds 2 percent, the central bank raises the interest rate above 4 percent. Note that the slope of the line depicting the policy rule is greater than 1, reflecting the fact that the Federal Reserve needs to increase the stated interest more than one-for-one with inflation in order to raise the real interest rate.

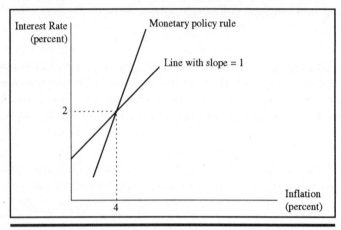

Figure 13.3

4. We now combine two concepts: the monetary policy rule that links the real interest rate to inflation and the dependence of aggregate expenditure on the real interest rate, to derive the aggregate demand/inflation (*ADI*) line. The derivation is illustrated in Figure 13.4. In order to learn this material, you should use pencil and paper to replicate the derivation.

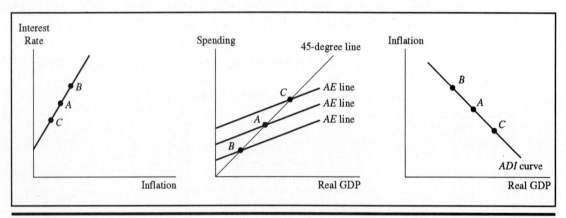

Figure 13.4

a. To derive the *ADI* line, first start with an inflation rate that, in accordance with the central bank's monetary policy rule, is consistent with the interest rate depicted by point *A* in the first panel. (The choice of how high or low the interest rate is at *A* is completely arbitrary.) The interest rate determined by the policy rule will produce values of consumption, investment, and net exports that define an *AE* line in the second panel. The *AE* line intersects the 45-degree line at the point of spending balance *A* to determine GDP. In the third panel, the inflation rate from the first panel and real GDP from the second panel are depicted by point *A*. Note that we have not yet defined a line, just a point.

b. Suppose that inflation rises. In accordance with its policy rule, the Federal Reserve increases the interest rate in the first panel to point *B*. Since the slope of the policy rule is greater than 1, this also raises the real interest rate, shifting the *AE* line down to intersect the 45-degree line at the point of spending balance *B* in the second panel. Through the multiplier effect, real GDP falls. The combination of higher inflation and lower real GDP defines point *B* in the third panel.

c. Suppose that inflation falls. The central bank lowers the interest rate to point *C*. This raises consumption, investment, and net exports, shifting the *AE* line up to intersect the 45-degree line at point *C* and increasing real GDP. Lower inflation and higher real GDP are depicted by point *C* in the third panel.

d. Connect the dots. The line *BAC* defines an inverse (downward-sloping) relationship between inflation and real GDP called the aggregate demand/inflation (*ADI*) curve. (Because the "curve" is a straight line, you really needed only two points.) Make sure you understand how the *ADI* curve (third panel) is derived from the policy rule (first panel) and spending balance (second panel).

e. Changes in inflation cause *movements along the ADI curve*. When inflation rises, the Federal Reserve raises interest rates, lowering real GDP and causing a movement up and to the left. When inflation falls, the Federal Reserve lowers interest rates, raising real GDP and causing a movement down and to the right.

f. What causes *shifts in the ADI curve*? First, anything that shifts the *AE* line will shift the *ADI* curve. This includes changes in government purchases, taxes, investment, and net exports. If the *AE* line shifts up, as with an increase in government purchases, the *ADI* curve shifts out (to the right). If the *AE* line shifts down, as with an increase in taxes, the *ADI* curve shifts in (to the left). Second, changes in the monetary policy rule will shift the *ADI* curve. If the policy rule changes toward a higher inflation target, the *ADI* curve shifts out. If the rule changes toward a lower inflation target, the *ADI* curve shifts in.

5. The price adjustment (*PA*) line is another important concept introduced in this chapter. There are three things that you need to understand about the *PA* line:

a. *The PA line is flat.* In Figure 13.5 inflation is on the vertical axis and real GDP is on the horizontal axis. The *PA* line is a horizontal (flat) line depicting the inflation rate. In the short run, the inflation rate is constant. It does not depend on the level of real GDP.

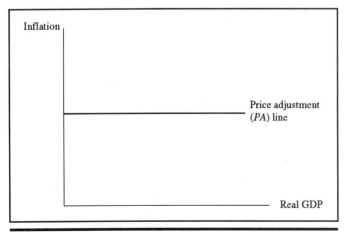

Figure 13.5

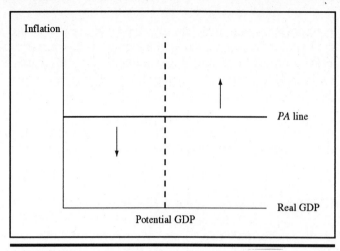

Figure 13.6

b. *The PA line moves over time when real GDP departs from potential GDP.* This is illustrated in Figure 13.6. When real GDP is greater than potential GDP, the *PA* line shifts up and inflation rises. When real GDP is less than potential GDP, the *PA* line shifts down and inflation falls. If real GDP equals potential GDP, the *PA* line stays in place and inflation is unchanged.

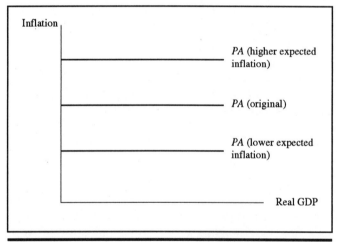

Figure 13.7

c. *Changes in expectations or raw materials prices shift the PA line.* Suppose that expected inflation rises. Firms and workers, as discussed above, raise wages and prices, and actual inflation rises. This is depicted as an upward shift of the *PA* line in Figure 13.7. Conversely, suppose that expected inflation falls. This causes actual inflation to fall and is shown as a downward shift of the *PA* line in Figure 13.7 Increases in the prices of raw materials, such as commodities or oil, raise inflation and shift the *PA* line up, whereas decreases in raw materials prices lower inflation and shift the *PA* line down.

6. The *intersection* of the aggregate demand/inflation (*ADI*) curve and the *PA* line gives an *equilibrium* level of real GDP and inflation. It is important to understand that this intersection does not have to be where real GDP equals potential GDP. As shown in Figure 13.8, the intersection can, in the short run, produce real GDP lower, above, or equal to potential GDP.

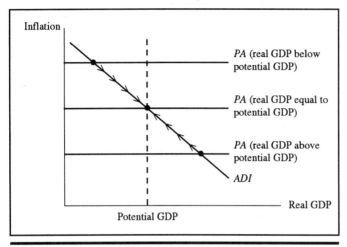

Figure 13.8

ACTIVE REVIEW

Fill-in Questions

1. The _____ curve is an inverse relation between inflation and real GDP.

2. The _____ is the annual rate of change in the overall price level.

3. Real GDP depends _____ on interest rates.

4. The _____ is the stated interest rate minus the expected rate of inflation.

5. The _____ is the part of the government that controls monetary policy.

6. In the United States, the central bank is called the _____.

7. Goals for inflation are called _____ inflation rates.

8. A _____ is a systematic response by the central bank to economic events.

9. The interest rate on overnight loans between banks is called the _____.

10. Consumption, investment, and net exports are _____ related to interest rates.

11. Changes in government purchases cause _____ the *ADI* curve.

12. Changes in inflation cause _____ the *ADI* curve.

13. The _____ line depicts the inflation rate at any point in time.

14. Price adjustment is influenced by _____ of future inflation.

15. A reason for slow price adjustment is _____ price and wage setting.

True-False Questions

T F 1. The aggregate demand/inflation curve is downward-sloping.

T F 2. When inflation is decreasing, prices are falling.

T F 3. If inflation is low, real and stated interest rates are similar.

T F 4. The central bank determines government purchases and taxes.

T F 5. Raising the interest rate when the exchange rate falls would be an example of a monetary policy rule.

T F 6. An increase in government purchases shifts the *ADI* curve to the right

T F 7. An increase in taxes shifts the *ADI* curve to the right.

T F 8. An increase in inflation shifts the *ADI* curve to the right.

T F 9. An increase in the target inflation rate shifts the *ADI* curve to the right.

T F 10. The price adjustment (*PA*) line is a downward-sloping relation between inflation and real GDP.

T F 11. The *PA* line moves when real GDP does not equal potential GDP.

T F 12. The *PA* line always moves over time.

T F 13. In the United States, wages in most industries are set at the same time.

T F 14. The setting of prices and wages by firms and workers is based only on expectations of future inflation.

T F 15. Potential GDP is determined by the intersection of the *ADI* curve and the *PA* line.

Short-Answer Questions

1. What are the two concepts used to derive the *ADI* curve?

2. Why does real GDP depend negatively on interest rates at the point of spending balance?

3. Why is the real interest rate, rather than the stated interest rate, the correct measure of the effect of interest rates on aggregate expenditure?

4. Describe the policy rule that the Federal Reserve System has used during the late 1980s and 1990s.

5. In order to raise the real interest rate when inflation increases, how must the central bank change the stated interest rate?

6. What is the relation between inflation and real GDP during a typical business cycle?

7. Why is the slope of the monetary policy rule greater than 1?

8. Why does the *ADI* curve slope downward?

9. What causes shifts in the *ADI* curve?

10. What is depicted by the price adjustment (*PA*) line?

11. Why is the *PA* line flat?

12. Describe the process of price adjustment in terms of the relation between inflation and real GDP.

13. How does the *PA* line move over time?

14. What causes the *PA* line to shift?

15. What is determined at the intersection of the aggregate demand/inflation (*ADI*) curve and the *PA* line?

WORKING IT OUT

1. The most important tool for you to learn in this chapter is how changes in aggregate expenditure shift the *ADI* curve. Let's examine a decrease in government purchases.

   a. The first step is to draw a diagram of the economy before the policy action occurs. The first panel of Figure 13.9 shows the *AE* line and the point of spending balance. The second panel shows the *ADI* curve. Although the *ADI* curve is drawn for a specific monetary policy rule, it is not necessary to diagram the rule because it will not change.

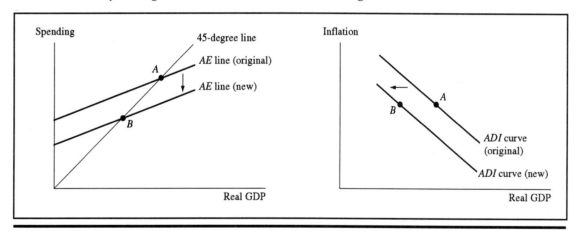

Figure 13.9

   b. The decrease in government purchases shifts the *AE* line down, moving the point of spending balance from *A* to *B*. This causes the *ADI* curve to shift to the left. If inflation is unchanged, as it will be in the short run before prices have time to adjust, the point of spending balance shifts from *A* to *B*.

2. A change in the monetary policy rule also shifts the *ADI* curve. We will consider a change toward a lower inflation target.

   a. The first step is again to diagram the economy before the policy change occurs. The three panels of Figure 13.10 depict the original policy rule, the *AE* line, and the *ADI* curve.

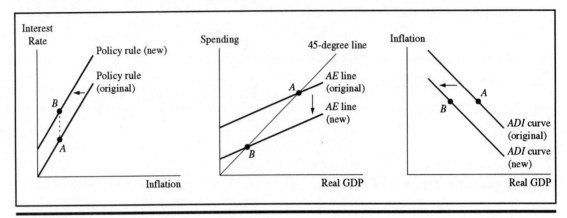

Figure 13.10

   b. A change in the monetary policy rule toward a lower inflation target shifts the policy rule to the left. In the short run, with inflation fixed, this raises the interest rate. The higher interest rate lowers aggregate expenditure, shifting the *AE* line in the second panel down and moving the point of spending balance from *A* to *B*. This causes the *ADI* line in the third panel to shift to the left.

Worked Problems

1. Suppose that people anticipate that taxes will be cut next year. How will this affect the *AE* line and the *ADI* curve?

Answer

According to the forward-looking theory of consumption, the anticipated tax cut will raise current consumption. This will shift the AE *curve up and shift the* ADI *curve to the right.*

2. The following table shows two monetary policy rules.

Inflation	Interest Rate Policy Rule A	Interest Rate Policy Rule B
0	3	1
1	5	3
2	7	5
3	9	7
4	11	9

Suppose that the Federal Reserve changes its monetary policy rule from policy rule A to policy rule B. Is this a switch to a higher or a lower inflation target? How would this change affect the *AE* line and the *ADI* curve?

Answer

To understand the switch in targets, start with equal interest rates and examine the resultant inflation rates. Compared to policy rule A, policy rule B produces higher inflation at each interest rate, implying a higher inflation target. To understand the effect on the AE *line, read across the columns. At each inflation rate, rule B has a lower interest rate than rule A, so the change from rule A to rule B shifts the* AE *line up and shifts the* ADI *curve to the right.*

Practice Problems

1. Suppose that the low U.S. exchange rate causes U.S. consumers to buy more American and fewer Japanese automobiles. How will this affect the *AE* line and the *ADI* curve?

2. Suppose that U.S. business firms, worried about a possible recession in the next few years, build fewer factories. How will this affect the *AE* line and the *ADI* curve?

3. Suppose that the price of imported oil increases, raising the U.S. inflation rate. How will this affect the *AE* line and the *ADI* curve?

4. Suppose that the Federal Reserve changes its policy rule to a higher inflation target. How will this affect the *AE* line and the *ADI* curve?

5. The following table shows two monetary policy rules.

Inflation	Interest Rate Policy Rule A	Interest Rate Policy Rule B
0	2	5
3	6	9
6	10	13
9	14	17
12	18	21

Suppose that the Federal Reserve changes its monetary policy rule from policy rule A to policy rule B. Is this a switch to a higher or to a lower inflation target? How would this change affect the *AE* line and the *ADI* curve?

CHAPTER TEST

1. The *ADI* curve illustrates the negative relation between
   a. inflation and unemployment.
   b. inflation and real GDP.
   c. interest rates and inflation.
   d. interest rates and real GDP.

2. If inflation is falling, then what is happening to prices?
   a. Prices are rising.
   b. Prices are falling.
   c. Prices are staying the same.
   d. There is not enough information to tell.

3. The components of aggregate expenditure that depend negatively on the interest rate are
   a. consumption, investment, and government purchases.
   b. investment, government purchases, and net exports.
   c. consumption, investment, and net exports.
   d. consumption, taxes, and net exports.

4. The real interest rate is the stated interest rate
   a. minus the expected rate of inflation.
   b. divided by the expected rate of inflation.
   c. minus the price level.
   d. divided by the price level.

5. The price adjustment (*PA*) line
   a. is downward-sloping.
   b. shifts with changes in expectations of the prices of raw materials.
   c. depicts real GDP in the economy at any point in time.
   d. remains constant over time when real GDP departs from potential GDP.

6. Suppose wages and prices have been rising at 3 percent per year over a period of time. In light of this, workers negotiate 3 percent annual wage increases. If expected inflation falls to 2 percent but wage increases remain at 3 percent, then
   a. firms remain equally well off.
   b. workers are worse off.
   c. workers are better off.
   d. firms are better off.

7. The policy rule recently followed by the Federal Reserve involves
   a. raising the real interest rate when real GDP rises.
   b. raising the real interest rate when inflation rises.
   c. raising the real interest rate when the exchange rate falls.
   d. raising the stated interest rate when the exchange rate falls.

8. The equilibrium level of real GDP and inflation is given by the intersection of
   a. the aggregate demand/inflation curve and the potential GDP line.
   b. the aggregate demand/inflation curve and the price adjustment line.
   c. the aggregate demand/inflation curve and the zero inflation line.
   d. the price adjustment line and the potential GDP line.

9. The federal funds rate is
   a. the interest rate on overnight loans between federal agencies.
   b. the interest rate on long-term loans between federal agencies.
   c. the interest rate on overnight loans between banks.
   d. the interest rate on long-term loans between banks.

10. In a typical business cycle,
    a. real GDP rises after inflation increases.
    b. real GDP falls after inflation increases.
    c. real GDP is unrelated to inflation.
    d. real GDP always equals potential GDP.

11. Higher inflation causes
    a. a positive departure of real GDP from potential GDP in the long run.
    b. a negative departure of real GDP from potential GDP in the long run.
    c. no departure of real GDP from potential GDP in the long run.
    d. the Federal Reserve Board (following its policy rule) to decrease interest rates.

12. Consumption is negatively related to interest rates because
    a. most consumption is financed by borrowing.
    b. consumer durables, such as automobiles, are often financed by borrowing.
    c. new houses are usually financed by borrowing.
    d. changes in interest rates affect exchange rates.

13. Suppose that inflation rises from 2 percent to 4 percent. If the Federal Reserve follows a policy rule of raising the real interest rate when inflation increases, then the stated interest rate would
    a. increase by less than 2 percent.
    b. increase by exactly 2 percent.
    c. increase by more than 2 percent.
    d. remain unchanged.

Use Figure 13.11 for questions 14–16.

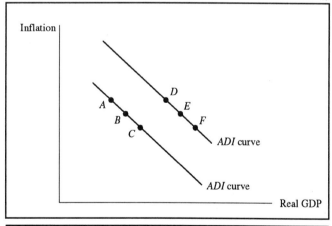

Figure 13.11

14. An increase in government purchases can be represented as a movement in the economy
    a. from A to B.
    b. from C to B.
    c. from B to E.
    d. from E to B.

15. An increase in taxes can be represented as a movement in the economy
    a. from *A* to *B*.
    b. from *C* to *B*.
    c. from *B* to *E*.
    d. from *E* to *B*.

16. An increase in inflation can be represented as a movement in the economy
    a. from *A* to *B*.
    b. from *C* to *B*.
    c. from *B* to *E*.
    d. from *C* to *D*.

17. An decrease in net exports causes a
    a. shift out of the *ADI* curve.
    b. shift in of the *ADI* curve.
    c. movement up the *ADI* curve.
    d. movement down the *ADI* curve.

18. A decrease in inflation causes a
    a. shift out of the *ADI* curve.
    b. shift in of the *ADI* curve.
    c. movement up the *ADI* curve.
    d. movement down the *ADI* curve.

Use the following table for questions 19 and 20.

Inflation	Interest Rate Policy Rule A	Interest Rate Policy Rule B
0	5	2
1	7	4
2	9	6
3	11	8
4	13	10

19. Suppose the government changes its monetary policy rule from policy rule A to policy rule B. How would this change affect the *AE* line?
    a. The *AE* line shifts up.
    b. The *AE* line shifts down.
    c. The *AE* line becomes steeper.
    d. The *AE* line is unaffected.

20. Suppose the government changes its monetary policy rule from policy rule A to policy rule B. How would this change affect the *ADI* curve?
    a. The *ADI* curve shifts left.
    b. The *ADI* curve shifts right.
    c. The *ADI* curve becomes steeper.
    d. The *ADI* curve is unaffected.

ANSWERS TO THE REVIEW QUESTIONS

Fill-in Questions

1. aggregate demand/inflation
2. inflation rate
3. negatively
4. real interest rate
5. central bank
6. Federal Reserve System
7. target
8. monetary policy rule
9. federal funds rate
10. negatively
11. shifts in
12. movements along
13. price adjustment (*PA*)
14. expectations
15. staggered

True-False Questions

1. **True**. It depicts a negative relation between inflation and real GDP.
2. **False**. Inflation can decrease but still be positive, in which case prices are still rising.
3. **True**. The real interest rate equals the stated interest rate minus the expected rate of inflation. If inflation is low, there is not much difference between the two interest rates.
4. **False**. The central bank determines monetary policy.
5. **True**. Although this is not the rule followed by the Federal Reserve, it would be a systematic response to economic events.
6. **True**. An increase in government purchases shifts the *AE* line up and shifts the *ADI* curve to the right.
7. **False**. An increase in taxes shifts the *ADI* curve to the left.
8. **False**. An increase in inflation causes a movement along the *ADI* curve.
9. **True**. An increase in the target inflation rate lowers the interest rate, shifting the *ADI* curve out.
10. **False**. The *PA* line is flat.
11. **True**. The *PA* line shifts up when real GDP is greater than potential GDP and shifts down when real GDP is less than potential GDP.
12. **False**. When real GDP equals potential GDP, the *PA* line is fixed.
13. **False**. They are staggered over different months and years.
14. **False**. Staggered price and wage setting imparts a backward-looking component to price and wage decisions.
15. **False**. The *ADI* curve and the *PA* line determine current real GDP, not potential GDP.

Short-Answer Questions

1. First, real GDP is negatively related to the interest rate at the point of spending balance. Second, because of the central bank's policy rule, the interest rate is positively related to the inflation rate.
2. Real GDP depends negatively on interest rates because investment, net exports, and consumption depend negatively on interest rates.
3. The real interest rate is the correct measure because it adjusts the stated interest rate for the effects of inflation.
4. The Federal Reserve System has raised the real interest rate when inflation has increased.
5. In order to raise the real interest rate, the central bank must raise the stated interest rate by more than the increase in inflation.
6. At the beginning of a cycle, the expansion of real GDP above potential GDP causes inflation. The Federal Reserve responds by raising interest rates, causing real GDP to fall.

7. The slope of the monetary policy rule is greater than 1 because, in order to raise the real interest rate, the Federal Reserve needs to increase the stated interest rate more than one-for-one with inflation.

8. The *ADI* curve slopes downward because higher inflation causes the Federal Reserve to raise interest rates, shifting the *AE* line down and lowering real GDP.

9. Changes in aggregate expenditure and changes in the money supply rule shift the *ADI* curve.

10. The *PA* line depicts the inflation rate in the economy at any point in time.

11. The *PA* line is flat because the inflation rate is constant in the short run. In particular, it does not depend on the level of GDP.

12. If real GDP exceeds potential GDP, inflation rises. If real GDP is less than potential GDP, inflation falls. If real GDP equals potential GDP, inflation does not change.

13. If real GDP is greater (less) than potential GDP, inflation increases (decreases) and the *PA* line moves upward (downward).

14. Changes in expectations or raw materials prices shift the *PA* line.

15. Inflation and real GDP are determined at the intersection of the *ADI* curve and the *PA* line.

SOLUTIONS TO THE PRACTICE PROBLEMS

1. U.S. imports will decrease, raising net exports. This shifts the *AE* line up and shifts the *ADI* curve to the right.

2. This will decrease investment, lowering the *AE* line and shifting the *ADI* curve out.

3. The higher inflation rate will cause the Federal Reserve, acting in accordance with its policy rule, to raise interest rates. This shifts the *AE* line down. The higher inflation rate represents a movement up and to the left along the *ADI* curve, not a shift of the curve.

4. A change in the monetary policy rule to a higher inflation target lowers the interest rate, shifting the *AE* line up and the *ADI* curve to the right.

5. The change from policy rule A to policy rule B represents a switch to a lower inflation target. This raises the interest rate at each inflation rate, shifting the *AE* line down and the *ADI* curve to the left.

ANSWERS TO THE CHAPTER TEST

1. b	6. c	11. c	16. b
2. d	7. b	12. b	17. b
3. c	8. b	13. c	18. d
4. a	9. c	14. c	19. a
5. b	10. b	15. d	20. b

CHAPTER 14

Toward Recovery and Expansion

CHAPTER OVERVIEW

We have constructed the economic fluctuations model from the aggregate demand/inflation (*ADI*) curve and the price adjustment (*PA*) line, and shown how the equilibrium level of real GDP and inflation is given by the intersection of the *ADI* curve and the *PA* line. In this chapter, we use the economic fluctuations model to study the effects, both in the short run and in the long run, of shocks to the economy, changes in aggregate expenditure, and changes in the monetary policy rule. The process of price adjustment is particularly important, for it allows us to understand the transition from short-run booms or recessions back to long-run potential GDP.

CHAPTER REVIEW

1. The **economic fluctuations model** is employed by academic, government, and private economists to study the effects of economic policy proposals such as changes in monetary policy rules and tax and spending changes. The economic fluctuations model, which was derived in Chapter 13, consists of three parts:

   a. The aggregate demand/inflation (*ADI*) curve is a negative relation between inflation and real GDP.

   b. The price adjustment (*PA*) line depicts the inflation rate in the economy at any point in time.

   c. The equilibrium level of real GDP and inflation is given by the intersection of the *ADI* curve and the *PA* line.

2. An important use of the economic fluctuations model is to analyze contemplated policy changes. The **baseline** is the path of an economic variable that would occur without the policy change under consideration. The model is used to compare the path of the economy with the policy change relative to the baseline.

3. The economy is never completely at rest. It is always subject to a number of shocks. **Demand shocks** are shifts in the *ADI* curve, including changes in government purchases, investment, net exports, or the monetary policy rule. **Price shocks** are shifts in the *PA* line, such as changes in the price of oil or other commodities. *Supply shocks* are shifts in potential GDP, such as technological progress that causes an increase in productivity growth.

4. A *boom* occurs when real GDP exceeds potential GDP, and a *recession* is when real GDP falls below potential GDP. A *temporary growth slowdown* is a decrease in the rate of growth of real GDP that is not large enough to make real GDP growth negative. **Stagflation** occurs when real GDP falls and inflation rises simultaneously. A **boom-bust cycle** is a complete economic fluctuation that occurs when the central bank lowers the interest rate too much. This causes a boom and inflation, leading the central bank to raise interest rates and cause a recession.

5. Changes in the monetary policy rule are an important source of economic fluctuations. A common objective is to lower the rate of inflation. **Disinflation** is a reduction in the rate of inflation. Be sure that you understand the difference between disinflation and **deflation**, a negative inflation rate, which is not a typical policy objective. **Reinflation**, the opposite of disinflation, is an increase in the inflation rate.

ZEROING IN

1. The *intersection* of the aggregate demand/inflation (*ADI*) curve and the *PA* line determines real GDP and inflation. It is important to understand that this intersection does not have to be where real GDP equals potential GDP. As shown in Figure 14.1, the intersection can, in the short run, produce real GDP lower, above, or equal to potential GDP.

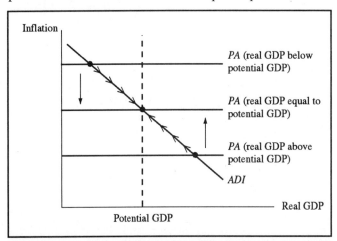

Figure 14.1

a. Suppose that the intersection of the *ADI* curve and the *PA* line produces real GDP that is less than potential GDP, causing inflation to fall. This is illustrated as a downward movement in the *PA* line in Figure 14.1. The economy moves down the *ADI* curve, in the direction of the arrows, until the long-run equilibrium is reached where real GDP equals potential GDP. Once the economy attains its long-run equilibrium, inflation stops falling and real GDP stops rising.

b. Suppose that the intersection of the *ADI* curve and the *PA* line produces real GDP that is greater than potential GDP, causing inflation to rise. As shown in Figure 14.1, the *PA* line moves up, causing the economy to move up the *ADI* curve until the long-run equilibrium is attained. At that point, inflation stops rising, real GDP stops falling, and real GDP equals potential GDP.

c. Suppose that the *ADI* curve intersects the *PA* line where real GDP equals potential GDP. End of story. The economy is in long-run equilibrium, and there is no reason for either inflation or real GDP to change.

2. *Changes in aggregate expenditure* are an important source of economic fluctuations. In Chapter 13, we saw how changes in expenditure shift the *ADI* curve and cause short-run departures of real GDP from potential GDP. Now we complete the story. Suppose that, starting with real GDP equal to potential GDP, government purchases increase.

    a. In the short run, the *ADI* curve shifts to the right and the *PA* line is fixed. As shown in Figure 14.2, the economy enters a boom at the point *SR* (short run), defined by the intersection of the *ADI* curve and the *PA* line.

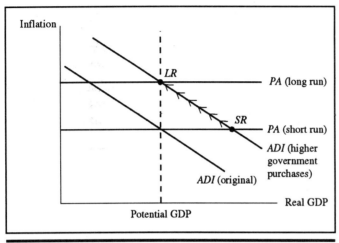

Figure 14.2

    b. At the point *SR*, real GDP exceeds potential GDP. Over time, inflation rises, shifting the *PA* line upward. Real GDP declines as the economy moves back along the *ADI* curve. The process stops when the long-run equilibrium is attained at point LR.

    c. What is the outcome of this policy? In the short run, real GDP increases at a constant inflation rate. In the long run, real GDP returns to potential GDP and inflation is higher.

3. A *change in the monetary policy rule* is the other important cause of a shift of the *ADI* curve. Suppose that, starting with real GDP equal to potential GDP, the monetary policy rule shifts to a lower inflation target.

    a. In the short run, the *ADI* curve shifts to the left and the *PA* line is fixed. As shown in Figure 14.3, the economy enters a recession at the point *SR*.

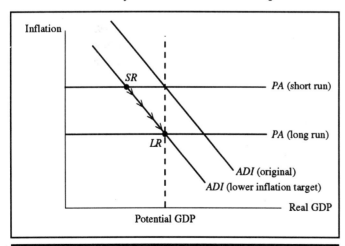

Figure 14.3

b. At the point *SR*, real GDP is below potential GDP. Over time, inflation falls, shifting the *PA* line downward. Real GDP recovers as the economy moves back along the *ADI* curve. The process stops when the long-run equilibrium is attained at point LR.

c. What is the outcome of this policy? In the short run, real GDP decreases at a constant inflation rate. In the long run, real GDP returns to potential GDP and inflation is lower. The central bank has achieved its target (lower inflation), but at a cost (the recession until the equilibrium is attained).

4. *Price shocks* are the other cause of economic fluctuations. Suppose that an oil price increase occurs at a long-run equilibrium with real GDP equal to potential GDP. Remember that an oil price increase is an example of a price shock.

a. In the short run, the oil price increase shifts the *PA* line upward. As shown in Figure 14.4, inflation rises and real GDP falls below potential, causing stagflation at point *SR*.

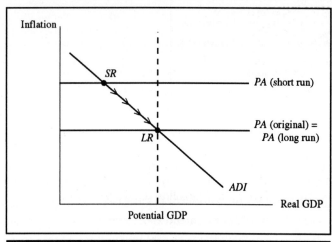

Figure 14.4

b. With real GDP below potential GDP at the point *SR*, inflation begins to fall, shifting the *PA* line downward. Real GDP rises, and the economy returns, over time, to potential GDP. Long-run equilibrium is attained at point LR, with inflation at its original level and real GDP equal to potential GDP.

ACTIVE REVIEW

Fill-in Questions

1. The _____ is used to study the effects of economic policy proposals.

2. The _____ is the path of an economic variable that would occur without the policy change under consideration.

3. _____ are shifts in the aggregate demand/inflation (*ADI*) curve.

4. _____ are shifts in the price adjustment (*PA*) line.

5. _____ are shifts in potential GDP.

6. A _____ is when real GDP falls below potential GDP.

7 A _____.is when real GDP exceeds potential GDP.

8. A _____ is a small decrease in the rate of growth of real GDP.

9. _____ occurs when real GDP falls and inflation rises simultaneously.

10. A(n) _____ is an economic fluctuation caused by the central bank.

11. _____ is a reduction in the rate of inflation.

12. _____ is a negative inflation rate.

13. An increase in the inflation rate is called _____.

14. In the _____ , real GDP can be above, below, or equal to potential GDP.

15. A long-run _____ is reached when real GDP equals potential GDP.

True-False Questions

T   F   1. The baseline is the predicted path of a variable following a policy change.

T   F   2. A change in net exports is an example of a demand shock.

T   F   3. A change in the monetary policy rule is an example of a price shock.

T   F   4. Price shocks are shifts in potential GDP.

T   F   5. Supply shocks are shifts in potential GDP.

T   F   6. A temporary growth slowdown causes a recession.

T   F   7. Stagflation occurs when real GDP and inflation fall simultaneously.

T   F   8. Deflation is a decrease in the price level.

T   F   9. Reinflation is the opposite of deflation.

T   F   10. Changes in investment shift the *ADI* curve.

T   F   11. Movements in the exchange rate shift the *PA* line.

T   F   12. Changes in the target inflation rate shift the *ADI* curve.

T   F   13. Oil price increases shift the *PA* line.

T   F   14. Changes in expected inflation shift the *ADI* curve.

T   F   15. Changes in government purchases shift the *PA* line.

Short-Answer Questions

1. What is the economic fluctuations model used for?

2. What are demand shocks?

3. What are price shocks?

4. What are supply shocks?

5. When do booms and recessions occur?

6. What is a temporary growth slowdown?

7. When does stagflation occur?

8. When does a boom-bust cycle occur?

9. What is the difference between disinflation and deflation?

10. Which is the more typical policy objective, disinflation or deflation?

11. When is the economy in long-run equilibrium?

12. Describe the behavior of inflation when the economy is in long-run equilibrium.

13. Starting from a long-run equilibrium, describe the path of inflation and real GDP following a decrease in government purchases.

14. Starting from a long-run equilibrium, describe the path of inflation and real GDP following a shift by the Fed to a higher inflation target.

15. Starting from a long-run equilibrium, describe the path of inflation and real GDP following a decrease in the price of oil.

WORKING IT OUT

1. The most important technique for you to learn in this chapter is how to work with the *ADI-PA* diagram. In the "Zeroing In" section, we presented a purely graphical approach. Here, we will combine numbers and graphs.

   a. The *ADI* curve is a downward-sloping relation between inflation and real GDP. Given a set of values for inflation and real GDP, you can graph the *ADI* curve. The following values are graphed in Figure 14.5. The numbers for inflation represent the inflation rate (in percent), whereas those for real GDP represent billions of dollars.

	Inflation				
	9	**7**	**5**	**3**	**1**
Real GDP	5,800	5,900	6,000	6,100	6,200

   b. The *PA* line is a flat (horizontal) line depicting the current inflation rate. Potential GDP is a vertical line. In Figure 14.5, the *PA* and potential GDP lines are drawn for a current inflation rate of 7 percent and a value of $6,000 billion for potential GDP. The *PA* line is labeled *PA* (*SR*) to indicate that it depicts the short-run (current) inflation rate.

c. In the short run, the economy is at the intersection of the *ADI* curve and the *PA (SR)* line. This point, with 7 percent inflation and $5,900 billion real GDP, is labeled *SR* in Figure 14.5.

d. At the point *SR*, real GDP is below potential GDP. Over time, the *PA* line moves downward, inflation falls, and the economy moves along the *ADI* curve as depicted by the arrows in Figure 14.5. In the long run, the *PA* line shifts down far enough, to *PA* (LR), so that real GDP equals potential GDP. At the long-run equilibrium point LR, real GDP equals $6,000 billion and inflation is 5 percent.

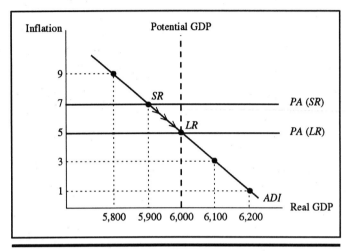

Figure 14.5

2. We have focused on movements of real GDP and inflation in the *ADI-PA* diagram. By looking at the other two diagrams used to derive the *ADI* curve, the policy rule and the AE line/45-degree line diagrams, we can trace out what happens to consumption, investment, and net exports during a cycle.

a. Suppose that we start from real GDP equal to potential GDP, and study the short- and long-run effects of an increase in government purchases. In the short run, the AE line shifts upward and the *ADI* curve shifts to the right. As shown by the points labeled *SR* in Figure 14.6, real GDP increases, but inflation and interest rates do not change.

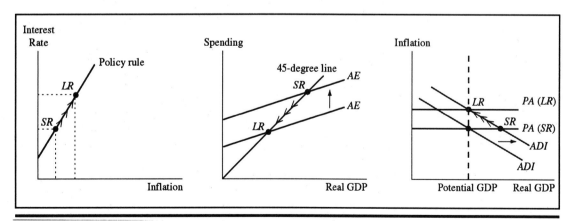

Figure 14.6

b. At the point *SR*, real GDP exceeds potential GDP, so the *PA* line moves up and inflation rises. According to the policy rule, the central bank raises interest rates when inflation rises. The higher interest rates shift the AE line downward, lowering real GDP. In the long run, labeled LR in Figure 14.6, real GDP returns to potential GDP. This is depicted as both a movement along the *ADI* curve and a downward shift of the AE line back to potential GDP. Inflation and interest rates are both higher.

c. We can now look at consumption, investment, and net exports. Remember that consumption depends positively on real GDP and negatively on interest rates, investment depends negatively on interest rates, and net exports depend negatively on both real GDP and interest rates. The key to tracing *C*, *I*, and *X* is to keep track of real GDP and interest rates. In the short run, real GDP increases and interest rates are unchanged. In the long run, the interest rate increases and real GDP returns to potential.

d. What happens to consumption, investment, and net exports when government purchases increase? In the short run, the increase in real GDP raises consumption and lowers net exports. Investment is unchanged. In the long run, the higher interest rates lower consumption, investment, and net exports. These results are summarized in the table below.

	Y	*C*	*I*	*X*
SR	↑	↑	—	↓
LR	—	↓	↓	↓

Worked Problems

1. Consider an economy characterized by the following relation between inflation and real GDP:

	Inflation				
	9	7	5	3	1
Original real GDP	6,700	6,800	6,900	7,000	7,100
New real GDP	6,900	7,000	7,100	7,200	7,300

Current inflation is equal to 3 percent, and potential GDP is equal to 7,000. Suppose that the economy moves in the short run from the original to the new relation.

a. Graph the original *ADI* curve, the new *ADI* curve, the *PA* line, and the potential output line. Describe the economy in the short run. Is the economy in equilibrium?

b. Show what happens to the economy over time. What is the long-run equilibrium?

Answers

a. *The original and new ADI curves are downward-sloping lines depicting the values of inflation and real GDP. The PA line is a horizontal line at 3 percent inflation, and the potential output line is a vertical line at 7,000 real GDP. The economy is originally in long-run equilibrium, with the intersection of the ADI curve and the PA line where real GDP equals potential GDP. In the short run, the economy is at the intersection of the new ADI curve and the PA line, with inflation at 3 percent and real GDP at 7,200. This is illustrated in Figure 14.7. Since real GDP exceeds potential GDP, the economy is not in long-run equilibrium.*

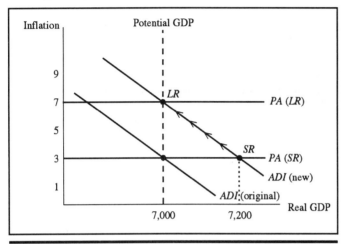

Figure 14.7

b. *In the short run, real GDP is greater than potential GDP, causing inflation. Over time, the PA line shifts up, inflation rises, and real GDP moves back toward potential. In the long-run equilibrium, real GDP is 7,000 and inflation is 7 percent. This is also shown in Figure 14.7.*

2. Starting from a long-run equilibrium with real GDP equal to potential GDP, suppose that a fall in oil prices causes a negative price shock. What are the effects, in both the short and the long run, on real GDP, inflation, consumption, investment, and net exports?

Answer

The negative price shock shifts the PA line downward, lowering inflation. The Fed, following its policy rule, lowers interest rates, shifting the AE curve up and raising real GDP above potential GDP. In the short run, consumption increases (real GDP rises), investment increases (interest rates fall), and net exports increase (the fall in interest rates dominates the rise in real GDP). Over time, the PA line moves up, inflation rises, and real GDP falls. In the long run, inflation, interest rates, and real GDP all return to their original levels, as do consumption, investment, and net exports. The effects are shown in Figure 14.8 and summarized in the table below.

	Y	**C**	**I**	**X**
SR	↑	↑	↑	↑
LR	—	—	—	—

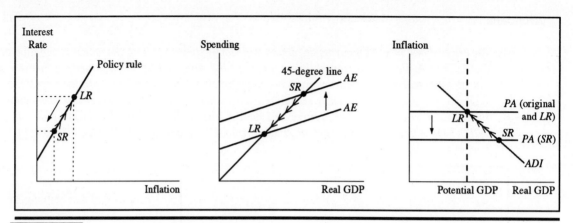

Figure 14.8

Practice Problems

1. Consider an economy characterized by the following relation between inflation and real GDP:

	Inflation				
	10	**8**	**6**	**4**	**2**
Real GDP	6,800	6,900	7,000	7,100	7,200

Current inflation is equal to 4 percent, and potential GDP is equal to 7,100.

a. Graph the *ADI* curve, the *PA* line, and the potential output line. Describe the economy in the short run. Is the economy in long-run equilibrium?

b. Show what happens to the economy over time. What is the long-run equilibrium?

2. Consider an economy characterized by the following relation between inflation and real GDP:

	Inflation				
	10	**8**	**6**	**4**	**2**
Original real GDP	5,700	5,800	5,900	6,000	6,100
New real GDP	5,400	5,500	5,600	5,700	5,800

Current inflation is equal to 8 percent, and potential GDP is equal to 5,800. Suppose that the economy moves in the short run from the original to the new relation.

a. Graph the original *ADI* curve, the new *ADI* curve, the *PA* line, and the potential output line. Describe the economy in the short run. Is the economy in long-run equilibrium?

b. Show what happens to the economy over time. What is the long-run equilibrium?

3. Consider an economy characterized by the following relation between inflation and real GDP:

	Inflation				
	9	**7**	**5**	**3**	**1**
Original real GDP	8,100	8,200	8,300	8,400	8,500
New real GDP	8,300	8,400	8,500	8,600	8,700

Current inflation is equal to 7 percent, and potential GDP is equal to 8,400. Suppose that the economy moves in the short run from the original to the new relation.

a. Graph the original *ADI* curve, the new *ADI* curve, the *PA* line, and the potential output line. Describe the economy in the short run. Is the economy in long-run equilibrium?

b. Show what happens to the economy over time. What is the long-run equilibrium?

4. Starting from a long-run equilibrium with real GDP equal to potential GDP, suppose that U.S. business firms purchase more computers. What are the effects, in both the short and the long run, on real GDP, inflation, consumption, investment, and net exports?

5. Starting from a long-run equilibrium with real GDP equal to potential GDP, suppose that the Fed changes its policy rule to a higher inflation target. What are the effects, in both the short and the long run, on real GDP, inflation, consumption, investment, and net exports?

6. Starting from a long-run equilibrium with real GDP equal to potential GDP, suppose that people expect higher inflation. What are the effects, in both the short and the long run, on real GDP, inflation, consumption, investment, and net exports?

CHAPTER TEST

1. The long run in the economic fluctuations model is determined by the intersection of the
   a. aggregate demand/inflation curve and the price adjustment line.
   b. aggregate demand/inflation curve, price adjustment line, and the potential GDP line.
   c. aggregate demand/inflation curve and the potential GDP line.
   d. price adjustment line and the potential GDP line.

2. The baseline is the path of an economic variable that would occur
   a. without an aggregate demand shock.
   b. after an aggregate demand shock.
   c. without the policy change under consideration.
   d. after the policy change under consideration.

3. In a boom,
   a. real GDP falls short of potential GDP, and inflation falls.
   b. real GDP falls short of potential GDP, and inflation rises.
   c. real GDP exceeds potential GDP, and inflation falls.
   d. real GDP exceeds potential GDP, and inflation rises.

4. A reduction in the rate of inflation is referred to as
   a. a temporary growth slowdown.
   b. deflation.
   c. disinflation.
   d. reinflation.

5. Demand shocks result from changes in
   a. government purchases, consumption, investment, or net exports.
   b. government purchases, investment, net exports, or the monetary policy rule.
   c. consumption, investment, net exports, or the monetary policy rule.
   d. government purchases, investment, net exports, or inflation.

6. Supply shocks are indicated by shifts in
   a. potential GDP.
   b. the price adjustment (*PA*) line.
   c. the aggregate demand/inflation (*ADI*) curve.
   d. the aggregate expenditure (AE) line.

7. If a fall in GDP coincides with a rise in inflation, then the economy is experiencing
   a. a temporary growth slowdown.
   b. stagflation.
   c. a boom-bust cycle.
   d. disinflation.

8. If the central bank reduces interest rates too much, then the economy experiences
   a. a supply shock.
   b. a temporary growth slowdown.
   c. stagflation.
   d. a boom-bust cycle.

9. When real GDP is less than potential GDP,
   a. the *PA* line shifts upward and inflation falls.
   b. the *PA* line shifts upward and inflation rises.
   c. the *PA* line shifts downward and inflation falls.
   d. the *PA* line does *not* shift and inflation remains unchanged.

10. If real GDP is less than potential GDP at the intersection of the *ADI* curve and the *PA* line, then the economy is in
    a. a long-run equilibrium, and there is no reason for inflation or real GDP to change.
    b. a recession, causing inflation to fall and GDP to rise until long-run equilibrium occurs.
    c. a boom, causing inflation to fall and GDP to rise until long-run equilibrium occurs.
    d. a boom, causing inflation to rise and GDP to rise until long-run equilibrium occurs.

11. Suppose the economy is in long-run equilibrium and the government subsequently decides to decrease purchases. In the short run,
    a. the *ADI* curve shifts left and the *PA* line is fixed.
    b. the *ADI* curve shifts right and the *PA* line is fixed.
    c. the *ADI* curve is fixed and the *PA* line shifts upward.
    d. the *ADI* curve is fixed and the *PA* line shifts downward.

12. Suppose the economy is in long-run equilibrium and the government subsequently decides to decrease purchases. In the long run,
    a. real GDP falls short of potential GDP, and inflation remains unchanged.
    b. real GDP equals potential GDP, and inflation remains unchanged.
    c. real GDP equals potential GDP, and inflation is higher.
    d. real GDP equals potential GDP, and inflation is lower.

13. If the central bank shifts to a monetary policy rule with a lower inflation target, then
    a. the *PA* line shifts upward.
    b. the *PA* line shifts downward.
    c. the *ADI* curve shifts right.
    d. the *ADI* curve shifts left.

14. Suppose the economy is in long-run equilibrium and the central bank subsequently decides to change the monetary policy rule to a higher inflation target. In the short run,
    a. real GDP decreases and the inflation rate remains constant.
    b. real GDP increases and the inflation rate remains constant.
    c. real GDP decreases and the inflation rate increases.
    d. real GDP increases and the inflation rate decreases.

Use Figure 14.9 for question 15.

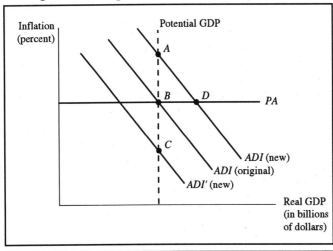

Figure 14.9

15. Initially the economy is in long-run equilibrium at point *B*. If the monetary policy rule changes to a higher inflation target, then which point in the above diagram represents long-run equilibrium?
    a. Point *A*
    b. Point *B*
    c. Point *C*
    d. Point *D*

16. Suppose the economy is initially in long-run equilibrium and subsequently the price of oil decreases. In the short run, the oil price decrease shifts
    a. the *ADI* curve right.
    b. the *ADI* curve left.
    c. the *PA* line upward.
    d. the *PA* line downward.

17. Suppose the economy is in long-run equilibrium and subsequently the price of oil decreases. In the long run,
    a. real GDP exceeds potential GDP, and inflation is higher.
    b. real GDP equals potential GDP, and inflation returns to its original level.
    c. real GDP equals potential GDP, and inflation is higher.
    d. real GDP equals potential GDP, and inflation is lower.

Use Figure 14.10 for questions 18 and 19.

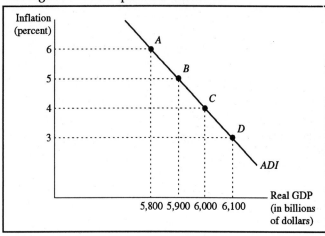

Figure 14.10

18. If the current inflation rate is 4 percent and the economy is in equilibrium, then potential GDP equals
    a. $5,800 billion.
    b. $5,900 billion.
    c. $6,000 billion.
    d. $6,100 billion.

19. If the economy is in long-run equilibrium at point *B*, movement from point *B* to point *A* represents
    a. a boom.
    b. a boom-bust cycle.
    c. stagflation.
    d. disinflation.

20. What are the short-run effects on real GDP, consumption, investment, and net exports when government purchases decrease?
    a. Real GDP, consumption, investment, and net exports fall.
    b. Real GDP, investment, and net exports fall, whereas consumption is unchanged.
    c. Real GDP, consumption, and investment fall, whereas net exports are unchanged.
    d. Real GDP, consumption, and net exports fall, whereas investment is unchanged.

ANSWERS TO THE REVIEW QUESTIONS

Fill-in Questions

1. economic fluctuations model
2. baseline
3. Demand shocks
4. Price shocks
5. Supply shocks
6. boom
7. recession
8. temporary growth slowdown
9. Stagflation
10. boom-bust cycle
11. Disinflation
12. Deflation
13. reinflation
14. short run
15. equilibrium

True-False Questions

1. **False**. The baseline is the path of an economic variable that would occur without the policy change under consideration.
2. **True**. Net exports, which shift the *ADI* curve, are a type of demand shock.
3. **False**. A change in the monetary policy rule is an example of a price shock.
4. **False**. Price shocks are shifts in the *PA* line.
5. **True**. Supply shocks cause permanent changes in real GDP.
6. **False**. A temporary growth slowdown lowers the rate of growth of real GDP, but does not make it negative.
7. **False**. Stagflation occurs when real GDP falls and inflation rises simultaneously.
8. **True**. Deflation is a negative inflation rate, which decreases the price level.
9. **False**. Reinflation is the opposite of disinflation.
10. **True**. Changes in investment change aggregate expenditure, which shifts the *ADI* curve.
11. **False**. Movements in the exchange rate affect net exports, changing aggregate expenditure and shifting the *ADI* curve, not the *PA* line.
12. **True**. Changes in the target inflation rate are changes in the monetary policy rule, which shift the *ADI* curve.
13. **True**. An oil price increase is an example of a price shock, which shifts the *PA* line.
14. **True**. Changes in expected inflation shift the *PA* line.
15. **False**. Changes in government purchases shift the *ADI* curve.

Short-Answer Questions

1. The economic fluctuations model is used to study the effects of economic policy proposals such as changes in monetary policy rules and tax and spending changes.
2. Demand shocks are shifts in the *ADI* curve, including changes in government purchases, investment, net exports, or the monetary policy rule.
3. Price shocks are shifts in the *PA* line, such as changes in the price of oil or other commodities.
4. Supply shocks are shifts in potential GDP, such as technological progress that causes an increase in productivity growth.
5. Booms occur when real GDP is greater than potential GDP. Recessions occur when real GDP is less than potential GDP.
6. A temporary growth slowdown is a decrease in the rate of growth of real GDP that is not large enough to make real GDP growth negative.
7. Stagflation occurs when real GDP falls and inflation rises simultaneously.

8. A boom-bust cycle occurs when the Fed lowers the interest rate too much, causing a boom and inflation. The Fed responds by raising interest rates, causing a recession..
9. Disinflation is a decrease in the inflation rate. Deflation is negative inflation.
10. Disinflation, a reduction in the rate of inflation, is a typical policy objective. Deflation, a negative inflation rate, is not.
11. The economy is in long run equilibrium when real GDP equals potential GDP.
12. Inflation is constant when the economy is in equilibrium.
13. The decrease in government purchases shifts the *ADI* curve to the left, lowering real GDP in the short run. Over time, inflation falls and the *PA* line moves downward. In the long run, real GDP equals potential GDP and inflation is lower.
14. The shift by the Fed to a higher inflation target shifts the *ADI* curve to the right, raising real GDP in the short run. Over time, inflation rises and the *PA* line moves upward. In the long run, real GDP equals potential GDP and inflation is higher.
15. The oil price decrease is a price shock that shifts the *PA* line downward, lowering inflation and raising real GDP in the short run. Over time, inflation rises and the *PA* line shifts back. In the long run, real GDP equals potential GDP at the original inflation rate.

SOLUTIONS TO THE PRACTICE PROBLEMS

1. a. The answer is illustrated in Figure 14.11. The *ADI* curve intersects the *PA* line at potential GDP. The economy is in equilibrium.

   b. Since the economy is in long-run equilibrium, nothing happens over time. The long run is the same as the short run.

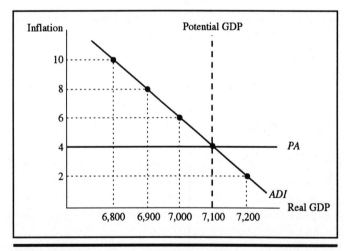

Figure 14.11

2. a. The answer is illustrated in Figure 14.12. The original *ADI* curve intersects the *PA* line with real GDP equal to potential GDP. The new *ADI* curve intersects the *PA* line with real GDP (5,500) below potential GDP (5,800). The economy is not in long-run equilibrium.

b. With real GDP below potential GDP in the short run, inflation falls. The *PA* line shifts down, and GDP rises. In the long-run equilibrium, real GDP equals potential GDP at 2 percent inflation.

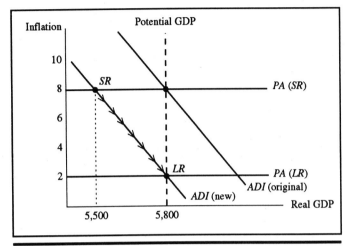

Figure 14.12

3. a. The answer is illustrated in Figure 14.13. The original *ADI* curve intersects the *PA* line with real GDP (8,200) below potential GDP (8,400). The new *ADI* curve intersects the *PA* line with real GDP equal to potential GDP. The economy is in long-run equilibrium.

b. Since the economy is in long-run equilibrium, nothing happens over time. The long run is the same as the short run.

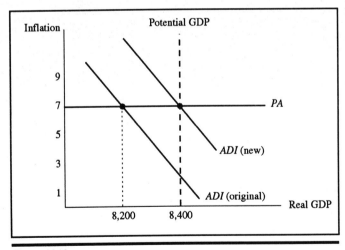

Figure 14.13

4. The purchase of more computers is an increase in investment, which shifts the *ADI* curve to the right. In the short run, real GDP increases and inflation and interest rates are unchanged. In the long run, real GDP returns to potential GDP at higher inflation and interest rates. The results, shown in Figure 14.14, are the same as those for an increase in government purchases except for investment, which is higher in both the short and the long run.

	Y	**C**	**I**	**X**
SR	↑	↑	↑	↓
LR	—	↓	↑	↓

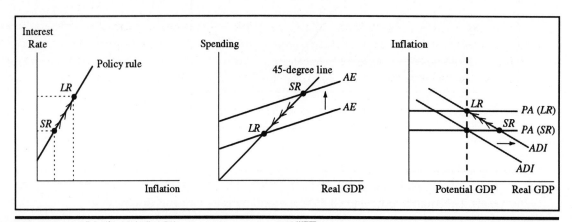

Figure 14.14

5. The policy rule shifts to the right, lowering interest rates and raising real GDP above potential GDP in the short run. Over time, inflation rises, causing the Fed to raise interest rates and real GDP to fall. In the long run, real GDP equals potential GDP at a higher inflation rate. The real interest rate returns to its original level, but, because of the higher inflation, the stated interest rate is higher. The results are shown in Figure 14.15 and summarized below.

	Y	**C**	**I**	**X**
SR	↑	↑	↑	↑
LR	—	—	—	—

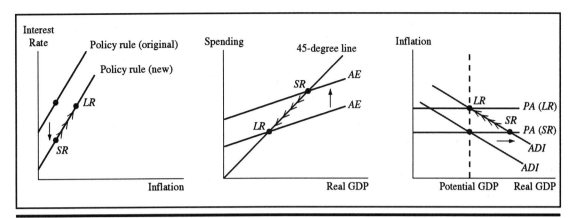

Figure 14.15

6. The expectations of higher inflation cause a positive price shock, increasing inflation, raising interest rates, and reducing GDP below potential GDP in the short run. Over time, inflation and interest rates fall. In the long run, real GDP returns to potential GDP at the original values of inflation and interest rates. The results are shown in Figure 14.16 and summarized below.

	Y	*C*	*I*	*X*
SR	↓	↓	↓	↓
LR	—	—	—	—

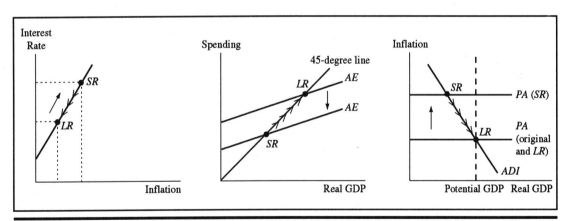

Figure 14.16

ANSWERS TO THE CHAPTER TEST

1. b	6. a	11. a	16. d
2. c	7. b	12. d	17. b
3. d	8. d	13. d	18. c
4. c	9. c	14. b	19. c
5. b	10. b	15. a	20. d

(CHAPTERS 11 - 14)
Economic Fluctuations

1. In practice, firms respond to increases in demand for their product by
   a. immediately raising prices.
   b. immediately expanding output.
   c. immediately decreasing output.
   d. immediately expanding output and raising prices.

2. According to real business cycle theory, economic fluctuations are caused by fluctuations in
   a. the money supply.
   b. aggregate demand.
   c. real GDP.
   d. potential GDP.

3. According to the consumption function, as income increases,
   a. consumption increases by the same amount.
   b. consumption increases by a greater amount.
   c. consumption increases by a smaller amount.
   d. consumption decreases by a smaller amount.

4. An increase in the marginal propensity to consume results in
   a. the aggregate expenditure line getting steeper.
   b. the aggregate expenditure line shifting up in a parallel direction.
   c. the aggregate expenditure line getting flatter.
   d. the aggregate expenditure line shifting down in a parallel direction.

5. If government expenditures decrease, the aggregate expenditure line will
   a. shift up in a parallel direction.
   b. shift down in a parallel direction.
   c. pivot up to the left.
   d. pivot down to the right.

6. Forward-looking theories of consumption explain why people
   a. let consumption fluctuate with year-to-year fluctuations in income.
   b. consume less than their income.
   c. consume more than they save.
   d. smooth their consumption over time.

7. One-year-ahead forecasts for real GDP
    a. are usually equal to the current year's GDP.
    b. are usually equal to a weighted average of real GDP over the past five years.
    c. reflect what forecasters believe will happen to the different spending components of real GDP.
    d. reflect forecasters' beliefs about the determinants of potential GDP over the next year.

Use Table 1 for question 8.

Income (Y) (in billions of dollars)	Consumption (C) (in billions of dollars)
0	250
500	500
1,000	750
1,500	1,000
2,000	1,200
2,500	1,500

TABLE 1

8. Suppose investment I is $400 billion, government purchases G are $200 billion, and net exports X are $200 billion. Using Table 1, at what level of income does spending balance occur?
    a. $1,000 billion.
    b. $1,500 billion.
    c. $2,000 billion.
    d. $2,500 billion.

9. The multiplier is defined as
    a. the change in consumption resulting from a change in aggregate expenditures.
    b. the change in real GDP resulting from a change in aggregate expenditures.
    c. the change in net exports resulting from a change in aggregate expenditures.
    d. the change in investment resulting from a change in aggregate expenditures.

10. If the marginal propensity to consume is 0.75 and investment declines by $5 billion, then real GDP will decline by
    a. $3.75 billion.
    b. $5.00 billion.
    c. $6.67 billion.
    d. $20.0 billion.

11. If net exports become more sensitive to changes in income, then the AE line
    a. gets flatter.
    b. gets steeper.
    c. shifts up in a parallel way.
    d. shifts down in a parallel way.

Use Figure 1 for question 12.

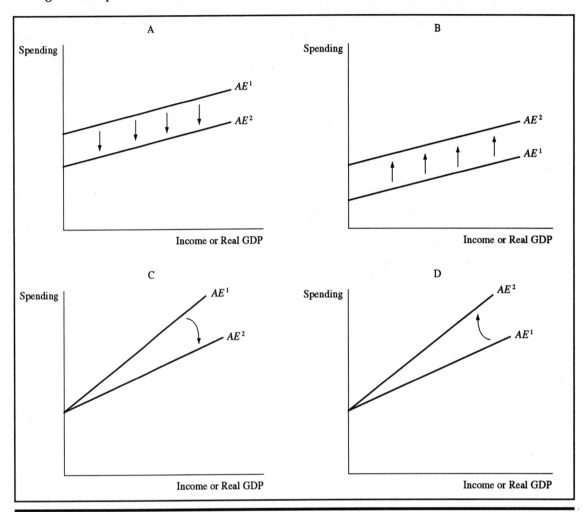

Figure 1

12. Which of the diagrams in Figure 1 represents the shape of the Phillips curve in the long run?
    a. A
    b. B
    c. C
    d. D

13. Under consumption smoothing,
    a. an individual's MPC is constant.
    b. consumption varies proportionally with income.
    c. individuals save in bad years and dissave in good years.
    d. individuals dissave in bad years and save in good years.

14. Which of the following statements is true?
    a. During a recession the MPC falls, but in a boom the MPC increases.
    b. During a recession the MPC increases, but in a boom the MPC decreases.
    c. The MPC is higher when changes in income are permanent than when they are temporary.
    d. The MPC is lower when changes in income are permanent than when they are temporary.

15. One reason consumption smoothing is not perfect is that
    a. some people are liquidity constrained.
    b. people have rational expectations.
    c. people are forward-looking.
    d. the marginal propensity to consume is constant.

16. According to the *ADI* curve, there is a(n)
    a. positive relationship between inflation and real GDP.
    b. positive relationship between inflation and the percentage deviation of real GDP from potential GDP.
    c. inverse relationship between inflation and real GDP.
    d. inverse relationship between the price level and the percentage deviation of real GDP from potential GDP.

17. An increase in interest rates leads to a(n)
    a. increase in both exports and imports.
    b. increase in exports and a decrease in imports.
    c. decrease in exports and an increase in imports.
    d. decrease in both exports and imports.

18. Which of the following is probably the *least* sensitive to changes in interest rates?
    a. Gross investment
    b. Residential investment
    c. Net exports
    d. Consumption expenditures

19. A decrease in inflation causes a
    a. movement up the *ADI* curve.
    b. movement down the *ADI* curve.
    c. shift out of the *ADI* curve.
    d. shift in of the *ADI* curve.

Use Table 2 for questions 20 and 21.

Inflation	Interest Rate Policy Rule A	Interest Rate Policy Rule B
0	3	5
1	5	7
2	7	9
3	9	11
4	11	13

TABLE 2

20. Suppose the government changes its monetary policy rule from policy rule A to policy rule B. How would this change affect the *AE* line?
    a. The *AE* line shifts up.
    b. The *AE* line shifts down.
    c. The *AE* line becomes steeper.
    d. The *AE* line is unaffected.

21. Suppose the government changes its monetary policy rule from policy rule A to policy rule B. How would this change affect the *ADI* curve?
    a. The *ADI* curve shifts left.
    b. The *ADI* curve shifts right.
    c. The *ADI* curve becomes steeper.
    d. The *ADI* curve is unaffected.

22. Which of the following is *not* one of the important features of the price adjustment line?
    a. The *PA* line is flat.
    b. The *PA* line moves over time when real GDP departs from potential GDP.
    c. The *PA* line is upward-sloping.
    d. The *PA* line shifts with changes in expectations or raw materials prices.

23. In a boom,
    a. firms raise their prices.
    b. firms reduce their prices.
    c. workers demand lower wages.
    d. firms experience low demand for their product.

24. When real GDP falls and inflation rises simultaneously, it is called
    a. disinflation.
    b. a supply shock.
    c. deflation.
    d. stagflation.

25. Staggered wages and prices
    a. slow down the speed of wage and price adjustment.
    b. accelerate the adjustment of prices and wages in the economy.
    c. do not affect the speed of wage and price adjustment.
    d. have an uncertain effect on the speed of wage and price adjustment.

26. The *PA* line will move up if there is a(n)
    a. decrease in real GDP.
    b. increase in potential GDP.
    c. increase in expected inflation.
    d. decrease in expected inflation.

27. If real GDP stays below potential GDP,
    a. the *ADI* curve will begin to shift to the right.
    b. the *ADI* curve will begin to shift to the left.
    c. the *PA* line will shift up.
    d. the *PA* line will shift down.

Use Figure 2 for question 28.

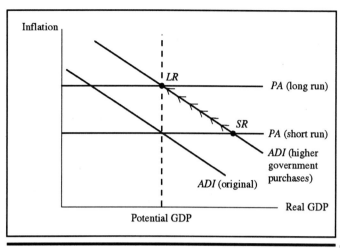

Figure 2

28. Starting with real GDP equal to potential GDP, Figure 2 depicts the response of the economy to
    a. an oil price shock.
    b. an increase in government purchases.
    c. a change in the monetary policy rule to a lower inflation target.
    d. an increase in potential GDP.

Use Figure 3 for question 29.

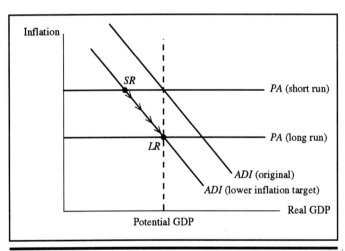

Figure 3

29. Starting with real GDP equal to potential GDP, Figure 3 depicts the response of the economy to
    a. an oil price shock.
    b. an increase in government purchases.
    c. a change in the monetary policy rule to a lower inflation target.
    d. an increase in potential GDP.

Use Figure 4 for question 30.

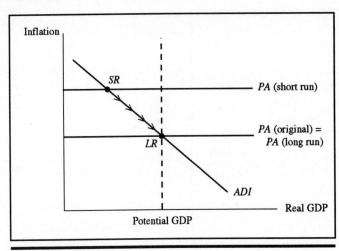

Figure 4

30. Starting with real GDP equal to potential GDP, Figure 4 depicts the response of the economy to
   a. an oil price shock.
   b. an increase in government purchases.
   c. a change in the monetary policy rule to a lower inflation target.
   d. an increase in potential GDP.

ANSWERS

1. b	7. c	13. d	19. b	25. a
2. d	8. c	14. c	20. b	26. c
3. c	9. b	15. a	21. a	27. d
4. a	10. d	16. c	22. c	28. b
5. b	11. a	17. c	23. a	29. c
6. d	12. b	18. d	24. d	30. a

PART 5

Macroeconomic Policy

We have studied long-run economic growth in Part 3 and short-run economic fluctuations in Part 4. Now we are ready to apply what we have learned. In Chapter 15, we study fiscal policy and the budget deficit. We learn about the federal government budget, automatic and discretionary aspects of fiscal policy, the long-run impact of budget deficits, and the desirability of a balanced budget amendment to the United States Constitution. Chapter 16 switches to monetary policy. We study central banks, how money supply and money demand interact to determine the interest rate, and how to evaluate alternative monetary policy rules.

We study the world's largest market, the international finance market, in Chapter 17. We learn how exchange rates are determined, study different types of exchange rate systems, see how concern about the exchange rate affects fiscal and monetary policy rules, and examine policy coordination between countries in practice. In Chapter 18, we learn about different schools of macroeconomic thought and see how they have evolved over time. We then examine two recent fiscal policy proposals by Presidents Bush and Clinton.

Chapter 19 looks at economic growth around the world. We first see that the predictions of growth theory work better for industrialized countries than for developing countries. We then consider developing countries in more detail and examine how their policy choices, both good and bad, have affected their growth rate. Emerging market economies are the subject of Chapter 20. We learn about how centrally planned economies operate, study how countries can make the transition to a market economy, and see how economic reform has actually worked in practice.

We study the gains from international trade in Chapter 21. We learn how gains from trade are related to comparative advantage and economies of scale, and see how the gains from international trade can be measured. Chapter 22 covers international trade policy. We study the effects of trade restrictions, both current and historical, learn about the arguments in favor of trade restrictions, and consider policies to reduce trade barriers.

CHAPTER 15

Fiscal Policy and
the Budget Deficit

CHAPTER OVERVIEW

The fiscal actions of the government—how much to spend on national defense or health care, whether taxes should be raised or cut, what to do about the deficit—are often front-page news. In this chapter, you will go beyond the headlines to understand how fiscal policy affects the economy. We study the federal government budget and learn how taxes, spending, debt, and deficits are related. We look at automatic and discretionary aspects of fiscal policy, and see how discretionary fiscal policy can either stabilize or destabilize the economy. We study the controversial issue of the long-run impact of the budget deficit. Finally, we investigate budget reform in practice and see whether a balanced budget amendment to the U.S. Constitution would be a good idea. Your investment in the long-run analysis in Part 3 and the economic fluctuations model in Part 4 will start to pay off. Issues involving debt and deficits span generations, and understanding them requires a long-run perspective. But fiscal policy also has major effects on the economy over the business cycle, which you will be able to analyze using the *ADI-PA* diagram.

CHAPTER REVIEW

1. **Fiscal policy** is the government's plans for spending, taxes, and borrowing. If *spending*, on national defense, social security, education, and all of the other activities of the government, is greater than *taxes*, the revenue used to pay for this spending, there is a **budget deficit**, which must be financed by *borrowing*. If taxes are greater than spending, the budget is in **surplus**, and if spending equals taxes, the budget is **balanced**.

2. As with any budget, it is useful to think about the federal budget from two sides: spending and revenue.

   a. The expenditure, or spending, side of the **federal budget** is divided into three major categories. The first is *purchases of goods and services*, mostly for national defense. The second is *transfer payments*: social security, welfare, unemployment compensation, Medicare, and Medicaid. The third is *interest payments* on the government debt. It might surprise you to learn that transfer payments are a larger portion of the federal budget than purchases of goods and services.

b. The revenue, or tax, side of the budget is divided into four major categories. *Personal income taxes* and *payroll taxes* are the two largest, whereas *corporate income taxes* and *sales taxes* are smaller. It also may surprise you to learn that payroll taxes, mostly social security taxes, are a larger source of revenue than personal income taxes.

3. The **budget cycle** is the process in which the federal budget is proposed, modified, enacted, and implemented. When the president submits a budget to Congress, it is a *proposal*. Actual spending and taxes differ from the proposed budget for two reasons. First, Congress always modifies the president's budget. Second, unexpected changes in the economy (wars and floods as well as booms and recessions) cause actual taxes and spending to differ from what was enacted. *Supplementals* are changes in spending programs or tax laws that affect the budget in the current fiscal year.

4. The federal budget for the United States has been in deficit, with spending greater than taxes, for every year since 1970 and, based on any plausible forecast, will be in deficit into the next century. Although deficits for the United States seem large, they are not out of line with those in other industrialized countries when measured as a percentage of GDP.

5. The **structural** or full employment **deficit** is the budget deficit that would occur, given existing tax and spending policies, if real GDP equaled potential GDP. It provides a measure of the deficit that is independent of the current state of the economy. The **cyclical deficit** is the difference between the actual deficit and the structural deficit.

6. The **federal debt** is the total amount of outstanding loans that the federal government owes. The deficit is the amount added to the debt each year. A surplus would be subtracted from the debt. The government borrows by selling government **bonds**. Many economists believe that the change in the **debt to GDP ratio** is a better measure of fiscal policy than the deficit. With a growing economy, the ratio of debt to GDP can be constant or fall even though the budget is in deficit. All this requires is for GDP to grow faster than the debt.

7. *State and local government budgets* look very different from the federal budget. Most state and local budgets are in balance or surplus, and many are required to be so by law. The major categories of spending include education, police, fire, roads, and prisons. Sales and property taxes, more than income taxes, are major sources of revenue.

8. The *instruments* of fiscal policy are government purchases, transfers, and taxes. *Discretionary* changes in the instruments of fiscal policy are specific changes in a spending program or in the tax system. The tax cuts of 1964 and 1981 are examples of discretionary policy. *Automatic* changes in the instruments of fiscal policy are changes in spending or revenues that occur without specific actions. The progressive income tax system, where tax payments rise when the economy is in a boom, is one example. Unemployment, social security, and welfare payments, all of which rise during recessions, are others.

9. **Countercyclical fiscal policy** is the attempt to use fiscal policy to offset, or counter, shocks that cause departures of real GDP from potential GDP.

   a. Automatic changes in the instruments of fiscal policy are called **automatic stabilizers** because they tend to stabilize the fluctuations of real GDP. Although they do not eliminate recessions, they make the effects less severe than they would otherwise be. The progressive tax system enhances the effectiveness of automatic stabilizers. With a **progressive tax** system, individual tax payments rise as a proportion of income as income increases. **Fiscal policy rules** that emphasize automatic stabilizers are considered desirable because of their stability and reliability.

b. **Discretionary fiscal policy** does not have a good track record in stabilizing the economy. Lags and uncertainty regarding the impact of policy make discretionary fiscal policymaking problematic. The large budget deficits experienced by the United States and Europe in recent years have also limited the scope for discretionary fiscal policy.

ZEROING IN

1. The structural deficit is a very useful concept for analyzing fiscal policy. In order to understand the structural deficit, we need to investigate the relation between the budget deficit and real GDP.

   a. The relation between the budget deficit and real GDP is shown in Figure 15.1, where the deficit is on the vertical axis and real GDP is on the horizontal axis. The horizontal line at deficit = 0 indicates a balanced budget. Above the line, there is a budget deficit; below the line, there is a budget surplus. The downward-sloping line indicates that the deficit falls as real GDP rises. The reason is automatic stabilizers. When real GDP rises, as in a boom, taxes increase and transfer payments fall, lowering the deficit. When real GDP falls, as in a recession, taxes decrease and transfer payments rise, raising the deficit. Points A, B, and C depict levels of real GDP that produce a budget deficit, budget balance, and budget surplus, respectively.

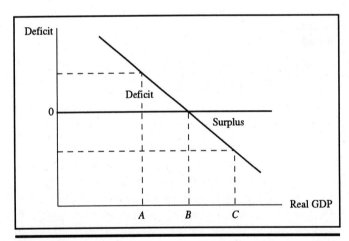

Figure 15.1

   b. Now we are ready to look at the structural deficit, the budget deficit when real GDP equals potential GDP. Figure 15.2 includes the potential GDP line, which is at a value of real GDP that produces a structural deficit. Of course, potential GDP that produced a structural balance or surplus could have been chosen. Figure 15.2 also incorporates a value for actual real GDP. Since actual GDP is less than potential GDP, the economy is in a recession. The actual deficit is greater than the structural deficit, and so the cyclical deficit is positive.

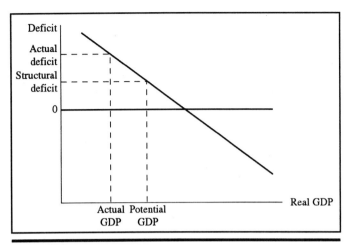

Figure 15.2

2. The long-run impact of budget deficits is a very controversial topic in macroeconomics. We focus on the differences between deficits caused by government spending increases and deficits caused by tax cuts.

    a. What is the long-run impact of a budget deficit caused by an increase in government purchases? You learned in Chapter 14 that in the short run, real GDP increases and inflation and interest rates are unchanged, but in the long run, real GDP returns to potential GDP at higher inflation and interest rates. The decrease in investment caused by the higher interest rates in the long run is called *crowding out*. The rise in interest rates also causes net exports to fall, raising the international *trade deficit*.

    b. What is the long-run impact of a budget deficit caused by a cut in taxes? If the tax cut stimulates consumption, the analysis is similar to that of a budget deficit caused by an increase in government purchases. The deficit causes debt, and therefore interest payments on the debt, to rise in the future, creating a *burden of the debt*, in the form of higher taxes, on future generations. But suppose consumers, being both very forward-looking and concerned about their children's welfare, anticipate these higher taxes and save, rather than spend, the tax cut. In this view, called **Ricardian equivalence**, consumption is not affected by budget deficits caused by tax cuts. If consumption is not affected, then neither are interest rates or investment. Economists are divided as to whether they believe that the evidence in support of Ricardian equivalence is convincing.

3. Deficit reduction has been an elusive goal for fiscal policymakers in recent years. We focus on the issue of **credibility**. When the government announces future policies, do people take these announcements seriously and act on them, or do they think that talk is cheap and ignore them?

    a. Why is credibility important? Deficit reduction through cuts in government purchases has adverse short-run consequences—a recession—before the fall in interest rates stimulates investment and net exports. If the government could announce a credible long-term deficit reduction plan, one that people believed, expected future interest rates would fall. Current long-term interest rates would also fall, mitigating the adverse short-run consequences.

    b. How can credibility be achieved? The existing record on credibility is not impressive. The most dramatic proposal for achieving credibility is the *balanced budget amendment* to the U.S. Constitution. Although the idea is appealing, and would have good long-term growth effects if it were adhered to, it is not clear that such a law could be enforced. In addition, a strict balanced budget amendment would not allow automatic stabilizers to expand the deficit during recessions, which could make recessions worse. Starting in 1997, the president of the

United States was given *line item veto authority*, which may help reduce budget deficits in the future. *Term limits* and *campaign finance reform* for Congress are other proposals for achieving fiscal policy credibility.

ACTIVE REVIEW

Fill-in Questions

1. _____ is the government's plans for spending, taxes, and borrowing.

2. If spending by the government is greater than taxes, there is a budget _____.

3. If taxes exceed spending, there is a budget _____.

4. If taxes equal spending, the budget is _____.

5. The three major categories of spending by the government are _____, _____, and _____.

6. The two largest taxes are _____ and _____ taxes.

7. The _____ or _____ deficit is the budget deficit that would occur if real GDP equaled potential GDP.

8. The _____ deficit is the actual deficit minus the structural deficit.

9. The _____ is the total amount of outstanding loans that the federal government owes.

10. _____ fiscal policy attempts to offset the effects of demand shocks.

11. Changes in the instruments of fiscal policy that do not require legislative action are called _____ stabilizers.

12. Structural budget balance implies a(n) _____ structural deficit.

13. The view that consumption is not affected by budget deficits caused by tax cuts is called _____.

14. Deficit reduction would be much easier if the government could achieve _____.

15. The most dramatic proposal for achieving credibility is the _____ to the U.S. Constitution.

True-False Questions

T F   1. The largest item in the federal budget is national defense.

T F   2. Corporate income taxes are the largest source of revenue in the United States.

T F   3. The president determines the federal budget.

T F   4. Even after the budget is passed, it is not final.

T F   5. The United States's budget deficits are the largest of any industrialized nation.

T F   6. State and local governments typically run large budget deficits.

T F   7. Deficits and surpluses are changes in the federal debt.

T F   8. Most economists believe that the deficit is the best measure of fiscal policy.

T F   9. Discretionary fiscal policy always stabilizes economic fluctuations.

T F   10. Unemployment insurance payments always stabilize economic fluctuations.

T F   11. The structural budget deficit is zero when real GDP equals potential GDP.

T F   12. The budget deficit is positively related to real GDP.

T F   13. In the long run, a budget deficit caused by an increase in government purchases lowers investment.

T F   14. According to the Ricardian equivalence view, budget deficits caused by tax cuts do not affect interest rates.

T F   15. The economy would be stabilized if the budget was always in balance.

Short-Answer Questions

1. How is fiscal policy related to the budget deficit?

2. During the past two decades, has the federal budget for the United States usually been in surplus or in deficit?

3. What is the budget cycle?

4. Why do actual spending and taxes differ from the president's proposed budget?

5. Why is the structural deficit a useful long-run measure of fiscal policy?

6. What is the difference between the federal debt and the federal budget deficit?

7. How does the government borrow?

8. What are the instruments of fiscal policy?

9. Give four examples of automatic stabilizers.

10. What is the relation between the structural deficit, the actual deficit, and real GDP?

11. What is the long-run relation between a budget deficit caused by an increase in government purchases and the international trade deficit?

12. How can budget deficits caused by tax cuts create a burden of the debt on future generations?

13. According to the Ricardian equivalence view, why is there no burden of the debt from deficits caused by tax cuts?

14. Why is credibility important for deficit reduction?

15. What proposals for gaining fiscal policy credibility have been advanced?

WORKING IT OUT

1. We start by reviewing the effects of changes in the instruments of fiscal policy—government purchases, transfers, and taxes—on the aggregate demand/inflation (*ADI*) curve.

   a. An increase in government purchases, as you should remember from Chapter 14, shifts the *ADI* curve to the right, and a decrease in government purchases shifts the *ADI* curve to the left. This is illustrated in Figure 15.3.

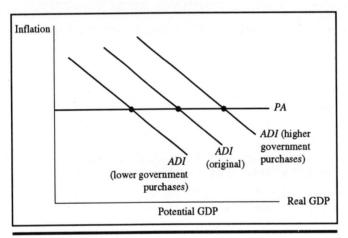

Figure 15.3

   b. The same diagram can be used for transfer payments and taxes. An increase in transfer payments or a decrease in taxes shifts the *ADI* curve to the right, whereas a decrease in transfer payments or an increase in taxes shifts the *ADI* curve to the left.

   c. Figure 15.3 does not include the potential GDP line. The reason for this omission is that the shifts in the *ADI* curve are the same whether the change in fiscal policy occurs when real GDP is above, below, or equal to potential GDP. Depending on the situation, fiscal policy can either move real GDP closer to potential GDP or move real GDP further away from potential GDP.

2. Countercyclical fiscal policy attempts to use changes in taxes, transfers, and spending to "counter" or reduce the size of economic fluctuations caused by demand shocks. The successful use of discretionary fiscal policy to counter a demand shock is illustrated in Figure 15.4.

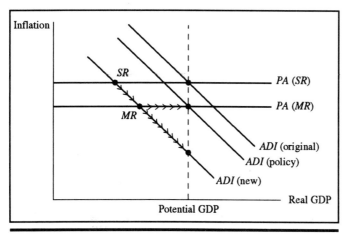

Figure 15.4

   a. Suppose that the economy is in long-run equilibrium with real GDP equal to potential GDP when a negative demand shock, such as a decrease in investment, shifts the *ADI* curve to the left. In the short run, real GDP is below potential GDP at unchanged inflation. This is shown by point *SR* at the intersection of *ADI* (new) and *PA* (*SR*).

   b. In the absence of a policy response, inflation will fall, the *PA* line will shift down, and the economy will eventually return to equilibrium at the intersection of *ADI* (new) and the potential GDP line. The cost of not responding is a recession, which may last a number of years, as the economy moves along the *ADI* curve.

   c. A countercyclical fiscal policy response, such as an increase in unemployment benefits or a tax cut, would shift the *ADI* curve back to *ADI* (policy). Since there are lags in the discretionary policy process, the economy first shifts down the *ADI* (new) curve to point *MR* (medium run), then shifts along the *PA* (*MR*) line. If the policy response exactly counters the shock, the economy moves to the intersection of the *ADI* (policy) curve and the potential output line.

   d. The major advantage of this policy is a shorter recession. Although you can't tell this by looking at the arrows in the diagram, the recovery along *PA* (*MR*) is much faster than the recovery along *ADI* (new). Automatic stabilizers could be even more effective. If they are activated quickly enough, the economy could move back along (or close to) the *PA* (*SR*) line, providing an even faster recovery.

3. Countercyclical fiscal policy does not always work well. An example of unsuccessful policy is shown in Figure 15.5.

a. Suppose that the economy starts in equilibrium and that the initial demand shock is the same as in Figure 15.4. In the short run, the *ADI* curve shifts to the left, and the economy is at point *SR*. In the medium run, the *PA* curve shifts down to point *MR*.

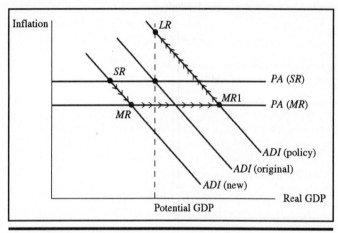

Figure 15.5

b. Now suppose that the policy response shifts the *ADI* curve too far. Real GDP increases above potential GDP to point *MR*1 at the intersection of *ADI* (policy) and *PA* (*MR*). With real GDP above potential GDP, inflation rises, shifting the *PA* line up along the *ADI* (policy) curve until potential GDP is restored. The long-run equilibrium is at a higher inflation rate, a completely unwanted result of the countercyclical fiscal policy.

c. The actual outcome could be even worse. When the inflation occurs, the president and Congress might cut spending or raise taxes, shifting the *ADI* curve back to the left. If the timing of this contractionary policy is no better than the timing of the expansionary policy, the economy could go into a recession.

Worked Problems

1. Consider an economy with the following relation between budget deficits and real GDP:

Deficit (millions of dollars)	220	210	200	190	180
Real GDP (billions of dollars)	5,800	5,900	6,000	6,100	6,200

Suppose that real GDP equals $5,900 billion and potential GDP equals $6,000 billion. What are the actual, structural, and cyclical deficits? Draw a diagram, using the values for real and potential GDP, to illustrate this example.

Answer

The actual deficit is the deficit at the current value of real GDP, $210 million, whereas the structural deficit is the deficit at potential GDP, $200 million. The cyclical deficit is the actual deficit minus the structural deficit, $10 million. Figure 15.6 illustrates the example. The deficit is on the vertical axis, and real GDP is on the horizontal axis. The values of the deficit at actual and potential real GDP are plotted. The line is downward-sloping, indicating that the deficit falls when real GDP is higher.

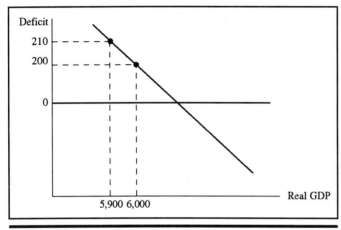

Figure 15.6

2. Consider an economy characterized by the following relation between inflation and real GDP:

		Inflation				
		10	**8**	**6**	**4**	**2**
Original	Real GDP	7,800	7,900	8,000	8,100	8,200
New	Real GDP	7,600	7,700	7,800	7,900	8,000
Policy	Real GDP	7,700	7,800	7,900	8,000	8,100

Current inflation is equal to 6 percent, and potential GDP is equal to 8,000.

a. Suppose that the economy moves in the short run from the original to the new relation. Graph the original *ADI* curve, the new *ADI* curve, the *PA* line, and the potential output line. Describe the economy in the short run.

b. Now suppose that inflation falls by 2 percent in the medium run. Show how the *PA* line shifts. Describe the economy in the medium run.

c. Finally, suppose that countercyclical fiscal policy moves the economy from the new to the policy relation. Graph the *ADI* curve under the new policy and describe the response of inflation and real GDP. Is the economy in equilibrium? If not, what will occur next?

Answers

a. *The original and new ADI curves are downward-sloping lines depicting the values of inflation and real GDP. The PA line is a horizontal line at 6 percent inflation, and the potential output line is a vertical line at 8,000 real GDP. The economy is originally in equilibrium, with the intersection of the ADI curve and the PA line where real GDP equals potential GDP. The short run is the intersection of the new ADI curve and the PA line, with inflation at 6 percent and real GDP at 7,800. This is illustrated in Figure 15.7.*

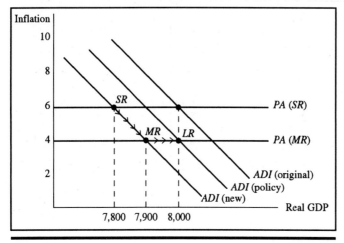

Figure 15.7

b. *In the short run, real GDP is less than potential GDP, so that, in the medium run, the PA line shifts down. The economy moves down the ADI (new) curve. Inflation is at 4 percent and real GDP at 7,900.*

c. *The countercyclical fiscal policy shifts the ADI curve to the right, intersecting the PA (MR) line at inflation = 4 percent and real GDP = 8,000. Real GDP = potential GDP, so the economy is in equilibrium.*

Practice Problems

1. Consider an economy with the following relation between budget deficits and real GDP:

Deficit (millions of dollars)	200	190	180	170	160
Real GDP (billions of dollars)	6,800	6,900	7,000	7,100	7,200

Suppose that real GDP equals $7,200 billion and potential GDP equals $7,000 billion. What are the actual, structural, and cyclical deficits?

2. Consider an economy with the following relation between budget deficits and real GDP:

Deficit (millions of dollars)	30	15	0	-15	-30
Real GDP (billions of dollars)	5,100	5,200	5,300	5,400	5,500

Suppose that real GDP equals $5,400 billion and potential GDP equals $5,500 billion. What are the actual, structural, and cyclical deficits?

3. Consider an economy with the following relation between budget deficits and real GDP:

Deficit (millions of dollars)	160	140	120	100	80
Real GDP (billions of dollars)	7,600	7,700	7,800	7,900	8,000

Suppose that real GDP equals $7,700 billion and potential GDP equals $7,700 billion. What are the actual, structural, and cyclical deficits?

4. Consider an economy characterized by the following relation between inflation and real GDP:

		Inflation				
		10	8	6	4	2
Original	Real GDP	6,500	6,600	6,700	6,800	6,900
New	Real GDP	6,700	6,800	6,900	7,000	7,100
Policy	Real GDP	6,600	6,700	6,800	6,900	7,000

Suppose that current inflation is equal to 4 percent and potential GDP is equal to 6,800. In the short run, the economy moves from the original to the new relation. In the medium run, inflation rises by 2 percent. Finally, a countercyclical policy response occurs. Using an *ADI-PA* diagram, describe the response of inflation and real GDP. Is the economy in equilibrium? If not, what will occur next?

5. Consider an economy characterized by the following relation between inflation and real GDP:

		Inflation				
		9	**7**	**5**	**3**	**1**
Original	Real GDP	4,900	5,000	5,100	5,200	5,300
New	Real GDP	4,700	4,800	4,900	5,000	5,100
Policy	Real GDP	5,000	5,100	5,200	5,300	5,400

Suppose that current inflation is equal to 7 percent and potential GDP is equal to 5,000. In the short run, the economy moves from the original to the new relation. In the medium run, inflation falls by 2 percent. Finally, a countercyclical policy response occurs. Using an *ADI-PA* diagram, describe the response of inflation and real GDP. Is the economy in equilibrium? If not, what will occur next?

6. Consider an economy characterized by the following relation between inflation and real GDP:

		Inflation				
		9	**7**	**5**	**3**	**1**
Original	Real GDP	6,600	6,800	7,000	7,200	7,400
New	Real GDP	6,200	6,400	6,600	6,800	7,000
Policy	Real GDP	6,300	6,500	6,700	6,900	7,100

Suppose that current inflation is equal to 5 percent and potential GDP is equal to 7,000. In the short run, the economy moves from the original to the new relation. In the medium run, inflation falls by 2 percent. Finally, a countercyclical policy response occurs. Using an *ADI-PA* diagram, describe the response of inflation and real GDP. Is the economy in equilibrium? If not, what will occur next?

CHAPTER TEST

1. If government spending is less than tax payments, then
   a. there is a budget deficit.
   b. there is a budget surplus.
   c. the budget is balanced.
   d. the government must borrow.

2. Which of the following is *not* considered on the expenditure or spending side of the federal budget?
   a. Purchases of goods and services
   b. Transfer payments
   c. Tax payments
   d. Interest payments

3. Federal budget deficits for the United States
   a. are large compared to those of other industrialized countries.
   b. are small compared to those of other industrialized countries.
   c. have been common in recent years.
   d. have been nonexistent in recent years.

4. The total amount of outstanding loans that the government owes is the
   a. federal debt.
   b. structural deficit.
   c. cyclical deficit.
   d. federal budget deficit.

5. The instruments of fiscal policy are
   a. government purchases, transfer payments, and interest payments.
   b. government purchases, interest payments, and taxes.
   c. government purchases, transfer payments, and taxes.
   d. transfer payments, interest payments, and taxes.

6. A structural budget balance
   a. requires a positive structural deficit.
   b. requires a zero structural deficit.
   c. is an unreasonable fiscal policy goal for the U.S. economy.
   d. would decrease investment and economic growth in the long run.

7. The major categories on the revenue side of the federal budget are
   a. personal income taxes, payroll taxes, property taxes, and sales taxes.
   b. personal income taxes, payroll taxes, property taxes, and corporate income taxes.
   c. personal income taxes, payroll taxes, sales taxes, and corporate income taxes.
   d. personal income taxes, property taxes, sales taxes, and corporate income taxes.

8. The cyclical deficit is
   a. the difference between the actual deficit and the structural deficit.
   b. the difference between the federal debt and the structural deficit.
   c. the budget deficit that occurs when real GDP equals potential GDP.
   d. a measure of the deficit that is independent of the current state of the economy.

9. Which of the following is *not* a major category of spending for state and local governments?
   a. Education
   b. Police
   c. Defense
   d. Prisons

10. Changes in the instruments of fiscal policy that do *not* require legislative action are referred to as
    a. supplementals.
    b. discretionary.
    c. automatic stabilizers.
    d. proposals.

11. When real GDP falls, as in a recession,
    a. tax payments increase and transfer payments decrease, decreasing the deficit.
    b. tax payments increase and transfer payments increase, causing an indeterminate effect on the deficit.
    c. tax payments decrease and transfer payments increase, increasing the deficit.
    d. tax payments decrease and transfer payments decrease, causing an indeterminate effect on the deficit.

12. The budget deficit and real GDP are
    a. positively related.
    b. negatively related.
    c. unrelated.
    d. either positively or negatively related, depending on other factors.

13. Crowding out is
    a. one of the long-run effects of a budget deficit caused by an increase in government purchases.
    b. one of the long-run effects of a budget deficit caused by tax cuts.
    c. one of the short-run effects of a budget deficit caused by an increase in government purchases.
    d. one of the short-run effects of a budget deficit caused by tax cuts.

14. According to Ricardian equivalence, budget deficits caused by tax cuts
    a. increase consumption, investment, and interest rates.
    b. decrease consumption, investment, and interest rates.
    c. have no effect on consumption, but increase investment and interest rates.
    d. have no effect on consumption, investment, and interest rates.

15. The most dramatic proposal for achieving credibility is
    a. term limitations.
    b. a line item veto for the president.
    c. a balanced budget amendment.
    d. campaign finance reform.

16. Which of the following shifts the *ADI* curve to the left?
    a. An increase in transfer payments
    b. An increase in taxes
    c. An increase in government purchases
    d. An increase in inflation

Use Figure 15.8 for questions 17–18.

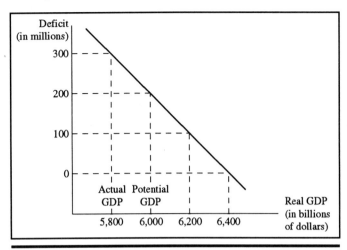

Figure 15.8

17. The structural deficit is equal to
    a. zero.
    b. $100 million.
    c. $200 million.
    d. $300 million.

18. The cyclical deficit is equal to
    a. zero.
    b. $100 million.
    c. $200 million.
    d. $300 million.

Use Figure 15.9 for questions 19–20.

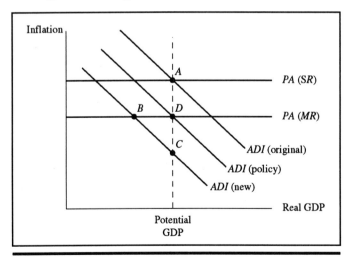

Figure 15.9

19. Suppose that the economy is in equilibrium at point *A* when a negative demand shock occurs, shifting the *ADI* curve from *ADI* (original) to *ADI* (new). In the absence of a policy response, which point on the diagram represents long-run equilibrium for the economy?
    a. *A*
    b. *B*
    c. *C*
    d. *D*

20. Suppose that the economy is in equilibrium at point *A* when a negative demand shock occurs, shifting the *ADI* curve from *ADI* (original) to *ADI* (new). If, after the *PA* curve shifts from *PA* (*SR*) to *PA* (*MR*), the government invokes a countercyclical fiscal policy response that exactly counters the shock, which point on the diagram represents long-run equilibrium for the economy?
    a. *A*
    b. *B*
    c. *C*
    d. *D*

ANSWERS TO THE REVIEW QUESTIONS

Fill-in Questions

1. Fiscal policy
2. deficit
3. surplus
4. balanced
5. purchases of goods and services; transfer payments; interest payments on the government debt
6. personal income; payroll
7. structural; full employment
8. cyclical
9. federal debt
10. Countercyclical
11. automatic
12. zero
13. Ricardian equivalence
14. credibility
15. balanced budget amendment

True-False Questions

1. **False**. Transfer payments are larger.
2. **False**. Both personal income taxes and payroll taxes are larger.
3. **False**. The president submits a proposal to Congress, but it is always modified.
4. **True**. Changes in tax laws and spending programs, called supplementals, affect the budget in the current fiscal year.
5. **False**. They are not out of line with those in other industrialized countries when measured as a percentage of GDP.
6. **False**. State and local budgets are usually in surplus or in balance.
7. **True**. Deficits represent additions to and surpluses subtractions from the debt.
8. **False**. Many economists believe that change in the debt to GDP ratio is a better measure.
9. **False**. Because of lags and uncertainty, discretionary fiscal policy can magnify business cycles.
10. **True**. Unemployment insurance payments rise during recessions and fall during booms, stabilizing fluctuations.
11. **False** When real GDP equals potential GDP, there can be a structural deficit surplus, or balance.

12. **False**. When real GDP increases, the deficit falls because of automatic stabilizers.
13. **True**. Higher government purchases raise interest rates in the long run, reducing (crowding out) investment.
14. **True**. According to Ricardian equivalence, deficits caused by tax cuts do not affect consumption. If consumption is not affected, neither are interest rates.
15. **False**. With a balanced budget, automatic stabilizers would not be able to reduce the effects of demand shocks.

Short-Answer Questions

1. Fiscal policy is the government's plans for spending, taxes, and borrowing. If spending exceeds taxes, there is a budget deficit, and the government must borrow.
2. The federal budget for the United States has been in deficit for every year since 1970.
3. The budget cycle is the process in which the federal budget is proposed, modified, enacted, and implemented.
4. First, the actual budget also depends on Congress, which modifies the president's proposed budget. Second, unexpected events cause actual spending and taxes to differ from the enacted budget.
5. The structural deficit measures what the deficit would be if real GDP equaled potential GDP, and so is not affected by current economic fluctuations.
6. The federal debt is the total amount of outstanding loans that the federal government owes. The federal deficit is the change in the debt, the amount added to the debt each year.
7. The government borrows by selling government bonds.
8. The instruments of fiscal policy are government purchases, taxes, and transfers.
9. The progressive tax system, unemployment benefits, social security payments, and welfare payments are four examples of automatic stabilizers.
10. When real GDP exceeds potential GDP, the actual deficit is less than the structural deficit. When real GDP is less than potential GDP, the actual deficit is greater than the structural deficit. When real GDP equals potential GDP, the actual and structural deficits are equal.
11. In the long run, deficits caused by higher government spending raise interest rates, causing net exports to fall and the trade deficit to rise.
12. The deficit causes debt, and therefore interest payments on the debt, to rise in the future, creating a burden of the debt on future generations.
13. If consumers, anticipating higher taxes in the future, save rather than spend the proceeds of the tax cut, there will be no burden of the debt.
14. If the government could announce a credible deficit reduction plan, long-term interest rates would fall, mitigating the adverse short-run consequences.
15. The balanced budget amendment, the line item veto, term limits, and campaign finance reform are some of the proposals for increasing credibility.

SOLUTIONS TO THE PRACTICE PROBLEMS

1. The actual deficit is $160 million, and the structural deficit is $180 million. The cyclical surplus is $20 million (the cyclical deficit is -$20 million).

2. The actual surplus is $15 million (the actual deficit is -$15 million) and the structural surplus is $30 million (the structural deficit is -$30 million). The cyclical deficit is $15 million.

3. Since real GDP equals potential GDP, the actual deficit is the same as the structural deficit, or $140 million. The cyclical deficit is zero.

4. The answer is illustrated in Figure 15.10. In the short run, real GDP rises to 7,000 at unchanged inflation as the *ADI* curve shifts to the right. In the medium run, the *PA* line shifts up, inflation rises to 6 percent, and real GDP falls to 6,900. The countercyclical policy response shifts the *ADI* curve to the left; real GDP falls to 6,800, and inflation stays at 6 percent. This is an equilibrium because real GDP equals potential GDP.

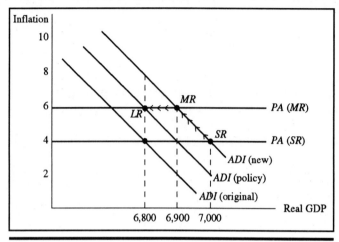

Figure 15.10

5. The answer is illustrated in Figure 15.11. In the short run, real GDP falls to 4,800 at unchanged inflation as the *ADI* curve shifts to the left. In the medium run, the *PA* line shifts down, inflation falls to 5 percent, and real GDP rises to 4,900. The countercyclical policy response shifts the *ADI* curve to the right; real GDP rises to 5,200, and inflation stays at 5 percent. This is not an equilibrium because real GDP exceeds potential GDP. In the absence of another policy response, the *PA* line will shift up along the *ADI* (policy) curve until potential GDP is reached at 9 percent inflation.

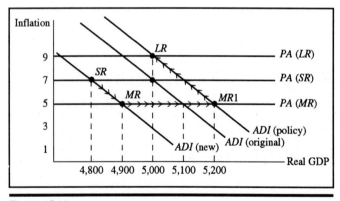

Figure 15.11

6. The answer is illustrated in Figure 15.12. In the short run, real GDP falls to 6,600 at unchanged inflation as the *ADI* curve shifts to the left. In the medium run, the *PA* line shifts down, inflation falls to 3 percent, and real GDP rises to 6,800. The countercyclical policy response shifts the *ADI* curve to the right; real GDP rises to 6,900, and inflation stays at 3 percent. This is not an equilibrium because real GDP is less than potential GDP. In the absence of another policy response, the *PA* line will shift down along the *ADI* (policy) curve until potential GDP is reached at 2 percent inflation.

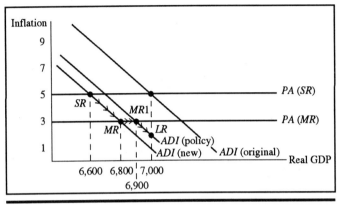

Figure 15.12

ANSWERS TO THE CHAPTER TEST

1. b	6. b	11. c	16. b
2. c	7. c	12. b	17. c
3. c	8. a	13. a	18. b
4. a	9. c	14. d	19. c
5. c	10. c	15. c	20. d

CHAPTER 16

Monetary Policy

CHAPTER OVERVIEW

Monetary policy is one of the most important topics in macroeconomics. By changing the money supply, the central bank affects interest rates, inflation, and real GDP. The head of the Federal Reserve System, the central bank for the United States, is often said to be the second most powerful person in America. In Chapter 10, we showed how long-run inflation is determined by the rate of growth of the money supply, while in Chapter 13, we showed how monetary policy affects short-run economic fluctuations. In this chapter, you will learn about monetary policy in both theory and practice. We see how money supply and money demand interact to determine the interest rate, how Fed policy actions work, and why independence of the central bank is desirable. Using the *ADI-PA* diagram, we evaluate alternative monetary policy rules and see how to choose a good rule.

CHAPTER REVIEW

1. *Monetary policy* is the set of actions taken by the government that affect the money supply and thereby interest rates, exchange rates, inflation, unemployment, and real GDP. The *central bank* — the *Federal Reserve System (Fed)* in the United States, the *Bundesbank* in Germany, and the *Bank of Japan* in Japan — is responsible for monetary policy in most countries. The most important feature of a central bank is *central bank independence*, the degree of independence the law gives it from the government.

2. **Money demand** is defined as a relationship between the interest rate and the amount of money that people want to hold at that interest rate. Money is only part of most individuals' wealth. Currency pays no interest, while checking accounts pay relatively low interest. Alternatives, such as certificates of deposit and Treasury bills, pay higher interest rates. The *opportunity cost* of holding money is the interest rate on the alternatives minus the interest paid on checking accounts for deposits. When the interest rates on the alternatives to holding money rise, the opportunity cost increases and money demand falls. When the interest rates on the alternatives fall, the opportunity cost decreases and money demand rises.

3. The Fed determines the *money supply* by changing the *monetary base*, currency plus reserves. How does it do this? Every day, bond traders at the New York Federal Reserve Bank buy and sell billions of dollars of government bonds. The other side of the market consists of banks, acting on their own or for customers. When the Fed buys government bonds, it pays for them by increasing bank reserves, the deposits banks have with the Fed. The increase in bank reserves increases the monetary base. When the Fed sells bonds, it lowers reserves, decreasing the monetary base. When the Fed buys or sells bonds, this is called an **open market operation**.

4. The *money multiplier* links the monetary base (*MB*) and the money supply (*M*). The money multiplier, which was derived in Chapter 11, is given by

$$\frac{M}{MB} = \frac{k+}{k+r}$$

where *r* is the required reserve ratio and *k* is the currency to deposit ratio. Although the Fed can, in theory, use changes in the required reserve ratio to affect the money multiplier and the money supply, in practice it affects the money supply by changing the monetary base through open market operations. Do not become confused by the term *multiplier*. The money multiplier is unrelated to the government purchases multiplier discussed in Chapter 12.

5. The interest rate is determined by the demand for money and the supply of money. When the Fed wants to lower the interest rate, it buys bonds, increasing the monetary base and increasing the money supply. When the Fed wants to raise the interest rate, it sells bonds, decreasing the monetary base and decreasing the money supply. The *federal funds rate* is the interest rate that the Fed looks at to make sure its actions have the intended effect. It is the short-term interest rate that banks charge one another on overnight loans. The federal funds rate is closely related to the longer-term interest rates on Treasury bills and certificates of deposit, which are relevant for money demand.

6. The **discount rate** is the rate that commercial banks are charged when they borrow from the Fed. The ability to borrow from the Fed increases people's confidence in the safety of their bank deposits, and the Fed is called the *lender of the last resort*. Changes in the discount rate always receive a lot of publicity, and the Fed sometimes changes the discount rate when it wants to bring public attention to its actions or provide a signal of its future intentions.

7. The **monetary transmission channel** describes how open market operations affect real GDP in the short run. The Fed buys bonds, increasing bank reserves, the monetary base, and, through the money multiplier, the money supply. Interest rates fall, increasing consumption, investment, and, through the exchange rate, net exports. Real GDP rises in the short run. When the Fed sells bonds, the opposite occurs and short-run real GDP falls.

8. In Chapter 13, we studied a monetary policy rule in which the Fed increases the interest rate when inflation rises and decreases the interest rate when inflation falls, and used the rule to derive a downward-sloping aggregate demand/inflation (*ADI*) curve. Including real GDP in the monetary policy rule is a slight modification of this rule. Along with reacting to inflation, the Fed raises the interest rate when real GDP rises above potential GDP and lowers the interest rate when real GDP falls below potential GDP. When the economy enters a boom, so that real GDP exceeds potential GDP, the Fed raises the interest rate even if inflation has not yet started to increase. This is called a **preemptive monetary strike** because the Fed raises the interest rate in anticipation of a rise in inflation, rather than waiting for inflation to actually increase before acting. When the economy goes into a recession, so that real GDP falls below potential GDP, the Fed lowers interest rates, stimulating investment and net exports and leading to a quicker recovery. Including real GDP in the monetary policy rule makes the *ADI* curve steeper. The Fed and other central banks appear to respond to real GDP, as well as to inflation, in this way.

9. The **constant money growth rule**, advocated by *monetarists*, is simply to keep the growth rate of the money supply fixed from year to year. Although this rule would keep inflation low in the long run, inflation would still be affected by price shocks and would not be perfectly stable from year to year. The slope of the *ADI* curve with a constant money growth rule would depend on the sensitivity of money demand to the interest rate. The **gold standard,** a monetary rule in which the value of money is linked to gold, was adopted by much of the would before 1914. Both a constant money growth rule and a gold standard world produce a downward-sloping *ADI* curve.

10. Central bank independence and clearly stated procedures for setting the interest rate are likely to increase the *credibility* of monetary policy. Two advantages of credibility are cited by advocates of policy rules. First, the Fed can take actions that appear contrary to its goals, explain its position, and be believed. In the absence of credibility, people would be more likely to interpret such actions as changes in the policy rule. Second, credibility lowers the cost of disinflation. The Fed can announce a disinflation path, and expectations of future inflation will adjust downward immediately. Without credibility it would take a recession that lowers actual inflation to affect people's expected inflation. If expected inflation can be brought down more quickly, so can actual inflation.

ZEROING IN

1. A unique aspect of monetary policy is that central banks have varying degrees of independence from the government. Although the Bank of Japan is closely tied to its government, the Bundesbank and, to a lesser extent, the Fed are able to act independently. In 1997, the Bank of England, which had been one of the least independent central banks, was given much more independence. At first glance, **central bank independence** seems like a strange idea. Why shouldn't the president and Congress, who are elected by the public, have control over monetary policy? In fact, some degree of independence is the most important attribute for a central bank to have in order to run a good monetary policy.

   a. There is a natural tendency toward higher inflation in the political system. We learned in Chapters 13 and 14 that, in the short run, a change in the monetary policy rule toward higher inflation would increase real GDP with little or no change in inflation, but in the long run, real GDP returns to potential at higher inflation. The government in power, looking toward the next election, would be tempted to raise the inflation target in order to make the economy look good at election time. If the government was reelected, the long-run inflation consequences could be dealt with later. If it was defeated, inflation would become the other party's problem. Countries in which the central bank has greater independence have lower long-run inflation than countries in which the central bank is more controlled by the government.

   b. The **political business cycle** refers to the tendency of governments to regularly use economic policy, either fiscal or monetary, to influence elections. This involves creating a boom just before the election, then slowing down the economy afterward. Although such cycles are possible in theory, recent evidence for a political business cycle in the United States is not strong. The independence of the Fed is the most important reason for the absence of a political business cycle in the United States.

c. Not all arguments for central bank independence involve such a cynical view of the political process. **Time inconsistency** describes the tendency of governments, attempting to improve the welfare of their citizens, to announce a low inflation policy, but then stimulate the economy in order to reduce unemployment. Unfortunately, a central bank that adopts this type of policy will lose credibility over time as people learn what it is doing, and this loss of credibility is very costly. Think of a professor who announces a final exam in order to get the students to study, but then walks into the classroom on the day of the final and cancels the exam. It may work the first time, but how hard do you think students would study for the same professor's final the next semester?

d. The need to finance government budget deficits provides another reason for central bank independence. When we discussed fiscal policy in Chapter 15, we assumed that deficits were financed by borrowing (issuing government bonds). But people will buy these bonds only if they expect to be paid back. If there is political instability, the government may not be able to borrow. In that situation, if the government, rather than the central bank, controls the money supply, it can print money to finance the budget deficit. With a large deficit, it does not matter if the government prints money directly, as in the American colonies during the Revolutionary War, or instructs the central bank to print money, as in Russia in the 1990s; the result is a large inflation.

2. We have seen in Chapter 14 how a change in the inflation target shifts the aggregate demand/inflation (*ADI*) curve. The Fed can also affect the *slope* of the *ADI* curve and influence by how much real GDP falls when inflation rises.

   a. Suppose that a price shock, such as an oil price increase, shifts up the price adjustment (*PA*) line and raises inflation. As shown in Figure 16.1, the amount that real GDP falls in the short run depends on the slope of the *ADI* curve.

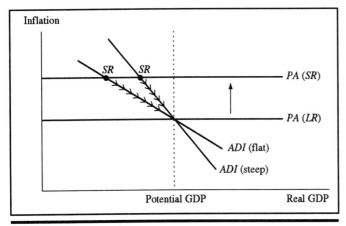

Figure 16.1

   b. How does the Fed influence the slope of the *ADI* curve? The Fed follows a *more aggressive* policy if, when inflation rises, it raises interest rates by a lot so that real GDP declines sharply. This produces a flat *ADI* curve. With a *less aggressive* policy, following a rise in inflation, the Fed raises interest rates less so that real GDP does not decline as much. This results in a steep *ADI* curve. The alternatives are shown in Figure 16.1. With a more aggressive policy, real GDP declines sharply after a price shock, but the return to the original inflation occurs quickly. With a less aggressive policy, the recession is smaller but the return to the original inflation takes longer.

c. The central bank faces a tradeoff between fluctuations in inflation and fluctuations in real GDP. A less aggressive policy, producing a steep *ADI* curve, will produce small real GDP fluctuations but large inflation fluctuations. A more aggressive policy, with a flat *ADI* curve, will produce large real GDP fluctuations but small inflation fluctuations.

ACTIVE REVIEW

Fill-in Questions

1. _____ is the set of actions taken by the government that affect the money supply and interest rate.

2. The central bank is called the _____ in the United States, the _____ in Germany, and the _____ in Japan.

3. The most important feature of a central bank is _____.

4. Money demand is a relationship between the _____ and the amount of money people want to hold.

5. The _____ equals currency plus reserves.

6. The _____ links the monetary base and the money supply.

7. The _____ is the interest rate that the Fed follows to make sure its actions have the intended effect.

8. The _____ is the rate that commercial banks are charged when they borrow from the Fed.

9. The _____ describes how open market operations affect real GDP in the short run.

10. The policy rule associated with monetarists is the _____ rule.

11. A _____ occurs when the Fed raises the interest rate in anticipation of a rise in inflation.

12. Central bank independence increases the _____ of monetary policy.

13. The _____ is the tendency of governments to regularly use economic policy to influence elections.

14. _____ describes the tendency of governments to announce a low inflation policy but then stimulate the economy in order to reduce unemployment.

15. The central bank faces a _____ between fluctuations in inflation and fluctuations in real GDP.

True-False Questions

T F 1. The actions of the Federal Reserve System are determined by the president and Congress.

T F 2. The opportunity cost of holding currency is the rate of inflation.

T F 3. The Fed exactly determines the money supply.

T F 4. The federal funds rate is the interest rate on Treasury bills.

T F 5. The discount rate is set by the Fed.

T F 6. At one time, much of the world was on the gold standard.

T F 7. With a preemptive monetary strike, the Fed raises the interest rate even though inflation has not started to increase.

T F 8. All major central banks are independent of their government.

T F 9. There is a natural tendency toward higher inflation in the political system.

T F 10. Central bank independence and inflation are unrelated.

T F 11. In recent times monetary policy has regularly been used to influence elections in the United States.

T F 12. An increase in government purchases makes the *ADI* curve steeper.

T F 13. A more aggressive policy by the Fed makes the *ADI* curve flatter.

T F 14. The central bank faces a tradeoff between the level of inflation and the level of real GDP.

T F 15. In practice, the Fed increases the interest rate only when inflation rises.

Short-Answer Questions

1. What is central bank independence?

2. How does the Fed change the monetary base?

3. What is the money multiplier?

4. What is preemptive monetary strike?

5. What is the policy rule most closely associated with the monetarists?

6. What two factors are likely to increase the credibility of monetary policy?

7. What are the two advantages of credibility for the Fed?

8. What is the political business cycle?

9. What is time inconsistency?

10. What is the cost to a central bank of adopting time-inconsistent policies?

11. What happens if a government budget deficit is financed by printing money?

12. How does the Fed shift the aggregate demand/inflation (*ADI*) curve?

13. How does the Fed change the slope of the *ADI* curve?

14. How is the slope of the *ADI* curve related to the tradeoff between inflation fluctuations and real GDP fluctuations?

15. What monetary policy rule does the Fed and other central banks follow?

WORKING IT OUT

1. We learned in Chapters 13 and 14 that a change in the monetary policy rule toward a higher inflation target would raise real GDP in the short run and increase inflation in the long run. Let's review that material.

   a. In Figure 16.2, inflation is on the vertical axis and real GDP is on the horizontal axis. The aggregate demand/inflation (*ADI*) curve is downward-sloping, and the price adjustment (*PA*) line is horizontal. The *ADI* (original) line is drawn to intersect the *PA* line at an equilibrium where real GDP equals potential GDP.

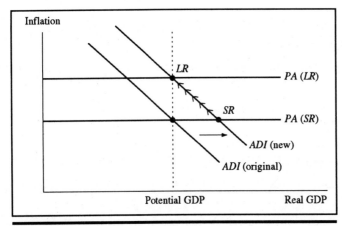

Figure 16.2

   b. A change in the monetary policy rule toward a higher inflation target shifts the *ADI* curve to the right. In the short run, depicted by the intersection of *ADI* (new) and *PA* (*SR*), real GDP rises with unchanged inflation.

   c. Over time, inflation rises and the *PA* line shifts up. The economy moves back toward potential GDP along the *ADI* (new) curve. In the long run, at the intersection of *ADI* (new) and *PA* (*LR*), inflation is higher and real GDP equals potential GDP.

2. We have learned that changes in the inflation target shift the *ADI* curve, whereas changes in the "aggressiveness" of policy, or how much interest rates are raised when inflation rises, change the slope of, or tilt, the *ADI* curve. In Chapter 14, we used a numerical example to illustrate shifts in the *ADI* curve. Now we use a similar example to examine changes in the slope of the *ADI* curve.

   a. Start with a relationship between inflation and real GDP:

	Inflation				
	9	**7**	**5**	**3**	**1**
Real GDP	5,800	5,900	6,000	6,100	6,200

The numbers for inflation represent the inflation rate (in percent), while those for real GDP represent billions of dollars. This defines an *ADI* curve. If potential GDP equals 6,000 and current inflation equals 5 percent, the *ADI* and *PA* curves can be drawn as in Figure 16.3.

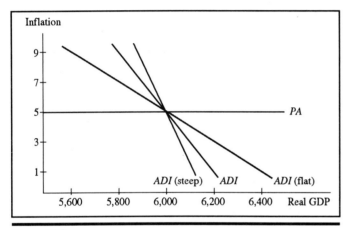

Figure 16.3

   b. Suppose that the relationship between inflation and real GDP changes to

	Inflation				
	9	**7**	**5**	**3**	**1**
Real GDP	**5,600**	**5,800**	**6,000**	**6,200**	**6,400**

The new *ADI* curve, *ADI* (flat), is drawn in Figure 16.3. It is flatter than the original *ADI* curve, indicating that policy has become more aggressive.

c. Now suppose that the relationship between inflation and real GDP changes to

	Inflation				
	9	**7**	**5**	**3**	**1**
Real GDP	5,900	5,950	6,000	6,050	6,100

The new *ADI* curve, *ADI* (steep), is also drawn in Figure 16.3. It is steeper than the original *ADI* curve, indicating that policy has become less aggressive.

3. We have discussed how the interest rate is determined by the supply of money and the demand for money. Let's look at this graphically.

a. Figure 16.4 shows a graph with the interest rate on the vertical axis and money on the horizontal axis. Money demand is a downward-sloping line because the interest rate is the opportunity cost of holding money. When the interest rate is higher, money demand is lower because other financial assets, such as Treasury bills, pay higher rates. Money supply is vertical because it is controlled by the Fed and does not depend on the interest rate.

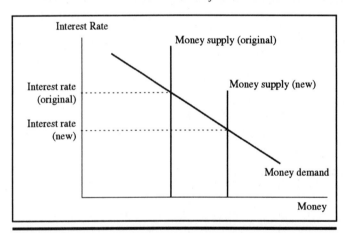

Figure 16.4

b. The interest rate is determined by the intersection of money demand and money supply. In Figure 16.4, this is at interest rate (original), at the intersection of money demand and money supply (original).

c. What happens if the Fed increases the money supply? The money supply line shifts to the right, lowering the interest rate from interest rate (original) to interest rate (new). This illustrates how the Fed lowers the interest rate by raising the money supply.

d. How does the Fed raise the interest rate? By lowering the money supply. Although this is not shown in Figure 16.4, you can see it for yourself. Draw a diagram like Figure 16.4 but instead of raising the money supply and shifting the money supply line to the right, lower the money supply and shift the money supply line to the left. The interest rate rises.

Worked Problems

1. Consider an economy characterized by the following relationship between inflation and real GDP:

	Inflation				
	10	**8**	**6**	**4**	**2**
Original real GDP	4,800	4,900	5,000	5,100	5,200
New real GDP	4,600	4,800	5,000	5,200	5,400

Current inflation is equal to 6 percent, and potential GDP is equal to 5,000. Draw the original *ADI* curve, the new *ADI* curve, and the *PA* line. Is the new *ADI* curve steeper or flatter than the original *ADI* curve? What change in policy caused the change in the slope of the *ADI* curve?

Answer

As shown in Figure 16.5, the ADI *curve is downward-sloping and the* PA *line is horizontal. The new* ADI *curve is flatter than the original* ADI *curve, indicating that policy has become more aggressive.*

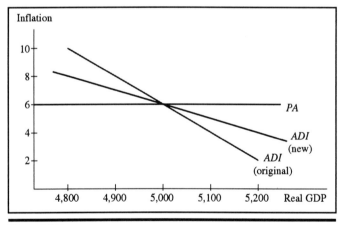

Figure 16.5

2. Consider an economy characterized by the following money demand line:

	Interest Rate				
	10	8	6	4	2
Money	300	400	500	600	700

The money supply is equal to $500 billion.

a. Draw the money demand and money supply lines. What is the interest rate?

b. Suppose that the money supply falls to $400 billion. What is the new interest rate?

Answers

a. *Money demand is downward-sloping and money supply is vertical, as shown in Figure 16.6. The interest rate, determined at the intersection of the two lines, is 6 percent.*

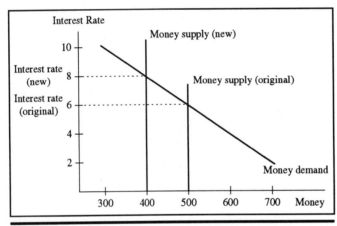

Figure 16.6

b. *If the money supply falls to $400 billion, the money supply line shifts left and the interest rate rises to 8 percent.*

Practice Problems

1. Consider an economy characterized by the following relationship between inflation and real GDP:

	Inflation				
	12	10	8	6	4
Original real GDP	6,500	6,750	7,000	7,250	7,500
New real GDP	6,800	6,900	7,000	7,100	7,200

Current inflation is equal to 8 percent, and potential GDP is equal to 7,000. Draw the original *ADI* curve, the new *ADI* curve, and the *PA* line. Is the new *ADI* curve steeper or flatter than the original *ADI* curve? What change in policy caused the change in the slope of the *ADI* curve?

2. Consider an economy characterized by the following relationship between inflation and real GDP:

	Inflation				
	5	**4**	**3**	**2**	**1**
Original real GDP	3,800	3,900	4,000	4,100	4,200
New real GDP	3,600	3,800	4,000	4,200	4,400

Current inflation is equal to 3 percent, and potential GDP is equal to 4,000. Draw the original *ADI* curve, the new *ADI* curve, and the *PA* line. Is the new *ADI* curve steeper or flatter than the original *ADI* curve? What change in policy caused the change in the slope of the *ADI* curve?

3. Consider an economy characterized by the following money demand line:

	Interest Rate				
	6	**5**	**4**	**3**	**2**
Money	300	400	500	600	700

The money supply is equal to $400 billion. Draw the money demand and money supply lines. What is the interest rate? Suppose that the money supply rises to $600 billion. What is the new interest rate?

4. Consider an economy characterized by the following money demand line:

	Interest Rate				
	11	**9**	**7**	**5**	**3**
Money	500	600	700	800	900

The money supply is equal to $800 billion. Draw the money demand and money supply lines. What is the interest rate? Suppose that the money supply falls to $700 billion. What is the new interest rate?

CHAPTER TEST

1. The most important feature of a central bank is
   a. the discount rate.
   b. the monetary transmission channel.
   c. central bank independence.
   d. preemptive monetary strikes.

2. Who makes decision regarding monetary policy in the United States?
   a. The president
   b. The Congress
   c. The Bundesbank
   d. The Federal Reserve System

3. When the interest rate on alternatives to holding money falls,
   a. the opportunity cost of holding money decreases and money demand rises.
   b. the opportunity cost of holding money decreases and money demand falls.
   c. the opportunity cost of holding money increases and money demand rises.
   d. the opportunity cost of holding money increases and money demand falls.

4. When the Fed buys government bonds, it
   a. lowers reserves, decreasing the monetary base.
   b. lowers reserves, increasing the monetary base.
   c. raises reserves, decreasing the monetary base.
   d. raises reserves, increasing the monetary base.

5. In practice, the Fed affects the money multiplier and the money supply by changing
   a. the required reserve ratio.
   b. the monetary base through open market operations.
   c. total government purchases.
   d. tax rates.

6. When the Fed wants to lower the interest rate, it
   a. buys bonds, increases the monetary base, and increases the money supply.
   b. buys bonds, decreases the monetary base, and decreases the money supply.
   c. sells bonds, increases the monetary base, and increases the money supply.
   d. sells bonds, decreases the monetary base, and decreases the money supply.

7. The discount rate is
   a. the short-term interest rate on overnight loans between commercial banks.
   b. the long-term interest rate on loans between commercial banks.
   c. the rate that commercial banks are charged when they borrow from the Fed.
   d. the long-term interest rate on Treasury bills.

8. The monetary transmission channel describes how open market operations affect
   a. nominal GDP in the short run.
   b. nominal GDP in the long run.
   c. real GDP in the short run.
   d. real GDP in the long run.

9. According to the money transition channel, when the Fed buys bonds,
    a. real GDP rises in the short run.
    b. nominal GDP rises in the long run.
    c. nominal GDP falls in the short run.
    d. real GDP falls in the short run.

10. The constant money growth rule, advocated by monetarists, is
    a. to keep the growth rate of the money supply fixed from year to year.
    b. to keep the growth rate of the money supply increasing from year to year.
    c. to keep the growth rate of money demand fixed from year to year.
    d. to keep the growth rate of money demand increasing from year to year.

11. Under the constant money growth rule,
    a. a boom-bust cycle would occur.
    b. inflation would be kept high in the long run.
    c. inflation would still be affected by price shocks.
    d. inflation would be perfectly stable from year to year.

12. The gold standard
    a. is advocated by monetarists.
    b. is a monetary rule in which the value of money is linked to gold.
    c. would keep the growth rate of the money supply constant.
    d. would keep inflation perfectly stable from year to year.

13. A political business cycle
    a. is a common occurrence in the United States.
    b. involves creating a boom just after an election.
    c. is commonly observed in countries in which the central bank is highly independent of the government.
    d. refers to the tendency of governments to regularly use economic policy to influence elections.

14. The Fed is said to follow a less aggressive policy if
    a. when interest rates rise, it raises inflation by a lot.
    b. when interest rates rise, it raises inflation by a little.
    c. when inflation rises, it raises interest rates by a lot.
    d. when inflation rises, it raises interest rates by a little.

15. A more aggressive policy by the Fed results in a
    a. leftward shift in the *ADI* curve.
    b. rightward shift in the *ADI* curve.
    c. flatter *ADI* curve.
    d. steeper *ADI* curve.

16. When the Fed follows a more aggressive policy, real GDP declines
    a. sharply after a price shock, but the return to the original level of inflation occurs rapidly.
    b. sharply after a price shock, but the return to the original level of inflation occurs slowly.
    c. slightly after a price shock, but the return to the original level of inflation occurs rapidly.
    d. slightly after a price shock, but the return to the original level of inflation occurs slowly.

17. The central bank faces a tradeoff between
    a. the level of inflation and the level of real GDP.
    b. fluctuations in inflation and fluctuations in real GDP.
    c. the level of inflation and fluctuations in real GDP.
    d. fluctuations in inflation and the level of real GDP.

18. In practice, the Fed and other central banks
    a. increase the interest rate when inflation rises and/or when real GDP falls below potential GDP.
    b. increase the interest rate when inflation falls and/or when real GDP rises above potential GDP.
    c. increase the interest rate when inflation rises and/or when real GDP rises above potential GDP.
    d. increase the interest rate when inflation falls and/or when real GDP falls below potential GDP.

Use Figure 16.7 for question 19.

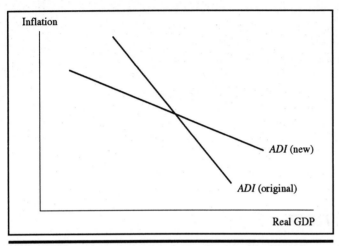

Figure 16.7

19. An adjustment from the original *ADI* curve to the new *ADI* curve indicates that
    a. the Fed is following a nominal GDP targeting rule.
    b. the Fed has moved to a higher inflation target.
    c. the Fed's policy has become less aggressive.
    d. the Fed's policy has become more aggressive.

Use Figure 16.8 for question 20.

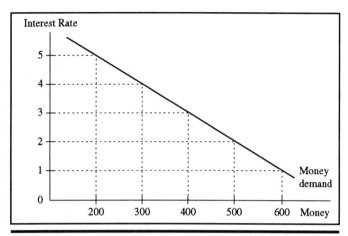

Figure 16.8

20. When the money supply equals $400 billion, what is the interest rate?
    a. 2 percent
    b. 3 percent
    c. 4 percent
    d. 5 percent

ANSWERS TO THE REVIEW QUESTIONS

Fill-in Questions

1. Monetary policy
2. Federal Reserve System; Bundesbank; Bank of Japan
3. central bank independence
4. interest rate
5. monetary base
6. money multiplier
7. federal funds rate
8. discount rate
9. monetary transmission channel
10. constant money growth
11. preemptive monetary strike
12. credibility
13. political business cycle
14. Time inconsistency
15. tradeoff

True-False Questions

1. **False**. The Federal Reserve System enjoys a degree of independence.
2. **False**. The opportunity cost of holding currency is the interest rate on the alternatives.
3. **False**. The Fed exactly determines the monetary base.
4. **False**. The federal funds rate is the interest rate on overnight loans between banks.
5. **True**. It is the rate that banks are charged when they borrow from the Fed.
6. **True**. Most of the world was on the gold standard before World War I.
7. **True**. The Fed raises the interest rate in anticipation of a rise in inflation.
8. **False**. The Bank of Japan is closely tied to its government.
9. **True**. The temptation to make the economy look good at election time imparts an inflation bias to the political system.

10. **False**. Countries with more independent central banks have lower long-run inflation than countries with less independent central banks.
11. **False**. Recent evidence does not support a political business cycle for the United States.
12. **False**. Increases in government purchases shift the *ADI* curve out. They do not affect its slope.
13. **True**. With a more aggressive policy, interest rates rise more when inflation rises, causing a greater decline in real GDP and a flatter *ADI* curve.
14. **False**. The central bank faces a tradeoff between fluctuations in inflation and fluctuations in real GDP. There is no tradeoff in levels; real GDP equals potential GDP at any level of inflation.
15. **False**. The Fed also increases the interest rate when real GDP rises above potential GDP.

Short-Answer Questions

1. Central bank independence is the degree of independence the law gives the central bank from the government.
2. The Fed changes the monetary base through open market operations, buying and selling government bonds with reserves.
3. The money multiplier is a number that describes by how much the money supply changes when the monetary base changes.
4. A preemptive monetary strike is when the Fed raises the interest rate in anticipation of a rise in inflation, rather than waiting for inflation to actually increase before acting.
5. The constant money growth rule is associated with the monetarists.
6. Central bank independence and clearly stated procedures for setting the interest rate are likely to increase the credibility of monetary policy.
7. With credibility, policy announcements by the Fed are more likely to be believed and inflation can be reduced with lower cost.
8. The political business cycle is the tendency of governments to regularly use economic policy in order to influence elections.
9. Time inconsistency is the tendency of governments to first announce a low inflation policy but later stimulate the economy to reduce unemployment.
10. The central bank will lose credibility if its policy is inconsistent.
11. Financing a deficit by printing money causes inflation.
12. If the Fed changes the inflation target, the *ADI* curve shifts.
13. If the Fed follows a more or less aggressive policy, the slope of the *ADI* curve changes.
14. A steep *ADI* curve will produce small real GDP changes but large inflation fluctuations. A flat *ADI* curve will produce large real GDP changes but small inflation fluctuations.
15. The Fed and other central banks increase the interest rate when inflation rises and/or when real GDP rises above potential GDP and decrease the interest rate when inflation falls and/or when real GDP falls below potential GDP.

SOLUTIONS TO THE PRACTICE PROBLEMS

1. As shown in Figure 16.9, the new *ADI* curve is steeper than the original *ADI* curve, indicating that policy has become less aggressive.

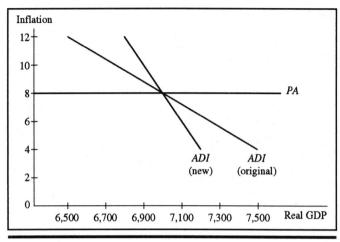

Figure 16.9

2. As shown in Figure 16.10, the new *ADI* curve is flatter than the original *ADI* curve, indicating that policy has become more aggressive.

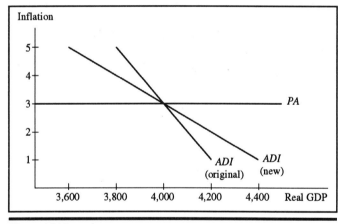

Figure 16.10

3. When the money supply is $400 billion, the interest rate is 5 percent. When the money supply rises to 600, the interest rate falls to 3 percent. This is illustrated in Figure 16.11.

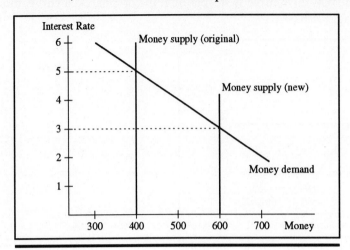

Figure 16.11

4. When the money supply is $800 billion, the interest rate is 5 percent. When the money supply falls to 700, the interest rate rises to 7 percent. This is illustrated in Figure 16.12.

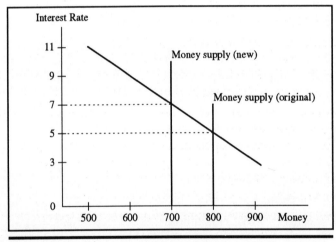

Figure 16.12

ANSWERS TO THE CHAPTER TEST

1. c	6. a	11. c	16. a
2. d	7. c	12. b	17. b
3. a	8. c	13. d	18. c
4. d	9. a	14. d	19. d
5. b	10. a	15. c	20. b

CHAPTER 17

International Finance

CHAPTER OVERVIEW

The international finance market is the world's largest market. Trade in currencies is more than 40 times the amount of trade in goods, and commodity and stock markets have become worldwide. In this chapter, we adopt a global perspective and move beyond the vantage point of the United States to consider how fiscal and monetary policy questions affect the world. We study the factors that determine trade balances, and learn why some countries have deficits while others have surpluses. We consider exchange rate determination, and see how purchasing power parity and interest rate differentials influence exchange rates. We study different types of exchange rate systems, both current and historical. Finally, we consider how concern about the exchange rate affects the implementation of the fiscal and monetary policy rules that we studied in Chapters 15 and 16, and see how policy coordination between countries works in practice.

CHAPTER REVIEW

1. A *trade surplus* for any single country occurs when exports exceed imports. When imports exceed exports, we say that there is a *trade deficit*. The world as a whole cannot have either a trade surplus or a trade deficit. If some countries have surpluses, others must have deficits. The United States has run a large trade deficit in recent years; it decreased in the late 1980s and, but then rose in the 1990s.

2. We have often used the term *net exports* to denote exports minus imports. When net exports are positive, there is a trade surplus. When net exports are negative, there is a trade deficit.

3. Exports and imports are divided into **merchandise trade**, such as automobiles and computers, and **services trade**, such as tourism and banking services. The **merchandise trade balance** equals merchandise exports minus merchandise imports, while the **services trade balance** equals services exports minus services imports. The trade balance equals the merchandise trade balance plus the services trade balance. Recently, the United States has run a merchandise trade deficit and a services trade surplus. The merchandise trade deficit has been larger than the services trade surplus, producing a total trade deficit.

4. **Factor income** consists of interest payments and profits earned by individuals and businesses operating in other countries. If a resident of the United States receives interest from a foreign bank account or an American firm receives profits from an affiliate abroad, this is called *receipt of factor income*. If a foreign resident receives interest or profits from operations in the United States, this is called *payment of factor income*. The difference between receipt and payment of factor income is **net factor income from abroad**.

5. **International transfer payments** consist of humanitarian and military aid paid to other countries. These payments can go in both directions; **net transfers from abroad** are the difference between transfers received and transfer payments made. The United States normally gives more aid than it receives, and so net transfers from abroad are usually negative.

6. The **balance of payments** accounts is a record of all the transactions between a country and the rest of the world. The two parts of the balance of payments accounts are the current account and the capital account.

7. The **current account balance** is the sum of the merchandise trade balance, the services trade balance, net factor income from abroad, and net transfer payments from abroad. Since each of the four categories can be positive or negative, there can be either a *current account surplus*, a positive value for the current account, or a *current account deficit*, a negative value for the current account. In recent years, the United States has run a current account deficit.

8. What determines whether the United States runs a trade surplus or a trade deficit. From reading newspapers and watching television, you would be tempted to conclude that trade barriers, specifically the closing of Japanese markets to American exporters, is the root cause. In reality, trade deficits and surpluses are caused by more the prosaic, but also more fundamental, factors of saving and investment. If the gap between investment and savings is positive, so that a country saves less than it invests, its net exports will be negative and it will have a trade deficit. If the gap between investment and savings is negative, so that a country saves mores hat it invests, its net exports will be positive and it will have a trade surplus.

9. If the United States runs a current account deficit, we must either borrow from abroad or sell assets to foreigners. In either event, **net foreign assets** held by U.S. residents decline. Conversely, a U.S. current account surplus would represent an increase in net foreign assets. During the 1980s, persistent current account deficits caused net foreign assets for the United States to decline from a positive to a negative value. Put differently, the United States shifted from a *net creditor* to a *net debtor* country. The **capital account** measures changes in loans and assets. Because of errors and omissions in counting foreign assets, the current and capital accounts do not always coincide.

10. The **bilateral trade balance** is the trade surplus or deficit between two countries. While bilateral deficits, such as the trade deficit of the United States with Japan in recent years, often receive a lot of attention, surpluses and deficits with individual countries are of little economic importance. **Sectoral trade balances**, such as the trade deficit for automobiles for the United States, also receive much attention. Like bilateral deficits, individual sectoral deficits are of little importance.

11. The *exchange rate* is the price of domestic currency in terms of foreign currency. For every pair of countries, there is a different exchange rate. For example, the exchange rate for the United States with Japan was about 115 yen per dollar in the summer of 1997. The **real exchange rate** is the exchange rate adjusted for inflation. The change in the real exchange rate equals the change in the exchange rate minus the difference in the inflation rate in the two countries.

12. The **law of one price** is a theory that says that exchange rates are determined so that the price of the same good would be about the same across different countries. This is sometimes called **purchasing power parity (PPP)**. PPP works well in the long run, but works very badly in the short run. It works better for **tradable goods**, where transport costs are low compared to the value of the good, than for nontradable goods, where transport costs are prohibitive.

13. *Interest rate differentials* are the most important reason for short-run deviations of exchange rates from purchasing power parity. When interest rates in the United States rise relative to interest rates abroad, investors switch from foreign to U.S. assets, causing the dollar to rise or appreciate. In the short run, these movements in exchange rates completely swamp the movements in exchange rates caused by equating goods prices according to PPP.

14. **Exchange market intervention** occurs when governments buy and sell currencies to prevent changes in the exchange rate. The world currency market is so large, however, that intervention does not affect exchange rates for long. Unless it is accompanied by changes in interest rates, exchange market intervention has only small effects.

ZEROING IN

1. The most basic issue for a country facing the world economy is what *exchange rate system* to adopt. The choice is between a **fixed exchange rate system**, where governments set, or fix, exchange rates between their currencies, and a **flexible exchange rate system**, where governments do not try to set the value of their currencies. Both throughout history and at the present time, countries have made a number of different choices.

   a. The *gold standard* was the exchange rate system for the 35 years preceding World War I. Under the gold standard, two or more countries agree to buy and sell gold at a fixed price. Because both currencies are tied to gold, the relative price of the two currencies, the exchange rate, is fixed. The gold standard is an example of a fixed exchange rate system.

   b. The **Bretton Woods system** was the exchange rate system between the end of World War II and 1971. Under the Bretton Woods system, only one country, the United States, bought and sold gold at a fixed price, and the other countries fixed their exchange rates to the dollar. The Bretton Woods system is another example of a fixed exchange rate system.

   c. The current flexible exchange rate system has been in place since 1973. Major countries such as the United States and Japan allow their currencies to fluctuate. As its name implies, the current system is an example of a flexible exchange rate system.

   d. The **European monetary system** (EMS) is an attempt by countries in Europe, including France, Germany, and the United Kingdom, to maintain fixed exchange rates among themselves while having flexible exchange rates with the rest of the world. While the EMS had much success in stabilizing exchange rates, in particular between France and Germany, in the 1980s, the strains caused by fixing exchange rates erupted into exchange rate crises in 1992 and 1993. The EMS is a third example of a fixed exchange rate system.

   e. The EMS is in the process of evolving beyond a fixed exchange rate system into a system with a single currency, called the *Euro*. While it is projected that the Euro will eventually replace national currencies, it is not clear which countries will join the system.

2. Why are fixed exchange rate systems desirable? Why do they break down? The answers to these questions help us understand why some countries, such as the United States and Japan, let their exchange rate fluctuate, whereas others, such as France and Germany, attempt to keep it fixed through the EMS.

a. Loss of **international monetary independence** is the most important characteristic of any fixed exchange rate system. Suppose that the Fed and the Bank of Japan (BOJ) agreed to fix the dollar/yen exchange rate. This can be accomplished by equalizing interest rates between the United States and Japan. Now suppose that the Fed wants to raise interest rates, maybe to move to a lower inflation target. Investors, looking for higher yields, would switch from yen- to dollar-denominated assets, causing the dollar to appreciate relative to the yen. The only way to keep the exchange rate fixed is for the Fed to not raise interest rates in the first place, a loss of international monetary independence.

b. The crises in the European monetary system during 1992 and 1993 can be explained by the loss of independence. In both cases, the Bundesbank, concerned with rising inflation because of the boom caused by increased expenditures to pay for the reunification of East and West Germany, raised interest rates. The United Kingdom (in 1992) and France (in 1993) did not want to raise interest rates because of fears that higher interest rates would cause a recession. The United Kingdom and France first attempted to keep their exchange rates with the deutsche mark stable by raising interest rates. Eventually, domestic economic considerations proved to be more important than fixing exchange rates. The United Kingdom left the EMS, and France allowed its currency to fall.

c. Why do countries form fixed exchange rate systems? One reason for fixed exchange rates, which was an important motivation in the establishment of the EMS, is the belief that flexible exchange rates, by increasing uncertainty, can interfere with trade. While reducing exchange rate risk is desirable, the development of **futures markets** in currencies allows firms to **hedge**, or protect against exchange rate risk, in a flexible exchange rate system.

ACTIVE REVIEW

Fill-in Questions

1. The _____ or _____ equals exports minus imports.

2. If net exports are negative, there is a trade _____.

3. Exports and imports are divided into _____ trade and _____ trade.

4. Interest payments and profits earned by individuals and businesses operating in other countries are called _____.

5. _____ consist of humanitarian and military aid between countries.

6. The _____ is the sum of net exports, net factor income from abroad, and net transfer payments from abroad.

7. The current account balance is the change in _____.

8. The _____ measures changes in loans and assets.

9. _____ trade deficits are between individual countries.

10. The _____ is the price of domestic currency in terms of foreign currency.

11. The _____ is the exchange rate adjusted for inflation.

12. _____ is a theory that says that exchange rates are determined so that the price of the same good would be about the same across different countries.

13. Exchange market _____ occurs when governments buy and sell currencies to prevent changes in the exchange rate.

14. In a(n) _____ exchange rate system, governments set the exchange rates between their currencies.

15. In a(n) _____ exchange rate system, governments do not try to set the value of their currencies.

True-False Questions

T   F   1. If there were only two countries in the world and one had a trade surplus, the other would have to have an equal trade deficit.

T   F   2. Net exports equal gross exports minus depreciation.

T   F   3. In recent years, the United States has run both a merchandise trade deficit and a services trade deficit.

T   F   4. Net transfers from abroad are usually negative for the United States.

T   F   5. During the 1980s, net foreign assets for the United States became negative.

T   F   6. The U.S. trade deficit with Japan is an example of a sectoral trade deficit.

T   F   7. Purchasing power parity (PPP) works better in explaining exchange rates in the long run than in the short run.

T   F   8. When interest rates in the United States rise relative to interest rates abroad, the dollar appreciates.

T   F   9. Exchange market intervention has large effects on exchange rates.

T   F   10. The most important cause of the U.S. trade deficit is Japanese trade barriers.

T   F   11. If the gap between investment and saving is positive, there is a trade surplus.

T   F   12. In a fixed exchange rate system, central banks cannot raise interest rates to lower inflation.

T   F   13. If there was a fixed exchange rate between the United States and Canada and the Fed raised U.S. interest rates, the Bank of Canada would have to raise Canadian interest rates.

T   F   14. Loss of international monetary independence is the most important characteristic of any flexible exchange rate system.

T   F   15. What exchange rate system is the EMS evolving toward?

Short-Answer Questions

1. In recent years, has the United States run a trade surplus or a trade deficit?

2. What are the two basic categories of exports and imports?

3. What are transfer payments?

4. What are the two parts of the balance of payments accounts?

5. What are the four items that make up the current account?

6. Has the United States run a current account surplus or deficit in recent years?

7. What is the real exchange rate?

8. What is the relation between purchasing power parity (PPP) and transport costs?

9. Which has more influence on the exchange rate in the short run, interest rate differentials or purchasing power parity?

10. What are the two basic alternatives available to a country when it chooses an exchange rate system?

11. What are the three major exchange rate systems adopted by industrialized countries in the last century?

12. What is the current exchange rate system in Europe?

13. What is the loss of international monetary independence in a fixed exchange rate system?

14. What caused the crises in the European monetary system during 1992 and 1993?

15. Describe two forms of coordination of monetary policy under fixed exchange rates.

WORKING IT OUT

1. Purchasing power parity (PPP) postulates that exchange rates are determined so that the price of the same commodity in two countries would be about the same. We will see how the algebra of PPP works.

   a. Let's first look at the law of one price for an individual good. Suppose that a watch sold for $100 in the United States and 200 marks in Germany. According to the law of one price, if transport costs are small, the exchange rate will adjust to equalize the price in the two countries. That exchange rate would be 2 marks per dollar.

   b. For the economy as a whole, PPP states that the exchange rate times the domestic price level equals the foreign price level. Written as an equation,

   $$E \times P = P^*$$

   where E is the exchange rate (marks per dollar), P is the domestic (U.S.) price level, and P^* is the foreign (Germany) price level. The U.S. price level is in dollars, and the German price level is in marks. The algebra is the same as above. If $P = 100$ and $P^* = 200$, then E must equal 2 for PPP to hold.

   c. Purchasing power parity can also be used to predict what will happen to the exchange rate if prices change. Suppose that the U.S. price level doubles to 200 but the German price level is unchanged. According to PPP, the exchange rate falls by half, from 2 marks per dollar to 1 mark per dollar.

2. We have discussed a number of ways to measure trade. The two most important are the total trade balance (net exports) and the current account.

   a. The terms *trade balance, total trade balance,* and *net exports* all mean the same thing, the sum of the merchandise trade balance and the services trade balance. To determine the trade balance, simply add the merchandise trade balance and the services trade balance. Since the value of either the merchandise or the services trade balance, or both, can be negative, net exports can be positive or negative. If net exports are positive, we say that there is a trade surplus. If net exports are negative, we say that there is a trade deficit.

   b. The current account is a more comprehensive measure of transactions with the rest of the world. To determine the current account, add net factor income from abroad and net transfers from abroad to the trade balance. Since these can be either positive or negative and net exports can be either positive or negative, the current account can be either positive or negative. If the current account is positive, we say that there is a current account surplus. If the current account is negative, we say that there is a current account deficit.

Worked Problems

1. Consider two countries with the following price levels:

Country	Price Level
United States (domestic)	100 dollars
Germany (foreign)	500 marks

a. What is the purchasing power parity exchange rate?

b. Suppose there is 25 percent inflation in the United States. What is the new PPP exchange rate?

Answers

a. *The PPP exchange rate is determined by the formula, $E \times P = P^*$, where E is the exchange rate, 100 dollars is the domestic (U.S.) price level, and 500 marks is the foreign (German) price level. From the formula, $E \times 100 = 500$, so $E = 5$ (marks per dollar).*

b. *If U.S. inflation is 25 percent, then the domestic price level P rises to 125. Using the formula, $E \times 125 = 500$, or $E = 4$ (marks per dollar). The exchange rate falls.*

2. Consider the following trade pattern for the United States, with values in billions of dollars.

	2000	2005
Merchandise trade balance	-100	-110
Services trade balance	20	25
Net factor income from abroad	10	5
Net transfers from abroad	-35	-40

a. What are the values of the trade balance and the current account for the years 2000 and 2005? Are they in deficit or in surplus?

b. Suppose that, in the year 2000, we sell $10 billion more computers to foreigners. How does this affect the trade surplus and current account?

Answers

a. *The trade balance is the sum of the merchandise and services trade balances; it equals -80 in the year 2000 and -85 in 2005. The current account adds net factor income and net transfers from abroad, and is -105 in 2000 and -120 in 2005. There are both a trade deficit and a current account deficit in both years.*

b. *The increased computer sales make the merchandise trade deficit less negative (-90). The trade deficit (-70) and the current account deficit (-95) both fall.*

Practice Problems

1. Consider two countries with the following price levels:

Country	Price Level
United States (domestic)	1 dollar
Japan (foreign)	100 yen

    a. What is the purchasing power parity exchange rate?

    b. Suppose there is 20 percent inflation in Japan. What is the new PPP exchange rate?

2. Consider two countries with the following price levels:

Country	Price Level
United States (domestic)	100 dollars
France (foreign)	400 francs

    a. What is the purchasing power parity exchange rate?

    b. Suppose there is 10 percent inflation in both the United States and France. What is the new PPP exchange rate?

3. Consider the following trade pattern for the United States, with values in billions of dollars.

	2000	2005
Merchandise trade balance	120	150
Services trade balance	-70	-65
Net factor income from abroad	15	10
Net transfers from abroad	-45	-40

    a. What are the values of the trade balance and the current account for the years 2000 and 2005? Are they in deficit or in surplus?

    b. Suppose that, in the year 2000, we give $10 billion more military assistance to foreign countries. How does this affect the trade balance and the current account?

4. Consider the following trade pattern for the United States, with values in billions of dollars.

	2000	2005
Merchandise trade balance	-20	-50
Services trade balance	30	65
Net factor income from abroad	5	10
Net transfers from abroad	-35	-30

a. What are the values of the trade balance and the current account for the years 2000 and 2005? Are they in deficit or in surplus?

b. Suppose that, in the year 2000, profits earned by U.S.-owned affiliates in foreign countries increase by $5 billion. How does this affect the trade balance and current account?

CHAPTER TEST

1. The trade balance for a country equals
   a. real GDP minus imports.
   b. exports minus imports.
   c. imports minus exports.
   d. imports plus exports.

2. The trade deficit for the United States
   a. decreased in the late 1980s, but rose in the 1990s.
   b. increased in the late 1980s, but fell in the 1990s..
   c. increased steadily from 1987 to 1997.
   d. decreased steadily from 1990 to 1997.

3. In recent years, the United States has run a merchandise trade
   a. surplus and a services trade surplus.
   b. surplus and a services trade deficit.
   c. deficit and a services trade deficit.
   d. deficit and a services trade surplus.

4. If an American firm receives profits from an affiliate abroad, the profits are called
   a. a transfer payment.
   b. a receipt of factor income.
   c. a payment of factor income.
   d. net factor income from abroad.

5. Net transfers from abroad are
   a. usually positive for the United States.
   b. the difference between the receipt and payment of factor income.
   c. the difference between transfers received and transfer payments made.
   d. the sum of the merchandise trade surplus, the services trade surplus, and net factor income from abroad.

6. If the United States runs a current account deficit,
   a. it must either lend abroad or buy assets from foreigners.
   b. it must either borrow abroad or sell assets to foreigners.
   c. net foreign assets held by U.S. residents rise.
   d. net foreign assets held by U.S. residents remain unchanged.

7. Purchasing power parity is the theory that
   a. is sometimes called the law of more than one price.
   b. says that exchange rates are determined so that the price of the same good varies across different countries.
   c. says that exchange rates are determined so that the prices of different goods vary across different countries.
   d. says that exchange rates are determined so that the price of the same good is about the same across different countries.

8. Purchasing power parity
   a. works badly in the long run, but works well in the short run.
   b. works well in the long run, but works badly in the short run.
   c. works better for nontradable goods.
   d. works equally well for both nontradable and tradable goods.

9. When interest rates in the United States fall relative to interest rates abroad,
   a. investors switch from foreign to U.S. assets, causing the dollar to rise or appreciate.
   b. investors switch from foreign to U.S. assets, causing the dollar to fall or depreciate.
   c. investors switch from U.S. to foreign assets, causing the dollar to rise or appreciate.
   d. investors switch from U.S. to foreign assets, causing the dollar to fall or depreciate.

10. If a country saves more than it invests, its net exports will be
    a. negative and it will have a trade deficit.
    b. negative and it will have a trade surplus.
    c. positive and it will have a trade deficit.
    d. positive and it will have a trade surplus.

11. Exchange market intervention
    a. has a lasting effect on exchange rates in the world currency market.
    b. occurs when governments buy and sell currencies to make changes in the exchange rate.
    c. occurs when governments buy and sell currencies to prevent changes in the exchange rate.
    d. accompanied by changes in interest rates has only small effects.

12. The gold standard
    a. *unlike* the Bretton Woods system, is an example of a fixed exchange rate system.
    b. was the exchange rate system for the 40 years prior to World War I.
    c. was the exchange rate system in which only one country, the United States, bought and sold gold at a fixed price.
    d. was the exchange rate system between the end of World War II and 1971.

13. The Bretton Woods system
    a. was a flexible exchange rate system.
    b. was the exchange rate system between the end of World War II and 1971.
    c. *unlike* the gold standard system is an example of a fixed exchange rate system.
    d. was the exchange rate system for the 40 years prior to World War I.

14. The projected single currency for the European Monetary System is called the
    a. Euro
    b. Bretton
    c. EMS
    d. Deutschmark

15. The development of futures markets in currencies allows firms to
    a. increase exchange rate risk in a flexible exchange rate system.
    b. reduce exchange rate risk in a flexible exchange rate system.
    a. increase exchange rate risk in a fixed exchange rate system.
    b. reduce exchange rate risk in a fixed exchange rate system.

16. Suppose that a can of soda that sells for 50 cents in the United States sells for 15,000 Turkish liras in Turkey. Assuming purchasing power parity holds, what is the exchange rate?
    a. 15,000 Turkish liras per dollar
    b. 20,000 Turkish liras per dollar
    c. 25,000 Turkish liras per dollar
    d. 30,000 Turkish liras per dollar

Use the following table for question 17.

Country	Price Level
United States (domestic)	1 dollar
Turkey (foreign)	36,000 Turkish liras

17. Suppose the U.S. price level doubles but the Turkish price level is unchanged. According to purchasing power parity, what is the new exchange rate?
    a. 9,000 Turkish liras per dollar
    b. 18,000 Turkish liras per dollar
    c. 36,000 Turkish liras per dollar
    d. 72,000 Turkish liras per dollar

Use the following table for questions 18 to 20. Consider the following trade patterns for a hypothetical country, with values in billions of dollars.

	2000
Merchandise trade balance	-30
Services trade balance	10
Net factor income from abroad	5
Net transfers from abroad	-15

18. What is the value of the trade balance in the year 2000?
    a. -10
    b. -20
    c. -30
    d. -40

19. What is the value of the current account in the year 2000?
    a. -10
    b. -20
    c. -30
    d. -40

20. Suppose that in the year 2000, $5 billion more in computers is sold by this hypothetical country to foreigners. What is the new value of the trade balance?
    a. -5
    b. -10
    c. -15
    d. -20

ANSWERS TO THE REVIEW QUESTIONS

Fill-in Questions

1. trade balance, net exports
2. deficit
3. merchandise, services
4. factor income
5. Transfer payments
6. current account
7. net foreign assets
8. capital account
9. Bilateral
10. exchange rate
11. real exchange rate
12. Purchasing power parity
13. intervention
14. fixed
15. flexible

True-False Questions

1. **True**. The world as a whole cannot have either a trade surplus or a trade deficit.
2. **False**. Net exports equal exports minus imports.
3. **False**. The United States has run a merchandise trade deficit and a services trade surplus in recent years.
4. **True**. The United States normally gives more aid than it receives.
5. **True**. The United States shifted from a net creditor to a net debtor country.
6. **False**. It is an example of a bilateral trade deficit.
7. **True**. PPP works very badly in the short run.
8. **True**. Higher U.S. interest rates cause investors to switch from foreign to U.S. assets, causing the dollar to rise or appreciate.
9. **False**. Unless it is accompanied by changes in interest rates, exchange market intervention has only small effects.
10. **False**. The United States runs a trade deficit because investment exceeds national saving, not because of trade barriers.
11. **False**. If the investment-saving gap is positive, there is a trade deficit.

12. **True**. Central banks must adjust interest rates to set the exchange rate in a fixed exchange rate system.
13. **True**. If the Bank of Canada did not act, the Canadian dollar would fall or depreciate against the U.S. dollar.
14. **False**. Loss of international monetary independence characteristics fixed exchange rate systems.
15. **False**. The development of futures markets in currencies allows firms to protect against exchange rate risk in a flexible exchange rate system.

Short-Answer Questions

1. The United States has run a large trade deficit in recent years; it decreased in the late 1980s, but rose in the 1990's.
2. Exports and imports are made up of merchandise and services.
3. Transfer payments consist of humanitarian and military aid between countries.
4. The two parts of the balance of payments accounts are the current account and the capital account.
5. The current account is the sum of the merchandise trade balance, the services trade balance, net factor income from abroad, and net transfer payments from abroad.
6. In recent years, the United States has run a current account deficit.
7. The real exchange rate is the exchange rate adjusted for inflation.
8. PPP works better for tradable goods, with relatively low transport costs, than for nontradable goods, where transport costs are prohibitive.
9. In the short run, interest rate differentials are much more important than purchasing power parity in determining the exchange rate.
10. Countries are faced with a choice between a fixed and a flexible exchange rate system.
11. The major exchange rate systems are the gold standard before 1914, the Bretton Woods system from 1945 to 1971, and the current flexible exchange rate system since 1973.
12. The European monetary system, in which countries fix exchange rates among themselves while floating jointly against other currencies, is the current exchange rate system in Europe.
13. In a fixed exchange rate system, central banks cannot adjust interest rates to achieve domestic economic objectives, but only to set the exchange rate.
14. Both crises were caused by the Bundesbank raising interest rates. France and the United Kingdom were faced with a choice between raising their interest rates, which they did not want to do, or letting their currencies depreciate against the mark.
15. The EMS is evolving toward a system with a single currency, called the Euro.

SOLUTIONS TO THE PRACTICE PROBLEMS

1. a. The PPP exchange rate equals 100 yen per dollar.

   b. The new PPP exchange rate is 120 yen per dollar.

2. a. The PPP exchange rate equals 4 francs per dollar.

   b. With equal inflation in both countries, the new PPP exchange rate is unchanged at 4 francs per dollar.

3. a. The trade balance equals 50 in the year 2000 and 85 in 2005. The current account is 20 in 2000 and 55 in 2005. There are both a trade and a current account surplus in both years.

    b. The increase in military assistance makes net transfers from abroad more negative (-55). This does not affect the trade deficit, but it decreases the current account surplus to 10.

4. a. The trade balance equals 10 in the year 2000 and 15 in 2005. The current account is -20 in 2000 and -5 in 2005. There are a trade surplus and a current account deficit in both years.

    b. The increase in profits makes net factor income from abroad more positive (10). This does not affect the trade balance, but it lowers the current account deficit to -15.

ANSWERS TO THE CHAPTER TEST

1. b	6. b	11. c	16. d
2. a	7. d	12. b	17. b
3. d	8. b	13. b	18. b
4. b	9. d	14. a	19. c
5. c	10. d	15. b	20. c

CHAPTER 18

Macroeconomic
Debates

CHAPTER OVERVIEW

As we have seen in the last three chapters, macroeconomics is often characterized as a battle between competing schools of thought. Policymakers in government and business draw on current theories to make their decisions. In the first part of this chapter, we look more deeply into the different schools of thought. Although the Keynesian, monetarist, and neoclassical growth schools dominated the debate from the 1930s through the 1960s, most of the issues that divided these schools have been resolved. Starting in the 1970s, the emergence of the new classical, new Keynesian, real business cycle, and supply side schools has raised new issues. The resolution of some of these issues is reflected in the theories of economic growth and economic fluctuations, whereas the jury is still out on others. In order to understand macroeconomic policy, you need to learn about macroeconomic practice as well as macroeconomic theories. In the second part of the chapter, you will study two recent fiscal policy proposals, one each by Presidents Bush and Clinton.

CHAPTER REVIEW

1. The **Keynesian school** dominated macroeconomics from the 1930s through the 1960s to such an extent that the changes in macroeconomic thought following the Great Depression are called the **Keynesian revolution**. Starting with the 1936 publication of John Maynard Keynes's book, *The General Theory of Employment Interest and Money*, Keynesian ideas were incorporated into textbooks, macroeconomic forecasting models, and national policymaking. The early 1960s, when Keynesian ideas greatly influenced the work of President Kennedy's Council of Economic Advisers, were the high point of the Keynesian school. The centerpiece of Keynesian economics is the concept that the total level of output or production in the economy is determined by aggregate demand. Declines in real GDP during recessions are therefore due to changes in aggregate demand. This provides a rationale for countercyclical fiscal policy, increases in government spending to reduce unemployment. The idea of the government spending multiplier, which shows the size of the impact on real GDP of a change in government purchases, is also attributable to Keynes. Paul Samuelson and James Tobin are two prominent current Keynesian economists.

2. The **monetarist school**, founded by Milton Friedman, mounted the earliest attacks on Keynesian economics. The key argument of monetarism is that monetary policy is a more powerful force than fiscal policy. During the 1960s, extensive debates centered on the question of whether changes in the money supply or changes in government spending mattered more for changes in real GDP. From the perspective of the 1990s, where it is clear that aggregate demand can change because of both monetary and fiscal policy, these debates seem rather pointless. Nevertheless, the monetarist criticism increased economists' understanding of the role played by monetary policy in economic fluctuations. A second aspect of monetarism, its criticism of the idea of a long-run tradeoff between inflation and unemployment in some Keynesian models, was also made by nonmonetarist economists and has become an accepted assumption of most macroeconomists.

3. The **neoclassical growth school** focuses on long-run growth rather than short-run fluctuations. Pioneered by Robert Solow, the neoclassical growth school emphasizes the production function to determine potential GDP and the growth accounting formula to explain the growth of potential GDP. Recently, the importance of technology for economic growth has been emphasized by growth economists such as Paul Romer.

4. Rational expectations, the concept that people look ahead to the future using all available information, has had such a profound impact on recent macroeconomic theories that the changes in macroeconomic thinking since the 1970s are called the **rational expectations revolution**. The ideas of credibility and time inconsistency, which you have applied in analyzing fiscal, monetary, and exchange rate policy, developed as a result of the use of rational expectations.

5. The **new classical school**, most closely associated with Robert Lucas, Thomas Sargent, and Robert Barro, combines rational expectations with the assumption that prices are perfectly flexible. The best-known result of the new classical school is the **policy ineffectiveness proposition**, that changes in monetary policy, if anticipated in advance, have no short-run effect on real GDP.

6. The **new Keynesian school** combines rational expectations with sticky, or slowly adjusting, prices. The main contribution of the new Keynesian school has been to combine rational expectations with a macroeconomic framework that includes the effects of aggregate demand, inflation, monetary policy, and potential GDP growth. One major focus of new Keynesian research, as in the work of Stanley Fischer, is to explain how anticipated monetary policy can affect real GDP in the short run. Another is to understand why prices are sticky. A third strand of new Keynesian research is the idea that fluctuations in the economy are due to **coordination failure**, which arises when people's actions depend on what they expect other people will do.

7. The **real business cycle school**, originated by Finn Kydland and Edward Prescott, views fluctuations in real GDP as due to fluctuations *in* potential GDP, rather than to movements in real GDP *around* potential GDP. Changes in potential GDP are usually assumed to be due to technological change in the production function. An important contribution of the real business cycle school has been to focus the attention of macroeconomists on changes in the production function and fluctuations of potential GDP.

8. **Supply side economics** is the idea that the growth rate of aggregate supply, or potential GDP, can be increased by cutting taxes or reforming the tax system. Supply side economics became widely publicized in the early 1980s by its association with the Reagan administration tax cuts. Although taxes clearly affect incentives, there is much disagreement over the size of the effects of tax cuts on potential GDP.

9. The schools of thought most relevant to the 1990s can be divided into two categories. The *freshwater* camp includes economists of the real business cycle and the new classical schools, many of whom teach in the central (Great Lakes and Mississippi River) region of the United States. The *saltwater* camp includes economists of the New Keynesian school, many of whom teach on either the East Coast or the West Coast.

10. By the late 1990s, a consensus of the two camps, which combines the sticky prices and implicit contracts of the saltwater camp with the careful treatment of information, policy rules, and equilibrium of the freshwater camp, seems to be developing. This consensus is reflected both in the academic work of many active researchers and in the models used at the Federal Reserve Board and the International Monetary Fund.

ZEROING IN

1. Two major examples of discretionary fiscal policy in the 1990s are the proposals made by President Bush in 1992 and President Clinton in 1993. There are many similarities between the two proposals, not the least of which is that neither was passed by Congress.

   a. The major aspects of President Bush's proposal were to enact an **investment tax credit** to encourage investment in 1992 and 1993 and to reduce the **capital gains tax**. Congress passed an alternative program that included a tax increase, which Bush vetoed. The veto was sustained, and so there was no stimulus program. Two parts of the Bush proposal did not require legislative approval: to shift $10 billion in government purchases from the future to the present and to temporarily decrease the amount of income taxes withheld by the government. These are both examples of temporary changes in fiscal policy, and their effects were small.

   b. The major parts of President Clinton's proposal were to increase government spending by $16 billion, to enact a temporary investment tax credit, and to reduce the capital gains tax for investments in certain small companies held for five years or more. Note that the investment tax credit and the reduction in the capital gains tax were also part of Bush's proposal. The Clinton program was also not enacted by Congress, but for a different reason. The proposal would have increased the budget deficit and reducing the deficit proved to be more important to Congress than stimulating the economy.

   c. When we discussed fiscal policy in Chapter 15, we argued that automatic stabilizers were more important than discretionary policy. This example seems to be in accord with that view. The budget deficit increased along with the unemployment rate in 1990 and 1991, and automatic stabilizers provided a much larger degree of fiscal stimulus than either of the proposed discretionary programs. The economy recovered from the 1990–1991 recession without discretionary fiscal stimulus. By 1994, the economy was close to full employment.

2. Which school of macroeconomics is taught in the text (and study guide)? There is not a simple answer to this question. The text presents a theory of economic growth and economic fluctuations. The theory of economic growth, based on the production function and the growth accounting formula, is obviously rooted in the neoclassical growth school. The theory of economic fluctuations is less obvious. The importance of aggregate demand and the use of the government spending multiplier are Keynesian, whereas the focus on monetary policy and the lack of a long-run tradeoff between inflation and unemployment are (at least partly) monetarist. Although the importance of rational expectations, credibility, and time inconsistency is part of both the new classical and new Keynesian schools, the assumption of sticky prices, the foundation of the price adjustment (*PA*) line, is clearly new Keynesian. Although the

contribution of the real business cycle school in focusing attention on shocks to potential GDP is acknowledged, these shocks are not emphasized as much as shocks to real GDP around potential GDP.

ACTIVE REVIEW

Fill-in Questions

1. The _____ revolution in macroeconomics followed the Great Depression of the 1930s.

2. According to the Keynesian school of macroeconomics, declines of real GDP during recessions are due to changes in _____.

3. The _____ school argued that monetary policy was more powerful than fiscal policy.

4. The production function and the growth accounting formula are important components of the _____ growth model.

5. The idea of rational expectations is that people look ahead to the future using _____.

6. The _____ revolution in macroeconomics began in the 1970s.

7. The _____ school combines rational expectations with flexible prices.

8. The _____ school combines rational expectations with sticky prices.

9. The _____ states that anticipated changes in monetary policy have no short-run effect on real GDP.

10. According to the _____ school, fluctuations in real GDP are due to fluctuations in potential GDP.

11. _____ refers to the concept that the growth rate of potential GDP can be increased by cutting taxes.

12. The schools of thought most relevant to the 1990s can be divided into the _____ and _____ camps.

13. The _____ is a tax break for firms that purchase new investment goods.

14. The _____ is a tax on the appreciation of assets.

15. The two most important discretionary fiscal policy proposals of the 1990s were those by President _____ in 1992 and President _____ in 1993.

True-False Questions

T   F   1. The Keynesian school of macroeconomics was most influential in the late 1970s.

T   F   2. According to the Keynesian school, declines in real GDP during recessions are caused by changes in potential GDP.

T   F   3. According to the monetarist school, monetary policy is a more powerful force than fiscal policy.

T   F   4. The existence of a long-run tradeoff between inflation and unemployment is a central concept of the monetarist school.

T   F   5. The neoclassical growth school focuses on short-run fluctuations.

T   F   6. According to rational expectations, forecasts of the future are always correct.

T   F   7. According to the new classical school, anticipated changes in monetary policy have no short-run effect on real GDP.

T   F   8. The new classical school combines rational expectations with flexible prices.

T   F   9. The idea that fluctuations in the economy are due to coordination failure is associated with the new classical school.

T   F   10. The new Keynesian school combines rational expectations with sticky prices.

T   F   11. According to the real business cycle school, fluctuations in real GDP are caused by changes in potential GDP.

T   F   12. According to the real business cycle school, changes in potential GDP are caused by monetary policy.

T   F   13. The schools of thought most relevant to the 1990s can be divided into the Keynesian and the monetarist camps.

T   F   14. There is no common ground between the freshwater and saltwater camps.

T   F   15. The fiscal stimulus programs proposed by Presidents Bush and Clinton helped end the 1990–1991 recession.

Short-Answer Questions

1. What is the central idea of Keynesian economics?

2. Name two prominent current Keynesian economists.

3. Is the question of whether monetary or fiscal policy is more important of great concern to macroeconomists today?

4. Who is the founder of the monetarist school of macroeconomics?

5. Who pioneered the neoclassical growth school?

6. Name two important concepts that developed as a result of the use of rational expectations in macroeconomics.

7. What is the policy ineffectiveness proposition?

8. Name three economists closely associated with the new classical school.

9. What is the main contribution of the new Keynesian school?

10. Name a prominent economist associated with the new Keynesian school.

11. Who are two of the originators of the real business cycle school?

12. What is the central idea of supply side economics?

13. What is the consensus of the freshwater and saltwater camps that appears to be developing in the late 1990s?

14. What programs were part of both the Bush and Clinton fiscal policy proposals?

15. What was the major difference between the two proposals?

WORKING IT OUT

1. The most important result of the new classical school is the policy ineffectiveness proposition, which is illustrated in Figure 18.1. The figure depicts the supply curve of an individual firm, with the perceived relative price of the good that the firm sells on the vertical axis and the quantity of the good on the horizontal axis.

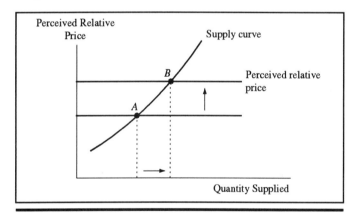

Figure 18.1

a. The supply curve is upward-sloping because if the firm receives a higher relative price for its good—a higher price relative to the prices of all other goods and services in the economy—it will want to supply more of the good. The perceived, rather than the actual, relative price matters because the firm may not know the actual relative price.

b. What happens if the price of the good produced by the firm increases? If the firm believes that other prices in the economy are not changing, it will think that the relative price of its good has increased and will produce more. However, if the firm believes that other prices are rising by the same amount, it will think that the relative price of its good is constant and will not change its production. The important point to understand is that the relative price perceived by firms is what matters for the production decision, not the actual (which may be unknown) relative price.

c. Suppose the Fed increases the money supply, and this increase is neither announced by the Fed nor expected by firms. In the new classical model, prices are perfectly flexible, and so the increase in the money supply will immediately raise all prices in the economy. The firm, operating with imperfect information, sees that the price of its good has risen but is not immediately aware that other prices have also risen. It (incorrectly) perceives that the relative price of its good has increased, and so increases the quantity supplied. This is shown as a movement from point A to point B in Figure 18.1. Because other firms in the economy make the same decision, real GDP rises.

d. Now suppose the Fed announces that it will increase the money supply. When firms see the price of their goods rising, they will know that other prices in the economy are also rising. Because there is no change in perceived (or actual) relative prices, firms will not change the quantity supplied, and so real GDP does not rise. This is the policy ineffectiveness proposition: An anticipated change in the money supply has no effect on real GDP.

The policy ineffectiveness proposition can also be illustrated by using an equation for the supply curve of an individual firm. The quantity supplied by the firm is determined by the difference between the price of the firm's good and the general price level perceived by the firm:

Quantity supplied = C + K(firm's price - perceived general price)

where C and K are positive numbers. If the firm's price equals the perceived general price, the firm produces the amount C. If the firm's price is above the perceived general price, it produces more than C.

Worked Problems

1. Suppose there is an unanticipated decrease in the money supply. According to the new classical school, what happens to real GDP? Use a diagram to illustrate your answer.

Answer

An unanticipated decrease in the money supply can be analyzed in the same way as an unanticipated increase in the money supply. When the Fed decreases the money supply, prices immediately fall, according to the new classical model. Firms see that their own prices have fallen, but they don't know the general price level, and so they think that their relative prices have decreased. The decrease in perceived relative prices lowers the quantity supplied and reduces real GDP. This is illustrated in Figure 18.2.

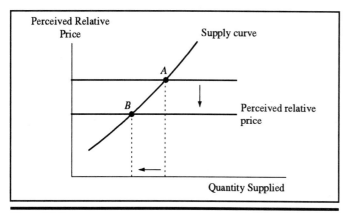

Figure 18.2

2. Let the supply curve for an individual firm be given by:

   Quantity supplied = 1,000 + 100(firm's price - perceived general price)

   with both the firm's price and the general price level initially equal to 1.00.

   a. Suppose there is an unanticipated increase in the money supply, so that all prices increase by 10 percent. What happens to the quantity supplied by the firm?

   b. Now suppose that the increase in the money supply that causes prices to increase by 10 percent was announced by the Fed and therefore anticipated. What now happens to the quantity supplied by the firm?

Answers

   a. *The firm's price increases to 1.1, but the perceived general price level does not change. The quantity supplied = 1,000 + 100(1.1 - 1.0) = 1,000 + 100(.1) = 1,000 + 10 = 1,010.*

   b. *In this case, both the firm's price and the perceived general price increase by 10 percent. The quantity supplied = 1,000 + 100 (1.1 - 1.1) = 1,000, and so is unchanged.*

Practice Problems

1. Suppose there is an anticipated decrease in the money supply. According to the new classical school, what happens to real GDP?

2. Let the supply curve for an individual firm be given by:

   Quantity supplied = 1,000 + 100(firm's price - perceived general price)

   with both the firm's price and the general price level initially equal to 1.00.

   a. Suppose there is an unanticipated decrease in the money supply, so that all prices decrease by 10 percent. What happens to the quantity supplied by the firm?

   b. Now suppose that the decrease in the money supply that causes prices to decrease by 10 percent was announced by the Fed and therefore anticipated. What now happens to the quantity supplied by the firm?

3. Let the supply curve for an individual firm be given by:

   Quantity supplied = 2,000 + 400(firm's price - perceived general price)

   with both the firm's price and the general price level initially equal to 1.00.

   a. Suppose there is an unanticipated increase in the money supply, so that all prices increase by 20 percent. What happens to the quantity supplied by the firm?

   b. Now suppose that the increase in the money supply that causes prices to increase by 20 percent was announced by the Fed and therefore anticipated. What now happens to the quantity supplied by the firm?

4. Let the supply curve for an individual firm be given by:

   Quantity supplied = 4,000 + 500(firm's price - perceived general price)

   with both the firm's price and the general price level initially equal to 1.00.

   a. Suppose there is an unanticipated decrease in the money supply, so that all prices decrease by 20 percent. What happens to the quantity supplied by the firm?

   b. Now suppose that the decrease in the money supply that causes prices to decrease by 20 percent was announced by the Fed and therefore anticipated. What now happens to the quantity supplied by the firm?

CHAPTER TEST

1. Which of the following schools of thought dominated macroeconomics from the 1930s to the 1960s?
   a. Keynesian school
   b. Monetarist school
   c. Neoclassical growth school
   d. New classical school

2. The monetarist school was founded by
   a. John Maynard Keynes.
   b. Paul Samuelson.
   c. Robert Solow.
   d. Milton Friedman.

3. Which of the following is a prominent current Keynesian economist?
   a. Robert Lucas
   b. Paul Samuelson
   c. Edward Prescott
   d. Milton Friedman

4. That monetary policy is a more powerful force than fiscal policy is the key argument of the
   a. Keynesian school.
   b. monetarist school.
   c. neoclassical growth school.
   d. real business cycle school.

5. That the total level of output or production in the economy is determined by aggregate demand is the centerpiece of the
   a. monetarist school.
   b. Keynesian school.
   c. neoclassical growth school.
   d. new classical school.

6. Which of the following schools of thought focuses on long-run growth rather than short-run fluctuations?
   a. Keynesian school
   b. Monetarist school
   c. Neoclassical growth school
   d. New classical school

7. Which of the following schools of thought was pioneered by Robert Solow?
   a. Monetarist school
   b. Neoclassical growth school
   c. New classical school
   d. New Keynesian school

8. The policy ineffectiveness proposition is the best-known result of the
   a. neoclassical growth school.
   b. monetarist school.
   c. new classical school.
   d. real business cycle school.

9. Which of the following schools of thought emphasizes the production function to determine potential GDP and the growth accounting formula to explain the growth of potential GDP?
   a. Neoclassical growth school
   b. New classical school
   c. Real business cycle school
   d. New Keynesian school

10. Combining rational expectations with a macroeconomic framework that includes the effects of aggregate demand, inflation, monetary policy, and potential GDP growth is the main contribution of the
    a. new classical school.
    b. neoclassical school.
    c. monetarist school.
    d. new Keynesian school.

11. Which of the following schools of thought is most closely associated with Robert Lucas, Thomas Sargent, and Robert Barro?
    a. Neoclassical growth school
    b. Monetarist school
    c. New classical school
    d. New Keynesian school

12. Focusing the attention of macroeconomists on changes in the production function and fluctuations in potential GDP has been an important contribution of the
    a. monetarist school.
    b. new classical school.
    c. new Keynesian school.
    d. real business cycle school.

13. Which of the following schools of thought is associated with Finn Kydland and Edward Prescott?
    a. Neoclassical growth school
    b. New classical school
    c. Real business cycle school
    d. New Keynesian school

14. Which of the following schools of thought combines rational expectations with the assumption that prices are perfectly flexible?
    a. Neoclassical growth school
    b. New classical school
    c. Real business cycle school
    d. New Keynesian school

15. Which of the following schools of thought explains fluctuations in real GDP by fluctuations in potential GDP?
    a. Neoclassical growth school
    b. Monetarist school
    c. New Keynesian school
    d. Real business cycle school

16. During the 1970s, explaining how anticipated monetary policy can affect real GDP in the short run was the major focus of the
    a. monetarist school.
    b. new Keynesian school.
    c. real business cycle school.
    d. new classical school.

17. Which of the following was *not* one of the parts of President Bush's fiscal policy proposal in 1992?
    a. To enact an investment tax credit to encourage investment
    b. To shift $10 billion in government purchases from the future to the present
    c. To temporarily decrease the amount of income taxes withheld by the government
    d. To raise the capital gains tax

18. Which of the following was *not* one of the parts of President Clinton's fiscal policy proposal in 1993?
    a. To increase government spending by $16 billion
    b. To enact a temporary investment tax credit
    c. To shift $10 billion in government purchases from the future to the present
    d. To reduce the capital gains tax

Use Figure 18.3 for questions 19 and 20.

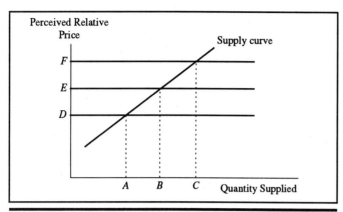

Figure 18.3

19. Suppose there is an unanticipated *increase* in the money supply that raises the perceived relative price from D to F. According to the new classical school, what would be the firm's output level?
   a. A
   b. B
   c. C
   d. E

20. Suppose there is an unanticipated *decrease* in the money supply which lowers the perceived relative price from F to E. According to the new classical school, what would be the firm's output level?
   a. A
   b. B
   c. C
   d. F

ANSWERS TO THE REVIEW QUESTIONS

Fill-in Questions

1. Keynesian
2. aggregate demand
3. monetarist
4. neoclassical
5. all available information
6. rational expectations
7. new classical
8. new Keynesian
9. policy ineffectiveness proposition
10. real business cycle
11. Supply side economics
12. freshwater, saltwater
13. investment tax credit
14. capital gains tax
15. Bush; Clinton

True-False Questions

1. **False**. The Keynesian school was most influential in the early 1960s.
2. **False**. According to the Keynesian school, changes in aggregate demand cause declines in real GDP during recessions.
3. **True**. This is the key argument of monetarism.
4. **False**. According to the monetarist school, there is no long-run tradeoff between inflation and unemployment.
5. **False**. The neoclassical growth school focuses on long-run growth.
6. **False**. Rational expectations is the concept that people look ahead to the future using all available information, not that their forecasts are always correct.
7. **True**. This is the policy ineffectiveness proposition.
8. **True**. These are the two central assumptions of the new classical school.
9. **False**. The idea that fluctuations are due to coordination failure is associated with the new Keynesian school.
10. **True**. These are the two key assumptions of the new Keynesian school.
11. **True**. This is the central idea of the real business cycle school.
12. **False**. Changes in potential GDP are assumed to be due to technological change in the production function.
13. **False.** They can be divided into the freshwater and the saltwater camps.
14. **False.** A consensus of the two camps seems to be developing.
15. **False.** Neither of the programs was passed by Congress.

Short-Answer Questions

1. The central idea of Keynesian economics is the concept that the total level of output or production in the economy is determined by aggregate demand.
2. Paul Samuelson and James Tobin are two prominent current Keynesian economists.
3. No. Since aggregate demand can change as a result of changes in both fiscal and monetary policy, the question of which is more powerful is of secondary importance.
4. Milton Friedman is the founder of the monetarist school.
5. Robert Solow pioneered the neoclassical growth school.
6. Credibility and time inconsistency developed as a result of the use of rational expectations.
7. The policy ineffectiveness proposition is that changes in monetary policy, if anticipated in advance, have no short-run effect on real GDP.
8. Robert Lucas, Thomas Sargent, and Robert Barro are three economists closely associated with the new classical school.
9. The main contribution of the new Keynesian school has been to combine rational expectations with a macroeconomic framework that includes the effects of aggregate demand, inflation, monetary policy, and potential GDP growth.
10. Stanley Fischer is a prominent economist associated with the new Keynesian school.
11. Finn Kydland and Edward Prescott are two of the originators of the real business cycle school.
12. The central idea of supply side economics is that the growth rate of potential GDP can be increased by cutting taxes or reforming the tax system.
13. The consensus combines the sticky prices and implicit contracts of the saltwater camp with the careful treatment of information, policy rules, and equilibrium of the freshwater camp.
14. An investment tax credit and reduction of the capital gains tax were included in both proposals.
15. Clinton's proposal included an increase in government spending, whereas Bush's did not.

SOLUTIONS TO THE PRACTICE PROBLEMS

1. According to the policy ineffectiveness proposition, an anticipated decrease in the money supply will not affect real GDP.

2. a. Quantity supplied = 1,000 + 100(.9 - 1.0) = 1,000 - 10 = 990.

   b. Quantity supplied is unchanged.

3. a. Quantity supplied = 2,000 + 400(1.2 - 1.0) = 2,000 + 80 = 2,080.

   b. Quantity supplied is unchanged.

4. a. Quantity supplied = 4,000 + 500(.8 - 1.0) = 4,000 - 100 = 3,900.

   b. Quantity supplied is unchanged.

ANSWERS TO THE CHAPTER TEST

1. a	6. c	11. c	16. b
2. d	7. b	12. d	17. d
3. b	8. c	13. c	18. c
4. b	9. a	14. b	19. c
5. b	10. d	15. d	20. b

CHAPTER 19

Economic Growth
Around the World

CHAPTER OVERVIEW

In Part 3, we studied how labor, capital, and technology combine to produce economic growth. Now we turn our attention to economic growth around the world, and see why some countries become rich while others remain poor. We start by looking at the predictions of growth theory, and see that, while they hold for states of the United States and for industrialized countries, they do not work well for developing countries. We then consider developing countries in more detail, and see how obstacles to the spread and adoption of new technology and obstacles to increases in capital per worker have hindered their growth. In this context, we look at issues ranging from restrictions on private enterprise and the importance of education to the role of international financial institutions. Finally, we study inward-looking versus outward-looking economic policies, and see that countries that have adopted outward-looking policies have experienced higher growth rates.

CHAPTER REVIEW

1. The *catch-up phenomenon* is that countries with low income (GDP) per capita will grow faster than, and therefore catch up to, countries with high income per capita. If technological advances can spread easily and if capital and labor have diminishing returns, then economic growth theory predicts catch-up.

2. **Economic development** attempts to explain why poor countries do not develop faster and to find policies to help them develop faster. There are large income disparities between relatively well-off countries, or **industrialized countries**, and the relatively poor countries, or **developing countries**. Developing countries are also called *less-developed countries*, or LDCs. **Newly industrialized countries**, such as Korea, are relatively poor countries that are growing rapidly whereas **countries in transition**, such as Poland, are relatively poor countries that are moving from central planning to market economies.

3. There are geographical patterns to economic development. The **North-South problem** describes the pattern that countries in the North are relatively rich and those in the South, with the exception of Australia and New Zealand, are relatively poor.

4. We learned in Chapter 17 that technological progress is necessary for sustained economic growth. In order to understand why some countries grow faster than others, it is natural to focus on the spread of technology.

   a. Why did the "miracle" of economic growth begin in Europe in the 1700s? The removal of restrictions on private enterprise seems to be the key. For the first time, entrepreneurs had the freedom to start businesses, hire workers, and ship products to market without political or religious restrictions.

   b. Why do poor countries remain poor? The most important reason seems to be restrictions on private enterprise. There is a tremendous amount of regulation in most developing countries. This regulation makes it so costly to start business enterprises that a huge **informal economy**, consisting of illegal businesses, has emerged. The centrally planned economies of the former Soviet Union, central Europe, and China also placed pervasive restrictions on entrepreneurs, which helps to explain both their large informal economies and their slow growth.

   c. Development of human capital, better educated and more highly skilled workers, is another important facet of technology. The newly industrialized countries, the developing countries that have been catching up most rapidly, have strong educational systems.

5. Increasing the amount of capital per worker, as we also learned in Chapter 17, is the second way to promote economic growth. Obstacles to increasing capital per worker can prevent developing countries from catching up to industrialized countries.

   a. High population growth in many developing countries is an obstacle to increasing the amount of capital per worker. With high population growth rates, more investment is necessary to increase, or even to maintain, the level of capital per worker. Remember that investment equals national saving plus net exports. In most developing countries, national saving is low, and they must look to net exports for investment.

   b. Foreign investment consists of **foreign direct investment**, when a foreign firm invests in more than 10 percent of the ownership of a business in another country, **portfolio investment**, when the ownership is less than 10 percent, and loans from banks and governments.

   c. The **International Monetary Fund (IMF)** and the **World Bank** make loans to developing countries, and the IMF also makes loans to economies in transition. The IMF often tries to induce countries to make difficult economic reforms by making its loans dependent, or conditional, on the reforms; this is the idea of conditionality. Most of the loans made by the World Bank are for specific projects.

6. Developing countries have adopted a variety of growth policies. Under an **import substitution strategy**, an example of an inward-looking policy, developing countries try to replace products that are imported from industrialized countries with products produced at home. Under an **export-led strategy**, an example of an outward-looking policy, developing countries encourage international trade by expanding exports. As predicted by economic growth theory, the evidence shows that countries that follow the export-led strategy grow faster than countries that follow the import-substitution strategy.

ZEROING IN

1. Understanding the catch-up phenomenon is the key to understanding the material in this chapter. We illustrate the catch-up phenomenon in Figure 19.1, where the *level* of income per capita is on the horizontal axis and the *growth rate* of income per capita is on the vertical axis. The **catch-up line** is a downward-sloping line that depicts the relation between the level and the growth rate of income per capita. A country on the upper left-hand part of the catch-up line, such as point *A*, is poor but growing rapidly. Although it has a relatively low level of income per capita, it has a relatively high growth rate of income per capita. A country on the lower right-hand part of the catch-up line, such as point *B*, is rich but growing more slowly. Although it has a relatively high level of income per capita, it has a relatively low growth rate of income per capita. The line is called the catch-up line because relatively poor countries are growing faster than, or catching up to, relatively well-off countries.

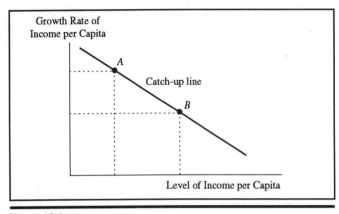

Figure 19.1

2. Why does economic growth theory predict catch-up, that poor countries will grow faster than rich countries? There are two parts to the answer: diffusion of technology and diminishing returns to labor and capital.

   a. A major difference between rich and poor countries is that rich countries, with high productivity, utilize advanced technology, whereas poor countries, with low productivity, use more basic technology. If the spread of technology is not difficult, countries with low productivity will adopt the more advanced technology, thereby raising their productivity. As we know from the growth accounting formula, increasing technology would raise the growth rates of the poor countries, narrowing the gap between rich and poor. In other words, poor countries would catch up to rich countries.

   b. Think about a poor country with a low level of capital per worker. While this country exhibits diminishing returns to labor, it has so little capital that diminishing returns to capital have not set in. In the absence of obstacles, investment would be very profitable, and capital per worker would grow rapidly. According to the growth accounting formula, this would raise output per worker. In contrast, think about a rich country with a high level of capital per worker that country exhibits diminishing returns to capital. This country would gain relatively little from investment that increases the amount of capital per worker. The flow of investment causes the poor country to grow faster than, or catch up to, the rich country.

   c. It is important to remember that growth theory does not predict catch-up under all circumstances. If there are obstacles to the spread of technology and/or obstacles to raising the level of capital per worker, the mechanism described above will not have the chance to operate and catch-up will not occur.

3. How does the catch-up prediction accord with the facts? We will look at three cases: states within the United States, industrialized countries, and the world as a whole.

   a. Suppose you think of the states within the United States as 50 different countries with a common language, a single currency, and free movement of capital and technology. Under these conditions, growth theory predicts catch-up, and that is exactly what has happened. Income per capita in states such as Florida and Texas, which were relatively poor in 1880, has grown quickly relative to income per capita in states such as California and Nevada, which were relatively well off in 1880.

   b. A similar picture emerges when we look at industrialized countries since 1960. Although capital and technology are not as mobile between industrialized countries as between states within the United States, there are relatively few obstacles to their diffusion. In accord with growth theory, catch-up has occurred. Countries such as Greece and Portugal, which were relatively poor in 1960, have grown faster than countries such as Canada and the United States, which were relatively well off in 1960.

   c. What about the world as a whole? When we consider developing countries, obstacles to the spread of technology and to raising the level of capital per worker become much more important. Under these conditions, economic growth theory no longer predicts catch up, and, in fact, it has not occurred. Some countries with low levels of income per capita in 1960, such as Korea and Singapore, have had very high growth rates, whereas others with equally low per capita incomes in 1960, such as Sri Lanka and Bangladesh, have had very low growth rates. The gap between rich and poor countries has not closed.

ACTIVE REVIEW

Fill-in Questions

1. The _____ phenomenon is that countries with low income per capita will grow faster than countries with high income per capita.

2. _____ attempts to explain why poor countries do not develop faster.

3. _____ countries are relatively well off.

4. _____ countries are relatively poor.

5. Developing countries are also called _____.

6. _____ countries, such as Korea, are relatively poor countries that are growing rapidly.

7. _____ are relatively poor countries that are moving from central planning to market economies.

8. The _____ describes the pattern that most countries in the North are relatively rich and those in the South are relatively poor.

9. The illegal sector is called the _____ economy.

10. Foreign investment consists of _____, _____, and _____.

11. The _____ makes loans to developing countries and to economies in transition.

12. _____ is the idea that the International Monetary Fund often tries to induce countries to make difficult economic reforms by making its loans dependent on those reforms.

13. Most of the loans made by the _____ are for specific projects.

14. Under a(n) _____ strategy, developing countries try to replace products that are imported from industrialized countries with products produced at home.

15. Under a(n) _____ strategy, developing countries encourage international trade by expanding exports.

True-False Questions

T   F   1. The catch-up phenomenon is that countries with low income per capita will grow faster than countries with high income per capita.

T   F   2. The differences in income per capita between industrialized and developing countries are small.

T   F   3. Newly industrialized countries are countries that are moving from central planning to market economies.

T   F   4. All countries in the South are relatively poor.

T   F   5. Obstacles to the spread of technology help explain why some countries grow faster than others.

T   F   6. Centrally planned economies are characterized by large informal economies.

T   F   7. Education is an important part of economic growth for developing countries.

T   F   8. Obstacles to increasing capital per worker help explain why catch-up does not always occur.

T   F   9. Portfolio investment occurs when a foreign firm invests in more than 10 percent of the ownership of a business in another country.

T   F   10. Both the International Monetary Fund and the World Bank make loans to developing countries.

T   F   11. Countries that follow outward-looking policies grow faster than countries that follow inward-looking policies.

T   F   12. Along the catch-up line, relatively poor countries are growing at the same rate as relatively well-off countries.

T F   13. According to growth theory, catch-up will occur if there are no obstacles to the spread of technology.

T F   14. Catch-up has occurred for industrialized countries since 1960.

T F   15. Catch-up has occurred for the world as a whole since 1960.

Short-Answer Questions

1. When does economic growth theory predict catch-up?

2. What is the goal of economic development?

3. What is the North-South problem?

4. What appears to have been the key factor that caused economic growth to begin in Europe in the 1700s?

5. What growth-limiting characteristic is shared by most developing and all centrally planned economies?

6. Why does a large informal economy exist in most developing countries?

7. Why is development of human capital an important determinant of economic growth?

8. Why is high population growth an obstacle to increasing the amount of capital per worker?

9. Why do most developing countries need to look abroad for investment?

10. What is conditionality?

11. What is the difference between an import substitution strategy and an export-led strategy to promote growth?

12. What is the catch-up line?

13. Under what conditions does economic growth theory predict catch-up?

14. How are diminishing returns to capital related to the catch-up phenomenon?

15. Why does growth theory predict catch-up for states within the United States?

WORKING IT OUT

1. The phenomenon of catch-up, that relatively poor countries grow faster than relatively well-off countries, is the central prediction of growth theory. We can use some algebra to test the catch-up prediction.

    a. We learned the formula for compound growth in Chapter 20. It states that the rate of growth depends on the initial level of income and the level of income at the end of n years, as follows:

    Rate of growth = (level of income at end of n years/initial level of income)$^{1/n}$ - 1

    Remember that you need a calculator with an exponent key to use this formula.

b. Consider income (GDP) per capita for industrialized countries. The data begin in 1960 and end in 1990, so that $n = 30$. The level of income per capita in 1960 and the level of income per capita in 1990 for five countries are:

Country	Level of GDP per Capita (1985 U.S. dollars)	
	1960	1990
Canada	7,288	17,415
Greece	2,088	6,679
Portugal	1,869	6,525
Spain	3,196	9,663
United States	9,776	18,399

c. Using the compound growth formula, you can calculate the annual rate of growth of income per capita. (Look at the "Working It Out" section of Chapter 20 of the *Study Guide* if you don't remember how.)

Country	Rate of Growth (percent)
Canada	2.95
Greece	3.95
Portugal	4.26
Spain	3.76
United States	2.13

d. The industrialized countries accord with the catch-up prediction. Those countries, Greece and Portugal, that were relatively poor in 1960 grew faster than those countries, Canada and the United States, that were relatively well-off in 1960.

2. The catch-up line plots the relation between the level and growth rate of income per capita. Another way of testing whether the catch-up prediction holds is to see how close groups of countries are to being on the catch-up line.

a. We will again look at industrialized countries. Set up a diagram with the growth rate of GDP per capita on the vertical axis and the level of GDP per capita on the horizontal axis. Using the level of GDP per capita in 1960 and the growth rates calculated above, plot the points for the five countries and draw a line through the points.

b. This is the catch-up line; it is illustrated in Figure 19.2. The catch-up line is downward-sloping, indicating that those countries with relatively low incomes per capita in 1960 grew faster than those countries with relatively high incomes per capita in 1960. In other words, the catch-up prediction holds for the industrialized countries.

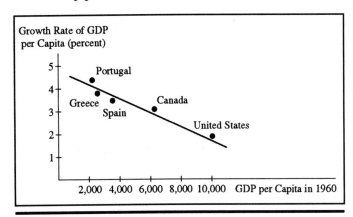

Figure 19.2

Worked Problems

1. Consider the following data on income (GDP) per capita for four developing countries. The data begin in 1960 and end in 1989, so that $n = 29$. The level of income per capita in 1960 and the level of income per capita in 1989 for the four countries are:

	Level of GDP per Capita (1985 U.S. dollars)	
Country	1960	1989
Hong Kong	2,210	14,035
Nigeria	560	742
Singapore	1,712	10,240
Sri Lanka	1,285	2,218

a. Using the compound growth formula, calculate the annual rate of growth of per capita income for each country.

b. Do these four countries accord with the catch-up prediction?

Answers

a. *Using the compound growth formula, the annual growth rates of income per capita are:*

Country	Rate of Growth (percent)
Hong Kong	6.58
Nigeria	0.98
Singapore	6.36
Sri Lanka	1.90

b. *These countries do not accord with the catch-up prediction. The countries with the highest incomes per capita in 1960, Hong Kong and Singapore, grew faster than those with the lowest incomes per capita in 1960, Nigeria and Sri Lanka.*

2. Consider the same four countries. Set up a diagram with the growth rate of GDP per capita on the vertical axis and the level of GDP per capita on the horizontal axis. Using the level of GDP per capita from 1960 and the growth rates calculated above, plot the points for the four countries and draw a line through the points. Does the catch-up prediction hold?

Answer

The answer is illustrated in Figure 19.3. There is no clear downward-sloping line through the four points, and so the catch-up prediction does not hold. This shows how the catch-up prediction does not hold for developing countries in general.

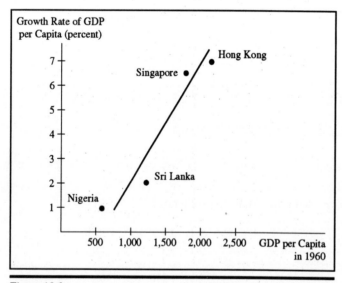

Figure 19.3

Practice Problems

1. Consider the following data on GDP per capita for five European countries. The data begin in 1960 and end in 1990, so that $n = 30$. The level of income per capita in 1960 and the level of income per capita in 1990 for the five countries are:

Country	Level of GDP per Capita (1985 U.S. dollars)	
	1960	1990
Denmark	6,751	13,801
Germany	6,637	14,498
Netherlands	6,122	12,868
Sweden	7,492	14,495
Switzerland	9,639	17,007

   a. Using the compound growth formula, calculate the annual rate of growth of income per capita for each country.

   b. Do these five countries accord with the catch-up prediction?

2. Consider the following data on GDP per capita for six South American countries. The data begin in 1960 and end in 1990, so that $n = 30$. The level of income per capita in 1960 and the level of income per capita in 1990 for the six countries are:

Country	Level of GDP per Capita (1985 U.S. dollars)	
	1960	1990
Argentina	3,293	3,513
Brazil	1,758	3,906
Chile	2,893	3,992
Colombia	1,652	3,186
Paraguay	1,215	2,258
Peru	1,917	2,041

a. Using the compound growth formula, calculate the annual rate of growth of income per capita for each country.

b. Do these six countries accord with the catch-up prediction?

3. Consider the five countries in Practice Problem 1. Draw the catch-up line. Does the catch-up prediction hold?

4. Consider the six countries in Practice Problem 2. Draw the catch-up line. Does the catch-up prediction hold?

CHAPTER TEST

1. The phenomenon that countries with low income per capita will grow faster than countries with high income per capita is called
   a. the catch-up phenomenon.
   b. the development phenomenon.
   c. the transition phenomenon.
   d. the industrialization phenomenon.

2. Which of the following countries is an example of a newly industrialized country?
   a. Germany
   b. Japan
   c. England
   d. Korea

3. The illegal sector is called
   a. the illegal economy.
   b. the informal economy.
   c. the unlawful economy.
   d. the unauthorized economy.

4. Which of the following are also called less-developed countries?
   a. Industrialized countries
   b. Newly industrialized countries
   c. Developing countries
   d. Countries in transition

5. Which of the following attempts to explain why poor countries do not develop faster?
   a. Economic development
   b. The catch-up phenomenon
   c. Import substitution strategy
   d. Export-led strategy

6. Which of the following is the key factor that caused economic growth to begin in Europe in the 1700s?
   a. Population growth
   b. Removal of restrictions on private enterprise
   c. Better industrial policies
   d. The French Revolution

7. Which of the following is *not* one of the main reasons for economic growth?
   a. Increasing the amount of capital per worker
   b. Development of human capital
   c. Deregulating industries
   d. High population growth

8. Investment by a foreign firm in more than 10 percent of the ownership of a business in another country is called
   a. portfolio investment.
   b. foreign indirect investment.
   c. foreign direct investment.
   d. capital investment.

9. Which of the following makes loans to countries in transition?
   a. International Monetary Fund
   b. World Bank
   c. Federal Reserve Bank
   d. Bank of America

10. Which of the following is *not* one of the reasons why economic growth theory predicts catch-up?
    a. Diffusion of technology
    b. Diminishing returns to capital
    c. Diminishing returns to labor
    d. Innovation

11. The catch-up line is
    a. upward-sloping.
    b. downward-sloping.
    c. horizontal.
    d. vertical.

12. The catch-up line depicts the relationship between the
    a. level of income and the growth rate of income.
    b. level of the money supply and the growth rate of the money supply.
    c. level of income per capita and the growth rate of income per capita.
    d. level of investment and the growth rate of investment.

13. Which of the following is *not* a true phenomenon for rich and poor countries?
    a. Rich countries utilize advanced technology, and poor countries use more basic techology.
    b. Rich countries have high productivity, and poor countries have low productivity.
    c. Rich countries have a high level of capital per worker, and poor countries have a low level of capital per worker.
    d. Rich countries do not exhibit diminishing returns, and poor countries exhibit diminishing returns.

14. The catch-up phenomenon will not occur if there are obstacles to
    a. the spread of technology.
    b. decreasing the level of capital per worker.
    c. increasing the money supply.
    d. raising the interest rate.

15. Which of the following countries has had very high growth rates since the 1960s?
    a. Sri Lanka
    b. Singapore
    c. Bangladesh
    d. Canada

Use the following table for questions 16 and 17.

Country	Level of GDP per Capita (1985 U.S. dollars)	
	1960	1990
Australia	7,879	14,300
Italy	4,638	12,557
Japan	3,032	14,839
United Kingdom	6,549	13,069

The data begin in 1960 and end in 1990, so that $n = 30$. Use the compound growth formula to answer question 16.

16. What is the annual rate of growth of GDP per capita for Australia, Italy, Japan, and the United Kingdom, respectively?
    a. 2.33, 5.44, 3.38, and 2.01 percent
    b. 2.33, 3.38, 5.44, and 2.01 percent
    c. 2.01, 5.44, 3.38, and 2.33 percent
    d. 2.01, 3.38, 5.44, and 2.33 percent

17. Do these four countries accord with the catch-up prediction?
    a. Yes, because the countries with the lowest incomes per capita in 1960, Italy and Japan, grew faster than those with the highest incomes per capita in 1960, Australia and the United Kingdom.
    b. Yes, because the countries with the lowest incomes per capita in 1960, Italy and Japan, grew slower than those with the highest incomes per capita in 1960, Australia and the United Kingdom.
    c. No, because the countries with the lowest incomes per capita in 1960, Italy and Japan, grew faster than those with the highest incomes per capita in 1960, Australia and the United Kingdom.
    d. No, because the countries with the lowest incomes per capita in 1960, Italy and Japan, grew slower than those with the highest incomes per capita in 1960, Australia and the United Kingdom.

Use Figure 19.4 for question 18.

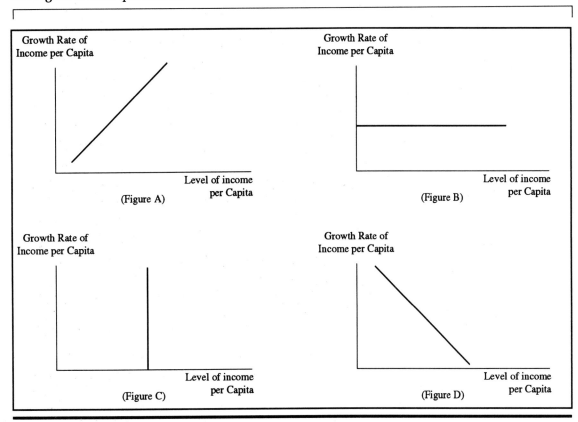

Figure 19.4

18. Which of the figures appropriately represents the catch-up line?
    a. Figure A
    b. Figure B
    c. Figure C
    d. Figure D

Use Figure 19.5 for questions 19 and 20.

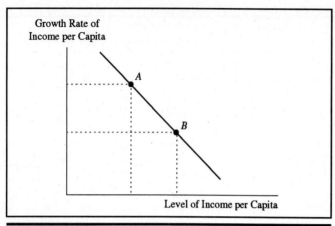

Figure 19.5

19. Country A, which is depicted by point *A*, is
    a. poor and growing rapidly.
    b. rich and growing rapidly.
    c. poor and growing more slowly.
    d. rich and growing more slowly.

20. Country B, which is depicted by point *B*, is
    a. poor and growing rapidly.
    b. rich and growing rapidly.
    c. poor and growing more slowly.
    d. rich and growing more slowly.

ANSWERS TO THE REVIEW QUESTIONS

Fill-in Questions

1. catch-up
2. Economic development
3. Industrialized
4. Developing
5. less-developed countries
6. Newly industrialized
7. Countries in transition
8. North-South problem
9. informal
10. foreign direct investment, portfolio investment; loans from banks and governments
11. International Monetary Fund
12. Conditionality
13. World Bank
14. import substitution
15. export-led

True-False Questions

1. **True.** The catch-up phenomenon is that countries with low income per capita will grow faster than, and therefore catch up to, countries with high income per capita.
2. **False.** There are large income disparities between industrialized and developing countries.
3. **False.** Newly industrialized countries are relatively poor countries that are growing rapidly. Countries in transition are moving from central planning to market economies.

4. **False.** Australia and New Zealand are relatively well-off countries in the South.
5. **True.** Technological progress is necessary for sustained economic growth.
6. **True.** Centrally planned economies place pervasive restrictions on entrepreneurs, which cause the development of large informal economies.
7. **True.** The newly industrialized countries, the developing countries that have been catching up most rapidly, have strong educational systems.
8. **True.** Obstacles to increasing capital per worker can prevent developing countries from catching up to industrialized countries.
9. **False.** When the ownership is more than 10 percent, it is foreign direct investment.
10. **True.** The International Monetary Fund also makes loans to countries in transition.
11. **True.** Countries that follow an export-led strategy grow faster than countries that follow an import substitution strategy.
12. **False.** Along the catch-up line, relatively poor countries are growing faster than, or catching up to, relatively well-off countries.
13. **True.** If the spread of technology is not difficult, countries with low productivity will adopt the more advanced technology, raising their growth rates and narrowing the gap between rich and poor.
14. **True.** Industrialized countries that were relatively poor in 1960 have grown faster than industrialized countries that were relatively well off in 1960.
15. **False.** Some countries with low levels of income per capita in 1960 have had very high growth rates, whereas others with equally low incomes per capita in 1960 have had very low growth rates.

Short-Answer Questions

1. Economic growth theory predicts catch-up if technological advances can spread easily and if capital and labor have diminishing returns.
2. Economic development attempts to explain why poor countries do not develop faster and to find policies to help them develop faster.
3. The North-South problem is that most countries in the North are relatively well off and most countries in the South are relatively poor.
4. The removal of restrictions on private enterprise seems to have been the most important factor.
5. Most developing and all centrally planned economies place stringent restrictions on private enterprise, which helps to explain their slow growth.
6. Regulation in most developing countries makes it costly to start legal business enterprises, causing a large informal economy to emerge.
7. Human capital is an important facet of technology, which is a vital element of growth.
8. With high population growth rates, more investment is necessary to increase, or even to maintain, the level of capital per worker.
9. Investment equals national saving plus net exports. In most developing countries, national saving is low, and so they must look abroad for investment.
10. Conditionality is the idea that the International Monetary Fund often tries to induce countries to make difficult economic reforms by making its loans dependent on those reforms.
11. Under an import substitution strategy, developing countries try to replace products that are imported from industrialized countries with products produced at home. Under an export-led strategy, developing countries encourage international trade by expanding exports.
12. The catch-up line is a downward-sloping line that depicts the relation between the level and the growth rate of income per capita.
13. Economic growth theory predicts catch-up if there are no obstacles to the spread of technology and no obstacles to raising the level of capital per worker.

14. Investment would be very profitable in a poor country that has so little capital that diminishing returns to capital have not set in. Capital per worker, and therefore output per worker, would grow rapidly.
15. States within the United States, with a common language, a single currency, and free movement of capital and technology, have no obstacles to catch-up.

SOLUTIONS TO THE PRACTICE PROBLEMS

1. a. The annual growth rates of GDP per capita are:

Country	Rate of Growth (percent)
Denmark	2.41
Germany	2.64
Netherlands	2.51
Sweden	2.22
Switzerland	1.91

   b. These countries accord with the catch-up prediction. The countries with the lowest incomes per capita in 1960, the Netherlands and Germany, grew faster than those with the highest incomes per capita in 1960, Sweden and Switzerland.

2. a. The annual growth rates of GDP per capita are:

Country	Rate of Growth (percent)
Argentina	0.22
Brazil	2.70
Chile	1.08
Colombia	2.21
Paraguay	2.09
Peru	0.21

   b. These countries accord in part with the catch-up prediction. The countries with the lowest incomes per capita in 1960, Colombia and Paraguay, grew faster than those with the highest incomes per capita in 1960, Argentina and Chile. The two countries in the middle in 1960, Brazil and Peru, exhibited the fastest and slowest growth, respectively.

3. The answer is illustrated in Figure 19.6. There is a downward-sloping line through the five points, and so the catch-up prediction holds.

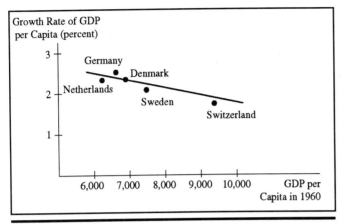

Figure 19.6

4. The answer is illustrated in Figure 19.7. There is a downward-sloping line through the six points, but the countries are not grouped as tightly as the industrialized countries. The catch-up prediction holds, but not as well as for the industrialized countries.

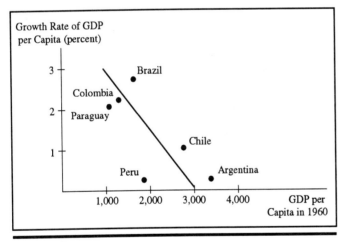

Figure 19.7

ANSWERS TO THE CHAPTER TEST

1. a	6. b	11. b	16. d
2. d	7. d	12. c	17. a
3. b	8. c	13. d	18. d
4. c	9. a	14. a	19. a
5. a	10. d	15. b	20. d

CHAPTER 20

Emerging Market Economies

CHAPTER OVERVIEW

The demise of communism, exemplified by the tearing down of the Berlin Wall, the reunification of Germany, and the breakup of the Soviet Union, is one of the major events of the twentieth century. The emergence of market economies in China, Eastern Europe, and the former Soviet Union is of similar importance. In addition, countries such as Argentina, Chile, Mexico, and India have reduced government control and increased reliance on markets in recent years. In this chapter, we study these and many other countries, called emerging market economies. We first learn about how centrally planned economies operate. We then study different paths that countries can follow as they make the transition to a market economy, and see how economic reform has actually worked in practice. Finally, we look at the relationship between economic freedom and political freedom. The success of these emerging market economies is perhaps the most important economic issue facing the world today, not only for themselves but for the United States, Europe, and Japan. We all have a lot to gain if these countries can make a successful transition to market economies, and a lot to lose if they cannot.

CHAPTER REVIEW

1. *Emerging market economies* are those countries that are making the transition from central planning or tight government control to an economy based much more on markets and freely determined prices. These include both former communist countries—China, Eastern Europe, and the republics of the former Soviet Union—and developing countries that are in the process of liberalizing their economies.

2. In a market economy, also called **capitalism**, individuals own the capital—factories, farms, and machines—and decisions about production and employment are decentralized. In contrast, **socialism** is an economic system in which the government owns the capital and decisions regarding the economy are made by those who run the government as part of a central plan. **Communism** is a situation in which all the people of the country *collectively* own the capital without direct government ownership. While the former Soviet Union was called a communist country, its economic system was socialism.

3. The former Soviet Union operated under a system of central planning, through which government commands determined what was produced. Private firms were taken over by the

government, in a process called **nationalization**. The state planning commission, called **Gosplan**, established **five-year plans** that stipulated **production targets** for the economy. Production of most industrial and agricultural goods took place at **state enterprises** and **collectivized farms**, business firms and farms that were owned and controlled by the government. Prices for individual goods were also controlled by the government. These were rarely set at levels that would equate the quantity supplied with the quantity demanded, with resultant shortages and surpluses. Central planning in China followed a similar pattern.

4. Reform of the central planning system in the Soviet Union began in 1985, when Mikhail Gorbachev became the leader of the Communist party. The process of reform began with **perestroika**, which translates as "restructuring." For example, enterprise managers were to be more accountable for their actions through worker and public criticism. Following the resignation of Gorbachev and the breakup of the Soviet Union in 1991, Boris Yeltsin, the President of Russia, disbanded central planning and began to enact more comprehensive reforms.

5. The goals of economic reform are simply the essential ingredients of a market economy. Prices must be freed and determined by competitive markets. A legal system must be established to specify property rights and enforce contracts. Freedom to trade at home and abroad is needed to realize economic efficiencies. A monetary system and a system of tax collections must be put into place.

6. How a centrally planned economy should make the transition to a market economy is more controversial than the ultimate goals of economic reform. A major question is how fast the transition should be. The alternatives are **shock therapy**, in which all the elements of the market economy are put in place at once, and **gradualism**, in which the reforms are phased in slowly.

7. **Privatization** is the process by which existing state enterprises are sold by the government, or privatized, and new private firms are allowed to start up. This process is necessary in order for a market economy to succeed.

ZEROING IN

1. How has economic reform worked in practice? For the countries of Eastern Europe and the republics of the former Soviet Union, the transition has been difficult. Most countries have deep recession, and for some the decline in real GDP has been comparable to that of the United States during the Great Depression.

2. While the transitions of all of the countries of Eastern Europe and the former Soviet Union have been difficult, their experiences have not been monolithic. While there are significant signs of improvement in most of the countries of eastern and central Europe, Russia and the central Asian countries continue to suffer transition problems.

3. Poland was the first country in Eastern Europe to attempt a transition to a market economy, with a reform program underway at the beginning of 1990. It is interesting to look at the Polish experience in more detail, for it may serve as a guide to the future prospects of other countries.

   a. The Polish stabilization program has several aspects. The government budget deficit was reduced sharply and most prices were deregulated. These reforms were instituted quickly, making Poland an example of the shock therapy approach to economic reform. Another important aspect of the Polish stabilization program involves the privatization of state enterprises. This part of the Polish reform program was instituted gradually.

b. The most dramatic effect of the stabilization program was on inflation, which declined from an average of 420 percent in 1989 and 1990 to 25 percent in 1992. The cost of bringing down inflation can be seen by the decline in real GDP, which fell by 12 percent in 1990 and 7 percent in 1991. By 1992, however, real GDP had stopped falling and, by 1994, economic growth was 6 percent.

4. Market reform in China began in 1978, much earlier than in the former Soviet Union. In the agricultural sector, where the reforms occurred first, the growth rate of production has doubled since 1978. In the mid-1980s, reform spread to the industrial sector, and GDP growth increased rapidly. China has also reduced restrictions on foreign trade, but reform of exchange rates and monetary policy did not begin until the early 1990s. One problem has been inflation, which reached 22 percent in 1994.

5. An interesting question raised by economic reform is the relationship between economic and political freedom. The two are not necessarily related, for it is possible that people would freely vote for central planning. How about the converse—does economic freedom lead to political freedom? Not necessarily, Chile under the Pinochet regime and China today are often cited as examples of countries in which the movement toward free markets has not been accompanied by a move to political freedom. Economic progress, however, does seem to be related to political freedom. Most countries today with high levels of real GDP per capita are also democracies. If economic freedom leads, over time, to economic progress, the link between economic and political freedom may be stronger than it first appears.

ACTIVE REVIEW

Fill-in Questions

1. _____ are those countries that are making the transition from central planning or tight government control to a market-based economy.

2. A market economy is also called _____.

3. _____ is an economic system in which the government owns the capital.

4. _____ is an economic system in which all the people of the country own the capital.

5. Under a system of _____, the government determines what is produced.

6. The state planning commission of the former Soviet Union was called _____.

7. In the former Soviet Union, Gosplan established _____.

8. Five-year plans in the former Soviet Union stipulated _____ for the economy.

9. Production of most industrial goods in the former Soviet Union took place at _____.

10. Production of most agricultural goods in the former Soviet Union took place at

    _____.

11. The process of reform in the former Soviet Union began with _____, which translates as "restructuring."

12. The goals of economic reform are to establish the essential ingredients of a(n)

    _____ economy.

13. Two alternative paths for making the transition to a market economy are _____

    and _____.

14. _____ is the process by which existing state enterprises are sold by the

    government.

15. _____ was the first country in Eastern Europe to attempt a transition to a market

    economy.

True-False Questions

T   F   1. Emerging market economies are those countries that are adopting central planning.

T   F   2. Capitalism is an economic system in which the government owns the capital.

T   F   3. The economic system of the former Soviet Union was communism.

T   F   4. In the former Soviet Union, government commands determined what was produced.

T   F   5. Central planning in the Soviet Union was disbanded in 1985.

T   F   6. The ultimate goals of economic reform are not a matter of much controversy.

T   F   7. In order for a centrally planned economy to make the transition to a market economy, the reforms need to be phased in slowly.

T   F   8. Economic reform can succeed without privatization.

T   F   9. Economic reform in the countries of Eastern Europe and the former Soviet Union has been relatively painless.

T   F   10. The countries of eastern and central Europe have had fewer transition problems than Russia and the central Asian countries.

T   F   11. Market reform in China began later than in the former Soviet Union.

T   F   12. Market reform in China has been a failure.

T   F   10. Economic and political freedom are not necessarily related.

T   F   11. Economic freedom necessarily leads to political freedom.

T   F   12. Economic progress is related to political freedom.

Short-Answer Questions

1. Which countries are classified as emerging market economies?

2. What is socialism?

3. Where did production of most goods in the former Soviet Union take place?

4. Why were there often shortages and surpluses of goods in the former Soviet Union?

5. How were production targets set for the economy in the former Soviet Union?

6. What was perestroika?

7. What are the goals of economic reform?

8. What are the alternative paths that a centrally planned economy can follow in order to make the transition to a market economy?

9. What is privatization?

10. What aspects of the Polish stabilization program were instituted quickly?

11. What aspect of the Polish stabilization program was instituted more gradually?

12. What happened to inflation during the Polish stabilization program?

13. What happened to real GDP during the Polish stabilization program?

14. What happened to economic growth in China following market reform?

15. How might economic and political freedom be related?

WORKING IT OUT

1. Analyzing economic performance during a transition from central planning is in some ways different from and in some ways the same as evaluating the performance of a market economy.

   a. A key element in macroeconomic analysis for the United States is the monetary policy rule that the Fed increases the interest rate when inflation rises. For the countries of Eastern Europe and the former Soviet Union, the policy rule is very different. During the past few years, government budget deficits have been very large. These deficits have been too large to finance through borrowing, and central banks have been forced to accelerate money growth in order to finance the deficits. With prices freed from central control, inflation has skyrocketed. The link between government budget deficits and inflation is much tighter for these countries than for the United States.

   b. The magnitude of the inflation and recession experienced by the countries of Eastern Europe and the former Soviet Union dwarfs the problems faced by the United States. When we discussed the rise of inflation in the United States in the 1970s and its fall in the 1980s, we were talking about an increase from 3 percent to 10 percent, with a subsequent fall back to 3 percent. For Russia and Ukraine, the two largest former republics of the Soviet Union, inflation was over 1,000 percent in 1992. In addition, the decline in real GDP in some of these countries has been nearly as large as the decline in real GDP in the United States during the Great Depression.

2. The issue of credibility, which we have discussed in the context of the cost of lowering government budget deficits and reducing inflation for the United States, is even more important for countries making a transition from central planning to a market economy.

   a. An important element in our macroeconomic analysis has been the assumption that prices are sticky. For the countries of Eastern Europe and the former Soviet Union, prices, which were suddenly freed from decades of government control, have fluctuated dramatically. If the government's anti-inflation policy is credible, it is possible, at least in theory, for inflation to be brought down at relatively low cost. This appears to be what has occurred in Poland. If the anti-inflation policy is not credible, a large recession will be needed to reduce inflation. While it is too early to evaluate most of the reform programs, this may characterize most of the countries of the former Soviet Union.

   b. Achieving credibility is one argument for a shock therapy program. When all of the elements of a market economy are put in place at once, there is no doubt about the government's commitment to reform. With a gradualist approach, where the reforms are phased in slowly, you are never sure if the next step toward reform will actually occur.

Worked Problems

1. Consider two emerging market economies characterized by the following data:

	Country A		Country B	
Year	Real GDP Growth	Inflation	Real GDP Growth	Inflation
2001	0	100	0	100
2002	-20	90	-5	95
2003	-15	20	-7	90
2004	-1	10	-9	85
2005	1	10	-7	80

   Both real GDP growth and inflation are measured in percent per year. Which of these countries is characterized by a policy of shock therapy, and which is an example of a policy of gradualism?

Answer

Country A is characterized by a policy of shock therapy. There is a very large recession, but inflation is brought down relatively quickly. Country B is an example of a policy of gradualism. The recession is smaller, but inflation is brought down only very slowly.

2. Consider two emerging market economies characterized by the following data:

Year	Country A		Country B	
	Real GDP Growth	**Inflation**	**Real GDP Growth**	**Inflation**
2001	0	100	0	100
2002	-30	90	-15	90
2003	-25	20	-10	20
2004	-5	10	0	10
2005	0	10	1	10

Both real GDP growth and inflation are measured in percent per year. Both countries have instituted shock therapy reform programs. Which government has greater credibility?

Answer

With credibility, inflation can be brought down at lower cost. Inflation falls at the same rate in the two countries, but the recession is more severe in country A than in country B. Therefore, the government of country B has greater credibility.

Practice Problems

1. Consider two emerging market economies characterized by the following data:

Year	Country A		Country B	
	Real GDP Growth	**Inflation**	**Real GDP Growth**	**Inflation**
2001	0	100	0	100
2002	-10	90	-25	95
2003	-15	87	-30	90
2004	-15	83	-9	20
2005	-12	80	-2	10

Both real GDP growth and inflation are measured in percent per year. Which of these countries is characterized by a policy of shock therapy, and which is an example of a policy of gradualism?

2. Consider two emerging market economies characterized by the following data:

Year	Country A		Country B	
	Real GDP Growth	**Inflation**	**Real GDP Growth**	**Inflation**
2001	0	100	0	100
2002	-40	90	-35	95
2003	-10	15	-30	90
2004	0	5	-5	15
2005	2	5	-1	15

Both real GDP growth and inflation are measured in percent per year. Are these two countries characterized by policies of shock therapy or by policies of gradualism?

3. Consider two emerging market economies characterized by the following data:

Year	Country A		Country B	
	Real GDP Growth	**Inflation**	**Real GDP Growth**	**Inflation**
2001	0	100	0	100
2002	-20	95	-35	95
2003	-15	30	-30	30
2004	-2	10	-20	10
2005	-1	10	-10	10

Both real GDP growth and inflation are measured in percent per year. Both countries have instituted shock therapy reform programs. Which government has greater credibility?

4. Consider two emerging market economies characterized by the following data:

Year	Country A		Country B	
	Real GDP Growth	Inflation	Real GDP Growth	Inflation
2001	0	100	0	100
2002	-4	95	-6	95
2003	-6	90	-8	90
2004	-4	85	-6	85
2005	-3	80	-5	80

Both real GDP growth and inflation are measured in percent per year. Both countries have instituted gradualist reform programs. Which government has greater credibility?

CHAPTER TEST

1. A market economy in which decisions about production and employment are decentralized and individuals own the factories, farms, and machines is called
   a. socialism.
   b. capitalism
   c. communism.
   d. central planning.

2. Which of the following countries is *not* classified as an emerging market economy?
   a. Hungary
   b. Romania
   c. Germany
   d. Bulgaria

3. An economic system in which the government owns the capital and decisions regarding the economy are made as part of a central plan is called
   a. socialism.
   b. capitalism.
   c. communism.
   d. a market economy.

4. An economic system in which all the people of the country own the capital is called
   a. socialism.
   b. capitalism.
   c. communism.
   d. a market economy.

5. Which of the following is *not* one of the essential ingredients of a market economy?
   a. Prices must be freed and determined by competitive markets.
   b. A legal system must be established to specify property rights and enforce contracts.
   c. A monetary system and a system of tax collections must be put in place.
   d. Protectionist trade policies should be followed.

6. The state planning commission of the former Soviet Union was called
   a. Gosplan.
   b. Central Planning.
   c. Perestroika.
   d. Gorbachev.

7. The process by which existing state enterprises are sold by the government and new private firms are allowed to start up is called
   a. gradualism.
   b. shock therapy.
   c. privatization.
   d. restructuring.

8. The process of reform in the former Soviet Union began with
   a. Gosplan.
   b. central planning.
   c. privatization.
   d. perestroika.

9. In a transition to a market economy, when the reforms are phased in slowly, this is called
   a. gradualism.
   b. shock therapy.
   c. Gosplan.
   d. perestroika.

10. Which of the following countries was the first in Eastern Europe to attempt a transition to a market economy?
    a. Hungary
    b. Poland
    c. Romania
    d. Bulgaria

11. What happened to real GDP during the Polish stabilization program in 1994?
    a. Real GDP rose by 6 percent.
    b. Real GDP rose by 12 percent.
    c. Real GDP declined by 7 percent.
    d. Real GDP did not change.

12. What happened to inflation in Poland between 1990 and 1992?
    a. Inflation declined from 42 percent to 25 percent.
    b. Inflation rose from 25 percent to 42 percent.
    c. Inflation declined from 420 percent to 25
    d. Inflation was unchanged.

13. Which of the following was *not* one of the aspects of the Polish stabilization program?
    a. The government budget deficit was reduced sharply.
    b. State enterprises were privatized.
    c. The government budget deficit was financed through borrowing.
    d. Most prices were deregulated.

14. Which of the following does not characterize market reform in China.
    a. Reform in China first occurred in the agricultural sector.
    b. Reform in China began after reform in the former Soviet Union.
    c. Restrictions on foreign trade have been reduced.
    d. Inflation has been a problem.

15. Following market reform in China, GDP growth
    a. increased rapidly
    b. increased slowly
    c. decreased rapidly
    d. decreased slowly

16. Which of the following was *not* one of the difficulties that the countries of Eastern Europe and the republics of the Soviet Union experienced during the transition?
    a. High inflation
    b. Deep recession
    c. Rising government budget deficits
    d. Deflation

17. For the countries of Eastern Europe and the former Soviet Union, central banks have financed government budget deficits by
    a. borrowing.
    b. accelerating money growth.
    c. increasing the interest rate.
    d. spending more.

18. In Russia, in 1992, inflation was over
    a. 5 percent.
    b. 50 percent.
    c. 1000 percent.
    d. 500 percent.

Use the following table for questions 19 and 20.

Year	Country A		Country B	
	Real GDP Growth	Inflation	Real GDP Growth	Inflation
2001	0	100	0	100
2002	-25	95	-6	95
2003	-20	25	-8	90
2004	-4	8	-6	85
2005	2	8	-5	80

19. Which of these countries is (are) characterized by a policy of gradualism?
    a. Country A
    b. Country B
    c. Neither country A nor country B
    d. Both country A and country B

20. Which of these countries experienced the largest recession?
    a. Country A
    b. Country B
    c. The recessions were equally severe.
    d. Not enough information to tell.

ANSWERS TO THE REVIEW QUESTIONS

Fill-in Questions

1. Emerging market economies
2. capitalism
3. Socialism
4. Communism
5. central planning
6. Gosplan
7. five-year plans
8. production targets
9. state enterprises
10. collectivized farms
11. perestroika
12. market
13. shock therapy, gradualism
14. Privatization
15. Poland

True-False Questions

1. **False**. Emerging market economies are those countries that are making the transition from central planning to an economy based much more on markets.
2. **False**. Under capitalism, individuals own the capital.
3. **False**. Although the former Soviet Union was called a communist country, its economic system was socialism.
4. **True**. The former Soviet Union operated under a system of central planning.
5. **False**. Although economic reform began in 1985, central planning was not disbanded until after the breakup of the Soviet Union in 1991.
6. **True**. The goals of economic reform, the essential ingredients of a market economy, are widely agreed upon.
7. **False**. An alternative is to put all of the elements of a market economy in place at once.
8. **False**. Privatization is necessary if a market economy is to succeed.
9. **False**. The transition has been difficult. Most countries have experienced high inflation and deep recession.
10. **True**. While there are significant signs of improvement in most of the countries of eastern and central Europe, Russia and the central Asian countries continue to suffer transition problems.
11. **False**. Market reform in China began in 1978, much earlier than in the former Soviet Union.
12. **False**. Economic growth in China has been very rapid since market reform.
13. **True**. It is possible that people would freely vote for central planning.
14. **False**. Chile under the Pinochet regime and China today are often cited as examples of countries in which the movement toward free markets has not been accompanied by a move to political freedom.
15. **True**. Most countries today with high levels of real GDP per capita are also democracies.

Short-Answer Questions

1. Emerging market economies include both former communist countries and developing countries that are in the process of liberalizing their economies.
2. Socialism is an economic system in which the government owns the capital and decisions regarding the economy are made as part of a central plan.
3. Production of most goods took place at state enterprises and collectivized farms.
4. Prices for individual goods, which were controlled by the government, were rarely set at levels that would equate the quantity supplied with the quantity demanded.
5. Gosplan, the state planning commission, established five-year plans that stipulated production targets for the economy.
6. Perestroika, which translates as "restructuring," was the beginning of the process of reform in the former Soviet Union.
7. The goals of economic reform are freely determined prices, property rights and incentives, competitive markets, freedom to trade at home and abroad, a role for government in establishing monetary and fiscal policy, and a role for nongovernment organizations.
8. The alternative paths are shock therapy, in which all the elements of the market economy are put in place at once, and gradualism, in which the reforms are phased in slowly.
9. Privatization is the process by which existing state enterprises are sold by the government and new private firms are allowed to start up.
10. The government budget deficit was reduced sharply and most prices were deregulated quickly.
11. Privatization of state enterprises is the aspect of the Polish stabilization program which was instituted more slowly.
12. Inflation fell dramatically in Poland between 1990 and 1992.
13. Real GDP in Poland declined sharply in 1990 and 1991, but rose significantly by 1994.
14. Economic growth in China has been very rapid.
15. If economic freedom leads, over time, to economic progress, there may be a link between economic and political freedom because most countries today with high levels of real GDP per capita are also democracies.

SOLUTIONS TO THE PRACTICE PROBLEMS

1. Country A is an example of gradualism, whereas country B is characterized by shock therapy.
2. Both country A and country B are examples of shock therapy.
3. The government of country A has greater credibility.
4. The government of country A has greater credibility.

ANSWERS TO THE CHAPTER TEST

1. b
2. c
3. a
4. c
5. d
6. a
7. c
8. d
9. a
10. b
11. a
12. c
13. c
14. b
15. a
16. d
17. b
18. c
19. b
20. a

CHAPTER 21

The Gains from International Trade

CHAPTER OVERVIEW

It may be an old cliché, but the world does get smaller every day. This author's running shoes were made in Korea; his digital watch was assembled in Malaysia; he is looking forward to French wine with dinner, but not before calling his editor in Boston on a Japanese portable telephone. How international is your world at this moment?

International considerations permeate virtually every nook and cranny of the economy. This chapter begins to explore the role of international trade in the economy by examining the microeconomic foundations of why countries exchange goods and services. While you are just beginning to look at these things, economics has a rich history of interest in international trade, going back to Adam Smith and the *Wealth of Nations* (1776). By comparing and contrasting free trade with mercantilism, Smith showed how countries benefit from trade. The reasons for trade were more formally developed by David Ricardo in his theory of comparative advantage. This theory stresses the importance of relative opportunity costs in determining what a country exports and what it imports. As a result of trade, the relative prices of products and of factors of production change. In fact, over time they tend to equalize between countries. This is shown using the already familiar production possibilities curve. Next, the Heckscher-Ohlin model is presented. This model addresses the determinants of comparative advantage. At its heart lies the abundance of factors of production and the intensity of their use. Within this discussion, the Leontief paradox is presented, and factor-price equalization is discussed.

Comparative advantage is not the only reason for trade. Economies of scale are also a reason to gain from trade. Here, complete specialization within a world market permits *ATC* to decline to a lower level than would have prevailed in a smaller market without trade. This is coupled with product differentiation to place the model of monopolistic competition into the world economy. Finally, the movement toward free trade and the resulting transition costs are discussed.

CHAPTER REVIEW

1. **International trade** offers many benefits to all countries. These can come in the form of increased specialization, a redistribution of existing supplies of goods, economies of scale in production, and increased competition. The importance of international trade in the world economy can be seen in the recent agreement between Mexico, Canada, and the United States to integrate their economies into a free trade area. In addition, there are many ongoing conversations among countries aimed at developing areas for expanded free trade. The **commerce clause** of the U.S. Constitution prohibits trade restraints between the states.

2. One of the first places we find an extensive discussion of the benefits from free trade is in the *Wealth of Nations* (1776) by Adam Smith. When Smith's writings initially appeared, the prevailing economic wisdom was **mercantilism**. This doctrine argued that a country's wealth was associated with its accumulation of gold and silver. This was accomplished by maximizing **exports** while minimizing **imports**, or maximizing **net exports**. Government regulations, **tariffs**, and quotas were used to maximize net exports. To Smith, **free trade** was better. It offered the benefits of (1) mutual gains from voluntary exchange of existing goods, (2) increased competition, (3) the division of labor, and (4) better use of skills and resources in different countries.

3. A basic foundation of international trade is the theory of comparative advantage. A country will export those goods in which it has a comparative advantage. Such an advantage exists when the opportunity cost of producing a good in a country is lower than the opportunity cost of producing the same good in another country. This is to say, a country that is relatively more efficient than another country in producing one good rather than another good has a comparative advantage in the production of that good. This is true even if one country has an **absolute advantage** in the production of both goods. If countries specialize in the goods in which they have a comparative advantage, the resulting trade flow will equate relative prices in each country. This can be shown with a production possibilities curve. If opportunity costs do not increase, countries will specialize in the production of goods in which they have a comparative advantage, and the total amount of goods available for consumption will increase, leading to **gains from trade**. The relative price after trade, or the quantity of imported goods that a country can obtain in exchange for a unit of exported goods, is called the **terms of trade**.

4. Comparative advantages can change over time; **dynamic comparative advantage** describes such changes, especially those that result when a country invests in physical and human capital and in technology. The Heckscher-Ohlin model attempts to identify the determinants of a country's comparative advantage. According to the model, a country has a comparative advantage in those goods that are intensively produced with its most abundant factor of production—that is, a country that is relatively **capital abundant** has a comparative advantage in goods whose production is relatively **capital intensive**, and a country that is relatively **labor abundant** has a comparative advantage in goods whose production is relatively **labor intensive**. An exception to this general rule—the tendency of the United States to export more labor-intensive goods—is referred to as the **Leontief paradox**; it is explained by the importance of human capital and research. Using the Heckscher-Ohlin framework, it can be argued that **factor-price equalization** will occur.

5. Gains from trade are also due to economies of scale. By specializing within a larger market brought about by free trade, a firm can take advantage of larger-scale economies. As a result, *ATC* and price fall as quantity grows. Trade flows founded in economies of scale tend to be **intraindustry** in character, whereas trade flows based on comparative advantage tend to be **interindustry**.

6. As the number of firms in a market of a given size increases, *ATC* tends to rise, as each firm has a smaller market share. However, as markets grow in size through trade, the *ATC* of existing firms falls. Also, as new firms enter the market, competition and product differentiation increase and, as a result, price falls, so that only normal profits are earned over the long run. Models of international trade based on economies of scale and product differentiation are referred to as **new trade theory**.

7. This chapter has endeavored to show that free trade creates benefits for participating economies. Over time, interest in moving toward free trade has increased. However, the **phaseout** of existing trade barriers may need to proceed slowly. Also, there may be a need for **trade adjustment assistance** for those hurt during the transition period.

ZEROING IN

1. One of the most important ideas in economics is that of comparative advantage. A specific example will be explored in "Working It Out." For now, one way to think about comparative advantage is by using opportunity costs, another important economic notion. *Absolute* productivity (or absolute advantage) really does not matter in the determination of what goods are traded. This is hard for many people to accept. If absolute productivity were the determinant of trade, the United States would export nearly everything it produces, as the United States has the most resources, the most physical capital, and many workers with large amounts of human capital. However, in comparative advantage, *relative* efficiency or productivity matters. This can be measured using opportunity cost, or what must be given up to produce another unit of some product. Given the fundamental problem of scarcity, net benefit maximization also includes the minimization of costs. Comparing opportunity costs across countries focuses trade on the most efficient producer. So absolute advantage does not necessarily matter.

2. The Heckscher-Ohlin model is one of the better known theories that attempts to identify the determinants of comparative advantage. This explanation is based on two things. First, comparative advantage depends on the relative abundance of inputs within a country. For a given demand, inputs that are relatively abundant have lower prices than they would if they were less plentiful. The second consideration is the way resources are used within the production process — the intensity of their use. Therefore, goods that are produced with a lot (intensity) of the most plentiful (abundant) resource are goods that can be produced by giving up the least amount of other things. Stated another way, the Heckscher-Ohlin model also identifies the determinants of opportunity costs.

ACTIVE REVIEW

Fill-in Questions

1. The movement of goods and services between countries is _____.

2. Although sovereign governments often restrict trade with other countries, the _____ of the U.S. Constitution prevents such restraint between states.

3. Recently Mexico, Canada, and the United States agreed to integrate their economies into a(n) _____

4. _____ held that the wealth of a country was related to its accumulation of gold and silver.

5. Positive _____ are achieved when _____ exceed _____.

6. _____ are taxes on imports.

7. In the _____, Adam Smith argued that _____ would create benefits for trading partners.

8. Adam Smith argued that international trade increases the size of the market, which allows for a(n) _____.

9. The theory of comparative advantage was initially developed by _____.

10. Comparative advantage can also be expressed in terms of _____.

11. A person with a lower opportunity cost of producing a good than another person has a(n) _____ in that good.

12. _____ efficiency is synonymous with comparative advantage.

13. The price of one good in terms of another is called its _____.

14. With trade, the relative prices of a good in different countries will _____ to the same value.

15. The after-trade relative price is called the _____.

16. A straight-line production possibilities curve will result in _____ within an economy after trade.

17. _____ describes changes in comparative advantage over time.

18. The _____ is used to describe an exception to the Heckscher-Ohlin model.

19. One implication of the Heckscher-Ohlin model is that trade will bring about factor-price _____ in different countries.

20. Not all gains from trade are based on comparative advantage; there are also gains based on _____.

21. The gains from trade that result from economies of scale are the _____.

22. Trade due to comparative advantage tends to be _____, whereas trade due to economies of scale tends to be _____.

23. There is a(n) _____ relationship between the number of firms and the *ATC* of each firm.

24. _____ means that trade barriers are reduced a little bit each year.

25. Transfer payments to workers hurt by a movement toward free trade are referred to as _____.

True-False Questions

T   F   1. International trade creates gains only by exploiting a country's comparative advantage.

T   F   2. Trade within the United States can be subject to tariffs levied by individual states.

T   F   3. International trade has been growing rapidly as a result of declining costs of transportation and communication, and the removal of restrictions on trade between countries.

T   F   4. Mercantilistic policies attempt to maximize net exports.

T   F   5. Adam Smith argued that mercantilism and free trade were synonymous.

T   F   6. International trade makes home markets more competitive.

T   F   7. "The division of labour is limited by the extent of the market."

T   F   8. David Ricardo's concept of absolute advantage shows how a country can improve the incomes of its citizens by allowing them to trade with others.

T   F   9. Comparative advantage can be expressed in terms of opportunity costs.

T   F   10. Trade has very little effect on the prices of goods within a country.

T   F   11. International trade allows countries to consume beyond their domestic (before trade) production possibilities curves.

T   F   12. Increasing opportunity costs produce complete specialization within a country in a free trade environment.

T   F   13. A straight-line production possibilities curve reflects constant opportunity costs.

T   F   14. A country's comparative advantage remains constant over time.

T   F   15. The Heckscher-Ohlin model is based, in part, on a country's factor supplies.

T   F   16. The Heckscher-Ohlin model implies factor-price equalization.

T   F   17. Trade that is a result of economies of scale tends to be interindustry in nature.

T   F   18. As the number of firms in a market of a given size grows, the *ATC* falls.

T   F   19. The movement toward free trade has no costs.

Short-Answer Questions

1. Give two reasons why international trade is beneficial.

2. How did mercantilism promote the wealth of nations?

3. What are the four reasons supporting free trade that Adam Smith put forth in the *Wealth of Nations*?

4. "The taylor does not attempt to make his own shoes, but buys them from the shoemaker." Explain.

5. Briefly explain David Ricardo's theory of comparative advantage.

6. Why do prices change with trade?

7. What are the terms of trade?

8. What does trade do to a country's production possibilities curve?

9. Is comparative advantage dynamic?

10. What is the purpose of the Heckscher-Ohlin model?

11. Is the Heckscher-Ohlin model always correct in predicting the nature of trade?

12. What is factor-price equalization?

13. Differentiate between intraindustry trade and interindustry trade.

14. Why does ATC tend to fall for a given number of firms as the market grows?

15. Why might trade adjustment assistance be necessary?

WORKING IT OUT

Because of the importance of the theory of comparative advantage, it is worthwhile to try to identify the comparative advantage in a specific example. There are several ways to determine comparative advantage. One way is to look at the relative productivity per worker in each country. Another way is to look at the opportunity cost of moving workers from one type of production to another.

Suppose that both wool yarn and beef are produced in both Australia and Argentina. Assume that both goods are made with only labor, and that the following relationships hold:

In Australia, 3 units of labor produce 105 pounds of beef, and 1 unit of labor produces 40 spools of wool yarn.

In Argentina, 2 units of labor produce 60 pounds of beef, and 2 units of labor produce 30 spools of wool yarn.

Furthermore, Australia has 600 units of labor and Argentina has 200 units of labor.

1. Figure 21.1 shows the production possibilities curves for Australia and Argentina. The production information may be used to determine the end points for each curve. For example, Australia can produce 21,000 pounds of beef [(600/3) × 105] or 24,000 spools of wool yarn [(600/1) × 40].

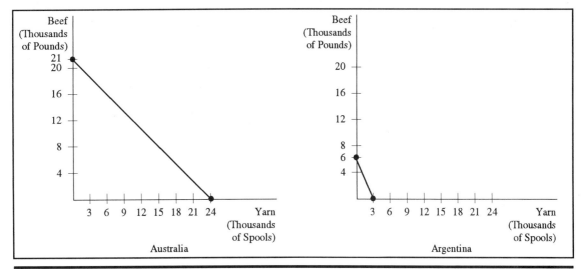

Figure 21.1

2. First, look at the absolute advantage in each good. Australia has an absolute advantage in the production of both beef and wool yarn. One Australian worker can produce more of both yarn and beef.

3. To describe the comparative advantage, let's look first at the relative productivity per worker in each country. In Australia, 1 worker produces 35 pounds of beef (105/3) or 40 spools of yarn (40/1). In Argentina, 1 worker produces 30 pounds of beef (60/2) or 15 spools of yarn (30/2). Thus, workers are relatively more productive in beef production in Argentina and in yarn production in Australia. Alternatively, to produce an additional 1,000 pounds of beef, it takes 28.6 workers in Australia (1,000/35), whereas it takes 33.33 workers (1,000/30) in Argentina. If those workers were moved into beef production from yarn production, Australia would lose 1,144 spools of yarn (28.6 × 40) and Argentina would lose approximately 500 spools of yarn. Obviously, beef is more expensive in terms of yarn in Australia than it is in Argentina. Thus, Australia has a comparative advantage in wool production and Argentina has a comparative advantage in the production of beef.

4. What happens to the price of the imported good in each country? Australia imports beef from Argentina. The supply curve for beef in Australia shifts to the right as a result of the imports. Assuming that demand is constant, the price of beef in Australia will fall. Argentina imports yarn from Australia. The supply curve of yarn shifts to the right and the price of yarn in Argentina falls, *ceteris paribus*.

Worked Problems

1. Assume that both Japan and France produce both cloth and computers. Assume that they are produced with only labor according to the following schedule:

   In France, 5 units of labor produce 100 bolts of cloth, and 2 units of labor produce 50 computers.

   In Japan, 6 units of labor produce 132 bolts of cloth, and 3 units of labor produce 45 computers.

   France has 1,000 units of labor and Japan has 1,200 units of labor.

   a. Construct the production possibilities curves.

   b. Which country has an absolute advantage?

   c. Identify the comparative advantage.

   d. How does trade flow?

Answers

   a. *First, determine the end points of the production possibilities curves. France can produce 20,000 bolts of cloth [(1,000/5) × 100] or 25,000 computers [(1,000/2) × 50]. Japan can produce 26,400 bolts of cloth or 18,000 computers. Figure 21.2 shows the production possibilities curves for Japan and France.*

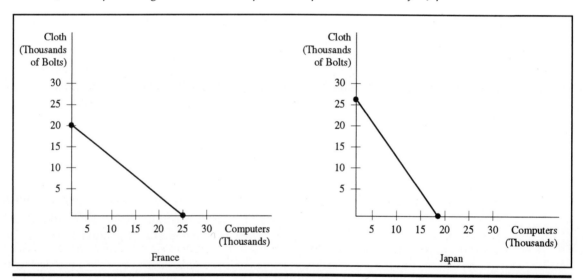

Figure 21.2

   b. *France has an absolute advantage in the production of computers, and Japan has an absolute advantage in the production of cloth.*

   c. *In France, 1 worker can produce 20 bolts of cloth or 25 computers. In Japan, 1 worker can produce 22 bolts of cloth or 15 computers. Thus, workers in Japan are relatively more efficient in cloth production than are French workers. Alternatively, to produce 100 additional bolts of cloth, France must give up 125 computers [(100/20 × 25], and Japan must give up 68 computers [(100/22) × 15]. Thus, the opportunity cost of cloth in terms of computers is lower in Japan. Japan has a comparative advantage in cloth production, whereas France has a comparative advantage in the production of computers.*

   d. *Computers flow from France to Japan, and cloth flows from Japan to France. The price of computers will fall in Japan, and the price of cloth will fall in France.*

2. Whenever possible, it is helpful to present a new concept using the familiar tool of supply and demand analysis. Here we will look at the Heckscher-Ohlin model from a market perspective.

   It was shown in "Working It Out" that Australia has a comparative advantage in wool production and Argentina has a comparative advantage in beef production. Assume that two kinds of labor, skilled and unskilled, are used to produce both wool and beef in both countries. Furthermore, assume that Argentina's comparative advantage is based on the fact that it has a very large number of unskilled workers and that they are employed intensively in beef production. Will the wage level of unskilled workers in Australia fall to that of unskilled workers in Argentina? Use the Heckscher-Ohlin model to support your answer.

Answer

Trade causes a reallocation of existing supplies of beef and wool between Argentina and Australia. It also causes a movement in each country toward specialization in the good in which that country has a comparative advantage. This movement causes shifts in the demand for skilled and unskilled workers. Assume that the supply curve of unskilled workers is upward-sloping (and not backward-bending). With trade, beef production in Australia falls. This results in a decline in the demand for unskilled workers in Australia, and their wages will fall. At the same time, the demand for unskilled workers in Argentina rises as the production of beef increases. As a result, their wages rise. In a perfect Heckscher-Ohlin model, factor prices will tend to equalize between the two beginning wages, not necessarily at the lowest one.

3. It may be useful to see some of the benefits offered by a trade agreement like GATT from the perspective of economies of scale and monopolistic competition. To do this, we will review Figures 17.5 to 17.8 in the text.

   GATT creates a process that lowers or removes trade barriers currently existing between many countries. As a result, firms will find it easier to access a larger market. Explain and graph the relationship between ATC and the number of firms in a market and between price and the number of firms. What happens to your diagram when the market gets bigger?

Answer

If the size of a market remains fixed, an increase in the number of firms reduces the market share of each. As firms become smaller, ATC rises. Thus, a positive relationship exists. This is shown in Figure 17.3 by line F.

   If the market increases in size but the number of firms remains constant, then each firm produces more. In a sense, each firm becomes larger, and, as a result, ATC falls. Accordingly, F would shift right to F_1, leading to a lower ATC (ATC_2 instead of ATC_1) for the same number of firms N_1.

   Assuming monopolistic competition, an increase in the number of firms reduces the market power of each firm; the market becomes more competitive. Thus, price falls with an increase in the number of firms, a negative relationship. This is shown by R in Figure 21.3. The intersection of R and F_1 (or F, depending on the size of the market) determines the long-run equilibrium number of firms (N_2) and price and ATC (ATC_3).

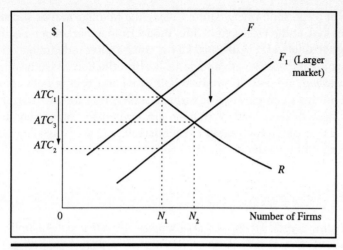

Figure 21.3

Practice Problems

1. Assume that Japan and France initially trade cloth and computers as described in worked problem 1. However, assume that the Japanese government subsidizes computer research so that 3 units of labor now produce 90 computers. Also, because of a unique environmental problem, Japanese cloth producers have had to cut back to 120 bolts per 6 workers.

   a. Identify the comparative advantage.

   b. Briefly discuss the trade flows.

2. Assume that the comparative advantage for Japan in worked problem 1 was due to an intensive use of abundant unskilled workers.

   a. What will happen to these workers' wages?

   b. What will happen to their wages based on the events in practice problem 1?

3. Using Figure 17.3, what happened to price, *ATC*, and the number of firms when NAFTA went into effect?

4. What happens to Figure 17.3 when a new technological discovery lowers the *ATC* for all firms?

5. Compare your answers in problems 3 and 4.

CHAPTER TEST

1. Recently, Mexico, Canada, and the United States formed a
   a. single country.
   b. free trade area.
   c. single baseball league.
   d. mutual defense pact.

2. Individual states in the United States are prohibited from restricting the free flow of goods by the
   a. Federal Reserve Act of 1914.
   b. Fair Labor Standards Act.
   c. Declaration of Independence.
   d. commerce clause of the U.S. Constitution.

3. In 1776, the prevailing economic wisdom was described as
   a. a disinterest in gold and silver.
   b. free trade.
   c. a system that discouraged tariffs.
   d. mercantilism.

4. Under a mercantilist policy, governments attempted to
   a. equate exports and imports.
   b. minimize exports and maximize imports.
   c. maximize exports and minimize imports.
   d. remove tariffs and quotas.

5. The benefits of free trade come from
   a. a redistribution of existing supplies of goods.
   b. a movement toward specialization.
   c. increased competition.
   d. all of the above.

6. Free trade increases the size of markets. As a result, firms
   a. can take advantage of economies of scale.
   b. can strengthen their monopoly positions.
   c. can maximize ATC.
   d. are guaranteed profits.

7. David Ricardo's theory of _____ advantage shows how a country benefits from trading with others.
   a. absolute
   b. constant
   c. comparative
   d. proportional

8. In explaining comparative advantage, economists often use the concept of
   a. demand.
   b. opportunity costs.
   c. monopoly.
   d. gravity.

9. With trade, relative prices within a country
   a. only rise.
   b. change.
   c. only fall.
   d. are unaffected.

10. Trade causes a country's production possibilities curve to
    a. change slope.
    b. shift inward in a parallel manner.
    c. shift outward in a parallel manner.
    d. remain constant.

11. If there are increasing opportunity costs, trade results in
    a. complete specialization.
    b. constant specialization.
    c. partial specialization.
    d. no specialization.

12. A major attempt at explaining the determinants of comparative advantage is found in
    a. the model of consumer behavior.
    b. diminishing returns to variable factors of production.
    c. the Taylor model.
    d. the Heckscher-Ohlin model.

13. According to the Heckscher-Ohlin model, a country will export goods
    a. produced intensively with its least abundant resource.
    b. not produced with its most abundant resource.
    c. produced intensively with no more than 10 percent of its most abundant resource.
    d. produced intensively with its most abundant resource.

14. If Sri Lanka exports products produced intensively with labor, its most abundant resource, then
    a. wages will fall relative to the prices of other resources.
    b. wages will remain unchanged.
    c. there is a Leontief paradox present.
    d. wages will rise relative to the prices of other resources.

15. Intraindustry trade refers to
    a. trade between different industries.
    b. trade within the same industry.
    c. trade within a country's own borders.
    d. trade determined by tariffs.

16. Interindustry trade refers to
    a. trade between different industries.
    b. trade within the same industry.
    c. trade within a country's own borders.
    d. trade determined by tariffs.

17. In a given market, as the number of firms increases,
    a. *ATC* falls.
    b. *MC* falls.
    c. *ATC* rises.
    d. *ATC* remains constant.

18. For a given number of firms, as the market grows,
    a. *ATC* rises.
    b. *AFC* rises.
    c. *ATC* remains unchanged.
    d. *ATC* falls.

19. Intraindustry trade is usually associated with
    a. a Leontief paradox.
    b. monopolies.
    c. comparative advantage.
    d. economies of scale.

20. Interindustry trade is usually associated with
    a. a Leontief paradox.
    b. monopolies.
    c. comparative advantage.
    d. economies of scale.

ANSWERS TO THE REVIEW QUESTIONS

Fill-in Questions

1. international trade
2. commerce clause
3. free trade area
4. Mercantilism
5. net exports, exports, imports
6. Tariffs
7. *Wealth of Nations*, free trade
8. greater division of labor
9. David Ricardo
10. opportunity cost
11. comparative advantage
12. Relative
13. relative price
14. converge
15. terms of trade
16. complete specialization
17. Dynamic comparative advantage
18. Leontief paradox
19. equalization
20. economies of scale
21. reduction in costs per unit
22. interindustry, intraindustry
23. positive
24. Phaseout
25. trade adjustment assistance

True-False Questions

1. **False**. Gains from trade also result from economies of scale.
2. **False**. The commerce clause of the U.S. Constitution prohibits the restriction of trade between the states.
3. **True**. Recently, the United States, Canada, and Mexico formed a free trade area.
4. **True**. A goal of mercantilist policy was the accumulation of gold and silver. This was accomplished by maximizing exports and minimizing imports.
5. **False**. Mercantilist policy attempted to manipulate trade flows through tariffs and other government restrictions. This is contrary to free trade. Smith wrote about the importance of free trade for maximizing social welfare.
6. **True**. International trade increases the number of suppliers in a country. When there are more sellers, the market power of each is reduced.

7. **True**. This is from the *Wealth of Nations*. Adam Smith argued that international trade promoted specialization by making markets larger.

8. **False**. Ricardo used the theory of *comparative* advantage. The benefits from trade between countries are based on the *relative* advantage of each country.

9. **True**. Opportunity costs are a way to define comparative advantage.

10. **False**. International trade is the movement of supplies of goods between countries. By changing the location of supplies, international trade does affect the prices of goods. In fact, trade flows will quickly eliminate price differences.

11. **True**. This is one way to show the gains from trade.

12. **False**. Under increasing opportunity costs, as more and more of a good is produced, the opportunity cost changes. These changes can reduce the gains from trade to the point where further specialization is no longer beneficial.

13. **True**. The tradeoff between the goods remains the same over the entire curve. Increasing opportunity costs are reflected by a production possibilities curve that bows outward.

14. **False**. Comparative advantage is a dynamic concept, especially if a country invests in human and physical capital and in technology.

15. **True**. According to the Heckscher-Ohlin model, a country will export those goods that are produced intensively with the country's most abundant resource.

16. **True**. Not only does trade change the location of the supplies of products, it also changes the demand for factors of production. Over time, shifts in demand and supply in product and input markets (in trading countries) will tend to equalize prices.

17. **False**. It tends to be intraindustry. Trade based on comparative advantage tends to be interindustry.

18. **False**. As the number of firms in a market of a given size rises, the market share of each falls. Thus, *ATC* will rise.

19. **False**. Often trade barriers need to be phased out over an extended period of time. Trade adjustment assistance programs may be necessary to help workers who are adversely affected by the movement toward free trade.

Short-Answer Questions

1. First, firms are able to reduce costs through economies of scale because trade makes markets larger. Second, trade allows countries to specialize in producing those goods in which they are relatively efficient.

2. According to mercantilist theory, a country would become wealthy through the accumulation of gold and silver. This was accomplished by maximizing exports while minimizing imports, or maximizing net exports. Government regulation of trade through tariffs and quotas is required for this to happen.

3. Gains from free trade would result because of (1) mutual gains from voluntary exchange of existing goods, (2) increased competition, (3) the division of labor, and (4) better use of skills and resources in different countries.

4. This is from the *Wealth of Nations*. In this passage, Adam Smith is arguing that free trade promotes specialization.

5. The theory of comparative advantage explains how a country can gain from trading with others. A country exports those products in which it has a comparative advantage. Simply stated, country A has a comparative advantage in a good relative to country B if the opportunity cost of producing that good in country A is less than it is in country B.

6. Trade reallocates the supplies of products. Assuming competition and negligible transportation costs, trade moves goods to the place (country) where they command the highest price. As a result, the price falls in one country and rises in the other.

7. Simply stated, the terms of trade for a country are given by the quantity of imported goods that it can obtain per unit of exported goods.

8. Trade causes the production possibilities curve to rotate out along the axis of the good that is imported. The change in the slope of the curve reflects the change in relative prices caused by trade.

9. Yes, comparative advantage can change. This can occur through investment in physical and human capital and in technology.

10. The Heckscher-Ohlin model attempts to explain the determinants of comparative advantage. The model argues that comparative advantage is based on the relative abundance of resource supplies and the relative intensity with which those supplies are used in production.

11. Not necessarily. The Leontief paradox describes a situation in which trade does not clearly reflect relative factor intensities.

12. Factor-price equalization is the tendency of the prices of factors of production to equalize across countries. As countries trade and specialize in production, the demand for inputs also changes. This causes the prices of factors of production to change. The wages of unskilled labor will fall in countries that import goods made with unskilled labor, whereas the wages of unskilled workers in countries that export these goods will rise as production expands.

13. Intraindustry trade means trade in goods from the same industry. Interindustry trade is trade in goods from *different* industries. Interindustry trade is usually associated with comparative advantage, whereas intraindustry trade is usually associated with economies of scale.

14. As markets grow, the amount produced by each firm increases. This allows firms to take advantage of economies of scale, and, as a result, *ATC* falls.

15. In moving into a free trade environment, some segments of the economy will experience a decline, and workers may lose jobs. These transition costs can be addressed through trade adjustment assistance. Such assistance may reduce the resistance of some to moving toward free trade.

SOLUTIONS TO THE PRACTICE PROBLEMS

1. a. In France, 1 worker still produces 20 bolts of cloth or 25 computers. In Japan, however, 1 worker now produces 20 bolts of cloth or 30 computers. Therefore, as a result of the research, Japan is now (relative to France) more productive in computer production than in cloth production — to get 100 more computers, Japan must give up 67 bolts of cloth [$(100/30) \times 20$], whereas France must give up 80 [$(100/25) \times 20$].

    b. Comparative advantage has shifted, and the flow of trade reverses.

2. a. As cloth production increases, the demand for unskilled workers in Japan will rise. This will cause the wages of the unskilled workers to rise, *ceteris paribus*.

    b. Comparative advantage has shifted. The demand for unskilled workers in Japan will fall, and their wages will fall.

3. NAFTA made the area of free trade larger. Thus, each firm had a larger market. As a result, firms should have become larger, and *ATC* should have fallen. This results in a rightward shift in F to F_1.

4. This will shift F to the right, indicating a lower *ATC* for a given number of firms in a market of given size.

5. The results are essentially the same. Expanding free trade is like discovering a new technique of production.

ANSWERS TO THE CHAPTER TEST

1. b	6. a	11. c	16. a
2. d	7. c	12. d	17. c
3. d	8. b	13. d	18. d
4. c	9. b	14. d	19. d
5. d	10. a	15. b	20. c

CHAPTER **22**

International Trade Policy

CHAPTER OVERVIEW

In the previous chapter, we explored the case for free trade. By exploiting comparative advantage and economies of scale, the citizens of a country (large or small) benefit from the free exchange of goods with other countries. However, free trade is not widely observed. For many reasons, governments restrict trade through tariffs, quotas, and other barriers. This chapter examines the consequences of these actions, looks at reasons supporting the use of trade restrictions, and presents ways of moving toward an environment of free trade. First, tariffs, quotas, and various nontariff trade barriers are examined, using the supply and demand model. Then a history of trade restrictions in the United States is presented. The discussion ranges from the tariff of abominations and Smoot-Hawley to GATT and the Uruguay Round. Next, many arguments supporting the use of trade barriers are discussed. These include strategic trade policy, infant industries, national security, and simple retaliation. Finally, the chapter ends with an examination of alternative policies to reduce trade barriers, including unilateral disarmament, bilateral and multilateral negotiations, customs unions, and free trade areas.

CHAPTER REVIEW

1. The United States is a relatively open economy. But this is a minority position in the world. Virtually all countries have **protectionist policies**; they impose **tariffs** (**ad valorem** and **specific**) and **quotas** on imported goods. Tariffs shift the **export supply curve** up by the dollar amount of the tariff, so that it intersects the **import demand curve** at a lower quantity. Tariffs generate duties or revenues for the government. Quotas can be analyzed in a similar fashion. Quotas, however, generate revenues for the individual(s) who hold the quota — those having the right to import the specific good.

2. In recent years, new alternatives to tariffs and quotas have been observed. Two of these are the **voluntary restraint agreement (VRA)** and **voluntary import expansion (VIE)**. Under a VRA, a government asks another country to "voluntarily" reduce its exports. This has market effects similar to those of a quota, except that the revenues go to the foreign producer. In a VIE arrangement, a government agrees to have firms in its country expand their imports of foreign goods from another country. While there is no real consensus on the effects of VIEs, some suspect that they raise the price of the imports of the country asking for increased usage of its exports. There are other trade barriers related to domestic policies. These include quality and performance standards and government procurement policies.

3. The U.S. economy has not always been a relatively free trade environment. The use of **revenue tariffs** can be traced back to before 1800. Some of the more infamous and disruptive tariffs include the "tariff of abominations" of 1828 and the **Smoot-Hawley tariff** of 1930, which led to a **trade war** as each country tried to beat the others with higher tariffs. In 1934 the **Reciprocal Trade Agreement Act** was passed, allowing President Roosevelt to reduce tariffs if other countries reciprocated. This process was made permanent in 1947 with the passage of the **General Agreement on Trade and Tariffs (GATT)**. Another form of trade restriction is **antidumping duties**, which address the problem of a foreign firm selling below its average cost or below the price in the home country (**dumping**). Other **nontariff barriers** to trade include the Multifiber Agreement (MFA).

4. Even though estimates suggest that removing trade restrictions from the economy would produce an annual gain of as much as $60 billion, arguments for the continuation of **trade restrictions** are many. One such argument is that trade restrictions create benefits if the output of a monopoly can be reduced. Others argue that trade restrictions can be used as a **strategic trade policy** by promoting the creation of firms with large economies of scale. Another argument suggests that tariffs and the like should be used to protect industries that are necessary for the national defense. Then there is the **infant industry argument**—trade restrictions should be imposed to give firms time to get established and become competitive. Finally, it is argued, if others restrict trade, why should we not also restrict trade. All of these arguments have weak points and disadvantages. It is also the case that there are alternatives to trade restrictions that are less harmful to the economy but that achieve the same ends.

5. There is a growing movement toward expanding free trade. There are five approaches to doing this. One approach is simply **unilateral disarmament**; this is difficult to achieve today. An alternative is **multilateral negotiation**, which allows opposing political interests to cancel each other out. An example is the recent **Uruguay Round** of GATT negotiations and the creation of the **World Trade Organization (WTO)**. Multilateral negotiations are almost always conducted on a **most-favored nation (MFN)** basis. Creating regional trading areas is another approach. With this approach, it is hoped that the increase in trade that results, or **trade creation**, will outweigh the replacement of low-cost firms from outside the area with high-cost firms within it, or **trade diversion**. There are two types of regional trading areas: **free trade areas** and **customs unions**. NAFTA is a recent example of a free trade area (FTA) involving the United States, Mexico, and Canada. With a free trade area, **domestic content restrictions** are needed to prevent external tariff avoidance.

6. **Managed Trade** refers to the actions of government agencies to affect trade by persuading firms to buy or sell larger or smaller quantities of goods in other countries.

ZEROING IN

The model of supply and demand was used to examine the effects of tariffs, quotas, VRAs, and VIEs. The first three can be examined by using one market. The effects of a VIE, however, require a little more imagination. In either case, practicing with supply and demand will reaffirm your developing knowledge of this essential economic paradigm.

1. Figure 22.1 shows the market for some imported good. D_1 is the import demand curve, and S_1 is the export supply curve before any trade restrictions are instituted. Thus, P_1 and Q_1 are the equilibrium price and quantity.

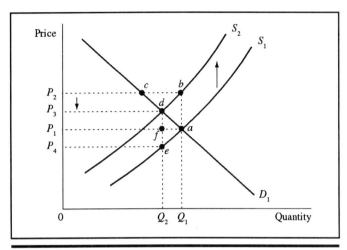

Figure 22.1

Assume that a tariff of amount ab is levied. As described in the text, this shifts the export supply curve up to S_2, where the vertical distance between S_1 and S_2 is equal to ab. Consumers must now pay P_1 plus the tariff, or P_2 ($P_2 = P_1 + ab$). At this point, however, there is a surplus on the market of cb. As a result, the price falls to P_3 with equilibrium quantity Q_2. Consumers now pay P_3 instead of P_1, and consumer surplus has fallen by the area P_1P_3da. However, although buyers pay P_3, foreign sellers get only P_4, where the difference de is the tariff collected by the government. Like consumer surplus, producer surplus has declined by the area P_1P_4ea. The tariff has made both domestic consumers and foreign producers worse off. The government, however, collects tariff revenue equal to the tariff per unit multiplied by the number of units subject to the tariff. In Figure 22.1 this is shown by the area P_3P_4ed. As you can see, the government is capturing some of the surplus lost by consumers and producers. The triangle dea is that part of the reduction in consumer and producer surplus that no one gets; this is the deadweight loss. So, a tariff is like a black hole in space—it makes some consumer and producer surplus disappear!

2. Figure 22.1 may also be used to review the effects of a quota. Assume that the free trade equilibrium is shown by P_1 and Q_1. One way a quota works is for the government to give someone an importing license. This allows this person to be the only importer of a product, making it easy for the government to keep track of imports to be sure the quota limit is not being violated. In terms of Figure 22.1, suppose that the license agreement says that no more than Q_2 may be imported. The quota holder now buys this amount from foreign suppliers for P_4 and sells it to domestic buyers for P_3. The area P_3P_4ed is the revenue earned by the quota holder. Also, there is still the deadweight loss of dea.

3. A VRA works like a quota, but we do away with the quota holder. The government sends an official representative to the foreign country and asks that country to export only Q_2. Alternatively, the official asks the country to hold Q_1Q_2 off the market. The foreign supplier now sells Q_2 at price P_3, and the area P_3P_4ed comes to the foreign firm as extra revenue. Also, like a tariff or quota, the VRA results in a deadweight loss of dea.

ACTIVE REVIEW

Fill-in Questions

1. A(n) _____ is a tax equal to a certain percentage of the value of an imported good.

2. A(n) _____ is a tax on the quantity sold of an imported good.

3. When the United States government imposes a tariff, the _____ shifts by the dollar amount of the tariff.

4. _____ set a maximum amount of a good that can be imported.

5. Tariffs generate _____ for the government.

6. A(n) _____ or _____ is similar to a quota, but it is imposed by a foreign government before goods are shipped to the United States.

7. Foreign firms have located factories in the United States to avoid VRAs. The products of these factories are called _____.

8. When foreign governments agree to promote the purchase of goods produced in the United States, this is called _____.

9. _____, _____, and _____ are examples of trade barriers related to domestic policies. These are often referred to as _____.

10. In general, over time, tariffs in the United States have _____.

11. The _____ was levied during the Depression of the 1930s and may have, in fact, increased its duration and depth.

12. The _____ allowed President Roosevelt to lower tariffs if certain conditions were met in other countries. This approach was made permanent in 1947 with the creation of the _____.

13. _____ occurs when a foreign firm sells a product at a price below average cost or the price in the home country. This has promoted the creation of _____.

14. Trade restrictions designed to permit firms to achieve economies of scale are referred to as _____.

15. Alexander Hamilton favored tariffs based on a(n) _____ argument.

16. The repeal of the Corn Laws in England is an example of the _____ approach to reducing trade barriers.

17. If a country is not granted _____, _____, are imposed on the imports of that country.

True-False Questions

T F   1. A tariff shifts the import demand curve upward.

T F   2. Quotas create revenue for the government.

T F   3. A VRA and a quota are both imposed by the importing country.

T F   4. Under a VIE, the French government might promote the use of California wines by Paris café owners.

T F   5. Fuel economy standards for cars sold in the United States are a form of trade restriction.

T F   6. Tariffs are a new and growing method used by the U.S. government to raise revenues for domestic transfer payments.

T F   7. The Smoot-Hawley tariffs of 1930 helped create a worldwide trade war.

T F   8. Dumping is permitted in the United States.

T F   9. Beggar-thy-neighbor policies are mutually beneficial.

T F 10. National security has been used as a rationale for trade restrictions.

T F 11. Unilateral disarmament is a more popular way of reducing trade barriers than multilateral negotiations.

T F 12. VRAs and VIEs are examples of tools used under a regime of managed trade.

T F 13. NAFTA created a common currency in Canada, Mexico, and the United States.

Short-Answer Questions

1. What are some differences between a tariff and a quota?
2. Is the effect of a VRA similar to that of a quota?
3. How does a VIE raise the price of U.S. imports when it is used to promote U.S. exports?
4. What is a transplant?
5. What is a nontariff trade barrier?
6. What is the Reciprocal Trade Agreement Act, and how is it related to GATT?
7. Why is it difficult to identify dumping?
8. What is the infant industry argument?
9. What is a beggar-thy-neighbor policy?

10. Describe the Uruguay Round.

11. Differentiate between free trade areas (FTA) and customs unions.

12. What is MFN?

13. Define managed trade.

WORKING IT OUT

International trade has linked markets in different countries, and, as a result, has changed the prices of products and of factors of production. These linkages created net benefits for all the economies involved. In this chapter we have examined the impact of blockages or restrictions to these connections. Let us look once again at the effects trade barriers have on supply and demand and expand the discussion to include price elasticity. We'll use Figure 22.2 to show the odd effects of a VIE.

Recall that a voluntary import expansion occurs when a government agrees to have firms in its country buy more of the exports of another country. Let us use supply and demand to show why the exporting country's imports might become more expensive. Market A is the Japanese market for American cars, with an initial equilibrium of P_A and Q_A. Market B is the market for Japanese cars in Japan, with a beginning equilibrium of P_B and Q_B. Finally, market C is the market for Japanese cars in the United States, with equilibrium of P_C and Q_C. A VIE would have the Japanese government expand Japanese demand for cars made in the United States. Thus, the first effect of a VIE is seen in market A as a shift in demand to D_{A1}. As a result, price rises to P_{A1} and more American cars are sold in Japan (Q_{A1}). This is the goal of the VIE—but don't stop! American cars in Japan are now relatively more expensive than Japanese cars in Japan. If these cars are viewed as substitutes by Japanese consumers, then the price rise in market A will cause the demand curve in market B to shift to the right to D_{B1}. This causes the price of Japanese cars in Japan to rise to P_{B1}. Japanese car producers can sell their cars in either Japan or the United States. A secondary effect of the VIE is to make it relatively more attractive to sell Japanese cars in Japan than in the United States because the price in Japan has increased. Therefore, Japanese car producers may decide to export fewer cars to the United States. If this occurs, the supply curve in market C will shift left to S_{C1}, and the price of Japanese cars in the United States will rise to P_{C1}. While there are many other effects that could have been developed, we have shown that by promoting Japanese consumption of United States products, a VIE can make Japanese products more expensive for American consumers!

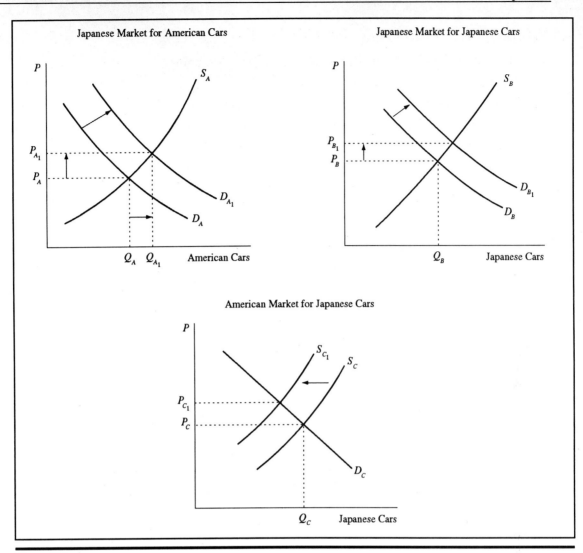

Figure 22.2

Worked Problems

1. Show the effects of a tariff on a market, assuming that demand is perfectly inelastic. How does your answer change if demand is less than perfectly inelastic?

Answer

Figure 22.3 shows the effects of a tariff and the role of differing elasticities.

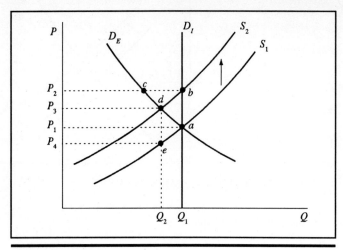

Figure 22.3

Assume that the pretariff supply curve is S_1. Two demand curves are indicated, D_I and D_E. For convenience, they both cross the supply curve at point a, making P_1 the pretariff equilibrium market price. As in previous examples, a tariff shifts the export supply curve up to S_2, where the distance ab is the amount of the tariff. If demand is perfectly inelastic (D_I), the effect of the tariff is to raise the market price to P_2. Here, quantity demanded is unaffected. Tariff revenue is shown by the area P_2P_1ab. Also, there is no deadweight loss. However, if the demand is relatively more elastic (D_E), the tariff raises the price only to P_3 — because demand has a negative slope (not vertical), at P_2 there is a surplus of cb, and quantity falls to Q_2. Tariff revenue is now P_3P_4ed, which is less than the revenue generated when demand was vertical. Also, a deadweight loss exists equal to the area dea. When demand is perfectly inelastic, more revenue is generated and the deadweight loss is minimized.

2. Using Figure 22.3, tell who bears the burden of the tariff.

Answer

When demand is D_I, price increases by the full amount of the tariff ($P_2P_1 = ba$); therefore, domestic consumers bear the burden. However, if demand is D_E, the price increases only to P_3. Thus, domestic consumers pay P_3P_1 of the tariff, while foreign producers pay the portion P_1P_4. From this it appears that consumers bear more of the burden the greater the inelasticity of demand.

Practice Problems

1. a. Draw a market in such a way as to make foreign sellers pay all of a tariff.

   b. Could this be a beggar-thy-neighbor policy?

2. a. Describe the market linkages in Figure 22.2. Start with A and go to C through B.

   b. What could you assume about the elasticity of demand in A that would prevent the transmission of a VIE into markets B and C?

3. Would a quota holder rather have a license for an imported product that had a relatively inelastic (not perfectly inelastic) demand or a relatively elastic demand? Draw a market diagram to support your answer.

CHAPTER TEST

1. Policies that restrict trade are called
   a. protectionist policies.
   b. GATT agreements.
   c. reciprocal trade agreements.
   d. free trade zones.

2. A tax equal to a certain percentage of the value of an imported good is a(n)
   a. specific tariff.
   b. ad valorem tariff.
   c. quota.
   d. nontariff trade barriers

3. Tariffs
   a. move the export supply curve right.
   b. move the import demand curve left.
   c. move the export supply curve left.
   d. do not generate revenue for the government.

4. The increased revenues that result from a quota are collected by
   a. the government.
   b. consumers through enhanced consumer surplus.
   c. foreign monopolies.
   d. the quota holder.

5. Managed trade includes the use of
   a. VRAs.
   b. IRAs.
   c. VIEs.
   d. any of the above; they are all tools of managed trade.

6. The revenue collected under a VRA goes to
   a. the government.
   b. the quota holder.
   c. the foreign producer.
   d. consumers as part of reduced consumer surplus.

7. Fuel economy standards for all cars sold in the United States may be considered a form of
   a. nontariff trade barrier.
   b. quota.
   c. tariff.
   d. government procurement policy.

8. Possibly the worst U.S. tariff policy
   a. was that under Smoot-Hawley.
   b. came from GATT.
   c. was started under the Reciprocal Trade Agreement Act of 1934.
   d. was passed in 1826 and was called the tariff of abominations.

9. The selling of a product by a foreign company at a price below average cost is called
   a. a tariff.
   b. dumping.
   c. a quota.
   d. a nontariff trade barrier.

10. The deadweight loss from a VRA is
    a. equal to the revenue collected by the government.
    b. equal to the revenue collected by the quota holder.
    c. the difference between the reduction in consumer surplus and the increase in producer surplus.
    d. the extra taxes paid by firms as a result of their higher profits.

11. Arguments in favor of trade restrictions include
    a. strategic trade policies.
    b. national defense considerations.
    c. infant industry arguments.
    d. all of the above.

12. To encourage firms in a particular country to achieve economies of scale is the aim of
    a. strategic trade policies.
    b. ad valorem tariffs.
    c. quotas.
    d. only European governments.

13. The stockpiling of strategic materials is an alternative to
    a. strategic trade policy.
    b. antidumping rules.
    c. infant industry arguments for restricting trade.
    d. national security arguments for restricting trade.

14. According to a story written by Frédéric Bastiat,
    a. French candlemakers wanted trade protection from the sun.
    b. infant industries need protection.
    c. quotas are better than tariffs in generating revenue for the government.
    d. it rains in Spain, but mainly on the plain.

15. GATT is an example of
    a. how nontariff trade barriers are formed.
    b. unilateral disarmament.
    c. multilateral negotiations.
    d. a customs union.

16. Recently, China
    a. signed VRA agreements with the United States.
    b. increased its quotas.
    c. was granted MFN status.
    d. was fined under its GATT status.

17. A disadvantage of a regional trading area is
    a. the lack of a common currency.
    b. trade diversion.
    c. the tendency to have trade wars within the area.
    d. that there are fewer countries involved than in multilateral negotiations.

18. If tariffs are reduced, the export supply curve
    a. does not shift.
    b. decreases(shifts upward).
    c. increases (shifts downward).
    d. becomes perfectly inelastic.

19. If a foreign country agrees to a VIE,
    a. the price of its imports will rise.
    b. the price of its exports may rise.
    c. the quantity of its exports may fall.
    d. all of the above could happen.

20. If import demand is perfectly inelastic and a tariff is levied,
    a. foreign suppliers will pay all of the tariff.
    b. the government will collect no revenue.
    c. quotas are needed to shift export supply downward.
    d. consumers will pay all of the tariff.

ANSWERS TO THE REVIEW QUESTIONS

Fill-in Questions

1. ad valorem tariff
2. specific tariff
3. export supply curve
4. Quotas
5. tax revenue
6. voluntary restraint agreement (VRA); voluntary export restraint (VER)
7. transplants
8. voluntary import expansion (VIE)
9. Quality and performance standards; government procurement policy; nontariff trade barriers
10. fallen
11. Smoot-Hawley tariff
12. Reciprocal Trade Agreement Act of 1934; General Agreement on Trade and Tariffs (GATT)
13. Dumping; antidumping duties
14. strategic trade policy
15. infant industry
16. unilateral disarmament
17. most-favored nation status (MFN); Smoot-Hawley tariffs

True-False Questions

1. **False**. It shifts the export supply curve upward.
2. **False**. Tariffs create revenues called duties. Quotas provide additional revenue for the quota holder.
3. **False**. A quota is imposed by the importing country. With a VRA, the foreign government (in the exporting country) agrees to limit exports. Quotas and VRAs have similar market effects.
4. **True**. A voluntary import expansion occurs when a foreign government agrees to promote the use of an imported product.
5. **True**. This is an example of a nontariff trade barrier.
6. **False**. Tariffs have a long history in the United States. However, tariffs are a declining source of revenue for the government. This has been especially true since 1910.
7. **True**. In fact, the Smoot-Hawley tariffs have been cited as one reason for the length and depth of the Great Depression of the 1930s.
8. **False**. Dumping occurs when a foreign producer sells in a foreign country at a price below average cost or below the price in the home country. There is antidumping legislation in the United States.
9. **False**. A beggar-thy-neighbor policy benefits one country at the expense of another. Thus, such policies cannot be mutually beneficial.
10. **True**. This argument claims that certain things need to be produced during times of war. Depending on foreign suppliers might be dangerous. Thus, domestic producers need to exist.
11. **False**. Some areas of the economy are hurt by unilateral disarmament. With multilateral negotiations, there is a simultaneous tariff reduction among many countries.
12. **True**. Managed trade is a phrase used to describe government actions that affect trade by persuading firms to buy or sell larger or smaller quantities of goods in other countries.
13. **False**. NAFTA only removed tariffs and quotas that existed between the three countries.

Short-Answer Questions

1. Tariffs are essentially taxes that are levied on an imported product. They generate duties, or tax revenue, for the government. Quotas simply limit the amount of a product that can be imported. Quotas generate revenue for the quota holder.
2. Yes. A VRA is a voluntary restraint agreement—for example, the U.S. government asks another government to voluntarily restrict exports to the United States. Thus, VRAs act like quotas. Foreign suppliers experience increases in profits.
3. With a voluntary import expansion, a government promotes imports from another country. For example, the Japanese government may encourage its citizens to buy more American cars. This causes the price of American cars to rise in Japan. In response, Japanese car producers may export less to the United States because they can get higher prices in Japan. Holding demand constant, such actions by Japanese producers will cause the price of Japanese cars to rise in the United States.
4. Often, foreign companies try to avoid VRAs by building factories in the restricted country. The products of these factories are called transplants.
5. A nontariff trade barrier is anything that limits trade that is not a tariff or a quota. Examples include quality and performance standards, government procurement rules, regulatory rules and standards, and minimum content or fiber requirements.

6. The Reciprocal Trade Agreement Act of 1934 gave President Roosevelt the authority to cut tariffs if other countries cut their own tariffs. This legislation successfully reduced tariffs from the levels imposed under Smoot-Hawley. This process of tariff reduction was so successful that it was made permanent by GATT in 1947.

7. Dumping is a form of predatory pricing, and it is difficult to differentiate between predatory pricing (discussed in Chapter 16) and aggressive pricing that results from active competition.

8. This is an argument in favor of tariffs in order to protect an industry that is just getting started. Once the industry is established, the tariff on imports can be removed and competition proceeds. A problem with this argument is that infant industries never seem to grow up.

9. This is a policy that benefits one country at the expense of another country. Trade wars may be encouraged if one country follows a beggar-thy-neighbor policy.

10. The Uruguay Round is the latest round of multilateral trade negotiations under GATT. This was a meeting (a round) of countries that tried to come to an agreement on a list of tariff reductions and the removal of other trade restrictions. The Uruguay Round included a reform of GATT. It created the World Trade Organization (WTO) to deal with trade disputes between countries.

11. Both are special trading areas within which barriers to trade between countries in the area are removed. However, external tariffs are the same for all countries in a customs union but may differ in a free trade area. Both forms may result in trade diversion.

12. MFN stands for most-favored nation status. When tariffs are reduced under GATT, they are reduced for all countries with MFN status.

13. The term *managed trade* refers to the actions of government agencies to affect trade by persuading firms to buy or sell large or small quantities of goods in other countries.

SOLUTIONS TO THE PRACTICE PROBLEMS

1. a. Figure 22.4 shows a tariff that is paid completely by foreign suppliers.

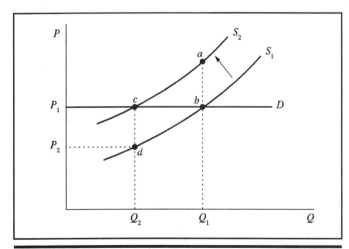

Figure 22.4

Assume that the pretariff export supply curve is S_1 and the pretariff demand curve is D. Note that demand is perfectly elastic at the free trade equilibrium price P_1. A tariff of amount ab shifts the export supply curve up to S_2. Given the perfectly elastic demand curve, the market price remains at P_1 even though the quantity supplied falls from Q_1 to Q_2. Domestic consumers pay the same price as before the tariff. However, foreign producers get only P_2. The distance P_1P_4 is equal to the tariff ab. Thus foreign producers pay all of the tariff.

b. This could be viewed as a beggar-thy-neighbor policy. The domestic government collects tax revenue (area P_1P_2cd) from foreign citizens and spends the money on its own citizens. Thus, one country benefits at the expense of another. This is the principal characteristic of a beggar-thy-neighbor policy.

2. a. The VIE caused Japanese demand for American cars to increase. This resulted in a price increase in market A. This price increase caused an increase in demand for Japanese-produced substitutes (market B). Japanese producers responded to this by keeping more of their products in Japan and cutting their exports to the United States. This is seen as a decrease in the supply of Japanese cars in the United States; the supply curve shifted upward in market C, causing the price to rise.

b. If the supply curve in market A had been perfectly elastic (horizontal) at the beginning market price (P_A), the increase in demand caused by the VIE would not have produced a price increase. Thus, there probably would not have been an effect on market B or market C.

3. Figure 22.5 can be used to communicate the value of a quota based on differing elasticities.

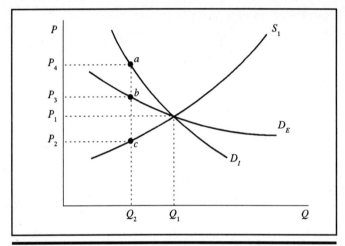

Figure 22.5

Assume that the export supply curve is S_1. Import demand curve D_E is relatively more elastic than import demand curve D_I. Further, assume that free trade equilibrium is at P_1 and Q_1. If the quota allows imports of only Q_2, the quota holder will purchase this quantity from foreign suppliers for P_2. The price at which the quota holder sells the imports to domestic consumers depends on the slope of the demand curve. Clearly, the quota holder can get a higher price if market demand is D_I. The revenue earned by the quota in this case is shown by area P_4P_2ca, as opposed to P_3P_2cb when demand is based on D_E. Thus, quota holders would like to face relatively inelastic import demand functions.

ANSWERS TO THE CHAPTER TEST

1. a
2. b
3. c
4. d
5. d

6. c
7. a
8. d
9. b
10. c

11. d
12. a
13. d
14. a
15. c

16. c
17. b
18. c
19. d
20. d

(CHAPTERS 15 - 22)
Macroeconomic Policy

1. Which of the following is the largest component of federal government expenditures?
   a. Defense purchases
   b. Nondefense purchases
   c. Transfer payments
   d. Interest payments

2. When tax revenues are equal to spending, there is a
   a. budget deficit.
   b. budget surplus.
   c. budget supplement.
   d. balanced budget.

3. The view that increases in the budget deficit will not affect consumption or the other components of real GDP is called
   a. monetarism.
   b. supply side economics.
   c. Ricardian equivalence.
   d. discretionary fiscal policy.

Use Table 1 for questions 4 and 5.

Deficit (millions of dollars)	250	230	210	190	170
Real GDP (billions of dollars)	6,000	6,200	6,400	6,600	6,800

TABLE 1

4. What is the structural deficit in this economy when real GDP equals $6,400 billion and potential GDP equals $6,800 billion?
   a. $170 million
   b. $210 million
   c. $40 million
   d. $380 million

5. What is the cyclical deficit in this economy when real GDP equals $6,400 billion and potential GDP equals $6,800 billion?
   a. $170 million
   b. $210 million
   c. $40 million
   d. $380 million

6. the central bank of the United States is the
   a. Unites States Treasury
   b. Bank of America
   c. Federal Reserve System
   d. International Monetary Fund

7. The most important feature of a central bank is
   a. the members of the Board of Governors.
   b. central bank independence.
   c. the ability to change the discount rate.
   d. the ability to print money.

8. When the Fed wants to raise the interest rate,
   a. it buys bonds.
   b. it sells bonds.
   c. it increases the money supply.
   d. it increases the monetary base.

9. The money multiplier links
   a. the monetary base and the money supply.
   b. the monetary base and the money demand.
   c. the monetary base and the interest rate.
   d. the monetary base and the savings rate.

10. When the Fed raises the interest rate in anticipation of a rise in inflation, it is called a
    a. constant money growth rule.
    b. aggregate demand/inflation (ADI) curve.
    c. gold standard.
    d. preemptive monetary strike.

9. Which of the following is a function of the Fed?
   a. Financing the budget deficit
   b. Determining the level of government spending
   c. Collecting taxes
   d. Supervising commercial banks
   e. Making loans to the public

10. According to the credit view of monetary policy, consumption and investment spending depends on
    a. the interest rate.
    b. the amount of money balances people hold.
    c. the ability of banks to make loans.
    d. real GDP.
    e. the exchange rate.

11. If the United States is running a current account deficit, then
    a. the U.S. Treasury will issue more bonds to fund it.
    b. taxes will be increased.
    c. the Federal Reserve will create more bank reserves.
    d. foreigners will increase their holdings of U.S. assets.

12. Purchasing power parity indicates that if the inflation rate is the same in the United States and in France,
    a. the U.S. dollar will depreciate against the French franc.
    b. the exchange rate between the U.S. dollar and the French franc has to equal $1 = 1$ French franc.
    c. the French franc will depreciate against the U.S. dollar.
    d. the exchange rate between the U.S. dollar and the French franc will remain unchanged.

13. Suppose a cup of coffee that sells for 50 cents in the United States sells for 16,000 Turkish liras in Turkey. Assuming that purchasing power parity holds, what is the exchange rate?
    a. 8,000 Turkish liras per dollar
    b. 16,000 Turkish liras per dollar
    c. 24,000 Turkish liras per dollar
    d. 32,000 Turkish liras per dollar

Use Table 2 for questions 14 and 15.

International Transactions for the Year 2000 (in billions of dollars)	
Merchandise trade balance	-100
Services trade balance	30
Net factor income from abroad	10
Net transfers from abroad	-50

TABLE 2

14. Using Table 2, what is the value of the trade balance in the year 2000?
    a. -130 billion
    b. -110 billion
    c. -70 billion
    d. -30 billion

15. Using Table 2, what is the value of the current account balance in the year 2000?
    a. -130 billion
    b. -110 billion
    c. -70 billion
    d. -30 billion

16. If the spread of technology is not difficult, then economic growth theory predicts
    a. -that only countries with low levels of income per capita will grow.
    b. - that only countries with high levels of income per capita will grow.
    c. -that countries with high levels of income per capital will grow faster than countries with low levels of income per capita.
    d. -that countries with high levels of income per capital will grow more slowly than countries with low levels of income per capita.

Use Figure 1 for question 17.

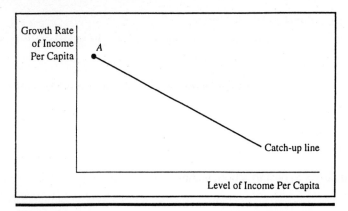

Figure 1

17. A country located at point A on the catch-up line in Figure 1 is
    a. a rich country enjoying rapid growth.
    b. a rich country experiencing a slow rate of growth.
    c. a poor country enjoying rapid growth
    d. a poor country experiencing a slow rate of growth.

18. The emergence of informal sectors in developing countries is due to
    a. the low income of the population.
    b. the lack of industrial base.
    c. the emergence of a service economy.
    d. heavy restrictions on business.

19. If a U.S. firm invests in a 15 percent ownership of a firm in France, the investment is referred to as
    a. foreign investment.
    b. foreign indirect investment.
    c. portfolio investment.
    d. capital investment.

20. An outward-looking development strategy involves
    a. government discouragement of international trade.
    b. replacing products imported from abroad with domestically produced products.
    c. manufacturing products to be used by other countries.
    d. imposing taxes on imports.

21. The idea that the growth rate of aggregate supply, or potential GDP, can be increased by cutting taxes or reforming the tax system is called
    a. monetarism.
    b. supply side economics.
    c. Ricardian equivalence.
    d. fiscal policy.

22. The theory of economic growth based on the production function and the growth accounting formula is rooted in the
    a. neoclassical growth school.
    b. monetarist school.
    c. new classical school.
    d. new Keynesian school.

23. The idea that people look ahead to the future using all available information best describes
    a. the Keynesian revolution.
    b. the monetarist challenge.
    c. the rational expectations revolution.
    d. the neoclassical growth school approach.

24. A distinguishing feature of the new Keynesian school is that
    a. prices are perfectly flexible.
    b. the MPC is not constant.
    c. there is no long-run trade-off between inflation and unemployment.
    d. prices are sticky.

25. The schools of thought most relevant to the 1990s are the
    a. monetarist and Keynesian schools.
    b. freshwater and saltwater schools.
    c. new classical and rational expectations schools.
    d. neoclassical growth and supply side schools.

26. Emerging market economics are
    a. countries making the transition from central planning or tight government control to an economy based much more on markets and freely determined prices.
    b. countries making the transition from markets and freely determined prices to an economy based much more on central planning or tight government control.
    c. countries making the transition from free trade to managed trade.
    d. countries making the transition from managed trade to free trade.

27. Which of the following is *not* one of the goals of economic reform?
    a. Prices must be freed and determined by competitive markets.
    b. A legal system must be established to specify property rights and enforce contracts.
    c. Decisions about production and employment must be centralized.
    d. A monetary system and a system of tax collections must be put into place.

Use Table 3 for question 28.

Year	Country A		Country B	
	Real GDP Growth	**Inflation**	**Real GDP Growth**	**Inflation**
1996	0	100	0	100
1997	-35	90	-20	90
1998	-20	20	-10	20
1999	-5	10	0	10
2000	0	10	1	10

TABLE 3

28. Based on the information in Table 3, which of the following statements is true over the period 1996–2000?
    a. The government of country A has greater credibility.
    b. The government of country B has greater credibility.
    c. Country A is characterized by a policy of gradualism.
    d. Country B is characterized by a policy of gradualism.

29. A communist system is best described as an economic system where
    a. the government owns the land and the capital and makes decisions about production and employment.
    b. the government is involved in the economy because of market failures.
    c. the people of a country collectively own the land and capital and make decisions about production and employment.
    d. prices are determined in a decentralized fashion.

30. Perestroika was
    a. an attempt by the Soviet Union to bring about market reform.
    b. an attempt to reform centralized planning.
    c. an attempt by the Soviet Union to make its economic system more centralized.
    d. a plan for dismembering the Soviet Union.

ANSWERS

1. c	7. b	13. d	19. b	25. b
2. d	8. b	14. c	20. c	26. a
3. c	9. a	15. b	21. b	27. c
4. a	10. d	16. d	22. a	28. b
5. c	11. c	17. c	23. c	29. c
6. c	12. d	18. d	24. d	30. b